MSE

Simulated MBE Workshop

barbri

BAR REVIEW

MULTISTATE TESTING

o be used in conjunction with the Summer 2007
nd Winter 2008 BAR/BRI Bar Review Courses

THOMSON
BAR/BRI

Celebrating XL years
one million students

barbri®

BAR REVIEW

Multistate Exam Workshop

Simulated Multistate Exam

Morning Exam

Afternoon Exam

Answer Key

Explanatory Answers

Lecture Handout

barbri

BAR REVIEW

Multistate Exam Workshop

Morning Exam

BAR REVIEW

Multistate Exam Workshop

Simulated Multistate Bar Examination

A.M. EXAM

Time—3 hours

You will be given three hours to work on this test. Be sure that the question numbers on your answer sheet match the question numbers in your test book. You are not to begin work until the supervisor tells you to do so.

Your score will be based on the number of questions you answer correctly. It is therefore to your advantage to try to answer as many questions as you can. Give only one answer to each question; multiple answers will not be counted. If you wish to change an answer, erase your first mark completely and mark your new choice. Use your time effectively. Do not hurry, but work steadily and as quickly as you can without sacrificing your accuracy.

YOU ARE TO INDICATE YOUR ANSWERS TO ALL QUESTIONS ON THE SEPARATE ANSWER SHEET PROVIDED.

DIRECTIONS

Each of the questions or incomplete statements in this test is followed by four suggested answers or completions. You are to choose the ***best*** of the stated alternatives. Answer all questions according to the generally accepted view, except where otherwise noted.

For the purpose of this test, you are to assume that Articles 1 and 2 of the Uniform Commercial Code have been adopted. You are also to assume relevant application of Article 9 of the U.C.C. concerning fixtures. The Federal Rules of Evidence are deemed to control.

The terms "Constitution," "constitutional," and "unconstitutional" refer to the federal Constitution unless indicated to the contrary.

You are also to assume that there is no applicable statute unless otherwise specified; however, survival actions and claims for wrongful death should be assumed to be available where applicable. You should assume that joint and several liability, with pure comparative negligence, is the relevant rule unless otherwise indicated.

DO NOT OPEN THE TEST UNTIL
YOU ARE INSTRUCTED TO DO SO.

Question 1

In which of the following fact situations does the defendant have the best argument that he was the victim of an illegal search or seizure?

(A) The police notice that the defendant's car is weaving erratically on the highway. The officers pull the defendant over. The defendant emerges from the car and appears incoherent and disoriented. The defendant is arrested and charged with driving under the influence of alcohol or drugs. The police search the defendant's glove compartment and find a plastic bag containing a large quantity of marijuana.

(B) Without a warrant, federal narcotics officers cross the defendant's fenced-in field and look through a window into the defendant's horse barn. The barn is located about 150 feet outside of the fence surrounding his house. The federal agents observe a large quantity of recently harvested marijuana within the barn. The agents then go to a magistrate, swear out a warrant, and arrest the defendant.

(C) Narcotics officers attached to the state police learn from an informant that the semi-opaque panes of glass on the defendant's greenhouse, adjacent to his house, are being replaced during the night with a newer type of glass that lets in more light without an increase in visibility. They fly over the defendant's greenhouse in a helicopter that night. One of the officers focuses on the greenhouse with a pair of infrared "night-vision" binoculars supplied by the Department of Defense and not available to the general public. He determines that marijuana is being grown. The officers then go to a magistrate, swear out a warrant, and arrest the defendant.

(D) Using a small plane of the type used for crop-dusting, county sheriff's officers take aerial photographs of the fields surrounding the defendant's farm. The pictures are later developed and show that there is marijuana growing in the defendant's fields. The sheriff's officers go to a magistrate, swear out a warrant, and arrest the defendant.

Question 2

One of the provisions of federal anti-smoking legislation imposes restrictions on federal economic development grants, which were awarded to states to promote and assist small businesses in urban areas. The legislation mandates that grants will be reduced by 10% for any state that fails to require businesses engaged in the sale of cigarettes to take steps to avoid sales to minors, including checking drivers' licenses or photo ID cards. A tobacco-growing state that receives several million dollars under the federal grant program challenged the constitutionality of the provision in federal district court.

Should the court uphold the federal provision?

(A) No, if the federal provision affects state regulation of businesses that do not operate in interstate commerce.

(B) No, because state distribution of economic development funds is an integral government function.

(C) Yes, because Congress may condition grants of money under its spending power.

(D) Yes, because the provision is substantially related to the important government interest of restricting minors' access to cigarettes.

Question 3

A large insurance company with many employees instituted a supplemental employee benefit plan. The plan provided that any employee who had worked for the company for at least 25 years would be permitted to designate a charity to receive, upon the employee's retirement, a donation in the employee's name of six months' worth of the employee's salary. The plan gave participating employees an unqualified right to change the beneficiary at any time before payment was made. A veteran employee had worked at the company for 26 years when the program was instituted and was planning to retire in 10 months. He enrolled in the program and named his favorite church as the beneficiary of the donation. The church, which was undergoing a highly publicized restoration of its historic chapel, received a letter from the company informing it that the employee had named it beneficiary of his plan and indicating the approximate amount that it would receive upon the employee's retirement in 10 months. The letter did not inform the church of the employee's right to change beneficiaries before that time. Church elders, anticipating the gift, hired a European artisan to restore the stained glass windows in the chapel. They planned to put up a plaque in the employee's honor and pay for the work with the funds from the employee's benefit program.

Six months later, the employee converted to a different religion and changed the beneficiary of his plan to his new church. When the employee retired, the company paid the benefit to his new church. His old church, which had paid for the stained glass restoration work upon its completion, demanded payment of the benefit from the company.

If the employee's old church sues the company for payment of the benefit, the court should rule in favor of:

(A) The church, because the church took steps to restore the windows in reliance on payment of the benefit.

(B) The church, because the employee did not have the power to change the beneficiary of his plan after the church's rights as third-party beneficiary had vested.

(C) The company, because the agreement between the employee and the company allowed the employee to change the beneficiary of the benefit plan.

(D) The company, because it had a duty to pay the employee's new church as the named beneficiary of his plan.

Question 4

A landowner sold a parcel of land to an investor for $100,000. The investor put the deed in her desk drawer without recording it and left for an extended sojourn in a foreign country. The landowner, aware of the investor's departure and seeing an opportunity to make a quick profit, partitioned the parcel of land and sold the front half to a friend in exchange for $50,000. The friend, who knew nothing about the investor's interest in the property, promptly recorded his interest. Two months later, the friend found a job in another city and sold the front parcel to a buyer in exchange for $55,000. The buyer was acquainted with the investor and was aware of her interest in the property but did not believe that she would return from her sojourn anytime soon. The buyer promptly recorded her deed to the front parcel. Meanwhile, the landowner executed a mortgage on the back half of the property to a bank in the amount of $40,000. The bank knew nothing of the landowner's transaction with the investor but neglected to record its mortgage interest. Six months later, the investor returned home and recorded her deed to the parcel of land.

The recording statute in the jurisdiction reads, in relevant part: "Any conveyance of an estate in land, other than a lease for less than one year, shall not be valid against any subsequent purchaser for value, without notice, unless the conveyance is recorded."

If the investor brings an action to quiet title in the parcel of land, which of the following statements is most accurate?

(A) The investor's claim to the parcel of land is superior to the landowner's rights in the back half and the buyer's rights in the front half, and not subject to the bank's mortgage on the back half.

(B) The investor's claim to the parcel of land is superior to the landowner's rights in the back half, inferior to the buyer's rights in the front half, and subject to the bank's mortgage on the back half.

(C) The investor's claim to the parcel of land is superior to the landowner's rights in the back half, inferior to the buyer's rights in the front half, and not subject to the bank's mortgage on the back half.

(D) The investor's claim to the parcel of land is superior to the landowner's rights in the back half and the buyer's rights in the front half, but subject to the bank's mortgage on the back half.

Question 5

A moving company specializing in local moves sent two employees on a typical job: a driver and a helper. The driver's responsibility was to drive the truck and load and unload the cargo. The helper's responsibility was to load and unload the cargo and generally assist the driver. While transporting furniture in a company truck, the driver failed to stop at a stop sign and collided with a car, causing the motorist to be seriously injured in the accident.

In a lawsuit brought by the motorist against the moving company on the theory of negligence by its employee, the motorist offered into evidence a written statement of the helper. The statement said that the driver was adjusting his portable radio and not observing the road when the accident occurred.

The helper's written statement is admissible if:

(A) The helper takes the witness stand and testifies that the driver was adjusting his radio and not observing the road.

(B) The helper is unavailable to testify.

(C) Evidence is introduced to establish that the helper is an employee of the moving company and his written statement is in the scope of his employment.

(D) The helper's statement was given under oath at a trial or other proceeding.

Question 6

A police officer went to the defendant's house and placed him under arrest for operating an auto theft ring. As the defendant was being arrested, he told his wife, "You had better call our lawyer; I don't want to sign anything unless she's with me." The defendant was given *Miranda* warnings on the way to the police station. Meanwhile, the defendant's lawyer called the station and told the desk sergeant that she was on her way and to have the defendant call her as soon as he arrived. The sergeant assured her that the defendant would be held without questioning for several hours until the district attorney arrived. When the defendant arrived at the station, the arresting officer and another officer immediately put the defendant in an interrogation room and questioned him about a bank robbery that had taken place two days ago. They did not inform him of the call from his lawyer, but he agreed to talk as long as he did not have to put anything in writing or sign anything without her okay. He made incriminating statements about the robbery, and he was eventually indicted for that crime as well.

At a preliminary hearing on the robbery charge, the defendant's lawyer moved to suppress the arresting officer's testimony about the defendant's statements. The court should:

(A) Deny the motion, because the questioning was about a different crime from the one for which the defendant was in custody.

(B) Deny the motion, because the defendant's statements were made voluntarily after receiving *Miranda* warnings.

(C) Grant the motion, because the defendant was not informed that his lawyer was trying to see him, and his lawyer was misinformed that he would not be questioned right away.

(D) Grant the motion, because the defendant's refusal to write or sign anything indicates that he did not knowingly and intelligently waive his right to the assistance of counsel.

Question 7

A landowner who had owned and operated a small airport notified the electric company that he was discontinuing operations and that it should shut down the electrical current that had supplied his communications equipment, which was surrounded by a fence with signs warning of high voltage. Because the electric company maintained a transformer next to the landowner's communications equipment that contained many valuable and reusable parts, it decided to leave the power on to prevent theft until it could schedule removal of the transformer. Three days later, a trespasser who knew that the airport had closed went onto the property looking for something to steal. He could find nothing of value except the transformer. He noticed the signs warning of the high voltage but believed that the power had been turned off by now. He scaled the fence with the intent to dismantle the transformer. As soon as he touched the transformer, he was seriously injured by the electric current.

If the trespasser asserts a claim against the electric company to recover damages for his injuries, the trespasser will:

(A) Prevail, because the electric company was not the owner of the land on which the trespasser trespassed.

(B) Prevail, because the electric company used unreasonable force to protect its property.

(C) Not prevail, because the trespasser was a trespasser on the landowner's land.

(D) Not prevail, because the trespasser intended to steal the electric company's transformer.

Question 8

To encourage minority business and foster pride in minority heritage, a state adopted legislation exempting magazines and other periodicals from the state's receipts tax if 20% of the magazine is devoted to articles concerning minorities (a commission was set up to sample magazines to determine on a yearly basis whether they should be exempt).

A publisher produced a sports magazine in the state that occasionally contained articles about minority athletes, but the commission determined that the publisher's magazine was not eligible for the receipts tax exemption. After paying the tax assessed on her magazine, the publisher sued for a refund.

The court will most likely find:

(A) Against the publisher, because taxpayers do not have standing to challenge tax exemptions.

(B) Against the publisher, because the state has a compelling interest in encouraging minority business.

(C) In favor of the publisher, because the tax violates the Equal Protection Clause.

(D) In favor of the publisher, because the tax violates the First Amendment freedoms of speech and press.

Question 9

A homeowner whose lawn mower broke down started borrowing his neighbor's mower once a week to mow his lawn. A running joke developed between the two men as to when the homeowner would break down and purchase a new mower. One fall day the homeowner decided to blow the leaves off his lawn before mowing. The homeowner went to the neighbor's house to borrow the neighbor's leaf blower, but the neighbor was not at home. His leaf blower, however, was in his unlocked garage with his other garden tools, and the homeowner took it. Unbeknownst to the homeowner, the neighbor had drained the oil from the leaf blower's motor. The homeowner ran the leaf blower for an hour; the motor was totally destroyed because it had no oil.

The value of the leaf blower at the time that the homeowner took it was $300. An identical, new leaf blower costs $500. The cost of repairing the motor is $150. A new motor will cost $250.

If the neighbor sues the homeowner on a theory of conversion and is successful, he is entitled to:

(A) $300, but the homeowner will keep the leaf blower.

(B) $500, but the homeowner will keep the leaf blower.

(C) $150.

(D) $250.

Question 10

The state of Palomar's legislature enacted a law that stated in relevant part, "No person who is not a citizen of the United States may be hired for Category C public employment positions by the state of Palomar or by any county, municipality, or other governmental unit within the boundaries of the state." One of the positions specified as Category C was civil engineer. At the time the statute was signed into law, Lourdes Delgado, a citizen of the Philippines, had been legally residing in Palomar for five years. She had been trained as an engineer in the Philippines and had been a public works engineer for 10 years in the Philippines before moving to Palomar. For the last three years, Lourdes has been taking additional classes at Palomar State University to stay abreast of the latest techniques and developments in her field. Lourdes read that the Palomar Department of Transportation needed a new drafting engineer. Lourdes Delgado applied for the position and had the required qualifications. However, Nekro, the assistant director of the department, turned down her application, telling Lourdes, "I'd really like to hire you but I can't." The sole reason Nekro gave was the recently enacted statute. Lourdes really wanted the job and filed suit in federal court, claiming that the statute violates her right to equal protection under the Fourteenth Amendment.

If Lourdes prevails, it will most likely be because:

(A) Lourdes has proved that the statutory provision is not necessary to achieve a compelling government interest.

(B) Lourdes has proved that the statutory provision is not rationally related to a legitimate government interest.

(C) The state has failed to prove that the law is necessary to achieve a compelling government interest.

(D) The state has failed to prove that the law is substantially related to an important government interest.

Questions 11-12 are based on the following fact situation:

Eddie suffered from a physical condition that caused him to periodically lapse into unconsciousness without symptoms that would indicate such a seizure was about to occur. Four years ago, Eddie visited Dr. Dock. At that time, Dock put Eddie on the medicine "Noseeze." Eddie was required to take six Noseeze pills daily. The medication successfully ended Eddie's lapses into unconsciousness. However, Noseeze caused some unpleasant side effects, such as periodic nausea. After one year on Noseeze, Dock cut Eddie's dosage in half, and one year later, Dock took Eddie off the medication altogether, although Eddie was required to visit Dock for a check-up every two months. In the two years since he was removed from the Noseeze medication, Eddie regularly appeared at his check-up appointments and told Dock that he had suffered no seizures while off the medication.

One day Eddie was driving his automobile along a busy highway. Eddie suddenly suffered a seizure and lapsed into unconsciousness. While Eddie was passed out, his car crossed the center line, which divided his lane from traffic proceeding in the opposite direction. The center line was marked with a double yellow line, and by statute the jurisdiction declares that it is illegal for any person operating a motor vehicle on the highways of the state to cross a double yellow line. When Eddie's car passed into the lane containing oncoming traffic, his car collided with a vehicle driven by Pompeia. Pompeia's car was damaged and Pompeia suffered physical injuries that required hospitalization.

11. If Pompeia sues Dr. Dock for personal injuries and property damage arising from the accident, is she likely to recover?

    (A) Yes, if it was reasonably foreseeable that removing Eddie from medication could cause harm to third parties.

    (B) Yes, if but for the removal of Eddie from medication, the accident would not have occurred.

    (C) No, unless Dr. Dock failed to warn Eddie about driving without medication.

    (D) No, if it was reasonable as to Eddie's treatment to suspend the medication.

12. Is Eddie liable to Pompeia?

    (A) Yes, because the vehicle he was operating crossed a double yellow line in violation of statute.

    (B) Yes, if Eddie lapsed into unconsciousness on prior occasions.

    (C) No, because Eddie was unconscious.

    (D) No, unless Eddie had reason to believe that he might lapse into unconsciousness.

Question 13

A parcel of property was located in a state with a statutory adverse possession period of 15 years. The current owner purchased the property 25 years ago. It was a suburban property containing a single-family dwelling in which the owner lived. Immediately adjoining the property was a five-foot-wide strip, which was a private right-of-way. When the owner took possession of the property, she was not sure where the exact boundaries of her property were located. Therefore, when she planted a garden and enclosed it with a wire fence two weeks after taking up occupancy, the five-foot right-of-way strip was included within the bounds of the fence.

The owner maintained the fence and garden for 20 years, at which time she tired of gardening chores. When she gave up gardening, she also removed the fence and smoothed out the ground where the garden had been located.

Five years later, the owner entered into a written contract to sell the property to a buyer. The description in the contract included the five-foot strip. After research in the county recorder's office, the buyer discovered that the strip was a private right-of-way when the owner purchased the property. After properly notifying the owner of the problem prior to closing, the buyer refused to tender the purchase money to the owner when the closing day arrived. The owner sued the buyer for specific performance of the real estate sales contract.

Who will prevail?

(A) The buyer, because the owner failed to provide a marketable title.

(B) The buyer, because the owner surrendered her adverse possession rights when she removed the fence, because her possession was no longer open, notorious, and continuous.

(C) The buyer, because one may not adversely possess a right-of-way.

(D) The owner, because she held the right-of-way for a longer time than the minimum required by the state adverse possession statute.

Question 14

On one of her daily constitutionals through the local park, Nicelady came across a stray dog. Because she was a dog lover, she coaxed the dog home with her and placed an ad in the paper, under "Lost and Found," to try to find the dog's owner. Soon thereafter, Dawglost, the owner of the dog, contacted Nicelady and arranged to come see the dog to see if it was in fact his precious stud poodle, Rambo.

The next day, Dawglost came to Nicelady's and saw that the dog was his Rambo. He was so overwhelmed with joy at finding his dog that he offered Nicelady a $200 reward, although he told Nicelady that he would not be able to pay her the reward until February 14, when he would receive the down payment on Rambo's stud fee. Nicelady thanked Dawglost but told him that she was happy that he and Rambo were reunited, and she did not want any money from him.

By February 14, however, Nicelady had a change of heart. She decided that she could use the extra money, and so she called Dawglost and said that she would like the reward after all. Dawglost refused to pay.

If Nicelady sues Dawglost for breach of contract, what will she recover?

(A) No compensation, because she rejected Dawglost's offer.

(B) No compensation, because there was no consideration to support a contract.

(C) $200, because the technical defense of the Statute of Frauds will be overcome by Dawglost's moral obligation to pay.

(D) $200, because Dawglost could not have revoked his offer until February 14, and he failed to do so before Nicelady accepted.

Questions 15-17 are based on the following fact situation:

The food and beverage manager of an exclusive country club received a letter in the mail dated January 3 and signed by the sales director of a distiller. The letter offered to meet the club's requirements for vodka in the current year, stating: "Beginning January 15, we will supply your requirements on the 15th of each month at $120 per case throughout the calendar year." The manager promptly wrote back, "Regarding your letter of January 3, we agree to have you meet our requirements for vodka at the club during the coming year, on the terms stated." The manager placed a modest order for the distiller's vodka, which was duly delivered at the stated price on January 15. The vodka proved exceedingly popular with the club members and the manager placed increased orders for February 15 and March 15, which were duly delivered at the stated price.

However, on March 17, the manager received a letter from the sales director, stating in relevant part, "Due to extraordinary conditions of social upheaval in the distiller's country of origin and concomitant increased production and import costs, it will be necessary for us to increase the price of our vodka to you to $200 per case." The manager telephoned the sales director and told him, "Our members aren't going to be happy if we change brands. We have a contract." The sales director replied, "No we don't, and in any case there's no way we can supply our product to you now at $120 per case." The manager ordered vodka from one of the distiller's competitors. The best price the manager could get for that vodka was $135 per case. The competitor's vodka proved to be far less popular than the distiller's vodka (which was the leading brand of imported vodka) and vodka consumption at the club declined, as did profits from the sale of vodka drinks. The club sued the distiller for damages.

15. The original agreement between the distiller and the club can be best described as:

(A) A single bilateral contract.

(B) A series of unilateral contracts.

(C) A series of option contracts.

(D) Not an enforceable contract.

16. Assume for purposes of this question only that the court decides that a single bilateral contract existed between the distiller and the club. The court considers the following damages to which the club might be entitled:

I. Nominal damages.

II. $15 times the number of cases of the competitor's vodka purchased from April through December.

III. The decline in profits that was caused by reduced sales of vodka drinks.

The court should award:

(A) I. only.

(B) II. only.

(C) III. only.

(D) II. and III.

17. The distiller's best defense against the club's suit is:

(A) The original promise by the club was illusory, because no maximum or minimum quantities were stated.

(B) The agreement between the distiller and the club was a series of monthly unilateral contracts, cancelable at will.

(C) Commercial impracticability.

(D) The distiller never made a valid offer to the club.

Question 18

Among his properties, Tommy owned Greenacres, a 300-acre operating farm. The farm was profitable, but Tommy received income from many other sources as well. When Tommy died, one of the provisions in his will left Greenacres "to my wife, Wanda, for life, then to my three daughters, Debi, Doreen, and Donna, in fee simple absolute."

Wanda occupied the farmhouse on Greenacres and operated the farm herself, occasionally hiring additional hands for busy times, such as planting and harvesting. After expenses of operation, Wanda earned about $25,000 per year from Greenacres. Neither Debi, Doreen, nor Donna did anything to assist Wanda with farm chores or expenses. Wanda has consistently failed to pay the annual $2,000 county tax assessment and continues to refuse to pay it, despite threats from county tax collection authorities.

With the taxes three years in arrears, the tax authorities made good on their threats. Using proper procedures authorized by state law, the county has ordered a tax sale of Greenacres.

You are an attorney with offices located in the county seat. Donna consults you regarding her rights and obligations.

You should advise her that:

(A) Wanda, as life tenant, is personally liable for the taxes, but a tax sale will cut off the rights of the remaindermen.

(B) The remaindermen are personally liable for the taxes if the life tenant does not pay them.

(C) Donna will have to pay one-third of the taxes if Debi and Doreen pay two-thirds.

(D) Wanda, as life tenant, is personally liable for the taxes, and the tax sale will affect only the rights of the life tenant and not the rights of the remaindermen.

Question 19

Donald was a defenseman for a professional ice hockey team in Detroit. Donald had a reputation for being a dirty, vicious player. During a game with New York, Victor, a New York player, skated towards Donald at a high rate of speed; his hockey stick was raised in a threatening manner. Victor did not intend to actually harm Donald, but wanted to show him how it felt to be threatened by a large man traveling at a high rate of speed with a hockey stick. As Victor approached Donald, Donald smashed his stick into Victor's face, causing permanent eye damage.

If Donald is charged with the crime of battery and found not guilty, it will be because:

(A) He did not intend to injure Victor.

(B) Professional hockey players consent to being hit by hockey sticks during a game.

(C) He reasonably believed that he was under attack and his actions were reasonable.

(D) Victor was the original aggressor.

Question 20

The town of Lilyville was the county seat and had a population of about 250,000. The city council of Lilyville consisted of 20 members, each of whom was elected at large. Although at one time Lilyville had had individual member districts, the city charter was revised in 1954 to provide for at-large election of all council members. The political life of the town had been dominated by members of the Good Ole Boys Club, and its full slate of candidates almost always won election. Among the population of Lilyville are now 60,000 blacks, 20,000 Hispanics, 3,000 Asians, and 2,000 Native Americans. During the long period that Lilyville had used the at-large election system, only one black person had ever served on the city council. Fifteen years ago, the Good Ole Boys Club had decided to slate Bill Johnson, who had been an outstanding scholar and athlete at the state university. Johnson, although black, was duly elected to the council with the Good Ole Boys' support. However, Johnson, during the course of his term, asked embarrassing questions about the housing conditions in predominantly black areas of the city and otherwise agitated for meaningful change. Although Johnson ran for reelection, he did not receive the Good Ole Boys' support and was soundly defeated, even though he received 95% of the black vote. Since then, no member of a minority group has served on the city council, nor has a member of a minority group been slated as a candidate by the Good Ole Boys Club.

If a minority coalition association brings suit to compel Lilyville to provide for single member districts, it would be most likely to win its case with arguments based upon which of the following provisions of the United States Constitution?

(A) Equal Protection Clause.

(B) Due Process Clause.

(C) The Fourteenth Amendment clause protecting the privileges and immunities of national citizenship.

(D) Article I, Section 2, Clause 4.

Question 21

Andy Carnopolous was well-known as a philanthropist. To ensure that his name would be long remembered, he planned to build the crown jewel of museums. He mentioned his plans to Mike, his longtime friend and governor of Massamont, an eastern state. Mike decided that the museum would bolster the economy and stature of wherever it was located and told Andy that if Andy put the museum in Massamont, he would arrange for the state to purchase the land and grant it to the museum. Andy agreed and the museum was built.

Andy appointed Adolph, an amateur painter, to be curator of Carnopolous Hall. Adolph was of German descent and was ashamed of Germany's actions during World War II. To assuage his own conscience, Adolph refused to hire anyone whom he believed to be of German descent. Henry applied for a job at the museum, but Adolph refused to hire him because of his German background. Henry discovered Adolph's rationale, and he brings suit against the museum.

The court will most likely find that Adolph's hiring policy is:

(A) Constitutional, because the museum is a private entity and so may constitutionally hire and fire as it desires.

(B) Constitutional, to the extent necessary to remedy past discrimination.

(C) Unconstitutional under the Equal Protection Clause, because the grant of the land is sufficient state involvement to render the museum's actions state action.

(D) Unconstitutional under the Equal Protection Clause, because the state will benefit from the museum and this creates a sufficient nexus to find state action.

Question 22

A retailer of personal watercraft and speedboats agreed to sell to a buyer a personal watercraft for $10,000. The written contract specified delivery within 30 days and a down payment of $2,000, but did not contain a liquidated damages clause. Two weeks after making the down payment, the buyer told the retailer that he lost his job and could not afford to go through with the purchase, and asked for his down payment back. The retailer, which could get as many of that model of watercraft as it required from the manufacturer for a wholesale price of $7,000, put the watercraft that it was going to deliver to the buyer back in its inventory. The retailer then sold it to someone else for $9,500.

The buyer sues the retailer to get back his deposit, and the retailer counterclaims for damages. Excluding incidental costs, which of the following amounts represents the most likely recovery?

(A) The buyer will recover $2,000.

(B) The buyer will recover $1,500.

(C) The retailer will recover $3,000.

(D) The retailer will recover $1,000.

Question 23

A fleeing bank robber ran into a school and took the principal hostage at gunpoint. The police, who had received a detailed description of the clothing the robber was wearing, surrounded the school and demanded that the robber come out with his hands up. When it began to get dark, the robber ordered the principal to undress, and the robber switched clothing with the principal. He tied the principal's hands to his side and pushed the principal out the door first. Seeing that the first person out of the door did not emerge with hands up and that the person was wearing clothing the robber was described as wearing, a police sharpshooter shot and killed the principal. The robber was captured and put on trial for the murder of the principal.

The jury should find the robber:

(A) Guilty, because the police were justified in using deadly force under the circumstances.

(B) Guilty, because changing clothes with the principal was an act taken with extreme indifference to an unjustifiably high risk to human life.

(C) Not guilty, because it was not foreseeable under the circumstances that the police would use deadly force.

(D) Not guilty, because the robber was not responsible for the police shooting the principal.

Question 24

The nephew of a financially successful farmer inherited a nearby farm with a tractor that was badly out of date. Because the local bank refused to extend credit solely to the nephew to buy a new tractor, the nephew asked his uncle to guarantee the loan. The uncle told him, "I'll guarantee that loan if you'll let me use the new tractor for 10 days without having to pay you rent." The nephew readily agreed to the uncle's proposal, so the uncle went to the local bank, where he kept his accounts, and told his loan officer, "I'm willing to guarantee that tractor loan for my nephew." This prompted the loan officer to agree to extend the requested credit to the nephew. Although the loan officer did not make the uncle sign any papers, he considered the uncle's word to be his bond and issued the nephew a loan commitment statement. That very evening the uncle learned that his nephew had a reputation for financial irresponsibility among his former classmates at the state agricultural college. The next day, the uncle telephoned the loan officer, telling him, "You can forget about me guaranteeing any loan to my nephew." Despite the uncle's phone call, the loan officer did not stop the check from being issued, and the nephew received the money to purchase the tractor. The nephew drove the tractor over to the uncle's farm and told him, "Here, you can have it for 10 days, just like I promised." The uncle replied, "I don't want to use your tractor and I'm not guaranteeing your loan."

Six months later, the nephew defaulted on the loan. Because of gross misuse, the new tractor was in terrible condition and its value would not cover anywhere near the amount of the loan. The nephew has departed for parts unknown.

If the bank sues the uncle for the unpaid portion of the loan:

(A) The bank will win, if the suretyship agreement was supported by consideration between the bank and the uncle.

(B) The bank will win, if the uncle's main purpose in making the agreement with the bank was to benefit himself rather than his nephew.

(C) The uncle will win, because the suretyship agreement was not in writing.

(D) The uncle will win, because he withdrew his promise before the nephew received the money or the tractor.

Question 25

Hal and Wallene, a married couple, owned Blackacre in joint tenancy. They conveyed a 10% interest in Blackacre to their daughter, Donna. Six months later, they conveyed a 10% interest in Blackacre to Donna's husband, Dan.

If the jurisdiction within which Blackacre is located does not recognize tenancy by the entirety, which of the following best describes the ownership of Blackacre after the conveyances?

(A) Hal and Wallene have an 80% interest as joint tenants, Donna has a 10% interest as tenant in common, and Dan has a 10% interest as tenant in common.

(B) Hal and Wallene have an 80% interest as tenants in common, Donna has a 10% interest as tenant in common, and Dan has a 10% interest as tenant in common.

(C) Hal and Wallene have an 80% interest as tenants in common, and Donna and Dan have a 20% interest as joint tenants.

(D) Hal and Wallene have an 80% interest as joint tenants, and Donna and Dan have a 20% interest as joint tenants.

Question 26

When Blandings decided to invest in the futures market, he borrowed $50,000 from Ace Financial Corporation, secured by a mortgage on his home. Shortly thereafter, when the bottom dropped out of the pork belly futures market, Blandings needed some ready cash, so he agreed to sell his home to Grant for $70,000. With the deed conveying the property to Grant was a recital signed by both parties stating that title passed "subject to" the indebtedness of $50,000 in favor of Ace, "which obligation grantee expressly assumes." Grant then paid Blandings $20,000, took possession of the house, and began making monthly payments of principal and interest to Ace. A few years later, Giant & Insensitive, Inc., a chemical manufacturing firm, built a huge sulfur processing plant just down the road from the home, which caused the house to immediately decline in value to $35,000. Grant's career as a dramatic actor similarly went into decline, and he was unable to continue making the monthly payments to Ace. Ace exercised its contractual right of nonjudicial foreclosure, and sold the house at a public auction for $34,000. Ace then brought suit against Blandings and Grant for $14,000, the difference between the proceeds of the foreclosure sale and the $48,000 principal remaining due on the original loan to Blandings. The jurisdiction does not bar deficiency judgments.

Ace should be granted a judgment for $14,000 against:

(A) Both Blandings and Grant.

(B) Only Blandings.

(C) Only Grant.

(D) No one.

Question 27

A patient sought psychiatric treatment from a psychiatrist. During the treatment, which consisted of hour-long analysis sessions twice a week, the psychiatrist, unknown to the patient, videotaped her. No sound recording was made of the sessions, but the psychiatrist was conducting a study on "body language" and planned to use the videotapes in those experiments. The patient learned that the psychiatrist had been videotaping their analysis sessions and brought an action against him on a theory of invasion of privacy.

Which of the following arguments best supports the patient's claims in this action?

(A) The psychiatrist has placed the patient in a false light.

(B) The psychiatrist has publicly displayed private facts of the patient's life.

(C) The psychiatrist has misappropriated the patient's likeness.

(D) The psychiatrist has intruded upon the patient's physical seclusion.

Questions 28-29 are based on the following fact situation:

Ken had a 1957 Chevrolet that he had restored using only original General Motors parts. He told his friend George that he was interested in selling it, but didn't know what price to ask. George said that he would pay $12,000 for the car, but would have to borrow the money and didn't know if he could get the financing. Ken said that he was going to put a classified ad in the auto section of the newspaper and really did not want to commit himself if George did not have the money. George then suggested that Ken postpone placing the ad in the newspaper and give him 10 days to obtain financing to buy the car. Ken agreed and wrote the following on a piece of paper and gave it to George: "I will sell my 1957 Chevrolet to George if he comes up with $12,000 within 10 days."

Later that day, Ken met an old college buddy, Lester, whom he had not seen in several years. Lester was in the business of selling customized cars, and when he learned of Ken's Chevrolet, said, "For 10% of the gross I could find you a buyer at no less than $15,000." Ken said nothing in reply.

The next morning, Lester telephoned Ken and told him that Mr. Jones was willing to pay $16,000 for the Chevrolet, sight unseen. Ken asked for Jones's phone number, which Lester gave, and then called Jones and arranged a sale. He then phoned George and said that he was revoking his offer.

28. Which of the following best describes the agreement between Ken and George?

(A) A promissory estoppel situation.

(B) A quasi-contract.

(C) An offer for a unilateral contract.

(D) An option contract.

29. If Lester is not paid by Ken and brings an action against Ken for breach of contract, seeking damages of $1,600, what will be the probable outcome?

(A) Ken will win, because 10% is unconscionably large as a finder's fee in such a transaction.

(B) Ken will win, because there was no consideration for any promise to pay that might have been implied from his conduct.

(C) Lester will win, because he obtained a buyer for Ken's Chevrolet and a purchase price over $15,000 was paid.

(D) Lester will win, unless Ken can show that he could have found another buyer who would pay at least $16,000 for the car.

Question 30

The following provision is on the statute books of the state of Central:

> No conveyance or mortgage of real property shall be valid against a subsequent purchaser for value and without notice whose conveyance is first recorded in accordance with the laws of the state of Central.

The following events all took place within the state of Central:

In January, Smith, the owner of Midacre, a parcel located in Lake County, executed and delivered a mortgage on the property to Senior Bank to secure a $50,000 loan. Due to a clerical error, the appropriate filing papers languished in the desk drawer of a bank officer, and so the mortgage was not recorded at that time. On February 15, Smith entered into a contract to sell Midacre to Jones for $150,000. On February 16, Smith took out a $30,000 mortgage on Midacre with Junior Bank. Junior Bank promptly and properly recorded the mortgage. Knowing nothing about either of the mortgages, Jones closed on Midacre on April 1, tendering $150,000 to Smith. Smith gave Jones a warranty deed to Midacre.

On April 3, the officer at Senior Bank finally found the papers for the Midacre mortgage in his drawer and properly recorded the mortgage that same day. Jones recorded his deed to Midacre on April 6.

Senior Bank brought an appropriate action to determine the status of its mortgage on Midacre. The court should hold that:

(A) Jones holds Midacre subject to both mortgages, and the Senior Bank mortgage is subordinate to the Junior Bank mortgage.

(B) Jones holds Midacre subject to both mortgages, and the Senior Bank mortgage is superior to the Junior Bank mortgage.

(C) Jones holds Midacre subject only to the Junior Bank mortgage.

(D) Jones holds Midacre subject only to the Senior Bank mortgage.

Question 31

A state enacted health care legislation to provide comprehensive insurance coverage on prescription drugs for all of its citizens. The legislation provided state reimbursement for the cost of all prescription drugs with one exception. Specifically excluded from the benefit plan was a drug commonly known as the "abortion pill," which was prescribed to induce early term abortions without surgery. All other prescription drugs for pregnant women were covered. A pregnant woman who had received a prescription for the drug and was subsequently denied reimbursement filed suit in federal district court challenging the constitutionality of the state's prescription drug benefit plan.

Which of the following best describes the appropriate standard by which the court should review the constitutionality of the state legislation?

(A) Because the state legislation does not improperly discriminate against a suspect class or burden a fundamental right, the woman will have to show that the legislation is not rationally related to any legitimate state interest.

(B) Because the state legislation discriminates against women by not providing coverage for all of their prescription medications as it does for men, the state will have to demonstrate that the legislation is substantially related to an important government interest.

(C) Because the state legislation impinges on a woman's constitutional right to choose whether to terminate her pregnancy, the state will have to show that the legislation does not constitute an undue burden on that right.

(D) Because the state legislation discriminates against women seeking to exercise their fundamental right to terminate their pregnancy in favor of women incurring the regular expenses of pregnancy, the state will have to demonstrate that the legislation is necessary to vindicate a compelling state interest.

Question 32

Pam sued Good Eats Restaurant, claiming that she injured her teeth, gums, and mouth when she bit into a hamburger that contained a large jagged piece of glass. Walter, working as a waiter for Good Eats at the time of the alleged incident, testified for Pam. Walter testified that, when he heard Pam scream, he looked in her direction and saw her remove a piece of glass from her bleeding mouth. On cross-examination, the defense asked Walter, "Isn't it a fact that three months ago you were fired by Good Eats for serving drinks to your friends and not charging for them?" Walter responded, "Yes, but I wasn't trying to steal anything. I just forgot to charge them." The defense then asked, "Isn't it a fact that last month you threw a rock through the plate glass window at Good Eats?" Walter replied, "That's not true; I was there but I didn't throw the rock." The defense then offered the testimony of Margaret. Margaret was prepared to testify that she also was there when the window was broken and that she saw Walter throw the rock.

Assuming that there have been no criminal charges filed as a result of the broken window, Margaret's testimony is:

(A) Inadmissible, because specific acts of misconduct that did not result in a conviction cannot be used to impeach a witness, either on cross-examination or through extrinsic evidence.

(B) Inadmissible, because specific acts of misconduct that did not result in a conviction cannot be established through extrinsic evidence.

(C) Admissible as evidence of bias.

(D) Admissible to establish that Walter lied under oath.

Question 33

In a wrongful death action for the death of his wife in an automobile accident, the plaintiff, Poshard, alleged that the accident was caused by a mudflap assembly that fell off the truck of Dean, the defendant. Poshard wishes to introduce the testimony of Willis, another truck driver who was on the same highway at the time, who heard someone tell Dean over CB radio that he had noticed at the truck stop that Dean's mudflap assembly on his truck was loose. Willis does not know the identity of the person who gave the warning.

If Dean objects to admission of the testimony, the court should rule that it is:

(A) Admissible to prove that Dean was notified that the mudflap assembly was loose.

(B) Admissible both to prove that Dean was notified that the mudflap assembly was loose and as substantive evidence that it was loose.

(C) Inadmissible, because Willis cannot identify who made the statement.

(D) Inadmissible, because it is hearsay not within any recognized exception.

Questions 34-35 are based on the following fact situation:

Agrigiant, Inc., a large midwestern farming corporation, and the Western Baking Company ("WBC"), a large food-selling corporation located on the Pacific coast, entered into a contract calling for Agrigiant to sell and WBC to buy 10,000 bushels of winter wheat for $5 per bushel. The contract stated that Agrigiant would deliver the wheat "F.O.B. St. Louis Railroad depot." Before the date on which performance was due, Agrigiant assigned all its rights under the contract to Pucker Farms, another large wheat producer. Pucker hired Acme Freight Lines to truck 10,000 bushels of winter wheat from the Pucker silos to a grain elevator in St. Louis, from which the wheat would be loaded onto Santa Fe Railroad hopper cars bound west. En route to St. Louis, the Acme trucks carrying the Pucker wheat were stopped by mobs of citizens maddened by the revelations that they and their children had been poisoned for years by the grain industry's practice of using highly toxic pesticides to fumigate grain and grain processing equipment. Although Pucker wheat was not fumigated with the pesticide, the mobs seized and burned the Acme trucks to protest the callousness and greed of the grain plutocrats and their government allies.

34. Pucker brings suit against WBC, which refused to pay the contract price for the wheat. What will be the probable outcome of this litigation?

(A) Pucker will lose.

(B) Pucker will recover the amount necessary to replace the destroyed wheat.

(C) Pucker will recover the full contract price.

(D) Pucker will recover the profits it would have realized under the contract.

35. WBC brings its own action against Agrigiant for breach of contract. What will be the probable outcome of this litigation?

(A) WBC will lose.

(B) WBC will recover the amount necessary to replace the destroyed wheat, over the contract price.

(C) WBC will recover the full contract price.

(D) WBC will be able to compel specific performance of the contract.

Question 36

A state statute prohibited the sale or possession of any food product containing more than one part per billion of a dangerous pesticide. An out-of-state driver taking her recreational vehicle through a corner of the state was stopped at a state inspection station. When the state trooper learned that the pantry of her RV was stocked with food, he asked to test a few samples of her baked goods. The samples contained about 600 parts per billion of the prohibited pesticide, and all of the other baked goods in her possession were tested and found to have the same level of pesticide. All of her baked goods, worth about $150, were confiscated and destroyed.

The state in which the driver lived has no laws governing the pesticide level of baked goods. A federal law designed to protect agricultural workers requires that any food product containing more than 500 parts per billion of the toxic pesticide must be labeled as such and be in special containers. The driver brings an action in federal court asserting that the state statute is invalid because it is preempted by the federal law.

How should the court rule as to this claim?

(A) For the state, because the purposes of the federal law are different from those of the challenged statute.

(B) For the state, because regulation of food quality is a power reserved to the states by the Tenth Amendment.

(C) For the driver, because the federal law does not expressly permit states to enact more stringent pesticide level controls.

(D) For the driver, because the federal law and the state statute regulate the same subject matter.

Question 37

A developer owned several acres in an old, dilapidated area of downtown. He was delighted when the city council decided to try to revitalize the city center, restoring some of the hundred-year-old buildings and creating a mixed use development that combined a variety of boutique shops and restaurants with small townhouse developments. The developer prepared a subdivision of his various parcels, filed a subdivision map showing commercial lots, obtained all the necessary approvals, and began selling the lots to merchants and businesspersons eager to join in the new prosperity of the development. Each of the deeds conveying lots sold by the developer contained the following:

> It is hereby covenanted by the seller that the property conveyed shall be used for commercial or residential purposes only, that no industrial, warehouse, or other manufacturing structures shall be erected or maintained thereon, and that this covenant shall bind the buyer, his heirs and assigns, and their successors.

Two years later, after all but two of the lots had been developed as small businesses, the developer was forced to raise funds immediately and sold his remaining two lots to a real estate speculation firm. The deed to the firm did not contain any language restricting the use of the property. The firm then sold the property to a giant supermarket chain, which intended to construct a warehouse and distribution center for its retail operations in the western states. The warehouse would involve the constant movement in and out of large trucks 24 hours per day, seven days a week.

A shopkeeper who had purchased a lot from the developer located next to the proposed warehouse operated a coffee shop specializing in local folk entertainment and poetry readings. She brings suit against the supermarket chain seeking to enjoin construction of the warehouse. Her attorney argues that the lots sold by the developer to the firm and then to the supermarket chain are bound by the same restrictions on use that are contained in the deed by which the shopkeeper took her property.

What is the likely outcome of this litigation?

(A) The shopkeeper will win unless the firm and the supermarket were not aware of the restrictions when they purchased the property.

(B) The shopkeeper will win if she can show that the developer established a common development scheme for his entire subdivision and that the subdivision appeared to conform to the scheme.

(C) The shopkeeper will lose because the restrictions in her deed binds only the purchaser of the land.

(D) The shopkeeper will lose because the deed by which the firm took the property from the developer did not contain any restrictions on use.

Question 38

Howard became very intoxicated one Saturday night, which was his custom, and as he was staggering homeward, he came upon a construction site where several large pieces of earthmoving equipment were parked. Having had heavy equipment training in the Army, Howard decided it would be fun to rearrange all the machines so that the operators would be very surprised when they returned to work on Monday. He started up a huge Caterpillar and drove it toward the edge of the site, but because he was so intoxicated, he lost control of it, and it rumbled out into the street, weaved along for about a quarter mile, and then crashed into Webster's house, demolishing the living room and kitchen.

In this jurisdiction, it is a misdemeanor to tamper with heavy equipment on a construction site. Howard is prosecuted on the tampering charge as well as for reckless damage of Webster's property.

Should he be convicted of the reckless damage charge?

(A) Yes, because he was tampering with heavy equipment on a construction site, in violation of law, when he damaged Webster's house.

(B) Yes, because he was intoxicated while driving a huge piece of earthmoving equipment.

(C) No, because at most he could be found guilty of criminal negligence.

(D) No, because he must have been aware that his conduct would cause damage to Webster's property in order to be found guilty of reckless damage.

Question 39

Dudley sent a computer virus to Harry attached to an e-mail. Dudley believed that the virus would just disable Harry's e-mail program for a short period of time without causing any additional damage. However, because of a hidden bug in Harry's e-mail program, the virus infected the hard drive of Harry's computer, eventually rendering it unusable. Harry not only lost important data, he had to replace the computer's hard drive at a cost of over $200.

The jurisdiction in which this occurred has a modern criminal code patterned after the Model Penal Code. One of its statutes makes it a criminal offense to "knowingly cause over $200 in damage to another's property."

Can Dudley be found guilty of violating the statute?

(A) No, because Dudley did not know that the virus would cause damage to the computer's hard drive.

(B) No, because Dudley did not intend to cause the damage to the computer's hard drive.

(C) Yes, because Dudley knew that he was sending a virus to Harry's computer.

(D) Yes, if Dudley was aware that in a very small percentage of cases the virus could cause damage to a computer's hard drive.

Question 40

In Robert's prosecution for robbery, the prosecutor asks the court to take judicial notice of the fact that, at that latitude, the sun is still up at 5:30 p.m. on June 21. The court so finds.

The effect of the court's action is that:

(A) The burden of persuasion is now on the defendant to prove otherwise as to the fact judicially noticed.

(B) The fact judicially noticed is established beyond a reasonable doubt.

(C) The prosecutor's burden of producing evidence on the fact judicially noticed is satisfied.

(D) The fact judicially noticed is conclusively established.

Question 41

A homeowner offered a roofer $500 to replace the bad shingles on his roof if the roofer could finish the job by October 1. The roofer told the homeowner he would get back to him after he had checked out prices at a local builder's supply store. The next day, the roofer phoned the homeowner, who was not at home, and left a message on his answering machine that he could not do the roof for less than $650. The roofer did not hear from the homeowner for several days; since October 1 was still two weeks away, the roofer phoned the homeowner again and left another message on his answering machine stating that "$500 is O.K. for the roofing job. I'll do it this weekend unless that would be inconvenient." The homeowner replayed the second message just as he was leaving town on a business trip and did not contact the roofer. That weekend, unknown to the homeowner, the roofer took his tools and materials to the homeowner's house and repaired the roof. When the homeowner returned from his trip several days later, the roofer presented him with a handwritten invoice for $500.

If the homeowner refuses to pay the roofer, and the latter brings an action solely for breach of contract to recover the $500 contract amount, who will likely prevail?

(A) The roofer, because he accepted the homeowner's offer before the latter materially changed his position in reliance upon the first telephone message.

(B) The roofer, assuming that the work he did was actually worth $500.

(C) The homeowner, because he was unaware that the roofer was doing the roof repair while he was out of town.

(D) The homeowner, because he did not accept the roofer's offer to do the roof repair for $500.

Question 42

Ogden owned Pineacre, an unimproved parcel of wooded land, in fee simple. He orally agreed to sell Pineacre to Burton under an installment land contract whereby Burton agreed to pay $5,000 down and $100 a month for the next 10 years, and Ogden would retain the deed until Burton finished paying the installments. Because Ogden and Burton were friends, they saw no need for a written contract and shook hands on the deal. After making the down payment, Burton moved onto the property and began clearing some of the trees for a road and a cabin. Ten months later, Burton, who had regularly made the monthly payments, was killed when a tree he was cutting fell on him. His estate consisted of a small quantity of personal possessions, $200,000 in cash, and his interest in Pineacre. His properly executed will conveyed his real estate to Rhonda and the remainder of his estate to Patrick. During the next several months, Burton's estate failed to make payments on the installment contract. Ogden then notified the estate that he was rescinding the deal and asserting ownership of Pineacre, and offered to return the amount Burton had paid him, less expenses, as restitution.

Burton's estate initiated a quiet title action, naming Ogden, Rhonda, and Patrick as parties. Papers filed in court by the estate indicated that it was prepared to pay the accelerated full balance of the contract from the proceeds of the estate in order to complete the conveyance and take title to the land, which it was permitted to do by the state's equity of redemption statutes.

If the court determines that Rhonda will receive title to Pineacre in fee simple free of any obligation on the installment contract, which of the following doctrines will the court use to reach this determination?

I. Doctrine of equitable conversion.

II. Doctrine of part performance.

III. Equitable mortgage doctrine.

(A) I., II., and III.

(B) I. only.

(C) I. and II.

(D) II. and III.

Question 43

Libby and her daughter Kimberly were driving home from an evening of Christmas shopping on December 21 when their car, which Libby was driving, was struck broadside by a car driven by Herman at an intersection controlled in all directions by stop signs. Libby and Kimberly were taken by ambulance to the hospital. In a personal injury action brought by Libby and Kimberly against Herman, pretrial discovery revealed that both cars were in perfect mechanical condition just before the accident, and Herman was on his way home from work at the time of the accident, but had stopped off at a bar before he reached the intersection at which he struck Libby's car.

At trial, Libby calls a co-worker of Herman, who testifies over objection that Herman has a reputation as a hard drinker who tolerates alcohol well but who always drinks a great deal at any one drinking occasion.

Was it error for the trial court to admit his testimony?

(A) Yes, because in a civil matter, evidence of a party's character may not be introduced until he has put his character at issue.

(B) Yes, because Libby may not attempt to prove that Herman acted in a particular way on one occasion in conformity with his reputation as to that behavior.

(C) No, as long as the co-worker had personal knowledge of Herman's drinking habits from having observed him while drinking.

(D) No, unless an unbiased eyewitness exists who can testify as to how much Herman actually drank at the bar before he had the accident with Libby.

Question 44

Paul Port spent the evening drinking at O'Hara's Bar in West Philadelphia. At 1 a.m., Port left O'Hara's to drive home. While driving home, Port passed out at the wheel. His car went through a red light at an intersection and was struck by a car driven by Dan Dane. Port, under the influence of alcohol, staggered from his car. Dane, believing that Port had been injured in the accident, said, "It's my fault. I was not paying attention. I'll take care of all your medical bills." Later that night, Port was treated for minor injuries at a nearby hospital.

Port sued Dane for damages, alleging that Dane was driving negligently at the time of the accident. Port offered the testimony of Wally Witness. Witness was prepared to testify that, after the accident, Dane stated in a clear, calm voice, "I was not paying attention. I'll take care of all your medical bills."

Assuming the proper objection, should Witness's testimony concerning Dane's statement be admitted?

(A) No, because Dane's statement is a settlement offer.

(B) Yes, as an admission by Dane.

(C) Dane's statement "I was not paying attention" should be admitted but the statement "I'll take care of all your medical bills" should not.

(D) No, if Port was negligent per se.

Question 45

Chuck had obtained a permit from the national forest service to cut some firewood in the national forest. He had driven his pickup to the designated area and had begun to cut down a marked tree with his axe when Chloe, a member of the Save the Vegetation movement, approached him and began berating him for cutting the tree. Chuck told her that he had a permit to cut and to leave him alone. Chloe persisted, however, shouting that Chuck was "a moronic, murdering plantkiller." Intending to frighten Chloe away, Chuck said, "Get away or I'll start cutting on people!" and swung his axe as if to strike her. The manufacturer of the axe had neglected to insert a metal pin that secured the axe handle to the blade, and Chuck's previous chopping had so loosened the head that it flew off the handle and struck Chloe in the upper chest, crushing her clavicle.

If Chloe brings an action for battery against Chuck, will she recover?

(A) No, if a reasonable person would have been angered by Chloe's remarks.

(B) No, because the defective axe was the cause in fact of Chloe's injuries.

(C) Yes, because Chuck intended to frighten her.

(D) Yes, unless she intended to provoke Chuck.

Question 46

The owner of three acres of lakefront property subdivided it and sold two acres to a buyer, retaining the one acre actually fronting upon the lake. The deed for the two acres expressly included an easement over the westernmost 30 feet of the one-acre parcel retained by the owner; the easement was for access to the lake for recreational purposes. Shortly after the transaction was completed, the buyer recorded his deed in the county containing the land. The county maintained an alphabetical grantor-grantee index only.

Fifteen years later, the owner died, leaving the one acre of beachfront property to his wife. She sold it to a real estate developer that planned to build beachfront condominiums. A month later, the buyer died, and his two acres passed by testamentary gift to his nephew. Three weeks after taking title to the property, the nephew and his family drove to the property, intending to spend a weekend of waterskiing at the lake. When they arrived, they discovered that the developer had erected a chain link fence all along the boundary between the nephew's land and the acre of beachfront land.

The nephew brings an action to enjoin the developer from obstructing his easement across the acre of beachfront property. Which of the following best describes why the nephew should prevail in this litigation?

(A) Since the developer and the nephew can trace their predecessors in interest to a common grantor whose covenants run with the land, the developer is estopped from interfering with the nephew's use of the easement.

(B) The nephew's easement is a legal interest that the developer has record notice of, even though there is no tract index.

(C) Since there is no tract index, the developer was under an obligation to determine the riparian rights of any adjacent landowners before erecting the chain link fence.

(D) The nephew's easement is a legal interest that attaches not just to a legal estate but to the land itself, and, running with the land, it binds successive owners of the servient estate whether or not they have notice of it.

GO ON TO THE NEXT PAGE

Questions 47-48 are based on the following fact situation:

Gordon's adult daughter Sheila smoked two packs of cigarettes a day, and he had often tried to persuade her to stop, to no avail. Gordon then learned that Sheila and her husband had decided to try to have a baby, and when he thereafter saw Sheila at a party, he told her, "If you will give up smoking for the next 11 months, at the end of that time I will give you $10,000." Sheila agreed to stop smoking that very day. After leaving the party, Sheila had second thoughts. She remembered that her father had once promised her that if she would refrain from wearing makeup until she was 16, he would buy her a car, and had never done so. Sheila called her mother, and asked her if she thought Gordon was serious. Nancy, her mother, said, "Go ahead and quit, honey—if your father won't pay, I'll see that you get the money he promised you from my own accounts."

Sheila quit smoking that day and never smoked again. Ten months after Gordon's conversation with Sheila, Gordon and Nancy were killed in an auto accident.

47. Assume for the purposes of this question only that, one month later, Sheila sought payment of the $10,000 only from her father's estate. Will Sheila prevail as to this claim?

    (A) No, because she will be unable to prove the terms of the oral contract between her and her father, because he is dead.

    (B) No, because her father's offer to pay was terminated upon his death.

    (C) Yes, because she has performed under a valid contract, and thus her father's estate must now perform.

    (D) Yes, because she changed her position for the worse in reliance on her father's promise, and thus his executor is estopped from denying that the contract existed.

48. Assume for the purposes of this question only that Sheila files a claim against her mother's estate for $10,000 on the promise her mother made to pay that amount if her father refused to pay. She proves that she has submitted a claim for $10,000 to the executor of her father's estate and has been refused payment. What is the best argument for the probate court's rejecting this claim against Nancy's estate?

    (A) The contract between Nancy and Sheila was illusory.

    (B) Sheila has not been damaged by any breach because the only effect—that she quit smoking—was salutary.

    (C) The contract between Nancy and Sheila was oral.

    (D) No consideration flowed to Nancy under the contract.

Question 49

Max was driving his beat-up old car along a narrow coast road overlooking the coastal bluffs when he was passed by Marcia in her new Mercedes. Marcia's daughter, Stephanie, was lying down in the back seat of the Mercedes and could not be seen. Max sped up, drew even with the Mercedes, and repeatedly rammed his car into the side of the newer car. After several collisions, the Mercedes was forced off the road, sliding down the cliff for several yards and being kept from falling the several hundred feet onto the rocks and surf below by a large tree growing out from the bluff.

Marcia and Stephanie were rescued and Max was charged with attempted murder of both of them. At his trial, he testifies that he was angry because of the cavalier way Marcia passed him in her new car, and that his only intent in smashing into her car was to scratch and dent it so that she would not be so haughty in the future.

Assuming that the trier of fact believes this testimony, Max may be convicted as to:

(A) Marcia.

(B) Stephanie.

(C) Both Marcia and Stephanie.

(D) Neither Marcia nor Stephanie.

Question 50

At the trial of the plaintiff's breach of contract action against the defendant, the plaintiff called as a witness her accountant to testify about the difference in gross sales, gross income, and net profit caused by the defendant's failure to supply the promised quantity of ice cream to the plaintiff's boutique ice cream shop/bookstore. When the plaintiff's attorney asked the accountant to state the gross income figures for the year prior to formation of the contract between the plaintiff and the defendant, the accountant replied that he could not remember the exact amounts. The plaintiff's counsel then handed the accountant a copy of the federal tax return submitted by the plaintiff for that year, and asked him to read it. Counsel then asked, "Now that you have read the tax return, can you remember what the gross income of the plaintiff's ice cream shop was for the relevant period?" The defendant's counsel objects.

How should the court rule?

(A) Sustained; the plaintiff's counsel is seeking to elicit testimony based on inadmissible hearsay.

(B) Sustained; the accountant's testimony is not the best evidence.

(C) Overruled; the accountant's hearsay testimony is admissible as a past recollection recorded.

(D) Overruled; the accountant's testimony is admissible evidence relating to the plaintiff's damages.

Question 51

Edward owns 15 acres of undeveloped property near the outskirts of Middleville. The land is mostly covered with grass and some old trees, and a small stream meanders through a portion of it. The parcel is adjacent to a small public park. Edward has been negotiating with the professional football league for assignment of an expansion franchise to Middleville, and believes that he has an excellent chance of being awarded a franchise two years from now. If so, he will build a stadium complex on the 15 acres to house the team. Until then, he would like to gain the goodwill of the city council and to get the citizenry in the habit of spending leisure time at or near his property. He wants to open the 15 acres to public use for picnicking and similar activities, and has asked you, his lawyer, for advice on the best manner of doing so while retaining the greatest freedom of action if the football franchise is awarded.

Which of the following would best suit Edward's needs?

(A) Dedicate the 15 acres for use as a public park.

(B) Lease the 15 acres to the city for two years.

(C) Grant the city an easement for public recreational uses for two years.

(D) Covenant that the city may use the 15 acres for recreation for two years.

Question 52

After leaving ceremonies at which Judge Burger had been named distinguished jurist of the year, while both Judge Burger and Judge Douglas were being interviewed by the press on the courthouse steps, Judge Douglas stated to a reporter, "Burger is a senile imbecile who lets his clerks write all his opinions. He hasn't had a lucid thought since 1975. In addition, he has been on the payroll of the mob for a decade." Enraged, Judge Burger attempted to choke Judge Douglas into unconsciousness, and was only pried away by the intervention of several reporters. Burger subsequently brought an action for defamation against Douglas.

Which of the following, if established by Burger in his defamation action, would permit recovery against Douglas?

(A) Douglas negligently made the statements, which were false, and caused Burger actual injury.

(B) Douglas made the statements knowing they were false.

(C) Douglas made the statements because he hated Burger and wished to destroy his reputation in the legal community.

(D) Douglas made the statements in order to ensure that Burger's political career was nipped in the bud.

Question 53

After a long period of marital problems, a wife told her husband that she was going to file for a divorce. Because the wife had recently inherited a large sum of money, the husband was determined not to let her go through with the divorce. He contacted an ex-convict and offered him $10,000 if he would kill his wife. The ex-convict agreed and they picked a time when the wife would be in the house by herself. When the ex-convict broke into the house, however, the wife called the police and fled out the back door. The ex-convict shot and wounded the wife as she was running away, but he was apprehended by the police before he could do any further harm.

After the ex-convict implicated the husband, both were charged with attempted murder and conspiracy to commit murder, and the husband was also charged with solicitation of murder. As part of a plea bargain, the ex-convict agreed to testify against the husband and plead guilty to aggravated battery in exchange for the attempted murder and conspiracy to commit murder charges being dropped.

Which of the following best states the crimes for which the husband can be convicted?

(A) Solicitation, attempted murder, and conspiracy to commit murder.

(B) Attempted murder and conspiracy to commit murder.

(C) Solicitation and attempted murder.

(D) Attempted murder only.

Question 54

Under which of the following circumstances would the named defendant be most likely to be convicted of common law murder?

(A) Huey, stopped by police for a traffic violation, gets into a fight with one of the officers and wrestles his gun away from him. The other officer fires his weapon, hitting Huey in the stomach. Rendered unconscious, Huey nevertheless fires the gun he took from the officer and hits the firing officer, killing him.

(B) Plagued by an infestation of rats in his house, Louie takes a flashlight and a pistol to the basement where the rats are worst, and begins picking off those that he can see. When one of the rats runs under a pile of gunny sacks, Louie aims at the movement he thinks is the rat burrowing to safety and shoots it. Unknown to Louie, the movement was a homeless person who had broken into Louie's home and crawled under the sacks for warmth, and who had been awakened by the previous shots. The person is killed by the pistol bullet.

(C) Despite the fact that he has had nine drunk driving arrests within the last year, and is on probation from his last drunk driving conviction, in which he pleaded guilty after smashing up another driver's car, Dewey drives to his favorite bar, gets extremely intoxicated, and then attempts to drive home. On his way, his car collides with another, killing the two occupants.

(D) While target shooting at some discarded soft drink cans on his ranch, Mickey takes aim at one of the cans and fires his rifle. The bullet passes through the can, hits a rock, ricochets to a nearby tree, ricochets off the tree, and strikes Mickey's companion, who is standing next to Mickey, and kills him.

Questions 55-56 are based on the following fact situation:

Barton entered into a contract with Currier to buy Texacre for $70,000. Although Barton was expecting to receive a large sum of money from an inheritance in a few weeks, he had very limited funds on hand and was able to obtain financing from Arco State Bank only in the amount of $40,000. He executed a promissory note in that amount secured by a mortgage on Texacre. To cover the remaining balance, Barton went to Currier and obtained a loan for $30,000, giving Currier a promissory note in that amount secured by a mortgage on Texacre and orally promising to pay Currier in full when he received his inheritance money. At the time the sale of Texacre was consummated, neither Currier nor Arco knew about the other's mortgage.

Currier learned from Barton a few days later that he would be receiving his inheritance sooner than he had thought. Currier promptly negotiated the mortgage note to Darwin for $25,000 without informing Barton. Darwin had no notice of Arco's interest in Texacre. The next day, Currier received a check from Barton in the amount of $30,000. A few days later, Currier left the country with the $95,000 he had made on the sale of Texacre. That same day, Arco properly recorded its mortgage on Texacre.

A statute in the jurisdiction provides:

> No conveyance of an interest in land, other than a lease for less than one year, shall be valid against any subsequent purchaser for value, without notice thereof, unless the conveyance is recorded.

The jurisdiction also permits a deficiency judgment against the mortgagor if the proceeds of a foreclosure sale are insufficient to satisfy the mortgage debt.

55. If a foreclosure action is instituted by Darwin, which of the following correctly states his rights against Barton?

    (A) Darwin has no enforceable interest in Texacre and no rights against Barton because Currier did not transfer the mortgage to him and Barton paid the mortgage amount in full.

    (B) Darwin has an enforceable interest in Texacre to the extent of $25,000, but cannot recover against Barton personally for any deficiency.

    (C) Darwin has an enforceable interest in Texacre to the extent of $25,000, and can recover against Barton personally for any deficiency.

    (D) Darwin has an enforceable interest in Texacre to the extent of $30,000, and can recover against Barton personally for any deficiency.

56. Assume for purposes of this question only that Darwin has an enforceable mortgage interest in Texacre. Which of the following correctly states Darwin's interest in relation to Arco's interest?

    (A) Arco's interest is superior to Darwin's interest because Arco has recorded its interest.

    (B) Arco's interest is superior to Darwin's interest because Arco provided a purchase money mortgage for Texacre.

    (C) Darwin's interest is superior to Arco's interest because neither Currier nor Darwin had notice of Arco's interest at the time of their transactions.

    (D) Darwin's interest and Arco's interest are equal in priority because they are both purchase money mortgages.

Question 57

Parker is suing Driver for injuries Parker suffered when his car was struck by Driver's truck, allegedly because Driver had fallen asleep at the wheel after driving all night. At trial, Glenda, Driver's girlfriend, testified that she had been with Driver in the truck and had taken over the driving duties for several hours that night while Driver napped. Parker calls Walker, an acquaintance of Glenda, to testify that Glenda told him that she had been unable to get out of bed the weekend the accident occurred because of severe back pain.

Walker's testimony is:

(A) Admissible for impeachment purposes only.

(B) Admissible for impeachment purposes and as substantive evidence as a declaration of physical condition.

(C) Inadmissible, because this means of impeachment can be done only through cross-examination.

(D) Inadmissible, because Parker has not first given Glenda an opportunity to explain or deny the statement.

Question 58

Robert is charged with having been one of two men who robbed the Roundup Bar and its patrons at gunpoint at 5:30 p.m. on December 16.

Robert calls Leon as a witness. Leon will testify that he was at Robert's house about 9:30 a.m. on December 16, and that as he was leaving, Robert said to him, "I'm going to my mother-in-law's house this afternoon for a birthday party."

Is Leon's testimony admissible?

(A) No, it is hearsay not within any exception.

(B) No, it is irrelevant.

(C) Yes, it is not being offered to prove the truth of the matter stated, so it is not hearsay.

(D) Yes, it is hearsay within an exception, and thus admissible.

Question 59

Concerned about the number of households headed by single teenage mothers and the deleterious effects of overpopulation, the state of Northwest enacted legislation requiring that any person under the age of 25 must obtain a certificate of responsibility before having children. Any fetus whose parents do not both have a certificate of responsibility must be aborted under the terms of the statutes, and any child born into the same circumstances will be placed up for adoption. Parents who violate the statute are subject to fine, imprisonment, or both.

If Ben, a 22-year-old resident of Northwest, brings an action in federal court seeking to enjoin enforcement of the legislation on the grounds that it violates his constitutional rights, alleging that he plans to marry and father children before he is 25, which of the following provides the strongest justification for dismissing the action?

(A) It involves a nonjusticiable political question.

(B) It is not ripe for adjudication.

(C) There is no substantial federal question involved.

(D) Ben has no standing to sue.

Question 60

State A's defamation statutes require as a prerequisite for the filing of a libel suit against a public newspaper that the plaintiff demand in writing that the defendant retract the allegedly defamatory material. In Rupert's defamation suit against Cellulose Corporation, publisher of the *Metropolis Times,* a public newspaper, Rupert calls as a witness Wilma, a former employee of the *Times* who was the secretary to the editor during the period in which the events underlying Rupert's suit occurred. Wilma will testify that two days after the allegedly defamatory story was run in the *Times,* she remembers receiving a letter to the editor of the *Times* delivered by Rupert. Rupert has already testified that he wrote a letter to the editor demanding a retraction, and that the letter was delivered by him the same day that the defamatory story was published.

Should the court admit Wilma's testimony over Cellulose Corporation's objection?

(A) No, because Wilma is no longer employed by the *Times.*

(B) No, because the letter itself is the best evidence.

(C) Yes, because Wilma's testimony is evidence of a matter in issue.

(D) Yes, because Wilma's testimony is an admission by a party-opponent.

Questions 61-62 are based on the following fact situation:

Decker owed Crieder $1,000 on a promissory note that was due on August 1. After Decker told Crieder that he might not be able to pay the note on its due date, Crieder agreed to extinguish the debt if Decker, who was the manager of a discount electronics store, purchased a new entertainment system that Crieder's girlfriend wanted and had it delivered to her home and set up by August 15. Since Decker would have to pay only $600 for the system because of his manager's discount, he agreed and the parties signed a writing to that effect on July 26.

61. Is the new agreement between Crieder and Decker legally enforceable?

    (A) No, because Decker incurred no additional detriment that would serve as consideration for the new agreement.

    (B) No, unless it would have cost Crieder $1,000 to purchase the entertainment system himself.

    (C) Yes, because Decker incurred a different obligation than he originally had.

    (D) Yes, because the new agreement between Decker and Crieder is enforceable with or without consideration as long as it was made in good faith.

62. Assume for purposes of this question only that Crieder filed suit against Decker on August 2 for failure to pay the $1,000 promissory note. May Decker have this action enjoined by introducing evidence of the July 26 agreement?

    (A) Yes, because the July 26 agreement between Decker and Crieder suspended Decker's obligation on the promissory note.

    (B) Yes, because the July 26 agreement between Decker and Crieder discharged Decker's obligation on the promissory note.

    (C) No, unless Decker has already initiated the purchase of the entertainment system in reliance on Crieder's promise to extinguish the debt.

    (D) No, because Decker's only remedy is to sue for damages for breach of the July 26 agreement.

Question 63

Ron, Mike, and Dick decided that they could make some easy money by going to a shopping center that catered to wealthy people, finding elderly women who were wearing a lot of expensive jewelry and furs, then following the women home and robbing them before they could get into their houses. The three agreed to meet at the shopping center the next evening. At the appointed time, each arrived, armed either with a gun or knife, and the three began checking out the shoppers, looking for a likely victim.

Ron began to have second thoughts when he considered that Mike had already done time for armed robbery and several assaults with deadly weapons, and that Mike had vowed that he would never "do time" again because "somebody finked to the cops." As Dick pointed out a frail-looking woman wearing what appeared to be a diamond necklace and a mink coat, Ron told Mike and Dick that he had changed his mind and wanted no part of the action. As the other two went off following the selected victim, Ron returned to his car and drove home.

The next day, Ron learned from the television news that an elderly woman had been robbed and brutally beaten as she got out of her car in her driveway after returning from a shopping trip the previous evening. Because of her ill health and age, the woman had died as a result of the beating.

The police later arrested Mike and Dick and obtained a full confession from Dick detailing the agreement and actions of all three, including the fact that Mike had beaten the woman to death after he and Dick had robbed her.

Ron is guilty of:

(A) No crime.

(B) Conspiracy.

(C) Murder.

(D) Murder and conspiracy.

Questions 64-65 are based on the following fact situation:

An elderly grocery store customer was doing his weekly shopping at the supermarket, and had left his grocery list at home. Somewhat absent-minded, he occasionally would reach into his coat pocket to take out the list, forgetting for the moment that it was not there. A clerk who saw the customer take his hand out of his pocket more than once alerted a security guard that the customer was shoplifting. After the customer had passed through the checkout counter, the security guard stepped in front of him and said, "Okay, Pops, what's in your pocket?" When the customer replied, "My car keys," the security guard said, "Let's go to the manager's office." The customer refused to move, demanding to know why he was being harassed. The security guard said, "Have it your way, then." Pulling a pair of handcuffs from his belt, he reached for the customer's arm. "I'll go," said the customer, and he went with the guard to the manager's office as some of his friends and neighbors looked on. The security guard told him to sit in a chair, left the office, and locked the door behind him from the outside with a key. An hour later, the manager, who had been supervising installation of a computer inventory system in another part of the store, returned with the security guard to his office, and told the employee who had originally alerted the security guard to identify the customer. After explaining what he had seen, including that he had never actually seen the customer put anything in his pocket, the employee left. When the customer explained the situation, the manager apologized profusely and escorted him out of the store.

64. If the customer brings an action against the supermarket for assault based on the security guard's attempt to handcuff him, will he likely recover?

    (A) No, because he suffered no injury from the guard's actions.

(B) No, if the guard did not intend to injure the customer when he pulled out the handcuffs and reached for the customer's arm.

(C) Yes, if the security guard was unreasonable in suspecting that the customer was a shoplifter.

(D) Yes, because he was afraid that the guard was going to handcuff him.

65. If the customer brings a false imprisonment action against the supermarket, will he be able to recover for the humiliation that he felt on being seized and taken to the manager's office in front of his friends and neighbors?

(A) No, humiliation is not actionable.

(B) No, unless the security guard and employee were negligent in suspecting that he was a shoplifter.

(C) Yes, but only if the store's actions were extremely outrageous.

(D) Yes, because he was falsely imprisoned.

Question 66

Upacre and Downacre are located in the state of New Cossack, which has a statutory 10-year prescription and adverse possession period. New Cossack follows the riparian doctrine of reasonable use.

Uri owned Upacre, a 15-acre undeveloped parcel of land, through which Timur Creek ran. Timur Creek also ran through Downacre, a 35-acre parcel located downstream from Upacre. Downacre was owned by Dmitri, and Dmitri began using Downacre to grow cotton and for other agricultural purposes. Dmitri drew off water from Timur Creek to irrigate his land and to water livestock thereon. Dmitri's use of Downacre and Timur Creek water has been continuous and uninterrupted for 18 years. Two years ago, Uri constructed a residence on Upacre, and began to draw off the waters of Timur Creek for his domestic use. During the first summer that Uri occupied the Upacre residence, there was adequate water in Timur Creek for all of Uri's domestic purposes and for all of Dmitri's agricultural purposes. However, the flow of Timur Creek is irregular and the water level dropped dramatically this summer. The amount of water in Timur Creek is sufficient to meet either all of Dmitri's needs and none of Uri's or all of Uri's needs and one-half of Dmitri's. Both Uri and Dmitri claim they are entitled to sufficient water from Timur Creek to meet all their respective needs. Each files suit against the other to enforce his rights.

In the resulting trial of the case, who will prevail?

(A) Dmitri, because he has a prior reasonable use of the water.

(B) Dmitri, because he is entitled to the water by prescription.

(C) Uri, because his use of the water does not totally deprive Dmitri of water for his needs.

(D) Uri, because Dmitri's use of the water is not a natural use.

Question 67

A state statute prohibited, under criminal penalties, the sale or furnishing of any alcoholic beverage to a minor. A 16-year-old minor went to his neighborhood liquor store and asked a patron who was about to enter if the latter would purchase some beer for him. The patron agreed, took the minor's money, and returned with a six-pack of beer. At the moment that the beer changed hands, an official of the State Bureau of Alcohol Control leapt from behind a nearby car and announced that both the patron and the minor were under arrest. The patron ran to his car and escaped. The minor is now being prosecuted under the statute as having aided and abetted the patron in its violation.

Which of the following is his best argument in defense?

(A) He cannot be convicted as an aider and abettor unless the principal is first convicted.

(B) He cannot be convicted as an aider and abettor of violating a statute designed to protect the class of which he is a member—minors.

(C) He cannot be convicted of aiding and abetting any crime because he is a minor.

(D) He cannot be convicted alone of committing a crime that requires at least two parties to commit a violation.

Question 68

In a civil action tried to a jury, Defendant objected to the introduction by Plaintiff of certain evidence without the judge first making a preliminary ruling on the admissibility of the evidence.

For which evidence is Defendant's objection ***not*** appropriate?

(A) Opinion testimony regarding the structural integrity of a building by an engineer called by Plaintiff, without a preliminary determination by the judge that the engineer is an expert.

(B) Hospital records pertaining to Plaintiff offered by Plaintiff, without a preliminary determination by the judge that they were made as a regular activity of the hospital staff.

(C) Contract negotiations between Plaintiff and a third party, without a preliminary determination by the judge that the third party was Defendant's agent.

(D) A paramedic's testimony that Plaintiff's wife, before she died, said that Defendant's car went through a red light before hitting her, without a preliminary determination by the judge that she made the statement under a sense of impending death.

Question 69

A criminal statute in the state of Leland adopted the common law definition of larceny. Another Leland statute provided as follows:

> It shall be an affirmative defense to a crime if the defendant establishes by clear and convincing evidence that, due to a mental disease or defect, he was unable to appreciate the criminality of his conduct or conform his conduct to the requirements of the law.

Victor Victim was leaving town for two weeks and he asked his cousin, Don, to stop by the house each day and water the plants. While at Victim's home, Don found the keys to Victim's new Corvette that was parked in the garage. Don took the car and drove it into town to show his friends. Don told all of his friends that he had purchased the Corvette. Victim returned home three days early, saw that the Corvette was missing, and called the police. Later that day, Don was arrested and charged with larceny.

At Don's trial, Don testified that he intended to return the car. In addition, two psychiatrists testified that, due to a mental defect, Don suffered from an extreme inferiority complex and delusions of grandeur. The doctors further testified that his mental condition caused him to take the car and to tell other people that he owned it. At the conclusion of the evidence, the court's instructions to the jury included the following:

I. If you find by a preponderance of the evidence that the defendant intended to return the car, you should find the defendant not guilty.

II. If you find by a preponderance of the evidence that, due to a mental disease or defect, the defendant was unable to appreciate the criminality of his conduct or conform his conduct to the requirements of the law, you should find the defendant not guilty.

Don was found guilty and he appealed, claiming that the jury instructions violated his constitutional rights. The appellate court should rule that:

(A) Both instructions were constitutional.

(B) Both instructions were unconstitutional.

(C) Instruction I was unconstitutional; Instruction II was constitutional.

(D) Instruction I was constitutional; Instruction II was unconstitutional.

Question 70

The legislature of the state of New Shire enacted a program by which students in the public schools could request instruction as to specific religions and religious beliefs, and thus participate in public school programs in which leaders of the religions involved gave religious instruction and performed religious practices on school grounds. The program provided instruction on any religion requested by a student.

Which of the following, if true, would be relevant in assessing the constitutionality of the state religious instruction program?

I. The substantial effect of the legislation is to promote the religions studied.

II. The primary purpose of the statute is to foster belief in the religions studied.

III. The state does not have a compelling interest in instructing public school students about specific religions.

IV. The legislation requires that religious leaders and school officials interact constantly and frequently.

(A) I., II., and III.

(B) I., III., and IV.

(C) II., III., and IV.

(D) I., II., and IV.

Question 71

A motorist purchased a new sport utility vehicle from his local dealer. Standard equipment on the vehicle included a set of top-of-the-line tires from a premium tire company. However, the motorist was able to save $400 on the purchase price by allowing the dealer to substitute a lower priced tire manufactured by a discount tire manufacturer. Unbeknownst to the motorist and the dealer, the tire manufacturer had negligently designed the tires, with the result that a tire would occasionally blow out when the car was traveling at a high rate of speed in hot weather. On July 4, the motorist was traveling 80 m.p.h. in a 55 m.p.h. zone. A tire exploded, resulting in damage to the vehicle and injury to the motorist.

If the motorist sues the dealer on a theory of strict liability, is he likely to prevail?

(A) Yes, because the tire was in a dangerously defective condition when the motorist purchased the car.

(B) Yes, because the dealer is responsible for the negligence of the tire manufacturer, because the dealer used its tires.

(C) No, because the motorist assumed the risk when he substituted the discount tires in exchange for $400.

(D) No, because the motorist was misusing the tire when he was traveling at 80 m.p.h.

Question 72

Jimmy McFinn, a resident of New Oregon, kept a pet bear, Horace, at his farm. Horace was very old in bear years. He had no teeth, no claws, and very little energy. The joke in the community was that Horace could not squeeze a lemon. Horace had not always been so tame. When Jimmy first obtained Horace, he had a large steel cage constructed to house the animal. The cage had an electronic lock that only opened with a security code. Even though Horace was currently harmless, he was always kept locked in the cage. One night during a severe storm while Jimmy was out of town, a bolt of lightning hit the cage and the door opened. Horace left the cage and wandered off. The next morning, 10-year-old Victoria was waiting on a rural road for her school bus. Horace emerged from a wooded area about 100 feet from where Victoria was standing and headed towards her. She screamed and turned to run, tripping on the road and breaking her arm when she fell.

If Victoria sues Jimmy on a theory of strict liability for her bodily harm, will she prevail?

(A) No, because Horace was in fact a non-dangerous animal.

(B) No, because the damage she suffered was not the type of damage that a bear would normally cause.

(C) Yes, because Horace is a wild animal.

(D) Yes, but only if she can establish that pet bears were uncommon in the community.

Question 73

Concerned about the rising death toll on the state's highways, the legislature of the state of Red enacted a statute providing for a summary one-year suspension of the driver's license of any person convicted of three speeding violations within a 12-month period. The statute provided that an administrative hearing is immediately available upon request. However, that hearing is limited to a determination of whether the licensee is the same person who was convicted of the speeding violations.

Donna received three speeding citations in a three-week period and was convicted of all three charges. Her license was promptly suspended under the authority of the state statute. Without first seeking an administrative hearing, Donna files a suit in federal district court challenging the constitutionality of the statute.

The court should rule that the state law is:

(A) Constitutional, because driving an automobile on the state's highways is a privilege and not a right.

(B) Constitutional, because the state's interest in promptly removing unsafe drivers from its roads outweighs Donna's right to a prior hearing under these circumstances.

(C) Unconstitutional, because the law creates an irrebuttable presumption that all drivers falling within the ambit of the statute are unsafe.

(D) Unconstitutional, as a denial of due process without a prior hearing.

Question 74

In connection with its agricultural products price support program, the United States Department of Agriculture regularly sent marketing and price information via telephone and teletype to its numerous field offices in various states. Recently, problems arose because sophisticated criminals were using electronic devices to intercept the transmitted information, which they then used to gain an unfair advantage over other traders in the nation's commodities markets. To alleviate this situation, Congress enacted legislation making it a criminally punishable offense to "intercept marketing and/or price information in any fashion or to transmit such intercepted information to any other person in any fashion."

Delbert, who opposed the federal agricultural price support program, learned the identity of the individuals who were intercepting the Department of Agriculture transmissions, and, in exchange for not revealing their identities, obtained copies of every transmission they intercepted. He published these in his weekly newsletter, the "Market Ripoff Report."

If Delbert is prosecuted for violation of the federal statute prohibiting transmission of intercepted marketing or price information, what is Delbert's strongest argument that the statute is unconstitutional as applied to him?

(A) The statute denies him the equal protection of the law as guaranteed by the Fourteenth Amendment.

(B) The statute violates his right not to be deprived of liberty without due process of law.

(C) The statute violates his First Amendment right to free speech.

(D) The statute is an undue burden upon interstate commerce.

Question 75

Cheryl had a bumper crop in her garden this year and decided to sell her surplus at a busy intersection near her home. She loaded her fruits and vegetables into her pickup truck and drove to the intersection, parking on the corner where there was a vacant lot, and put up a small sign advertising her products and prices. Business was fairly good, so she returned for the next four days. A statute provides that it is a misdemeanor, punishable by a fine of up to $500 and/or imprisonment in county jail for up to one year, to sell any product without a business license, except for informal sales held on the property of the seller no more often than once every three months.

At Cheryl's trial, she requested but was refused appointed counsel. Assuming that she would otherwise qualify as indigent, if she is convicted of violating the statute, what is the maximum penalty that may be imposed upon her?

(A) Imprisonment for six months.

(B) A $500 fine.

(C) Imprisonment for six months and a $500 fine.

(D) No penalty, because her conviction is void as having been obtained in violation of her right to counsel under the Sixth Amendment.

Question 76

Porter sued Data Exchange, a computer dealer engaged in buying and selling used computers, alleging that he was not given credit for a CD-ROM drive that he had on the computer that he had sent back for resale. Warden, the bookkeeper, testified that it was company practice when a boxed computer was returned to have one clerk open the box and identify the type of computer and its components and have another clerk record the information in the inventory ledger. Data Exchange seeks to enter into evidence the original ledger entry, which Warden authenticated, showing that a CD-ROM drive was not checked off on the components list for Porter's computer. Porter objects to the admission of the ledger.

The ledger is:

(A) Admissible, because it is a record of a transaction for which Warden does not have any present recollection.

(B) Admissible, because it was regular company practice to record receipt of the components in the inventory ledger.

(C) Inadmissible as hearsay within hearsay, because even if a hearsay exception permits introducing the record itself rather than requiring testimony by the employee who made it, that employee was just recording hearsay because he had no personal knowledge of what he was recording.

(D) Inadmissible hearsay, because absence of the notation implies a statement that no CD-ROM return was received, and the evidence is being offered as proof of that assertion.

Question 77

To combat fraud and misuse of driver's licenses, the state of Elbonia's Department of Motor Vehicles enacted new regulations for the issuance of driver's licenses. One of the regulations, which were authorized by state law, required for the first time that driver's licenses display a photograph of the person whose name is on the license. The regulations did not provide for any exemptions from this requirement. Living entirely within Elbonia was the Flemarite sect, which devoutly believed that allowing oneself to be photographed was sinful. However, because much of Elbonia was rural and sparsely populated, the Flemarites needed to travel by automobile to obtain necessary services and to gather for worship. A Flemarite who was refused a driver's license because he would not allow himself to be photographed challenged the state regulation in federal court.

Is the court likely to uphold the application of the regulation to the religious group?

(A) Yes, because exempting the church's members from the regulation would not have a secular purpose and would constitute improper state advancement of, and entanglement with, religion.

(B) Yes, because enactment of the regulation was not motivated by a desire to interfere with religion.

(C) No, unless the state shows that the regulation is necessary to promote a compelling governmental interest.

(D) No, because the opposition to the regulation arises from a sincerely held religious belief.

Question 78

Billy entered into a contract with Sherm to purchase Sherm's farm, upon which the latter grew wheat and soybeans. The contract of sale referred to the farm by name and location, and recited that it contained 250 acres of prime farmland. The agreed-upon price was $1 million. Before the date upon which escrow was to close, Billy learned from a surveyor he had hired that the farm actually contained 248 acres. On the date the sale was to close, Billy instructed the escrow agent to release all but $8,000 of the purchase money. Sherm refused to proceed with the sale.

If Billy brings an action for specific performance and also seeks a reduction of the agreed-upon contract price, what will be the probable outcome of the litigation?

(A) Sherm will win, because Billy refused to tender the contract price when Sherm tendered substantially what the contract called for him to perform.

(B) Sherm will win, because both parties had seen the farm before the contract was formed.

(C) Billy will win, because he is not receiving what he bargained for under the contract.

(D) Billy will win, if the difference of two acres is found to be material and if the reduction in price is not an excessive variance from the parties' agreement.

Question 79

Pinkerton owned Lowacre, a strawberry farm that he held open to the public for a fee. Pinkerton's business consisted primarily of families, who would often eat as many strawberries out in the field as they would bring home with them. Accordingly, Pinkerton advertised that no chemical pesticides or fertilizers were used on his strawberries, so that they could be eaten right off the plant. Adjacent to Lowacre was Highacre, owned by Dalton, on which a soap factory was located. Flakes of calcium silicate, a chemical byproduct of the process, would drift over onto Lowacre whenever the wind was blowing in that direction and settle onto the strawberry plants. The flakes caused no harm to the plants themselves, but detracted from the appearance of the strawberries as well as their taste if eaten right off the plant; consequently, Pinkerton's business sharply declined. On several occasions Pinkerton complained to Dalton about the discharge, but Dalton did nothing, in part because a visit to the county recorder of deeds office had convinced him that he was the true owner of a large part of Lowacre. After a heavy discharge had ruined what should have been a peak weekend of berry picking, Pinkerton sued Dalton.

Can Pinkerton recover damages for the harm caused to his business?

(A) Yes, because the discharge from Dalton's factory entered Pinkerton's land.

(B) Yes, because Dalton intended to conduct the activities that caused the particles to fall on Pinkerton's land.

(C) No, because Dalton had no intent to cause harm to Pinkerton's property.

(D) No, if Dalton's belief that he owned the property, although erroneous, was reasonable.

Question 80

At Donald's BAR-B-QUE Restaurant, the barbecue was prepared in a large, outdoor pit in the back of the restaurant. Cooking meat outdoors in a commercial establishment violated a city health code regulation, designed to assure that the food was not exposed to flies and other insects. On windy days, smoke from the barbecue pit sometimes blew into Paul's backyard. Paul had extremely sensitive eyes. They watered and stung every time that he was exposed to any form of smoke. When the barbecue smoke drifted onto his property, Paul could not use his backyard.

If Paul sues Donald's on a theory of private nuisance, should Paul prevail?

(A) Yes, because Donald's action interfered with Paul's use and enjoyment of his yard.

(B) Yes, because Donald's was violating a health code regulation.

(C) No, if the smoke would not disturb a person of ordinary sensibilities in the community.

(D) No, because the health code regulation was not designed to protect against the type of harm suffered by Paul.

Questions 81-82 are based on the following fact situation:

Late one night in Valleytown, a young couple in a small foreign car were struck by a speeding Cadillac as the couple's car crossed an intersection with the light green in their favor. The impact sent the smaller car spinning into one of the street light poles near the intersection, and the larger car rolled over several times before coming to rest in a nearby field. Witnesses saw a male get out of the Cadillac and run away, but could not describe him sufficiently to permit the police to make an arrest. The Cadillac was not registered with the State Department of Motor Vehicles, and its last registered owner lived in another part of the state and could prove that he had sold it several years ago.

Several weeks later, Jorge, awaiting trial on burglary charges, called the officer who had arrested him to the jail cell where he (Jorge) was incarcerated and asked to speak to a Highway Patrol officer. When the Highway Patrol officer came to the cell, Jorge told him that he had been the driver of the Cadillac that had struck the small foreign car. Jorge said that he just wanted to get it off his chest, since the female passenger in the small car had been killed in the accident. Jorge told the Highway Patrol officer that he had been drinking heavily before driving the Cadillac that night.

81. Jorge is tried for second degree murder on the theory that his driving of the Cadillac at high speed while intoxicated showed a wanton disregard for human life sufficient to provide the malice necessary to constitute murder. The prosecution seeks to introduce the statements made by Jorge to the Highway Patrol officer regarding the events of the night of the accident. Jorge's attorney objects, seeking suppression of the statements. Which of the following is the strongest argument for permitting the statements into evidence?

    (A) Jorge had not been charged in connection with the auto accident at the time the statements were made to the Highway Patrol officer.

    (B) Jorge made the statements spontaneously, without inducement or interrogation by the police.

    (C) The Highway Patrol officer had no connection with the burglary investigation for which Jorge had been incarcerated.

    (D) Jorge's statements were not the product of coercion by the police officers.

82. During Jorge's murder trial, a critical issue is the amount of alcoholic beverages he had drunk before driving his Cadillac that evening. At the start of the second day of trial, a bailiff conducting Jorge from his holding cell to the courtroom persuades Jorge to admit that he had had at least half a fifth of vodka shortly before driving the Cadillac and hitting the small foreign car. When the trial resumes, Jorge testifies that he had nothing to drink that night. In rebuttal, the prosecution attempts to put the bailiff on the stand to testify as to Jorge's statements, but Jorge's attorney again objects. Which of the following is the strongest argument in favor of excluding the statements from evidence?

    (A) The bailiff did not give Jorge *Miranda* warnings.

    (B) The bailiff did not tell Jorge's attorney that he was going to question him.

    (C) The statements were made in the absence of Jorge's counsel.

    (D) The statements were made to a law enforcement officer and therefore were not voluntary.

Question 83

At Jason's trial for armed robbery, the prosecutor offers evidence tending to show that Jason committed two other armed robberies in the year preceding the present offense, and that Jason committed all three robberies to obtain money for his heroin habit.

Should the court admit this evidence over Jason's objection?

(A) No, unless Jason was convicted of the other robberies.

(B) No, if Jason has not testified at his trial.

(C) Yes, unless the court determines that the probative value of the evidence is substantially outweighed by its prejudicial effect.

(D) Yes, if the prosecution establishes by clear and convincing evidence that Jason committed the robberies.

Question 84

Darrel was out backpacking with friends when he came upon another hiker, who had been bitten by a rattlesnake. Darrel and his companions carried the bitten hiker back to Darrel's four-wheel-drive vehicle, and Darrel drove him toward the nearest hospital. On the way there, while exceeding the posted speed limit, Darrel lost control of his vehicle and crashed into a tree by the side of the road. He was uninjured, but the snakebitten hiker's leg was broken. An ambulance soon arrived and took the hiker to the hospital. The emergency room physician committed malpractice that resulted in the loss of the hiker's leg. The hiker is now suing Darrel.

Which of the following is the most likely reason why Darrel will be held liable for the hiker's injuries?

(A) Having undertaken to rescue the hiker, Darrel is strictly liable for injuries resulting from the rescue.

(B) The emergency room physician's malpractice is a foreseeable intervening cause that does not relieve Darrel of liability.

(C) Darrel did not conduct himself as a reasonably prudent person in carrying out the rescue of the hiker.

(D) Darrel committed negligence per se when he exceeded the posted speed limit.

Question 85

If Congress enacted a statute that provided for direct money grants to the various states to be distributed by them to police agencies within their jurisdictions for the purpose of purchasing gas-efficient patrol vehicles, to help reduce the dependency of the United States on imported oil, which of the following would provide the best constitutional justification for the statute?

(A) The Commerce Clause.

(B) The power to tax and spend for the general welfare.

(C) The Necessary and Proper Clause.

(D) The power to conduct the foreign relations of the United States.

Question 86

Peron was a passenger on a commuter train operated by Northeast Transit, Inc. During the commute, Peron left his seat to go to the lavatory at the front of the car. While he was in the aisle, the car moved across intersecting tracks, causing the car to rock. He stumbled and bumped his knee against the lavatory door, aggravating a preexisting circulation problem in his leg that had been controlled by medication. As a result, he had to have several surgeries to correct the circulation problem.

Peron brought suit against Northeast for his damages. At the jury trial, the following evidence was presented: Peron testified as to how he was injured and introduced evidence of his medical expenses. His physician testified that the bump aggravated the circulation problem. The engineer of the train testified that the train had not been exceeding the speed limit for that stretch of track, and Northeast introduced a report indicating that a subsequent inspection disclosed no problems with the track.

At the close of the evidence, Northeast moved for a directed verdict. The court should:

(A) Grant the motion, because there is no evidence that Northeast operated the train negligently.

(B) Grant the motion, if Northeast introduced uncontroverted evidence that a person in normal health would not have been injured by the bump.

(C) Deny the motion, because the jury could find that Northeast, as a common carrier, breached its high duty of care to Peron.

(D) Deny the motion, because the fact that the severity of Peron's injuries was not foreseeable does not cut off Northeast's liability.

Questions 87-88 are based on the following fact situation:

On August 5, Walter and Yogi entered into a written agreement that specified, among other things, that "if the Seals win the pennant, Walter will deliver to Yogi's concession stand at Seals Stadium 500 hot dogs on each of the following days: September 5, 7, and 9. Price to be 25¢ per hot dog. Payment to be made by Yogi to Casey, a creditor of Walter, on September 10."

87. On August 15, Walter wants to avoid his obligation to deliver the hot dogs to Yogi. Casey has not become aware of any agreement between Walter and Yogi. Which of the following is the most accurate statement?

    (A) Walter can rescind if Yogi and Casey give their permission.

    (B) Walter can rescind if Yogi gives permission.

    (C) Walter can repudiate the agreement because Yogi's promise to perform is illusory.

    (D) Walter can revoke the offer to sell hot dogs if the Seals have not won the pennant.

88. Assume for the purposes of this question only that Casey first learned of the agreement between Walter and Yogi on September 5. On September 10, after Yogi refused to pay any money to Casey, the latter filed suit against Yogi for $375. Which of the following would provide a partial defense for Yogi in the litigation?

    I. Walter and Yogi agreed on September 1 that the contract price for the hot dogs would be 20¢ instead of 25¢.

    II. Walter and Yogi had originally agreed that the contract price for the hot dogs would be 15¢, but Walter had inadvertently written 25¢ in the contract, and neither Walter nor Yogi noticed before signing.

    (A) I. only.

    (B) II. only.

    (C) I. and II.

    (D) Neither I. nor II.

Question 89

The state of Northern enacted a gross receipts tax on all businesses operating in that state. The tax was a proportional tax based on revenue derived by businesses in the state. Westco, which had its corporate headquarters and most of its manufacturing plants in Northern, was the leading manufacturer in the United States of widget assembly devices, known as widgebots, which are purchased by widget users across the country.

If Westco challenges the constitutionality of Northern's assessment of the tax against Westco, what is its strongest argument?

(A) Eighty percent of Westco's revenue is derived from widgebot purchases by the federal government.

(B) The tax applies to revenue derived from all of Westco's manufacturing plants, including those not located in Northern.

(C) The state of Northern also imposes a use tax on component parts purchased outside of the state by Westco to make its widgebots that is equivalent to Northern's sales tax for similar purchases within the state.

(D) Sales taxes are imposed by other states on Westco's widgebots sold in those states.

Question 90

During a nationwide trucker's strike, striking drivers committed repeated acts of violence against independent truckers and railroad shipments that had replaced truck transportation. This prompted Congress to enact an emergency measure directing the President to dispatch United States Army troops to specified cities and rail and highway locations to preserve order and ensure the continued flow of commerce.

This enactment is probably:

(A) Unconstitutional, because it infringes the President's authority to faithfully execute the laws of the United States.

(B) Unconstitutional, because it infringes the President's authority as Commander in Chief of the armed forces.

(C) Constitutional, under Congress's power to regulate commerce.

(D) Constitutional, under Congress's power to raise and support the armed forces.

Question 91

In which of the following cases would the offered evidence most likely be admissible?

(A) In a civil defamation action arising from media allegations that the school board president had embezzled funds, testimony from the director of a homeless shelter that the president volunteers her services at the shelter every weekend.

(B) In a criminal action for aggravated battery in which a witness for defendant has testified that defendant is a peaceful and law-abiding citizen, a certified copy of defendant's two-year-old felony conviction for armed robbery.

(C) In a civil fraud action for making false and misleading statements in a stock offering, evidence that defendant had made intentional misrepresentations on other stock offerings.

(D) In a criminal action for shoplifting, testimony by a restaurant cashier that defendant, a regular customer, had several times corrected an undercharge on her bill.

Question 92

Abigail was scheduled to undergo surgery for removal of her appendix. Doctor Smith, her family doctor, was to perform the operation. The day of the surgery, Doctor Smith was called out of town because of a family illness. Even though there was no emergency, it was decided by the hospital to go ahead with the operation and substitute Doctor Michaels for Doctor Smith. Doctor Michaels is considered to be an expert in appendectomies. Abigail was not informed of the switch in doctors.

If Abigail sues Doctor Michaels on a battery theory, who will prevail?

(A) Abigail, only if the operation did not improve her physical well-being.

(B) Abigail, regardless of whether the operation improved her physical well-being.

(C) Doctor Michaels, because he was at least as qualified as Doctor Smith.

(D) Doctor Michaels, if Doctor Smith approved the substitution of doctors.

Question 93

Beavis and Butthead, both 15 years old, attended Southside High School, located in Arkla. They were best friends. For over a year, Butthead had been dating Ashley, but they broke up when Ashley declared that Butthead was "smothering her" and that she needed "more space." Both Beavis and Butthead knew that the real reason for the breakup was that Ashley had developed a crush on Tony, a new kid in school. Beavis appeared more upset over the breakup than Butthead. He continually urged Butthead to do something to embarrass Ashley and to get back at her. One day Butthead brought his pet snake, a small boa constrictor, to school to show to his science class. Beavis encouraged Butthead to put the snake in Ashley's desk, so that when she opened it up, she would scream, jump, and make a fool of herself. Butthead agreed and placed the snake in Ashley's desk. When she opened the desk, she screamed, jumped, and fell backwards, injuring her hip in the fall.

A statute in Arkla provides that "anyone who recklessly causes bodily injury to the person of another is guilty of battery in the third degree." In all other criminal matters, Arkla follows the common law.

If Beavis is charged with battery in the third degree under the theory of accomplice liability, he will most likely be found:

(A) Not guilty, because he did not engage in the act prohibited by the statute.

(B) Not guilty, if he did not intend to cause Ashley bodily injury and was not reckless with respect to her bodily injury.

(C) Guilty, because he intended to encourage Butthead, and Butthead recklessly caused bodily injury to Ashley.

(D) Guilty, because he encouraged Butthead to commit the crime.

Question 94

One provision of the federal Return to Decency Act, recently passed by Congress and in effect for all relevant purposes of this question, provided that state governments may enact legislation regulating any form of pinball machine or video game, including location and hours of operation. Shortly thereafter, Arizona enacted legislation providing, among other things, that no establishment could operate more than five video games at a single location, that no location where any video games were operated could be within 1,000 yards of any other location operating video games, and that no video game could be operated in any location during the hours when any school with grades kindergarten through twelve was in session. The Arizona statute also mandated that any video game sold or operated within the state use a particular LCD screen designed to minimize eyestrain.

Funtime, Inc. is a California corporation that designs and manufactures video games for sale throughout the United States and in Europe. Approximately 10% of their gross sales arises from sales of their machines in Arizona. Funtime machines are not manufactured using the special eye-protecting LCD screen; to install such screens in all machines manufactured would cause the price of the machines to increase by 20%, and to use the screens in machines sold only in Arizona would increase the cost of the Arizona machines by 50%. Funtime files suit in federal district court in Arizona seeking to enjoin enforcement of the Arizona video game statute.

How should the court rule?

(A) For the state, because the challenged legislation is within the powers specifically reserved to the states by the Tenth Amendment.

(B) For the state, because Congress has acted within its power to authorize video game regulation by the states.

(C) For Funtime, because the challenged statute violates the Commerce Clause.

(D) For Funtime, because the challenged statute is overbroad and exceeds the permissible bounds of regulation as authorized by Congress.

Question 95

Lamont applied for a job at the Jones Security Agency. He was required to fill out an application listing references and indicating whether he had any prior convictions of felonies or violent misdemeanors, which would disqualify him from a position as a security officer. Lamont listed as references some aunts and uncles who had not seen him in some time, and stated that he had no prior convictions. In fact, Lamont had several times been convicted of violent assaults using firearms as a juvenile, but the official records were sealed to the public when he attained age 21, several months before he applied for the job at Jones. Lamont was hired, given training in security procedures and firearm use, and placed on assignment at a shopping mall.

After he had been working for a month, Lamont was at a bar with his girlfriend when he got into an argument with another patron over whether the city's football team would make it to the Super Bowl. When the patron made a remark disparaging the abilities of a certain running back, Lamont drew the pistol he had been given at work, which he kept in his waistband, and shot the patron in the chest, killing him.

If the survivors of the dead patron bring an action against Jones Security Agency for wrongful death, who is likely to prevail?

(A) Jones, because Lamont's actions occurred while he was acting outside the scope of his employment.

(B) Jones, because it owed no duty to the patron which was violated.

(C) Plaintiffs, because Jones employed Lamont and gave him the pistol he used to kill the patron.

(D) Plaintiffs, if they can show that a reasonable employer would have discovered Lamont's prior convictions.

Question 96

Norma was injured when the bus in which she was riding braked too abruptly and threw her into a support stanchion, breaking her hip. She has brought an action against the bus company for damages from personal injuries on theories of respondeat superior and negligent hiring.

During its case in chief, the bus company counsel calls Walden, personnel director for the company, as a witness and asks him if the driver of the bus had been required to provide proof that he had had no convictions for crimes relating to vehicle use before being hired. Walden answers, "It's been several years since he was hired, but my best recollection is that we did not ask for such proof." Counsel then prepares to question Walden about his statement, made at a deposition taken 18 months before trial, that he had personally requested and received a statement from the driver before he was hired that he (the driver) had no such convictions.

May counsel for the bus company pursue this matter in this fashion?

(A) Yes, if it is being done to refresh Walden's recollection.

(B) Yes, but the jury must be instructed that the evidence may only be considered for impeachment of Walden.

(C) Yes, the evidence may be admitted for both impeachment and substantive purposes.

(D) No, counsel may not impeach its own witness.

GO ON TO THE NEXT PAGE

Questions 97-98 are based on the following fact situation:

Proctor and Gamble owned large adjoining tracts of land. The boundary line between the two properties was never properly determined or clearly known.

In 1976, Proctor installed a gas-powered generator on land he thought he owned, but which was in fact owned by Gamble. The generator was housed in a small shed and surrounded by a fence. During the summer months, Proctor ran electrical wires from the generator to a guest house across land he knew belonged to Gamble. Gamble orally consented to the wiring's crossing his land.

In 1989, Gamble was found to be mentally incompetent. He died in 2000, and his executor filed suit to eject Proctor and quiet title. The statute of limitations in ejectment is 20 years.

97. With respect to the land on which the generator was installed:

    (A) Proctor cannot claim title by adverse possession because the statute of limitations was tolled by Gamble's incompetency.

    (B) Proctor cannot claim title by adverse possession because his occupation was not under claim of right.

    (C) Proctor has acquired title by adverse possession.

    (D) Proctor has acquired a prescriptive easement.

98. With respect to the land over which the electrical wires were laid:

    (A) Proctor has acquired title by adverse possession.

    (B) Proctor has acquired a prescriptive easement.

    (C) Proctor cannot claim any right on title because his use of the land in question was not continuous.

    (D) Proctor cannot claim any right on title because Gamble consented to his use of the land for the wires.

Question 99

Douglas Corporation manufactured parachutes, which it sold exclusively to the United States Army. To meet the standards required by the Army, each parachute was subjected to a 15-point inspection by Douglas before it could be approved for sale. When a parachute did not pass inspection, it was stored in another section of the Douglas plant. At a later time, a further inspection of the defective parachute would be made to determine whether the defects could be corrected or whether the parachute should be destroyed.

One night, the Douglas plant was burglarized and a large number of parachutes, including the defective ones, were stolen. The defective parachutes eventually were sold on the black market to Paul, the president of High-Flying Sky Divers, a private group of parachute enthusiasts. Sky Divers members were delighted to get Douglas parachutes, as the parachutes were seldom available to nonmilitary people. One week later, Paul was killed when his Douglas parachute failed to open.

If Paul's estate brings a wrongful death action against Douglas on a theory of strict liability in a jurisdiction retaining traditional contributory negligence rules, Douglas's best defense would be that:

(A) Douglas acted reasonably in storing the defective parachutes.

(B) Douglas did not sell or place into the stream of commerce the defective parachute.

(C) Paul did not purchase the parachute from Douglas.

(D) Paul was negligent when he purchased the parachute on the black market.

Question 100

After a routine background check of his references, John Jones was hired as a security guard at First Bank. Jones had been a security guard at another local bank, First Federal, but took the job at First Bank for a higher salary. The bank issued Jones a gun that he was allowed to take with him during his off-duty hours. However, First Bank policy required that all bullets be removed from the gun when the guard was off duty. Each security guard was required to sign a statement that he would abide by the unloaded gun policy.

One evening, John was driving home on the expressway. Another car, driven by Victor, cut sharply in front of John's car. John and Victor exchanged obscenities as their cars traveled at a high rate of speed on the expressway. On one occasion, John almost ran Victor off the road. Both vehicles took the same exit and when they pulled up next to each other at a stop light, the argument intensified. In a rage, John jumped out of his car, waving his gun. It was loaded and accidentally went off. Victor suffered a gunshot wound.

Victor brought an action against both First Bank and John Jones for his injuries. He alleged that First Bank was negligent in entrusting the weapon to John, and that John was negligent in his handling of the weapon. Victor offers the testimony of Warren, a security guard who worked with Jones for 10 years at First Federal. Warren is prepared to testify that, while an employee at First Federal, Jones had a reputation for being a hothead, keeping his weapon loaded during off-duty hours, and threatening people with his gun whenever he got into an argument.

Assuming proper objection, how should the court rule regarding the admissibility of Warren's testimony?

(A) Warren's testimony is character evidence, inadmissible in a civil case.

(B) Warren's testimony is character evidence admissible against First Bank if it can be established that First Bank knew of John's reputation.

(C) Warren's testimony is character evidence admissible against First Bank whether or not First Bank knew of John's reputation.

(D) Warren's testimony is admissible to help establish that John may have acted negligently at the time of the accident.

STOP

ANSWER SHEET

1. __________
2. __________
3. __________
4. __________
5. __________
6. __________
7. __________
8. __________
9. __________
10. __________
11. __________
12. __________
13. __________
14. __________
15. __________
16. __________
17. __________
18. __________
19. __________
20. __________
21. __________
22. __________
23. __________
24. __________
25. __________
26. __________
27. __________
28. __________
29. __________
30. __________
31. __________
32. __________
33. __________
34. __________
35. __________
36. __________
37. __________
38. __________
39. __________
40. __________
41. __________
42. __________
43. __________
44. __________
45. __________
46. __________
47. __________
48. __________
49. __________
50. __________
51. __________
52. __________
53. __________
54. __________
55. __________
56. __________
57. __________
58. __________
59. __________
60. __________
61. __________
62. __________
63. __________
64. __________
65. __________
66. __________
67. __________
68. __________
69. __________
70. __________
71. __________
72. __________
73. __________
74. __________
75. __________
76. __________
77. __________
78. __________
79. __________
80. __________
81. __________
82. __________
83. __________
84. __________
85. __________
86. __________
87. __________
88. __________
89. __________
90. __________
91. __________
92. __________
93. __________
94. __________
95. __________
96. __________
97. __________
98. __________
99. __________
100. __________

BAR REVIEW

Multistate Exam Workshop

Afternoon Exam

BAR REVIEW

Multistate Exam Workshop

Simulated Multistate Bar Examination

P.M. EXAM

Time—3 hours

You will be given three hours to work on this test. Be sure that the question numbers on your answer sheet match the question numbers in your test book. You are not to begin work until the supervisor tells you to do so.

Your score will be based on the number of questions you answer correctly. It is therefore to your advantage to try to answer as many questions as you can. Give only one answer to each question; multiple answers will not be counted. If you wish to change an answer, erase your first mark completely and mark your new choice. Use your time effectively. Do not hurry, but work steadily and as quickly as you can without sacrificing your accuracy.

YOU ARE TO INDICATE YOUR ANSWERS TO ALL QUESTIONS ON THE SEPARATE ANSWER SHEET PROVIDED.

DIRECTIONS

Each of the questions or incomplete statements in this test is followed by four suggested answers or completions. You are to choose the ***best*** of the stated alternatives. Answer all questions according to the generally accepted view, except where otherwise noted.

For the purpose of this test, you are to assume that Articles 1 and 2 of the Uniform Commercial Code have been adopted. You are also to assume relevant application of Article 9 of the U.C.C. concerning fixtures. The Federal Rules of Evidence are deemed to control.

The terms "Constitution," "constitutional," and "unconstitutional" refer to the federal Constitution unless indicated to the contrary.

You are also to assume that there is no applicable statute unless otherwise specified; however, survival actions and claims for wrongful death should be assumed to be available where applicable. You should assume that joint and several liability, with pure comparative negligence, is the relevant rule unless otherwise indicated.

DO NOT OPEN THE TEST UNTIL YOU ARE INSTRUCTED TO DO SO.

Question 101

A petroleum company operated refineries in several states and was also engaged in the manufacture of a variety of petrochemical products. The company hired an industrial cleaning service to thoroughly clean one of its refineries. While one of the cleaning service's employees was engaged in routine cleaning activities at the refinery, one of the support legs on a crane suddenly gave way, causing part of the crane to fall onto a pipe carrying hot oil, cracking it open. The employee had his back to the pipe at the time and hot oil squirted over his back and legs, causing severe burns. The employee filed suit against the petroleum company for his injuries.

The parties stipulated for trial that the crane had been designed and constructed by a crane construction specialist and was serviced at regular intervals by a reputable crane maintenance company selected by the crane construction company. The employee testified at the trial that he was injured when the pipe cracked open and submitted his medical bills and other evidence of damages. The employee introduced no further evidence. At the conclusion of the employee's case, the petroleum company moved for a directed verdict in its favor.

Should the directed verdict be granted?

(A) Yes, because the employee has done nothing to connect the petroleum company to any negligent activity that might have caused the accident.

(B) Yes, because the petroleum company did not owe a duty to an employee of an independent contractor.

(C) No, because the petroleum company is strictly liable to the employee for his injuries.

(D) No, because based on the evidence presented by the employee, a jury could reasonably conclude that the petroleum company was negligent.

Question 102

On July 26, a manufacturer of computer accessories received a purchase-order form from a retailer of computer and office equipment, in which the latter ordered 2,000 ergonomic mouse pads for delivery no later than September 1 for a total price of $10,000, as quoted in the manufacturer's current catalog. Two days later, the manufacturer faxed its own purchase-order acceptance form to the retailer, which had not previously done business with the manufacturer. The purchase-order acceptance form stated that it was an acceptance of the specified order, was signed by the manufacturer's shipping manager, and contained all of the terms of the retailer's form, but it also contained an additional printed clause stating that all disagreements under this sale are subject to arbitration by the American Arbitration Association.

Assuming that there was no further communication between the parties, which of the following is an accurate statement of the legal relationship between the manufacturer and the retailer?

(A) There is an enforceable contract between the parties whose terms do not include the arbitration clause in the manufacturer's form.

(B) There is an enforceable contract between the parties whose terms include the arbitration clause in the manufacturer's form.

(C) There is no enforceable contract between the parties because the manufacturer's form constituted a rejection of the retailer's offer and a counteroffer by the manufacturer.

(D) There is no enforceable contract between the parties because the manufacturer's form added an additional term that materially altered the terms of the retailer's offer.

Question 103

A defendant was charged with embezzling $1 million from his employer, a bank. The theory of the government's case was that $1 million of the bank's funds had been wired to a secret, off-shore account in the bank's name, and that only the defendant and a bank vice-president were authorized to draw funds from the account. The vice-president had been indicted with the defendant but had committed suicide on the day that the grand jury indictments came down.

At trial, the defendant testified that he had wired $1 million to the account but had done so at the direction of the vice-president, who had told him that the bank was acting as a secret agent for one of its largest depositors, which was attempting to acquire an off-shore property with a minimum of publicity. The defendant stated under oath that he had no intent to embezzle bank funds. The government's cross-examination of the defendant concentrated exclusively on his relationship and conversations with the vice-president.

The defense now seeks to call a second witness, who is prepared to testify that he had worked with the defendant for 10 years and that the defendant had a reputation in both the business and general communities as being a very honest person.

The witness's testimony is:

(A) Admissible, because a defendant has a constitutional right to call witnesses in his own behalf.

(B) Admissible to help show that the defendant did not embezzle funds.

(C) Inadmissible character evidence.

(D) Inadmissible, because you cannot bolster the credibility of your own witness unless the credibility of the witness has been attacked.

Question 104

Prex came to Doctor Dillamond, a dermatologist, for treatment of a skin condition on his face that had resisted standard treatment. Doctor Dillamond prescribed a new topical antibiotic cream that was recommended by an associate of hers. Doctor Dillamond gave Prex instructions on how and when to apply the cream but did not discuss potential side effects. Prex purchased the cream at his local pharmacy and applied it as instructed. Shortly thereafter his skin turned a vivid shade of green and he felt a strong burning sensation when he tried to wash it off. The color took almost a week to fade away, during which time he avoided going out in public and took time off from work.

The cream was packaged with a lengthy printed insert that listed a number of possible side effects of varying degrees of probability. A "green pallor" and "irritation" were listed as uncommon side effects.

If Prex sues Doctor Dillamond for prescribing the medicine, is he likely to prevail?

(A) No, if a reasonable person in Prex's position would have used the cream even when told of the potential side effects.

(B) No, because the printed insert that came with the cream listed possible side effects similar to the reaction Prex experienced.

(C) Yes, unless the severity of the reaction Prex experienced was unforeseeable.

(D) Yes, because Doctor Dillamond, as a specialist, owes a high duty of care and is liable even for slight negligence.

Questions 105-107 are based on the following fact situation:

On January 1, Farnsworth entered into a written contract with Jones by which Farnsworth was to sing nightly at Jones's nightclub for a period of two years at $54,000 per year, commencing February 1.

105. Assume that on January 25 Farnsworth phoned Jones and told him, "I still haven't finished moving all my belongings into my new apartment. It's going to take me awhile to get settled and I might not be ready to start singing until February 10."

Can Jones bring an immediate suit against Farnsworth?

(A) Yes, because Farnsworth's telephone call was a repudiation.

(B) Yes, if Jones changes his position in reliance on Farnsworth's telephone call.

(C) No, because Farnsworth's telephone call did not constitute a repudiation.

(D) No, because a repudiation must be in writing to be given effect.

106. Assume that Jones had no communication with Farnsworth between January 1 and February 1. On February 1, Jones received a telegram from Farnsworth stating:

> Due to circumstances beyond my control, I will not be able to start my singing engagement at your club until February 10. I'm sorry for any inconvenience this causes you.

On February 10 Farnsworth appeared at Jones's nightclub, ready to sing.

May Jones cancel the contract?

(A) Yes, because Farnsworth failed to start singing when he contracted to do so.

(B) Yes, because Farnsworth's actions constitute a material breach.

(C) No, unless Jones was materially prejudiced by Farnsworth's failure to start singing on February 1.

(D) No, because Farnsworth notified Jones of his delay in performance in a timely fashion.

107. Assume that after Farnsworth failed to appear at Jones's nightclub on February 1, Jones read in the newspaper that Farnsworth had been in a traffic accident and was expected to be in the hospital for two months. Jones hired Young to sing in his nightclub for two months at a salary of $5,000 per month. Can Jones recover from Farnsworth the additional $500 per month salary he must pay Young?

(A) Yes, because Farnsworth failed to give Jones timely notice of his hospitalization.

(B) Yes, because Farnsworth knew that Jones had spent a considerable amount of money advertising live entertainment at his nightclub commencing February 1.

(C) No, because Farnsworth was not at fault for the delay since he did not cause the accident.

(D) No, because in a personal services contract, performance is excused by illness of the party performing the personal service.

Question 108

A debtor owed a creditor $5,000, but the debt was barred by the applicable statute of limitations. During a conversation between the debtor and the creditor, the debtor agreed to assign to the creditor a debt of $4,000 that was owed to the debtor by a third party and was coming due in a week, and called the third party to inform him of the assignment. When the debt became due, the third party refused to pay the creditor.

If the creditor brings an action to collect the debt against the third party, will he likely prevail?

(A) Yes, because the creditor's agreement to accept a lesser amount than the original debt constituted consideration for the assignment.

(B) Yes, because an assignment need not be in writing to be enforceable.

(C) No, because the third party may raise the debtor's statute of limitations defense on the original debt.

(D) No, because a new promise to pay a legal obligation barred by law must be in writing.

Question 109

A homeowner decided to destroy his home by fire in order to collect the insurance. A neighbor's house was located a short distance from the homeowner's home. The homeowner knew that there was a strong wind blowing towards the neighbor's home; while he did not want to burn the neighbor's home, he nevertheless set fire to his own home. The fire department was unable to save the homeowner's house. They did manage to put out the fire moments before it spread to the neighbor's home, which suffered damage from smoke and soot. The jurisdiction's arson statute covers burning one's own dwelling as well as the dwelling of another, but is otherwise unchanged from the common law.

If the homeowner is charged with attempted arson of the neighbor's home, he will most likely be found:

(A) Not guilty, because he did not intend to burn the neighbor's house.

(B) Not guilty, because the fire was put out before any part of the neighbor's home was burned.

(C) Guilty, because he intended to burn his own home and took a substantial step toward burning the neighbor's house.

(D) Guilty, because he acted with malice and took a substantial step toward burning the neighbor's house.

Question 110

Recently enacted legislation required farmers in certain counties of a western state to use drip irrigation systems instead of traditional methods in order to conserve water for agricultural and other uses. A farmer who refused to use the drip system was charged pursuant to the enforcement provisions of the legislation. A state court enjoined him from using other irrigation methods and fined him.

The farmer appealed to the state supreme court, renewing his trial court claims that the irrigation legislation violated a state constitutional provision prohibiting certain governmental intrusions into private commercial activities and that it was preempted by federal water management statutes. The state supreme court held that the state constitution prohibited the challenged legislation, and construed the relevant statutes as being within the parameters of the federal statutes, and thus preempted.

If the state petitions for certiorari to the United States Supreme Court, how should the Court rule on the petition?

(A) Grant the petition, if it appears that the state court's interpretation of the scope of the federal statutes was incorrect.

(B) Grant the petition, because, under principles of federalism, a state court cannot be the final arbiter of the validity of its own legislation when it is alleged to be in conflict with federal law.

(C) Deny the petition, because there is no substantial federal question that is dispositive of the case.

(D) Deny the petition, because a state government may not seek review of decisions of its own courts in the United States Supreme Court.

Question 111

Rupert's uncle decided, as a surprise birthday present, to give Rupert a beach house which Rupert had visited often and expressed his great admiration for. The uncle's attorney prepared and the uncle validly executed a deed conveying the property to Rupert, and the attorney then validly recorded the deed.

Unknown to the uncle, Rupert was experiencing severe financial difficulty and was contemplating filing for bankruptcy. When Rupert learned of the recordation of the deed at his birthday party, he immediately told his uncle that he did not want the beach house and could not accept such an expensive gift anyway.

Later, Rupert filed for bankruptcy and the trustee in bankruptcy asserted an ownership interest in the beach property on behalf of the debtor's estate. The bankruptcy court ruled that the property belonged to Rupert's uncle and not to Rupert, and thus was not part of the debtor's estate subject to distribution.

Which of the following is the strongest reason in support of the bankruptcy court's ruling?

(A) There was no presumption of delivery created by recordation of the deed because Rupert did not know of the recordation.

(B) Rupert's statements to his uncle at the birthday party were a constructive reconveyance of the property.

(C) There was never an effective acceptance of delivery of the deed by Rupert.

(D) The recordation of the deed was invalid because it was done without Rupert's permission.

Question 112

An elderly woman who lived alone in a large house invited her niece, a registered nurse, to live with her. The niece accepted and moved into the house. For the next several years, the niece took care of most of the housework and the shopping despite her busy schedule. The aunt decided that when she died she should reward the niece by giving her the home. The aunt had her attorney prepare a valid warranty deed conveying the property to the niece, then executed and delivered it to the niece. The niece did not record the conveyance.

Two years after the conveyance, the aunt was involved in an auto accident that left her bedridden. She had allowed her auto insurance to lapse and the other driver's insurance company obtained a judgment against her for $100,000, which it recorded. A statute in the jurisdiction provides: "Any judgment properly filed shall, for 10 years from filing, be a lien on the real property then owned or subsequently acquired by any person against whom the judgment is rendered."

When the aunt died five years later, her will left all of her property to the niece. The insurance company filed a claim in probate against the estate for $100,000. The niece, as executrix, seeks a determination from the probate court that the home is not part of the aunt's estate, having already been conveyed to the niece.

What should the court's ruling be?

(A) That the home is part of the estate and must be utilized to satisfy the $100,000 claim.

(B) That the home is part of the estate, but is not subject to the $100,000 claim.

(C) That the home is not part of the estate and thus is not subject to the claim.

(D) That the home is not part of the estate, but is nevertheless subject to a $100,000 lien in favor of the insurance company.

Question 113

At trial of Priscilla's personal injury action against Delbert, Bill, who was near the accident scene but did not see what happened, testifies that Oscar, a witness to the accident, shouted, "Good Lord! The green car just ran through a red light and hit the red car!" Previous evidence had established that Delbert drove a green car and Priscilla a red one. Delbert offers to call as a witness Arthur, who will testify that he spoke with Oscar the next day, and Oscar said that the light was green when the green car drove through the intersection. Oscar had moved to Sri Lanka prior to trial.

Should this evidence be admitted over Priscilla's objection?

(A) No, because Oscar is not available to explain or deny the contradiction.

(B) No, because it is hearsay not within any exception.

(C) Yes, for the purpose of impeachment and as substantive evidence.

(D) Yes, for the purpose of impeachment only.

Question 114

A developer with a large plot of unimproved land divided it into 30 small plots and two much larger ones, intending to develop a "flea-market" or "swap meet" where nontraditional retailers could market their wares. He built covered stalls on the small plots and larger, permanent buildings on the two large plots. He leased the small plots and stalls to retailers for lease terms ranging from six months to two years. One of the larger plots and the building thereon were offered for lease to an auctioneer, who planned to use the building mainly for storage and as a "show area," while auctions would be conducted outside, from the raised porch at the front of the building. Because rain was frequent in the area, the auctioneer insisted that the developer construct a structure in front of the building that would keep rain off the heads of the auctioneer's prospective customers. The developer agreed to do so and the auctioneer signed a 10-year lease. The developer built a large wooden roof supported by wooden columns. A term in the auctioneer's lease stated, "Lessor agrees to maintain all structures on the property in good repair." The auctioneer's business was a success.

Four years after the auctioneer entered into the lease, the developer sold the property to a buyer. The buyer did not agree to perform any obligations under the lease. As instructed, the auctioneer began paying rent to the buyer. In the fifth year of the lease, the wooden roof began to leak. Citing the lease terms, the auctioneer asked the buyer to repair the roof. He continually refused to do so. The auctioneer finally repaired the roof herself at a cost of $2,000. The auctioneer then brought an appropriate lawsuit to recover the money.

Absent any other facts, the auctioneer is likely to recover:

(A) $2,000 from the developer only, because the sale of the property did not sever his obligation to the auctioneer.

(B) $2,000 from the buyer only, because a covenant to repair runs with the land.

(C) $1,200 from the buyer and $800 from the developer, because that represents their pro rata shares.

(D) $2,000 from either the buyer or the developer, because they are both in privity with the auctioneer.

Question 115

On the way out of Dinah's Diner after enjoying a wonderful meal, Eaton made a detour into the kitchen to personally compliment the chef. However, before he could get the attention of the chef, he slipped on a puddle of grease that had congealed on the floor by the stove. He fell, hitting his head and sustaining a severe head injury.

If Eaton sues Dinah's for damages, is he likely to recover?

(A) Yes, because Dinah's Diner is a place of public accommodation and breached its duty of care owed to its patrons.

(B) Yes, because a Dinah's employee could have discovered the dangerous condition of the floor by making reasonable inspections.

(C) No, unless patrons were welcomed into the kitchen to compliment the chef.

(D) No, if the puddle of grease was visible on the floor.

Questions 116-117 are based on the following fact situation:

NatureFoods, Inc. owned a number of natural food stores in the state of Vegas, and had contracted with landowners and construction firms in the neighboring state of Oro in preparation for the opening of several NatureFoods outlets in that state.

NatureFoods products are stored and sold in bulk, the consumers removing and packaging the amount of food they desire from large bins, and then presenting their assembled purchases at a checkout counter. Oro statutes prohibited the sale of food in bulk due to the health hazards associated with bulk storage and contamination from consumer access to food sold from bins. Oro has prosecuted other grocers' violations of the statute in the past.

116. NatureFoods, Inc. seeks an injunction in state court in Oro prohibiting that state from enforcing its statute barring bulk sale of foodstuffs on the ground that it is an unreasonable interference with interstate commerce. If the state court rules that the relevant statute is valid and denies injunctive relief, which of the following is the proper next step for the corporation to take to obtain review of the state court decision?

(A) Appeal to the state appellate courts.

(B) Petition for removal to the federal district court with jurisdiction in the state of Oro.

(C) Appeal to the federal circuit court of appeals with jurisdiction in the state of Oro.

(D) Petition for certiorari to the Supreme Court of the United States.

117. If NatureFoods had sought an injunction against state officials in the United States District Court with jurisdiction in the state of Oro, and the state officials had sought dismissal on the ground that the corporation lacked standing to sue, what would be the probable outcome?

(A) The suit would be dismissed, because NatureFoods has suffered no injury in the state of Oro.

(B) The suit would be dismissed, because the challenged state legislation had no effect on civil liberties.

(C) The federal court would hear the suit, because a federal question—interstate commerce—is involved.

(D) The federal court would hear the suit, because NatureFoods has undertaken substantial steps to open outlets in the state of Oro.

Question 118

In which of the following situations would the defendant be most likely convicted of manslaughter instead of murder (ignoring the felony murder doctrine)?

(A) Defendant, angry at his girlfriend for going out with another man, sets fire to the house he thinks is hers, but in fact the house set afire is the neighbor's very similar residence. The neighbor and his wife are killed in the blaze.

(B) Defendant, as part of a fraternity initiation ritual, throws a burning mattress onto the front porch of a sorority house late at night, intending to douse the mattress with a garden hose after the women inside the house have run outside in their nightclothes. He discovers that the hose has been disconnected and the sorority house burns down, killing several of the residents.

(C) Defendant, in order to punish his neighbor for filing a complaint with the city government about his (defendant's) pet hogs, ignites the utility shed a few feet from his neighbor's home. The blazing shed causes the house to catch fire, killing the neighbor.

(D) Defendant, seeking to gain a competitive advantage over a business rival, sets fire to the rival's warehouse in the deserted commercial district, not knowing that his rival decided to sleep in the warehouse that night to guard his inventory. The warehouse burns to the ground, killing the rival.

Question 119

Oscar and Henry were suspected of having murdered, for pay, the rival of a local union leader. Both were under constant surveillance. One evening, the police arrested Henry at his home. After he was taken to the police station, the officers who remained at Henry's house asked Henry's housekeeper if she knew where any firearms could be found in Henry's home. She went into the bedroom and returned with a pistol. Ballistics experts established that the pistol had been used to murder the victim, and Oscar's fingerprints were all over the pistol. At subsequent grand jury proceedings, the district attorney introduces the pistol and the related ballistics and fingerprint evidence, and the grand jury indicts Oscar.

If Oscar seeks to quash the indictment, he will:

(A) Not prevail, because the evidence was offered before a grand jury, not a court.

(B) Not prevail, because the pistol was obtained by a private citizen, not the police.

(C) Prevail, unless the police had probable cause to seize the pistol.

(D) Prevail, because Henry's housekeeper was acting as an agent of the police when she obtained the pistol.

Questions 120-122 are based on the following fact situation:

Linda is charged with arson for hire in the burning down of an old office building, Watson Towers, in downtown River City.

120. The prosecution offers to introduce the testimony of Libby, an acquaintance of Linda, who will state that the day after the fire, she went to Linda's apartment. Linda had burnt a roast in her oven, and the apartment was full of smoke. Libby, coughing and choking, said, "What did you do, burn down Watson Towers again?" Linda made no reply. Should this evidence be admitted over Linda's objection?

    (A) No, it is hearsay not within an exception.

    (B) No, if the court determines that Linda would not reasonably deny such a statement under the circumstances.

    (C) Yes, it is an admission by silence.

    (D) Yes, it is a declaration against penal interest.

121. The prosecution offers to introduce the testimony of Officer Brown, who will testify that he showed a photographic lineup containing Linda's picture to a witness who saw the arsonist run from Watson Towers, and the witness selected Linda's picture. The witness has moved out of state and cannot be persuaded or compelled to return to testify. Should this evidence be admitted over Linda's objection?

    (A) Yes, it is a past recollection recorded.

    (B) Yes, it is a prior identification.

    (C) No, it is hearsay not within an exception.

    (D) No, unless the picture of Linda is properly authenticated.

122. During the prosecution's case in chief, evidence was introduced establishing that a can of turpentine, a highly flammable liquid, was discovered in Linda's closet when she was arrested. On direct examination by her own attorney, Linda states that when she was arrested and the can of turpentine was found, she told the officers, "I use that to clean my paint brushes after art class." If the prosecution moves to strike this testimony, how should the court rule?

    (A) For Linda, since it is a prior consistent statement.

    (B) For Linda, since it tends to explain prosecution evidence.

    (C) For the prosecution, because it is hearsay not within an exception.

    (D) For the prosecution, because it is a self-serving statement.

GO ON TO THE NEXT PAGE

Question 123

While walking down a city street, Paul was seriously injured when a rotten limb fell off of a tree and hit him on the head. The tree was located on a vacant lot next to Don's house. The lot appeared to be a part of Don's property. Paul sued Don to recover damages for his injuries, alleging that Don was negligent with respect to the care of the tree. Don's defense was that he did not own the lot or the tree, and that both the lot and the tree were the property of the city. At trial, Paul calls Wally to testify that shortly after Paul was taken to the hospital, he observed Don cutting down the rotten limbs on a number of trees on the vacant lot.

Wally's testimony is most likely:

(A) Admissible, to help prove that Don was negligent in not removing the rotten limbs sooner.

(B) Admissible, to help prove that Don owned the lot.

(C) Inadmissible, because subsequent repairs are encouraged for reasons of public safety.

(D) Inadmissible, because the evidence does not prove that Don owned the lot.

Question 124

Debbie owed Cyndy $1,250. Cyndy's best friend, Francis, had recently lost his job and was facing a number of serious financial problems. He told Cyndy that he might have to file for bankruptcy unless he could deal with some pressing overdue credit card bills. Cyndy wanted to help Francis, but most of her money was tied up in certificates of deposit, none of which came due in less than six months. Cyndy therefore told Debbie to pay the $1,250 to Francis when the debt became due in three days. Immediately after directing Debbie to pay Francis, Cyndy called Francis and told him he should expect to get $1,250 from Debbie in three days. Debbie did not know Francis and was doubtful of the wisdom of paying someone she did not know. When her debt became due, Debbie tendered $1,250 to Cyndy, and Cyndy accepted the money.

If Francis sues Debbie for $1,250, which of the following is the most likely result?

(A) Francis will recover, because Cyndy effectively assigned her right to collect the $1,250 to Francis.

(B) Francis will not recover, because Cyndy's acceptance of $1,250 from Debbie revoked Cyndy's gift to Francis.

(C) Francis will not recover, because Debbie was never indebted to Francis and cannot be forced to pay him.

(D) Francis will not recover, because Debbie's tender of $1,250 to Cyndy and Cyndy's acceptance thereof constituted a novation.

Question 125

Alan wanted to have his driveway resurfaced. He called a number of commercial establishments which do such work and received bids ranging from $4,200 to $5,000. Bert submitted a bid to do the work for $4,000, and Alan entered into a contract with him to have the driveway resurfaced.

Shortly before Bert was scheduled to begin work, he called Alan and said, "I just found out my secretary made a mistake in adding figures. I know we signed a contract, but I couldn't possibly do the work for less than $4,400 or it would not be worth it."

Can Alan enforce the contract for $4,000?

(A) No, if Alan had reason to know that $4,000 was too low a bid.

(B) No, because there was no mutual assent.

(C) Yes, because a $400 change in price has a material effect on the agreement.

(D) Yes, because Bert assumed the risk of bid computation errors.

Question 126

Darryl and Ernie were 17-year-old seniors at Millard Fillmore High School. Ernie's father was a petroleum engineer whose work took him all over the world. He frequently brought back presents for his family from the exotic lands he visited. His last trip involved a mineral exploration project in Australia and he brought Ernie a boomerang, a heavy curved piece of dense wood used for the hunting of small game by traditional Australian Aborigines. The boomerang had beautiful hand carvings and felt good in Ernie's hand. He wanted to try the boomerang out, so Ernie telephoned his friend Darryl and asked Darryl to join him in Recreation Park where they could practice throwing the boomerang. Ernie threw the boomerang a couple of times and explained to Darryl that the knack to throwing it was all in the snap of the wrist.

Just as Darryl made his first throw, George, a Park District gardener, came riding into view on a large lawn mower. The boomerang missed George by about three feet and came sailing back to where Ernie and Darryl were standing. George began yelling curses at Darryl. Thus, Darryl decided to repeat his actions and so he hurled the boomerang in George's direction. It again passed over George's head by about three feet. However, when it sailed back in the direction from which it was originally thrown, it struck George on the head. The blow from the boomerang caused George to suffer a fatal cerebral hemorrhage.

Darryl was charged with homicide for George's death. At trial, the jury was given instructions on common law murder and manslaughter.

If the jury believes Darryl's testimony that he did not intend to hit George with the boomerang, the most serious crime for which the jury could find him guilty is:

(A) Murder.

(B) Voluntary manslaughter.

(C) Involuntary manslaughter based on criminal negligence.

(D) No homicide crime.

Questions 127-128 are based on the following fact situation:

Based on a tip from a reliable informant that an attorney was illegally selling automatic weapons and ammunition from his storefront office, the police obtained a warrant to search for weapons at the office. When they arrived at the building, they saw a client exiting the attorney's office and placing what appeared to be a weapon inside his jacket. The police stopped the client on the street and an officer patted down his outer clothing but found no weapon. However, the officer felt a bag with several small tube-shaped objects in it, and she immediately placed him under arrest. The contents of the bag were later determined to be marijuana cigarettes.

Meanwhile, other officers had entered the attorney's office and seized a quantity of weapons, records, and cash, and placed the attorney under arrest. The weapons seized from the attorney's office were determined to have been stolen. The records seized from the office indicated that the client had purchased a weapon, and the client's fingerprints were found on some of the cash that was seized. After further searching, the police found a gun in a trash bin near where the client was stopped that was the same type that he was recorded as having purchased. The client was charged with possession of illegal narcotics and purchase of an unlicensed and stolen weapon.

127. At a preliminary hearing on the narcotics charge, the client sought to suppress introduction of the marijuana as evidence. The arresting officer testified at the suppression hearing that, based on her long experience as a narcotics officer, she concluded immediately that the bag contained marijuana cigarettes when she first touched it. If the officer's testimony is believed, the motion to suppress the marijuana evidence should be:

(A) Denied, because the search was incident to a lawful arrest.

(B) Denied, because the police had a reasonable suspicion that the client might be armed and dangerous.

(C) Granted, because the scope of an officer's patdown during an investigatory detention is limited to a search for weapons.

(D) Granted, because the search warrant did not authorize the police to search the client despite the fact that he was just present at the place to be searched.

128. At a preliminary hearing on the weapons charge, the client established that, at the attorney's preliminary hearing, the court held that the search warrant for the attorney's office was not supported by probable cause and suppressed introduction of the evidence seized. The client moved to suppress introduction of the records and the cash on the same basis. If the court agrees that the search warrant of the attorney's office was not supported by probable cause, the client's motion should be:

(A) Granted, unless the police acted reasonably in relying on the issuance of the warrant.

(B) Granted, because the evidence is the fruit of an unlawful search.

(C) Denied, because the client's legitimate expectation of privacy was not constitutionally violated.

(D) Denied, because discovery of the gun would have led the police to the records and cash under the inevitable discovery exception to the exclusionary rule.

Question 129

Turbo entered into a written five-year lease to rent an office from Blaze for $6,000 per year. The lease term was scheduled to begin on October 1, and the lease required that rent in the amount of $500 be paid on or before the first of each month. During Turbo's occupancy, he paid his rent promptly each month. Two months before the five-year term was up, Turbo received a letter from Blaze. It contained a new lease identical to the lease Turbo had already signed, except that the lease term began on the upcoming October 1 and the stated amount of rent per month was $600. The envelope also contained a note stating, "The rent goes up to $600 per month on October 1. If you want to renew, sign this and return it to me by September 15. Sorry about the rent increase. Taxes went up. —Blaze." Turbo returned the lease to Blaze unsigned, with a letter stating that he did not intend to renew the lease, and would be moving on September 30. Turbo did not move on September 30, and would not return Blaze's phone calls. On October 1, Blaze received a check for $500 from Turbo. The notation on the check indicated that it was for the October rent. Blaze deposited the check in her account. She then sent a letter to Turbo stating that he was $100 in arrears in his rent. Turbo did not move out of the office during October, and Blaze did nothing to remove him.

Most courts would hold that:

(A) Turbo has a month-to-month tenancy at a rent of $500.

(B) Turbo has a month-to-month tenancy at a rent of $600.

(C) Turbo has a year-to-year tenancy at $500 per month.

(D) Turbo has a year-to-year tenancy at $600 per month.

Question 130

Walter owned a large citrus farm in southern California. The marketing and sale of oranges was subject to the control of a local marketing authority created pursuant to federal legislation. The marketing authority determined what quantity of oranges could be sold by each grower, the price, and the location of sale. These decisions were made by a council of local growers whose members were selected by the federal Department of Agriculture.

The applicable federal legislation provided, in part, that when any grower subject to a marketing order challenged the propriety of that order, the council of the marketing authority must submit the controversy to the United States District Court with geographical jurisdiction for a recommendation as to whether the order should be confirmed, modified, or rescinded. After the hearing in district court, the council must revote on the challenged marketing order.

Walter brings suit in United States District Court, seeking to enjoin enforcement of the federal legislation providing for the marketing order that the council issued with regard to his orange crop. He asserts that the federal legislation is unconstitutional.

As to the constitutionality of the challenged legislation, Walter will probably:

(A) Lose, because the federal government may properly regulate items in interstate commerce.

(B) Lose, because the marketing order system is a necessary and proper means of effectuating the commerce power.

(C) Win, because the federal legislation permits the federal district court to give an advisory opinion.

(D) Win, because the federal legislation deprives him of his property without due process of law.

Question 131

Richard owned a skate rental business that he operated out of a specially equipped van. He would drive to various parks and public beaches in the southern California area and rent roller skates, related safety equipment and lightweight stereo/earphone sets to passersby on an hourly basis. He also sold skates and skating equipment.

About 50% of Richard's time is spent in the city of Beachfront, and he earns about 70% of his gross rental and sale income at its beach areas. After receiving numerous complaints from beachgoers about the sidewalks congested with roller skaters, the city council of Beachfront passed an ordinance prohibiting roller skating on public property between the hours of 7 a.m. and 9 p.m.

If Richard seeks to enjoin enforcement of the ordinance in federal district court on the basis that it is unconstitutional, that court will probably:

(A) Reach the merits of Richard's challenge to the ordinance, because it interferes with his right to free association.

(B) Reach the merits of the challenge, because enforcement of the ordinance will harm Richard's business and the rights of the public are linked to Richard's rights.

(C) Decline to hear the case, because the ordinance does not prohibit the rental of skating equipment.

(D) Decline to hear the case, because skating is not prohibited on private property, nor on public property from 9 p.m. to 7 a.m.

Question 132

A landowner owned a strip mall in a suburban commercial district. She leased one of the stores to a grocer for a term of five years at $10,000 per year, payable in monthly installments. The lease permitted assignments and subleases. After occupying the premises for two years and paying the rent, the grocer transferred the remaining three years of the term to a florist. The agreement between the parties did not have a specific provision regarding payment of rent, instead just referring to the original lease provisions. The florist occupied the premises for two years but paid rent only for the first year. With one year left on the original lease, the florist transferred her leasehold interest to a barber. The barber occupied the premises for one year but did not pay any rent.

The landowner brought an appropriate action against the grocer, the florist, and the barber to recover the rent. Against whom may the landowner recover?

(A) The grocer and the florist jointly and severally for $10,000, and the grocer individually for $10,000.

(B) The grocer and the florist jointly and severally for $10,000, and the grocer and the barber jointly and severally for $10,000.

(C) The grocer and the florist jointly and severally for $10,000, and the grocer, the florist, and the barber jointly and severally for $10,000.

(D) The grocer and the florist jointly and severally for $20,000.

Question 133

Bobby, age 12, was dedicated to his hobby of flying radio-controlled model airplanes that he built himself. One Saturday, Bobby invited his friends to the park to watch him fly his plane. The weather that day was rainy, and the instruction manual for the plane warned against flying it in the rain, but Bobby did not want to miss this opportunity to impress his friends with the tricks it could do. He therefore forged ahead and was able to get the plane off of the ground, but he had trouble controlling it with the transmitter because of the rain. He tried to have the plane make a loop but it veered off course and crashed through the fabric roof of Hank's convertible, which was parked nearby on the street.

If Hank sues Bobby for damages to his car and prevails, it will be because:

(A) A child of Bobby's age, education, intelligence, and experience would not have flown the airplane that day.

(B) A reasonable person would not have flown the airplane that day.

(C) The airplane instruction manual warned against flying in the rain.

(D) Bobby committed a trespass to chattel with his airplane.

Questions 134-135 are based on the following fact situation:

Aaron and Sean hatched a scheme to kidnap an Australian film star, Russell Byrd, and hold him for ransom. After conducting a surveillance of Byrd's home, they decided that they would have to have inside help to disable the security system at the home. They agreed that Aaron would contact Byrd's gardener, Ralph, who they learned was heavily in debt and frequented a local racetrack during his time off. Ralph would be offered $10,000 to disconnect the security system on the night of the planned kidnapping. Shortly before Aaron was to go to the track to make contact with Ralph, Sean had a change of heart about the scheme and contacted Ralph. He warned Ralph not to have anything to do with Aaron. Ralph met with Aaron anyway and pretended to go along with his proposal, accepting the down payment that Aaron offered. After meeting with him, Ralph contacted the authorities.

134. Aaron and Sean are charged with conspiracy in a jurisdiction that follows the common law rule for conspiracy. The most likely result will be:

(A) Both Aaron and Sean are guilty of conspiracy because Sean agreed with Aaron to commit the offense.

(B) Sean is not guilty of conspiracy because he withdrew from the conspiracy by contacting Ralph.

(C) Sean is not guilty of conspiracy because he withdrew from the conspiracy by contacting Ralph, and Aaron is not guilty of conspiracy with Sean because one cannot be a conspirator by oneself.

(D) Aaron is guilty of conspiracy with Ralph.

135. Aaron and Sean are also charged with attempted kidnapping in a jurisdiction following the modern rules for attempt. Which of the following statements is most accurate?

(A) Aaron can be found guilty, because he paid Ralph to disable the security system.

(B) Both Aaron and Sean can be found guilty, because they conspired to kidnap Byrd.

(C) Aaron cannot be found guilty, because Ralph only pretended to agree to the proposal.

(D) Neither Aaron nor Sean can be found guilty, because they did not form the mental state necessary for attempt.

Question 136

A homeowner wanted to have his house repainted. He called a number of businesses which do such work and received bids ranging from $8,500 to $9,000. A local painter submitted a bid to do the work for $8,000, and the homeowner entered into a contract with him to have the house repainted. Shortly before the painter was scheduled to begin work he discovered that he could not make a profit unless the homeowner agreed to pay him $8,600. He called the homeowner with that information. The homeowner responded, "O.K., I'll pay you the extra $600, but I think you're being unfair." After the painter finished the painting he asked the homeowner for his money. The homeowner handed the painter $8,000 in cash and said, "This is all I'm going to pay you because you had no right to up the price on me."

If the painter sues the homeowner for the additional $600, who will prevail?

(A) The homeowner, because the promise to pay the additional money was not in writing.

(B) The homeowner, because the painter was already under a preexisting duty to paint the house for $8,000.

(C) The painter, because he relied to his detriment on the homeowner's promise to pay the additional money.

(D) The painter, because the promise to pay the additional money was the settlement of a good faith dispute.

Questions 137-138 are based on the following fact situation:

A balloonist sued the manufacturer of deflation panels for hot air balloons after one of the panels failed while his balloon was descending, causing the balloon to crash and the balloonist to suffer severe injuries.

137. At trial, the balloonist calls as a witness a structural engineer, who testifies that she read several reports done by an independent laboratory on the burst strength and material composition of the deflation panel closures. His attorney then asks the engineer whether, in her opinion, the closures caused the deflation panel to give way. The manufacturer objects. Should the court admit this testimony?

(A) No, unless the balloonist establishes that the engineer performed the laboratory tests herself.

(B) No, because the laboratory reports are hearsay not within an exception.

(C) Yes, if the balloonist offers into evidence the reports to which the engineer referred, so that the manufacturer may cross-examine as to them.

(D) Yes, if structural engineers reasonably rely on such reports in the course of their profession.

138. During his testimony, the balloonist stated that he purchased the deflation panels two days before installing them and taking the test flight. During its case in chief, the manufacturer presents the testimony of a clerk at the aviation supply store where the balloonist purchased the panels. The clerk testifies that she remembers the balloonist coming into the store and purchasing the panels a week before the date testified to by him, because he signed the purchase order with such an unusual signature. If the balloonist objects to this testimony, should the trial court admit it?

(A) No, because the content of the purchase order is hearsay not within any exception.

(B) No, because the date of purchase of the panels is a collateral matter.

(C) Yes, because the purchase order is a past recollection recorded.

(D) Yes, because the clerk's testimony is relevant evidence as to the date the panels were purchased.

Question 139

Overhill owned Lawnacre, a 20-acre tract of land in a formerly rural area that was rapidly becoming developed. She conveyed Lawnacre "to Tract and his heirs, provided that no multi-family dwellings may be built on the property for a period of 25 years. If such construction is undertaken, the grantor may terminate the conveyance and retake Lawnacre." Two years later Overhill died, leaving her nephew, Verdi, as the sole beneficiary under her will. Shortly thereafter Verdi discovered that Tract was constructing multi-family dwellings on Lawnacre. He promptly brought an ejectment action against Tract.

The jurisdiction in which Lawnacre is located has a statute providing that all future interests are freely devisable and alienable inter vivos. There are no other applicable statutes.

The court should rule that ownership of Lawnacre belongs to:

(A) Verdi, because Tract began constructing multi-family dwellings on Lawnacre.

(B) Verdi, because Tract began constructing multi-family dwellings on Lawnacre and Verdi brought an action for ejectment.

(C) Tract, because the Rule Against Perpetuities applies.

(D) Tract, because the restriction in the conveyance is an invalid restraint on alienation.

Question 140

At a defendant's trial for assault with a deadly weapon, the defendant's counsel calls a witness to the stand and asks him, "What is the defendant's reputation for honesty and veracity in your community?" The prosecutor objects before the witness can answer.

Should the court admit the testimony?

(A) Yes, because reputation evidence is admissible under these circumstances to establish a character trait.

(B) Yes, because the prosecution put the defendant's character at issue when they filed charges against him.

(C) No, because the evidence offered is irrelevant to any material issue in the case.

(D) No, because the evidence offered is inadmissible hearsay.

Question 141

In litigation over whether an uncle conveyed a parcel of land to his nephew, the nephew wishes to offer into evidence a tape recording of his uncle made by a well-known oral historian at the nearby state university. The voice on the tape is discussing various conveyances of the parcel of land and other property owned by the uncle. The nephew wishes to have the historian testify that the voice on the tape is the uncle's.

If the court allows the historian to testify, it will be because:

(A) The historian is testifying regarding an admission by a party-opponent.

(B) The historian has heard the uncle speak before.

(C) The historian became familiar with the uncle's voice before the dispute over the property arose.

(D) The historian's experience as an oral historian qualifies him as an expert in voice recognition.

Question 142

On March 1, School District 726 faxed a "quotation request form" to various suppliers of school furniture requesting offers for the sale of 20 student chairs. The form was on school district letterhead and signed by Paul Boone, the district's purchasing director. It specified that the offer must be held open for four months and that the price term must be no higher than $30 per chair. Joe Smith, the president of Multistate Institutional Furniture, telephoned the next week and told Boone that Multistate will sell the school district 20 chairs at $20 per chair, and agreed to hold the offer open for four months. Boone thanked Smith for the offer and indicated that he would get back to him within that time period. On May 1, before the school district had responded to Multistate's offer or taken any action in reliance on it, Smith faxed a letter to Boone stating that demand for student chairs had been higher than expected and that the offer was terminated. On May 2, Boone called Smith and told him that the school district was treating Multistate's offer as still being open and was accepting it on its terms.

Did Boone's call on May 2 create a legally enforceable contract with Multistate?

(A) Yes, because the contract is for the sale of goods valued at less than $500.

(B) Yes, because the school district accepted the offer within three months.

(C) No, because Multistate did not sign the form specifying the length of time that the offer would be held open.

(D) No, because a firm offer under the Uniform Commercial Code is not effective if its term is more than three months.

Questions 143-144 are based on the following fact situation:

Rafael Guzman was an undercover agent for the United States Drug Enforcement Agency ("DEA"). He had infiltrated an international drug cartel in Juarez, Mexico. Through his position in the cartel, Rafael sometimes learned the details surrounding a shipment of illegal drugs to the United States. When that occurred, Rafael would notify the appropriate DEA agents in the United States. In August 1999, Guzman informed the DEA that a large amount of cocaine was being mailed from Mexico City to Ms. Mary Ash in Topeka, Kansas. The cocaine would be mailed in a large box, wrapped in bright-colored, festive paper with "Happy Birthday, Mary" printed in large letters on the package. Guzman further informed the DEA that Mary was not the purchaser of the cocaine, but was only acting as an intermediary. The cocaine would be picked up within a few days by the buyer, a businessman from Des Moines, Iowa.

The DEA immediately placed Mary's house under surveillance. In a few days, a large box wrapped in bright-colored paper was delivered by the post office. The DEA did not make an arrest, but kept the house under surveillance. Two days later, a well-dressed man driving a car with Iowa plates arrived at Mary's home. He entered the house and, within an hour, he came out carrying what appeared to be the same box. The suspect placed the box in the trunk of his car and drove off. Two blocks later, acting without a warrant, the car was stopped, the suspect arrested, and the DEA agents searched the entire vehicle. The box in the trunk was opened and cocaine was found. In addition, the DEA agents found two pounds of marijuana in the back seat of the car.

The suspect, identified as Donald Dawson of Des Moines, Iowa, was charged with possession of cocaine and marijuana. At a preliminary hearing, Dawson moved to suppress evidence of both the cocaine and the marijuana.

143. As to the cocaine, the motion should be:

(A) Denied, because the DEA agents had probable cause to search the trunk.

(B) Denied, because the search was incident to a valid arrest.

(C) Granted, because the DEA agents should have obtained a warrant before opening the package.

(D) Granted, because the DEA agents had no way of knowing that it was the same package that was delivered to Mary Ash.

144. As to the marijuana, the motion should be:

(A) Denied, because when the police stopped the car, they had probable cause to search the car.

(B) Denied, because the search was incident to a lawful arrest.

(C) Granted, because the DEA did not have probable cause to search the back seat.

(D) Granted, because, after arresting the driver, the car should have been impounded and a warrant obtained before the search.

Question 145

Donna and Ed entered into a written contract whereby Donna contracted to sell and Ed to purchase Whiteacre at a price of $200,000. The closing date was set at August 8. Before the closing date, Ed received the title search report. The records on Whiteacre in the County Recorder of Deeds office indicated that Alan conveyed Whiteacre to Belle by quitclaim deed in 1975 and that Cornelius conveyed Whiteacre to Donna by warranty deed in 1987. Ed notified Donna that the records did not indicate how Whiteacre was conveyed to Cornelius (Donna's immediate transferor), and that Ed was concerned about this. Donna replied that she had no knowledge of the matter, but that she would look into it. At the date and time appointed for closing, Donna informed Ed that she could not locate Cornelius, or obtain any information as to the conveyance of Whiteacre to him. Upon hearing this, Ed refused to tender the purchase money, and told Donna that he was rescinding the contract. Donna sued Ed for specific performance.

Which party is more likely to prevail?

(A) Donna, because land is unique and therefore a proper subject for a specific performance action.

(B) Donna, because she took title from Cornelius by warranty deed.

(C) Ed, because there is a gap in the title.

(D) Ed, because Donna cannot supply marketable title.

Question 146

Based on recommendations of a state commission studying the effect of pornographic films on violent criminal activity, the state of Pilgrim adopted legislation banning films intended for commercial distribution that appealed as a whole to the prurient interest in sex of the average person in the community, portrayed sex in a patently offensive way to citizens of the state, and which a reasonable person in the United States would find had no serious literary, artistic, political, or scientific value.

In ruling on a constitutional challenge to the legislation from a film distributor in Pilgrim who was convicted of distributing films in violation of the legislation, the federal court will likely find the legislation:

(A) Constitutional, because it uses a national reasonable person standard for determining the social value of the work.

(B) Constitutional, because it uses a statewide standard rather than a community standard for determining whether the material is patently offensive.

(C) Unconstitutional, because it uses a statewide standard rather than a national standard for determining whether the material is patently offensive.

(D) Unconstitutional, unless the court finds that the legislation is necessary to advance the state's compelling interest in reducing violent criminal activity.

Question 147

On March 1, a builder entered into a contract with a buyer to build a home on a specified lot and sell the lot and house to the buyer for $350,000. The buyer had the following language added to the contract: "Because my current lease will expire on September 1, time is of the essence on this contract." The builder and the buyer agreed that construction would be completed on August 1, and that escrow would close on the transaction on August 15.

State law required that a home builder have an architect's certificate of completion before any residence could be conveyed to a purchaser. The builder employed his own architect to design and oversee construction of his custom homes. Due to a materials shortage resulting from a dockworker's strike in early summer, construction of the buyer's house was not completed until August 5. On August 8, the builder discovered that his architect had left for a long-planned overseas trip without preparing the certificate of completion for the home. The builder was not able to obtain a certificate until August 20 from a local architect, who had to study the plans and make inspections that had already been completed by the builder's architect. When the builder attempted to place the deed and certificate of completion into escrow, he learned that the buyer had canceled escrow on August 16 and that she refused to proceed with the purchase.

The builder sold the home nine months later for its then reasonable market value of $330,000. He brings an action for damages against the buyer, seeking $20,000, the difference between the contract price and the amount he ultimately received for sale of the house.

Will the builder recover?

(A) No, because the duty to certify completion of the home cannot be delegated to an architect unfamiliar with the construction.

(B) No, because he was late in delivering the deed and certificate of completion into escrow.

(C) Yes, because the short time the builder was late in delivering the deed was not a material breach of the contract.

(D) Yes, unless the buyer can prove that she suffered damages as a result of the delay.

Question 148

Bylon, the owner of an apparel store, faxed an order to Seltex, one of her regular suppliers, for 100 pairs of xylon gloves at $10 a pair, Seltex's list price, delivery within five days. Seltex checked its inventory and discovered that it only had 90 pairs of xylon gloves. It shipped to Bylon the 90 pairs of xylon gloves as well as 10 pairs of zeelon gloves, which also had a list price of $10 a pair. Seltex also faxed to Bylon the following message: "Did not have enough stock of xylon gloves to fill your order. In the hope that you will be able to use them, we are sending zeelon gloves at the same list price to make up the balance of the shipment."

Upon receipt of the shipment and the fax, what are Bylon's options?

(A) Bylon may accept the shipment, in which case she must pay Seltex $1,000 less any damages sustained because of the nonconforming shipment, or she may reject the shipment, in which case she has no further remedy against Seltex.

(B) Bylon may accept the shipment, in which case she must pay Seltex $1,000, or she may reject the shipment, in which case she may recover against Seltex for breach of contract.

(C) Bylon may accept the shipment, in which case she must pay Seltex $1,000, or she may reject the shipment, in which case she has no further remedy against Seltex.

(D) Bylon may accept the conforming part of the shipment and reject the nonconforming part, in which case she must pay Seltex $900 less any damages sustained because of the nonconforming part of the shipment, or she may reject the entire shipment, in which case she may recover against Seltex for breach of contract.

Question 149

Howard and Marty were brothers who each owned 80-acre parcels of farmland adjacent to each other. They decided to combine their acreage in order to benefit from economies of scale, and operated the combined 160 acres as a single farm. After a few years, during which each got married and had children, they began to worry that the very successful farm would be broken up if either of them died, since at least half might be divided among the deceased brother's survivors. Consequently, they each executed identical documents providing: "I hereby grant to my brother and his heirs and assigns a right of first refusal as to my 80 acres, exercisable within 45 days of any proposed sale or transfer of ownership by me." Each brother gave the other valuable consideration for their respective agreements. Each brother promptly recorded his document in the county where their land was located.

Fifteen years later, Marty died, devising his interest in his 80 acres to his oldest child, Charlene. Two weeks later, Howard learned that Charlene had entered into a contingent contract with Boxhomes Developers for the sale of the 80 acres, the contract to take effect when the property was out of probate. Howard notified the executor of Marty's estate that he wished to purchase the 80 acres at the contract price, but on instructions from Charlene, the executor refused. The jurisdiction in which the land is located has a Rule Against Perpetuities unmodified by statute.

If Howard brings an action for specific performance of the agreement giving him a right of first refusal, how should the court rule?

(A) Against Howard, because the interest created by the document violates the Rule Against Perpetuities.

(B) Against Howard, because the document created an unreasonable restraint on alienation.

(C) For Howard, because the document granted him a valid and existing interest in Marty's property.

(D) For Howard, because the document was recorded prior to Marty's death.

Question 150

Oscar, the owner of Wolfacre, conveyed Wolfacre by will as follows: "To Harry Lupus, so long as one or more dogs are kept on the property; if dogs are no longer kept on the property, then to the American Society for the Prevention of Cruelty to Animals (ASPCA)." The will also provided that the residuary estate would go to Oscar's nephew, Remus.

In a jurisdiction that has not modified the common law Rule Against Perpetuities, what are the respective interests in Wolfacre on Oscar's death?

(A) Harry has a fee simple subject to a condition subsequent and Remus has a right of entry.

(B) Harry has a fee simple determinable and Remus has a possibility of reverter.

(C) Harry has a fee simple determinable and the ASPCA has a remainder.

(D) Harry has a fee simple determinable subject to an executory interest and the ASPCA has a shifting executory interest.

Question 151

Under recently passed health care legislation in the state of Lincoln, generous state-subsidized health benefits were provided to all residents who did not have an employer-funded program that met specified minimum requirements. To alleviate the burden on the state's budget, the legislation provided that a person must have resided in the state for at least one year to be entitled to any health benefits provided by the state. Partridge moved to the state of Lincoln last month to take a consulting job with a computer firm. The position does not provide health benefits, so she sought coverage through the state program and was denied. She then filed suit in federal district court, challenging the denial of the state benefits to her.

If the court finds in favor of Partridge, it will most likely be because:

(A) The restriction does not have a rational relationship to a legitimate state interest as required by the Equal Protection Clause of the Fourteenth Amendment.

(B) The restriction deprives Partridge of certain privileges and immunities in violation of the Interstate Privileges and Immunities Clause of Article IV, Section 2.

(C) The restriction improperly burdens the fundamental right of interstate travel in violation of the Equal Protection Clause of the Fourteenth Amendment.

(D) The restriction deprives Partridge of a property interest without due process of law in violation of the Due Process Clause of the Fourteenth Amendment.

Questions 152-153 are based on the following fact situation:

The owner of a self-propelled mower started the engine in preparation to mow when the clutch of the mower suddenly engaged, and it jerked forward rapidly. The owner was unable to grab the handle in time before the mower was out of reach and heading for the street. As he caught up with the mower and attempted to restrain it in the street, a motorist driving down the street swerved to avoid the mower and struck another car traveling in the opposite direction. Both the motorist and the other driver were injured and their cars damaged. The jurisdiction follows traditional contributory negligence rules. The owner purchased the mower 15 years ago.

152. The owner brings an action against the manufacturer of the mower for indemnity based on claims asserted against him by the motorist and the other driver. Assuming for the purpose of this question only that the latter claims are valid and that traditional indemnity rules are followed by the jurisdiction, what will be the probable outcome of this litigation?

(A) The owner will lose, because the mower was 15 years old.

(B) The owner will lose, unless he can show that the mower clutch engaged because of some defect in manufacture.

(C) The owner will win, if his conduct is found not to have been negligent.

(D) The owner will win, because the manufacturer is strictly liable for damages caused by its product.

153. In the motorist's action for personal injuries and property damage against the owner, will she prevail?

(A) No, because the owner was so startled by the mower's sudden movement that he was unable to react swiftly enough.

(B) No, unless the owner was negligent in his maintenance of the mower.

(C) Yes, because her damages resulted from the defective condition of the owner's mower.

(D) Yes, if a reasonable person under the circumstances would have restrained the mower before it entered the street.

Question 154

To gain progress on critical treaty negotiations with another country, the President issued an official pardon to the leader of a radical group who was in a state prison after being convicted of a violent crime in the state. The President directed the governor of the state to free the leader but the governor refused. The Justice Department brought an action in federal district court seeking an order compelling his release.

The federal court most likely will rule:

(A) For the state, since a state official acting pursuant to his state's constitution need not obey inconsistent orders from a federal official.

(B) For the state, because the President's constitutional power to pardon prisoners extends only to those convicted of federal offenses.

(C) For the state, because the President's order and the pardon given the convicted leader violate his duty to see that the laws of the United States are faithfully executed.

(D) For the federal government, since the President's actions are authorized by his power to enter into treaties with other nations.

Question 155

The state of Sequoia's pension program provided supplemental state pension benefits to surviving spouses and children of state employees. The program provided that when the spouse remarried, that spouse's benefits would be gradually terminated based on a statutory formula. Because of statistics showing past disparities between the household income levels of male surviving spouses and female surviving spouses, different formulas were used for the termination schedule depending on whether the surviving spouse was male or female.

Paul, the widower of a state employee, was informed after he remarried that his pension benefits would be terminated in 90 days according to the applicable formula. Upon learning that a similarly situated widow would have continued to receive benefits for six months after remarrying, he decided to file suit in federal court, alleging that the state program is unconstitutional because it is discriminatory and it unfairly burdens his right to marry.

Which of the following best states the burden of persuasion in this case?

(A) The state must demonstrate that the program is narrowly tailored to achieve a compelling government interest.

(B) The state must demonstrate that the program is substantially related to an important government interest.

(C) Paul must demonstrate that the program is not substantially related to an important government interest.

(D) Paul must demonstrate that the program is not rationally related to a legitimate government interest.

Questions 156-157 are based on the following fact situation:

A testing lab used a wind tunnel to test the aerodynamic characteristics of components of vehicles, boats, and planes. The wind tunnel was sold to the lab as a complete unit by a machinery company, which contracted with an electronics company for the design and installation of the electronic systems that regulated air speed and triggered the emergency shut-off devices.

A technician was installing a scale model of a prototype aircraft that was to be tested in the wind tunnel when the electronic control system of the tunnel malfunctioned and started the huge fans that created the air flow. The powerful air flow pinned the technician against the grating covering the intake ducts, asphyxiating him before he was discovered and the fans could be shut off.

156. If the technician's survivors bring an appropriate action against the machinery company for negligently causing the technician's death, they will recover if they prove that:

(A) The control system of the wind tunnel was defective.

(B) The control system of the wind tunnel was defective and the machinery company failed to inspect it before selling the tunnel to the lab.

(C) The control system of the wind tunnel was defective and the machinery company inspected it but failed to discover the defect.

(D) The control system of the wind tunnel was defective, the machinery company inspected the tunnel and failed to discover the defect, and the defect was such that it should have been discovered in the exercise of reasonable care.

157. The technician's survivors bring an appropriate action against the electronics company for damages. Proof by the plaintiffs that the machinery company failed to inspect the wind tunnel has which of the following legal effects?

(A) If the electronics company is held liable to the plaintiffs, it may bring an action for indemnity against the machinery company based upon the failure to inspect.

(B) The failure of the machinery company to inspect the tunnel is a superseding cause that relieves the electronics company of liability to the plaintiffs.

(C) The failure of the machinery company to inspect the tunnel is attributable to the electronics company under the doctrine of respondeat superior.

(D) The failure of the machinery company to inspect the tunnel has no legal effect on the electronics company's liability.

Question 158

As part of legislation enacted for the stated purpose of improving computer literacy of schoolchildren, Congress appropriated funds to permit public school teachers who had been certified by state school districts as remedial computer instructors to provide supplemental computer instruction to any students in either public or private schools who did not have access to computer resources. To help insure content neutrality, the statute required the instructors coming to the private schools to use the laptop computers supplied by the public school districts, which contained the programs that the instructors used for the same purpose in the public schools.

A citizens' group filed suit in federal district court to challenge the constitutionality of funding the computer teachers for private schools, alleging that most of the private schools covered by the statute were religiously affiliated schools. No members of the group have any children in either public schools or private schools affected by the statute.

How is the court likely to rule?

(A) Dismiss the case on the pleadings, because the citizens' group does not have a sufficient stake in the controversy to have standing to challenge Congress's expenditure, which was authorized under its power to spend for the general welfare.

(B) Decide the case on the merits in favor of the government, because the legislation defines the context in which instruction can be provided in private schools so as to avoid excessive government entanglement with religion.

(C) Decide the case on the merits in favor of the citizens' group, because the appropriation's primary effect advances religion in violation of the Establishment Clause of the First Amendment.

(D) Decide the case on the merits in favor of the citizens' group, because the court will presume that any instruction provided on the premises of a religiously affiliated school will be influenced by religion.

Question 159

Ogden owned Blackacre, a one-acre tract of land containing a gift shop and general store, that was located adjacent to a national park. Thirty years ago, he delivered a deed of Blackacre "to Merch for so long as tobacco is not sold on the premises, because careless smokers are the second leading cause of fires in the park." The deed was promptly and properly recorded. A few years later, Ogden died, leaving Harry as his only heir but devising "all of my interests in any real property" to Devlin by a duly probated will. The next year, Devlin conveyed "all of my interest in Blackacre" to Purch by means of a quitclaim deed supported by valid consideration. Purch promptly and properly recorded the deed. Two months ago, Merch began selling tobacco at the general store located on Blackacre.

In a jurisdiction in which the common law Rule Against Perpetuities is unmodified by statute, who currently has title to Blackacre?

(A) Harry, because Devlin received an executory interest that was void under the Rule Against Perpetuities.

(B) Devlin, because the interest he holds in Blackacre is not transferable inter vivos.

(C) Purch, because tobacco is being sold on Blackacre.

(D) Merch, because no party has taken action to terminate his interest in Blackacre.

Question 160

In January of 1996, Dan, a drug dealer in south Florida, became engaged to Wanda. During the engagement, Dan confided in Wanda about various drug deals in which he was participating. Wanda, hopelessly in love, swore to Dan that she would never reveal any of his confidences. On January 1, 1997, Dan and Wanda were married. Dan continued to share with Wanda information concerning his illegal drug activity. Wanda's only rule was that Dan could not participate in any illegal drug transactions in their home. On one occasion, Wanda came home unexpectedly and saw Dan completing a drug transaction in the living room. Dan was not aware that Wanda had observed the event. In 1998, Dan was charged with 57 counts of illegal drug sales that occurred between 1995 and 1998. The prosecutor wishes to call Dan's wife, Wanda, as a witness for the state.

Assuming that Dan's attorney makes appropriate objections, which of the following statements is correct regarding testimony by Wanda?

I. Wanda can testify about Dan's 1996 and 1997 statements if she desires.

II. Wanda must testify to the 1996 statements of Dan.

III. Dan can keep Wanda from testifying about his 1997 statements.

IV. Wanda can testify to the drug sale that she observed if she wants to.

(A) Only III. and IV. are correct.

(B) Only I. and IV. are correct.

(C) Only II. and III. are correct.

(D) None of the above.

Question 161

Under which of the following circumstances would the named defendant ***least*** likely be found guilty of arson?

(A) Walter hires a "torch"—a professional firestarter—who burns down the restaurant of a competitor.

(B) Rico, angry because he has been ejected from a dance party at a private club, prepares a "Molotov cocktail" and throws it at the entryway of the club, causing a fire that destroys the building.

(C) Nancy, as a sorority initiation prank, puts several powerful firecrackers in the fireplace of another sorority, and when the members light their evening fire, the firecrackers explode, sending flaming debris into the room, which results in a fire that severely damages the sorority house.

(D) Leon, preparing to barbecue steaks in his backyard, douses the charcoal liberally with gasoline. When he throws a lighted match onto the charcoal, the gasoline explodes, igniting the can of gasoline that Leon had set down next to the barbecue. The resultant explosion sets both Leon's and his neighbor's houses afire, destroying both.

Question 162

Victoria sued Specialty Cleaners, claiming that Specialty had permanently ruined her $10,000 mink coat. The theory of her case was that Specialty had cleaned the mink coat with a solvent that left an extremely offensive odor that smelled like "skunk." Further attempts to have the odor removed by other cleaning services were unsuccessful. The odor was so bad that she could no longer wear the coat.

At the trial, Victoria testified to the above facts. She then identified a mink coat as her coat that the defendant had ruined. She testified that it still smelled the same as it did after Specialty had cleaned it. Victoria's counsel offered to introduce the coat for the purpose of having the jury smell it. Defense counsel objected.

How should the court rule?

(A) The coat is admissible based on Victoria's testimony.

(B) The coat is admissible, but only if Victoria presents extrinsic evidence sufficient to support a finding that the coat is the coat that she had cleaned at Specialty.

(C) The coat is not admissible because Victoria's testimony has not been impeached.

(D) The coat is not admissible because its limited probative value in resolving the case would be substantially outweighed by the prejudice that would result from the jury smelling the coat.

Question 163

Wanda is an employee of the National Park Service. The Park Service recently created a new personnel level for field employees—Senior Ranger III, which is the highest salaried position available to Park Service field employees. The position is restricted to employees over six feet in height. Wanda seeks your advice as to whether she can challenge the validity of the height restriction in federal court.

If you decide to file suit on her behalf (she is five foot three inches tall), which of the following would be your strongest argument against the validity of the restriction?

(A) Since most women are less than six feet tall, the restriction is unconstitutional as a violation of the Equal Rights Amendment.

(B) Since most women are less than six feet tall, the restriction is an invalid discrimination on the basis of gender in violation of the Due Process Clause of the Fifth Amendment.

(C) Since most women are less than six feet tall, the restriction is an invalid gender-based discrimination in violation of the Equal Protection Clause of the Fourteenth Amendment.

(D) The restriction denies Wanda a property right without an opportunity for a hearing before a neutral decisionmaker, in violation of the Due Process Clause of the Fifth Amendment.

Question 164

After drinking heavily at his bachelor party at a beachside resort, Vinnie was helped into a speedboat by a few of his friends and transported to a small island off the coast. They left him on the island, which had a small shelter but no communication facilities, without telling anyone else. As a result, Vinnie missed his wedding the next day.

One of the participants, Dennis, was charged with kidnapping, which is defined in the jurisdiction as the unlawful movement or concealment of a person without his consent. In his defense, Dennis claims that he was so intoxicated that he did not realize what he was doing, and that Vinnie had consented to his being left on the island.

Which of the following would be ***least helpful*** to his defense?

(A) Vinnie was not legally intoxicated that evening.

(B) Kidnapping is a general intent crime in the jurisdiction.

(C) Kidnapping is a specific intent crime in the jurisdiction.

(D) Dennis had overheard Vinnie say that he was not sure about going through with the wedding.

Question 165

Darwin was driving his expensive sports car down the highway at 90 m.p.h. in a heavy rainstorm. Just after cresting a hill, Darwin observed a large tree that had been hit by lightning and was blocking the highway. To avoid hitting the tree, Darwin drove off the road and onto the property of Peter. In so doing, Darwin destroyed Peter's mailbox and flower bed.

If Peter sues Darwin for damages to his mailbox and flower bed, he will:

(A) Prevail, but only if he can establish that Darwin was not exercising due care.

(B) Prevail, regardless of whether Darwin was exercising due care.

(C) Not prevail, because Darwin was acting under necessity when he drove onto Peter's property.

(D) Not prevail, because even though Peter was exceeding the speed limit, the tree in the road was an act of God, and a superseding intervening cause.

Question 166

A state statute prohibits leaving a child under the age of five years unattended in an automobile. A mother parked her car at a supermarket parking lot. She left her four-year-old son in the car with his seatbelt fastened while she did her grocery shopping. While the mother was shopping, the son undid his seatbelt, left the car, and started riding on the grocery carts that customers had left in the parking lot. The son crashed one of the carts into another shopper's car, causing damage.

The shopper brought a negligence action against the mother to recover for the damage caused by the son. At trial, the shopper presented evidence of the statute and the facts stated above. At the conclusion of the shopper's case, the mother moved for a directed verdict in her favor.

Should the court grant the mother's motion?

(A) No, because the shopper has established negligence per se based on the mother's violation of the statute.

(B) No, because the jury could find that it was foreseeable that the son would cause damage to cars in the parking lot if the mother left him unattended.

(C) Yes, because the shopper has not presented evidence that the statute was designed to prevent children from causing damage to the cars of other customers.

(D) Yes, because a parent is not vicariously liable for the negligence of her child.

Question 167

Structo entered into a contract with Devlo to build a warehouse for $500,000 by August 1. The agreement provided for five progress payments of $100,000 each at various stages of completion. On June 20, after Structo had spent $350,000 on performance and received $300,000 in progress payments, Structo notified Devlo that it was not going to continue with the project because its crews were needed to start some other building projects. Devlo hired Buildco, another contractor, to complete the warehouse by August 1 for $250,000, which was a reasonable price, given the short deadline.

Which of the following statements regarding the parties' remedies is correct?

(A) Structo can recover $50,000, the difference between the amount Structo expended on performance and the amount it was paid, to prevent Devlo's unjust enrichment.

(B) Neither party can recover anything, because the $50,000 extra that Devlo had to pay to complete the building is offset by the $50,000 difference between Structo's expenditures and the payments Devlo made to Structo.

(C) Devlo can recover $50,000, the difference between the contract price and the total amount it paid for completing the building.

(D) Devlo can recover $100,000, the difference between the contract price and the total amount expended in construction of the building.

Question 168

Lester owned Forestacre, a parcel of land on which he built a single-family residence. To pay for the construction, he obtained financing from Multistate Mortgage Company in exchange for a mortgage on Forestacre. Multistate promptly and properly recorded its mortgage in the appropriate recording office. When the house was completed, Lester agreed to lease the house to Terrence for a three-year term. At the time Terrence moved in, the house was complete except for the absence of an oven in the kitchen, and there was no provision in the lease agreement regarding kitchen appliances. Terrence bought a state-of-the-art professional chef model oven from Applianceco and had it installed in the space provided around the built-in cabinets in the kitchen. To make the purchase, Terrence signed a security agreement with Applianceco granting it a security interest in the oven in exchange for financing. Applianceco did not file or record its security interest in the oven.

By the end of the lease term, Lester was in serious default on his mortgage payments to Multistate and Terrence was in serious default on his loan payments to Applianceco. In preparing foreclosure proceedings against Lester, Multistate learned that Terrence was planning to remove the oven and take it with him when he moved out within the next few weeks. Multistate filed an action against Terrence claiming ownership of the oven, and joined Lester and Applianceco as parties.

Which party has a superior claim to the oven?

(A) Multistate, because its mortgage interest attaches to all fixtures on the real estate and it has priority over Applianceco.

(B) Terrence, because removal of the oven will not cause substantial damage to the real estate.

(C) Lester, because the oven was annexed to the real estate after the mortgage was given.

(D) Applianceco, because it has a valid security interest in the oven even though it was not recorded.

Question 169

A parcel of oceanfront property was devised to a husband and wife "as joint tenants with right of survivorship" through the will of the husband's mother. After title had passed to them, the husband and wife experienced marital difficulties. Unknown to the husband, the wife quitclaimed her interest in the oceanfront property to a bona fide purchaser for value. Shortly thereafter, the husband and the wife reconciled. The next month, the wife was killed in an auto accident.

The purchaser of the wife's interest filed a suit for partition of the property so that he could build a beach house on the portion of which he would become sole owner. The husband filed an appropriate counterclaim for quiet title, asserting that he was owner of the entire parcel by right of survivorship.

How should the court rule?

(A) For the purchaser, because he owns an undivided one-half interest in the property.

(B) For the purchaser, if the husband and the wife are found to have taken title from the mother as tenants in common.

(C) For the purchaser, if he can show that the husband and the wife were legally separated when he purchased his interest from the wife.

(D) For the husband, because he succeeded to the entire ownership when the wife died.

Question 170

To encourage the development of local integrated circuit manufacturing operations, the state of Eastern Seaboard enacted legislation requiring that at least 50% of the units sold by retailers of electronic products within the state utilize locally manufactured microprocessors. Rudy, who owned several personal and business computer stores in Eastern Seaboard, sells electronic devices manufactured entirely in other states, primarily personal computers that he purchases from a manufacturer in the state of Oro.

If Rudy attacks the Eastern Seaboard legislation as being unconstitutional, which of the following would provide the strongest support for his position?

(A) The Equal Protection Clause of the Fourteenth Amendment.

(B) The Due Process Clause of the Fourteenth Amendment.

(C) The Commerce Clause.

(D) The Privileges and Immunities Clause of Article IV.

Questions 171-172 are based on the following fact situation:

Grainco, a large grain dealer in the Midwest, contracted with Petchow, Inc., a pet food manufacturer, to supply "100 tons of cornmeal" to Petchow after Grainco had processed the grain from the fall corn harvest, but in any case no later than November 15. The purchase price and delivery terms were specified in the contract, which permitted partial shipments. On November 1, Grainco delivered 50 tons of cornmeal to Petchow with the notification that the balance would be shipped by November 15. Petchow rejected the shipment because the written documentation accompanying the shipment did not establish that the cornmeal came from corn that was not genetically modified, and therefore Petchow could not use it.

171. Assume for purposes of this question only that Grainco seeks an injunction to force Petchow to accept the shipment. Petchow claims that both parties to the contract understood that the term "cornmeal" meant only cornmeal documented to be from corn that was not genetically modified. If Petchow seeks to introduce evidence of trade usage supporting that understanding of the term, should the court permit it?

(A) Yes, because there was a latent ambiguity in the expression of the parties' agreement.

(B) Yes, because trade usage is admissible to explain or supplement the terms of a contract.

(C) No, because the term "cornmeal" in the contract is not ambiguous.

(D) No, if the court finds that the writing is a complete integration.

172. Assume for purposes of this question only that Grainco responded to Petchow's rejection by conceding that the shipment did not conform to the contract and promising Petchow that it would deliver all 100 tons of cornmeal by November 15 with proper documentation showing that it was not from genetically modified corn. Which of the following best expresses Petchow's options?

(A) Petchow may notify Grainco that the entire contract is terminated and that Petchow is going to obtain the 100 tons of cornmeal from another source.

(B) Petchow may notify Grainco that the contract is terminated as to the 50 tons of cornmeal that was shipped and did not conform to the contract, but must accept the additional 50 tons when it is shipped if it conforms to the contract.

(C) Petchow must allow Grainco a commercially reasonable time to ship cornmeal that conforms to the contract before it can terminate the contract.

(D) Petchow must allow Grainco until November 15 to ship cornmeal that conforms to the contract before it can terminate the contract.

Question 173

After winning a long and grueling civil trial, Brett and several other attorneys from a prestigious litigation firm went out to celebrate at a private club. After consuming numerous alcoholic beverages over a period of two hours, Brett attempted to drive home, ignoring the pleas of others in his group. Two blocks away, he allowed his car to cross over the center line because of his intoxicated condition and the car collided head-on with Terry's car, killing her instantly. The district attorney, who was an acquaintance of Brett's from law school, charged Brett with driving while intoxicated. After a bench trial, he was convicted and sentenced to two years of probation. The resulting public outcry and media attention cost the district attorney the next election. His successor immediately filed a charge of reckless homicide against Brett for causing Terry's death while driving drunk.

Brett was tried and convicted of the reckless homicide charge and sentenced to five years in prison. If Brett asserts on appeal that his trial and conviction on the reckless homicide charge violates the Fifth Amendment provision against double jeopardy, will he be likely to prevail?

(A) No, because the driving while intoxicated charge and the reckless homicide charge each require proof of an additional element that the other crime does not require.

(B) No, because the fact that the charges arose out of the same transaction does not prevent the imposition of separate punishments as long as they are imposed in separate trials.

(C) Yes, because the reckless homicide charge will require proof of the same conduct that constituted the driving while intoxicated charge.

(D) Yes, because the sentence for the reckless homicide conviction was greater than, and not concurrent with, the driving while intoxicated sentence.

Question 174

The state of North Central's Commercial Code provides, in part, that "the minimum price of cheese sold in this state shall be $2.50 per pound."

As to which of the following persons would the North Central statute be most likely constitutionally applied?

(A) A resident of North Central selling cheese in that state to a manufacturer of snack foods whose plant is located in the neighboring state of South Central.

(B) A resident of Canada selling cheese made in Canada to the citizens of North Central.

(C) A resident of North Central selling cheese to the Commissary at the United States Air Force base in Capitol City, North Central.

(D) A resident of North Central selling cheese to the North Central State Department of Education for its use in its school lunch program.

Question 175

Tess, the owner in fee simple of Farmacre, made the following provision in her will:

> I grant Farmacre to Harold, my husband, for life, then to my nieces for life, then to the children of my nieces in fee simple.

When Tess died, she had one niece, Anne, who had a son, Edward. While Harold was alive, another niece, Beth, was born. One year after Harold died, another niece, Caryn, was born. At the time Caryn was born, Anne, Anne's son Edward, and Beth were also alive. The jurisdiction's Rule Against Perpetuities is unmodified by statute.

What are the respective interests of the parties in Farmacre at this point in time?

(A) Anne and Beth have a life estate, and Edward has a remainder.

(B) Anne and Beth have a life estate, and Tess's heirs have a reversion.

(C) Anne, Beth, and Caryn have a life estate, and Edward has a remainder.

(D) Anne, Beth, and Caryn have a life estate, and Tess's heirs have a reversion.

Question 176

Patterson purchased Sandacre from Alphonse for $100,000. She financed the purchase by obtaining a loan from Alphonse secured by a mortgage on Sandacre. Alphonse promptly and properly recorded his mortgage. Shortly thereafter, Patterson obtained a loan from Bradford Credit Union secured by a mortgage on Sandacre for remodeling. Bradford promptly and properly recorded the mortgage. One year later, Patterson obtained a home equity loan from Charter Bank secured by a mortgage on Sandacre. Charter promptly and properly recorded its mortgage. A few months later, Patterson stopped making payments on the debt owed to Bradford. With proper notice to all parties, Bradford brought an action to foreclose on its mortgage. At that time, Patterson owed $20,000 on the Alphonse mortgage, $25,000 on the Bradford mortgage, and $30,000 on the Charter mortgage. At the foreclosure sale, the property was sold for $45,000. The jurisdiction in which Sandacre is located permits deficiency judgments.

After the $25,000 debt owed to Bradford is satisfied from the proceeds, which of the following statements is most correct?

(A) Alphonse's mortgage and Charter's mortgage are both reduced by $10,000 and remain on Sandacre.

(B) Alphonse's mortgage is satisfied in full and extinguished, while Charter's mortgage remains on Sandacre.

(C) Alphonse's mortgage remains on Sandacre, while Charter's mortgage is reduced by $20,000 and extinguished, leaving Patterson personally liable to Charter for the deficiency of $10,000.

(D) Alphonse's mortgage is satisfied in full and extinguished, and Charter's mortgage is also extinguished, leaving Patterson personally liable to Charter for the deficiency of $30,000.

Questions 177-178 are based on the following fact situation:

A chemical company located in a small city manufactured the components of a deadly nerve gas under government license. It contracted with an ordnance company to design and manufacture the delivery system, which would hold the chemical agents in chambers and then combine them effectively upon deployment. The chemical company's detailed specifications for creation of the delivery systems required that the chemical agents be held harmlessly in the separate chambers for at least 15 years without deterioration. After receiving the filled delivery systems from the ordnance company, the chemical company stored them in its underground vaults, which were adjacent to an old underground storage chamber of the city's cable car system. Unknown to the chemical company or the city, children living nearby had gotten access to the city's underground chamber and played in there from time to time.

About three weeks after the nerve gas weapons had been placed in their underground storage vaults, several of the canisters in the delivery systems began to leak, permitting mixture of the two harmless agents into the deadly nerve gas. The chemical reaction of the mixture released a great deal of heat energy, which eventually melted through the walls of the storage vault where it adjoined the city's underground storage chamber. The children playing in the chamber at the time were able to scramble out through a ventilation shaft, but one of the children fell and broke his arm while escaping. Fortunately, the intense heat of the chemical reaction rendered the nerve poison inert, and no one was harmed by its effects.

177. Through his parents, the injured child brings an action against the chemical company. Will he prevail?

(A) Yes, because the chemical company was engaged in an abnormally dangerous activity.

(B) Yes, because the chemical company was negligent.

(C) No, because his injuries were not foreseeable.

(D) No, because the underground chamber in which the child was injured was owned by the city, not by the chemical company.

178. Through his parents, the child brings an action against the ordnance company. Will he prevail?

(A) Yes, because the ordnance company caused the accident that resulted in his injuries.

(B) Yes, because the ordnance company will be found negligent pursuant to the doctrine of res ipsa loquitur.

(C) No, because the canisters that leaked were most recently in the custody and control of the chemical company before they caused the injuries to the child.

(D) No, because the ordnance company was unaware and could not have discovered that the children were playing in the underground chamber.

Question 179

Denny is on trial for first degree murder for the shooting of a rival gang member. Denny's defense is that the gun accidentally discharged while he was cleaning it and that he is not in any gang. The prosecution seeks to offer the testimony of Warden, an experienced police officer in the gang crimes unit who interrogated Denny. Warden is prepared to testify that he saw a distinctive tattoo on Denny's leg and that he recognized the tattoo as one worn by members of a gang that was a rival of the victim's gang. Denny's attorney objects to this testimony.

How should the court rule?

(A) The testimony is inadmissible because Warden does not have personal knowledge that Denny is in the gang.

(B) The testimony is inadmissible unless Warden is qualified by the court as an expert on gangs.

(C) The testimony is admissible as circumstantial evidence that Denny was a member of the rival gang.

(D) The testimony is admissible only if the tattoo is either displayed in court or shown by the prosecution to be no longer available.

Question 180

The manager of a bank branch announced to bank employees at a meeting that the corporate security staff would be staging a mock bank robbery that evening just at closing time, so that the employees could learn the proper responses to such a stressful situation and view bank security measures. At closing time that evening, the main bank's security chief, dressed in grubby clothes, entered the bank with an assistant and pointed his empty handgun at a bank teller, shouting, "Put all your money in this bag now! Get moving or I'll blow your head off!" The teller, who had been too busy with a crossword puzzle to listen to the manager's announcement at the meeting, thought that a real robbery was in progress. He nervously attempted to stuff the contents of his cash drawer into the bag while the security chief was threatening him and waving the gun at him. Believing that the teller was playing along, the security chief then demanded the teller's wallet and wristwatch, threatening to shoot the watch off if he did not hurry up. After giving the security chief what he wanted and watching him exit, the teller collapsed into a chair and suffered a mild heart attack before the security chief could return with his "loot" to discuss the exercise with the bank employees.

Which of the following crimes has the security chief committed with regard to the teller?

(A) Robbery.

(B) Larceny.

(C) Assault.

(D) No crime.

Question 181

Bonnie brought an action against a major national department store alleging that the electric blanket she bought from them overheated, causing a fire that destroyed her home and all that it contained. The defendant contends that its blanket could not have overheated unless it was left on after Bonnie left for work on the day of the fire. Bonnie offers in rebuttal the testimony of her husband, Clyde, who will state that he has been married to Bonnie for seven years, that he has slept in the same bed with her for most of that period, and that the first thing Bonnie does every morning upon awakening is to turn the control on the electric blanket to "off."

Should this testimony be admitted?

(A) Yes, because prior conduct may be used to show conformance with habit.

(B) Yes, because evidence of habit may be used to show that a person acted in conformance with the habit on a particular occasion.

(C) No, because habit may only be established by opinion or reputation evidence, not specific conduct.

(D) No, because there is no corroboration of Clyde's testimony by a nonparty witness.

Questions 182-183 are based on the following fact situation:

Sutter owned a gold mine in California and a silver mine in Nevada. His will provided that the property on which the gold mine was located, Golden Acres, would go "to my wife Karen, for life, remainder to my nephew, Lester." The property on which the silver mine was located, Silver Creek, was devised "to my sister Ida, her heirs, and assigns; but if Ida should die without producing issue, then to the American Cancer Society."

When Sutter died, the gold mine was producing a net annual value of $100,000 in gold and had proven reserves valued at $2 million. The silver mine was producing a net annual value of $25,000 in silver and had proven reserves of $250,000.

182. Shortly after Sutter's death, Lester brings an action to enjoin Karen from operating the Golden Acres mine. What should be the outcome of this litigation?

(A) Issue the injunction, because Lester has a vested remainder subject to partial divestment.

(B) Issue the injunction, because Lester has a vested remainder.

(C) Deny the injunction, because Karen has a freehold estate.

(D) Deny the injunction, because of the open mines doctrine.

183. Shortly after Sutter's death, the American Cancer Society brings an action to enjoin Ida from operating the Silver Creek mine. What should be the outcome of this litigation?

(A) Issue the injunction, because the Society has a contingent remainder.

(B) Issue the injunction, because the Society has an executory interest.

(C) Deny the injunction, because Ida has a defeasible fee simple.

(D) Deny the injunction, because of the open mines doctrine.

Question 184

The state of Idarodo was the sole habitat of the leafy wortplant, a large, fast-growing bush with a massive root system that grew naturally only on steep hillsides exposed to the sun. The roots of the wortplant were highly prized by chefs, who used them in numerous local recipes. The roots were also used for a very popular herbal remedy in the region. Krell owned several large tracts of hilly land in Idarodo that were covered with wortplants, and he regularly harvested a substantial quantity of the roots and sold them to local wholesalers.

After the most recent rainy season, a number of the communities in the lower-lying areas of Idarodo suffered flooding and mudslides that caused extensive property damage to public and private property. A study commissioned by the state legislature determined that the extensive removal of wortplants from the hillsides was a significant factor contributing to the floods and mudslides. The legislature passed a statute requiring, among other measures, that property owners leave intact at least 50% of the wortplants growing on any hillside.

Krell challenged the state statute on federal constitutional grounds, alleging that he had regularly harvested substantially more than 50% of the wortplants from his property and needed to do the same this year to meet the demand for the root.

Is he likely to prevail in his challenge?

(A) Yes, because the statute substantially impairs the economic value of Krell's land.

(B) Yes, because the statute effects a taking of private property for public use without just compensation.

(C) No, because the statute is rationally related to the legitimate government interest of preventing flooding damage to property.

(D) No, because the statute promotes an important public purpose and permits the continued use of Krell's property.

Question 185

Venn entered into a written contract with Purch for the sale of Scrubacre, a large tract of land in a sparsely populated area of the state. The contract set forth an accurate metes and bounds description of the land based on a survey that Venn had undertaken before putting the property up for sale. At closing, Purch discovered that the deed was incorrectly transcribed and did not agree with the description of the land in the contract. Purch refused to proceed with the closing and brought an action to reform the deed to make it conform to the intention of the parties.

The deed described the property to be conveyed as follows:

I. From the southwest corner of Section 25 of Township 2 North, Range 6 West, Cimmaron Base and Meridian, proceed South 45 degrees East 200 feet to the Scrub Basin Irrigation Canal;

II. From that point, proceed South 45 degrees West 100 feet along the Scrub Basin Irrigation Canal to its intersection with State Highway 11;

III. From that point, proceed North 45 degrees West 200 feet along State Highway 11;

IV. From that point, proceed South 45 degrees East 100 feet to the starting point.

Which of the following corrections should be made for the deed to properly describe Scrubacre?

(A) Direction I. should be changed to "South 45 degrees East 100 feet."

(B) Direction III. should be changed to "North 45 degrees West 100 feet."

(C) Direction III. should be changed to "North 45 degrees East 200 feet."

(D) Direction IV. should be changed to "North 45 degrees East 100 feet."

GO ON TO THE NEXT PAGE

Question 186

A gun collector ordered a rifle from a gun catalog. The rifle had a barrel 16 inches long and a pistol-type grip instead of the more usual rifle stock, so that the entire weapon was only 22 inches long. The collector was aware of a state penal statute that prohibited the possession of "any sawed-off shotgun or rifle." He was also aware that another statute defined sawed-off shotgun or rifle so as to include any such weapon whose barrel was less than 16 inches in length. He was unaware that the same statute also included in its definition of the prohibited weapons any shotgun or rifle whose overall length was less than 24 inches. When the rifle he had ordered arrived in the mail, he carefully measured it to confirm that its barrel was exactly 16 inches in length.

While driving to the target range one day, the collector was stopped for having a defective taillight, and the traffic officer saw the rifle he had ordered lying on the back seat of his car in plain view. The collector was arrested and subsequently prosecuted for possession of a sawed-off rifle.

What will be the probable outcome of the trial?

(A) He will be acquitted, because he honestly did not know that a weapon with an overall length of less than 24 inches was in violation of the statute.

(B) He will be acquitted, because he conducted a reasonable investigation to ensure that he was in compliance with the statute.

(C) He will be convicted, unless the trier of fact determines that his failure to realize that the overall length of the weapon was in violation of the statute was reasonable.

(D) He will be convicted, because his reasonable investigation does not vitiate violation of the statute arising from a mistake of law.

Question 187

In a civil lawsuit arising from a car accident, the plaintiff's witness testified that she observed the defendant drive through a red light before striking the plaintiff's car. The defendant then presented evidence impeaching the plaintiff's witness. The plaintiff now wishes to call someone else to testify as to his witness's good reputation for truthfulness.

The court is most likely to permit this testimony if the impeachment was by evidence that:

(A) The plaintiff's witness was convicted of the felony of aggravated battery five years ago.

(B) The plaintiff's witness had a previous dispute with the defendant.

(C) The plaintiff's witness was not wearing her prescription eyeglasses at the time of the accident.

(D) The plaintiff's witness was his mother.

Question 188

When Dottie learned that the boyfriend of her roommate, Pam, had a motorcycle, she advised Pam that they should both wear helmets when they were on it. Pam responded that they had no intention of wearing helmets because they were too restricting. Dottie, whose brother died in a motorcycle accident because he was not wearing a helmet, wanted to impress upon Pam how important helmets were. One day when Pam was at work, Dottie called her and left a message that her boyfriend was in a motorcycle accident and was in the hospital on life support. Pam was very upset when she got the message and left immediately for the hospital. When she found out later that the message was not true, she became even more upset.

If Pam brings an action against Dottie to recover for her emotional distress, is she likely to prevail?

(A) Yes, if Pam suffered physical injury from her distress.

(B) Yes, if Dottie knew that it was very likely that Pam would suffer severe emotional distress.

(C) No, unless Dottie's purpose was to cause Pam severe emotional distress.

(D) No, because Pam and her boyfriend were not related.

Question 189

Vanessa collapsed at her desk while drinking her morning coffee. Her secretary, Will, came rushing to her aid. Gasping for breath, Vanessa said, "I don't think I have much time left. I want you to remember when they come looking for suspects that I believe Debbie would kill for my job." Vanessa soon lost consciousness. She regained consciousness briefly after arriving at the hospital, but the doctors would not allow her to speak to anyone, including the police. She again lapsed into a coma, and she remains in this vegetative state. It was determined that she was poisoned. Debbie is arrested and charged with attempted murder.

At Debbie's trial, the prosecution wishes to call Will to testify to Vanessa's statement to him at the office before the ambulance arrived.

The court should find the statement:

(A) Admissible, because it is a dying declaration.

(B) Admissible, because it is a declaration of Vanessa's state of mind.

(C) Inadmissible, because dying declarations are not admissible unless the declarant is dead.

(D) Inadmissible, because it is hearsay not within any exception.

Questions 190-192 are based on the following fact situation:

Dick took his six-year-old son Doug to the shopping mall to do some Christmas shopping. As Dick was looking at the mall directory in order to locate a store he was seeking, Doug walked over to a nearby "Santa's Reindeer Ride," a small electric trolley made to look like a sleigh being pulled by reindeer, which traveled over a small oval track in a winter holiday setting. The sleigh held four children, and as Doug watched, four youngsters whose parents had paid the 50¢ admission climbed into it for a ride. Doug climbed over the low fence surrounding the ride and ran to the rear of the sleigh, catching onto the upper edge and riding on a narrow ledge at the bottom. Dick, who looked up and saw Doug on the end of the sleigh, ran toward it, attempting to hurdle a small pile of construction materials that had been left by workers who set up the ride. Dick sprawled onto his face, breaking his collarbone. Doug, who turned to see what the commotion was about, lost his grip on the sleigh and fell backward onto the track, injuring his head.

190. Doug brings an action, through his guardian ad litem, against the manufacturer of the sleigh ride on a theory of strict liability. Assume that the jurisdiction follows traditional contributory negligence rules. Which of the following would provide the best defense for the manufacturer in this litigation?

(A) There is not privity of contract between Doug and the manufacturer.

(B) Doug was contributorily negligent in riding on the rear of the sleigh.

(C) The sleigh was not being used by Doug in a reasonably foreseeable manner.

(D) Dick was negligent in his supervision of Doug.

191. Dick brings an action in negligence against the shopping mall to recover for his injury. Assume that the jurisdiction follows traditional contributory negligence rules. Who will prevail?

(A) The mall, if its employees were unaware of the pile of construction materials left by the sleigh ride builders.

(B) The mall, because Dick assumed the risk of injury when he attempted to vault the pile of materials.

(C) Dick, unless he is found to have been contributorily negligent when he attempted to vault the pile of materials.

(D) Dick, on a theory of res ipsa loquitur.

192. Assume for purposes of this question only that the jurisdiction has adopted pure comparative negligence and has replaced its traditional contribution rules with a pure comparative contribution statute, but has retained joint and several liability. Assume further that parent-child immunity does not apply in this situation. Doug brought a negligence action, through his guardian ad litem, against the shopping mall. The trier of fact determined that Doug has suffered \$100,000 in damages and that the shopping mall was 60% at fault, Doug was 10% at fault, and Dick was 30% at fault in failing to supervise Doug. How much can Doug recover from the shopping mall?

(A) \$60,000, because the jurisdiction has adopted comparative contribution rules.

(B) \$90,000, but the shopping mall can recover \$30,000 from Dick.

(C) \$90,000, and the shopping mall cannot recover from Dick because its fault was greater than the combined fault of Dick and Doug.

(D) \$100,000, because the jurisdiction has retained joint and several liability.

Question 193

In which of the following situations is Debbie most likely to be guilty of larceny?

(A) Coming out of a bar quite drunk, Debbie mistakes Susan's car for her own and drives off.

(B) Mistakenly believing that a porch swing attached to the house that she had just sold was not a "fixture" that became part of the realty, Debbie goes onto the property while the new owner is away and removes the swing.

(C) Mistakenly believing that it is not a crime to accept services without paying for them, Debbie eats a meal at Kim's restaurant and cannot pay the bill.

(D) Debbie borrows Jim's bicycle without his permission, intending to return it the next day, but it is stolen from her before she can do so.

Question 194

The legislature of State, concerned that the numerous and strident television, radio, and newspaper advertisements by auto dealerships annoy and mislead the public, enacted comprehensive legislation regulating the timing and content of such ads, limiting their duration, frequency, and the types of claims and information made and given.

Which of the following statements is most accurate as to the constitutionality of the advertisement regulation of State?

(A) It is unconstitutional, because it infringes upon the First and Fourteenth Amendment rights of auto dealers to free speech.

(B) It is constitutional if it does not prohibit the dissemination of truthful information about price and the availability of products, and is narrowly tailored to serve a substantial government interest.

(C) It is constitutional, because it is within the police power of the state and no federal constitutional rights are infringed.

(D) It is unconstitutional, because it infringes upon the rights of the auto dealers to enter into contracts for advertising.

Questions 195-196 are based on the following fact situation:

Laura and Emily wanted to open a restaurant, but were only able to raise $40,000 of the $160,000 needed for its construction. Bill, a contractor who had suffered greatly in the decline in residential construction, learned of Laura and Emily's problem and suggested that they enter into the following agreement: Laura and Emily would pay Bill $20,000 in cash on commencement of construction, scheduled for April 15 after the spring thaw. On completion of the restaurant on September 30, Bill would be paid an additional $20,000 in cash. He would agree to take the remaining $120,000 of the cost of building the restaurant in monthly payments of $1,000 principal plus 12% annual interest on the outstanding balance, once the restaurant started earning a profit. Laura and Emily were delighted, and a written contract setting forth those plus other terms was executed on March 30.

195. Assume for the purposes of this question only that the region had a late spring and that on April 30, Bill had not yet commenced construction of the restaurant. He has:

(A) Not breached the contract, but Laura and Emily need not make the initial $20,000 payment.

(B) Not breached the contract, and Laura and Emily must make the initial $20,000 payment.

(C) Breached the contract in a nonmaterial particular; thus, Laura and Emily need not make the initial $20,000 payment.

(D) Breached the contract in a material particular; thus, Laura and Emily may treat the contract as at an end and sue for damages.

196. Assume for the purposes of this question only that despite several months' effort, Laura and Emily are unable to attract enough customers to earn any profit from the operation of the restaurant. They are able to find a buyer who pays them $170,000 for the facilities. Bill brings an action against Laura and Emily for the remaining $120,000 owing on the contract. Will he recover?

(A) No, because Laura and Emily never earned a profit from their operation of the restaurant.

(B) No, because the failure to earn profits from the operation of the restaurant was an unforeseeable intervening event.

(C) Yes, because the provision governing payment of the outstanding balance of the construction cost merely established the time frame in which payment was to be made.

(D) Yes, because all of the conditions precedent to Laura and Emily's duty to pay had occurred.

Question 197

Belching Rapids was an industrial city in the Midwest with approximately 300,000 inhabitants. Of these, approximately 150,000 were members of a recognized racial minority, and the latest Census figures indicated that 33,501 minority residents of Belching Rapids could be classified as "poor" under federal poverty guidelines. Of the approximately 150,000 nonminority residents of Belching Rapids, only 7,328 could be classified as "poor." The 10-member city council of Belching Rapids, containing no minority members and no poor members, decided that it was time to deal with the large operating deficit incurred by the city-owned transit system. The council decided to raise bus fares during rush hour periods from 80¢ to $1. Because poor people and members of minority groups placed greater reliance on the city's bus lines than did the bulk of the nonpoor and nonminority population (many of whom drove to work), the effect of the transit-fare increase was hardest on the poor and minority communities. Several activist groups representing the poor, various minority organizations, and some community action coalitions vowed to fight the fare increase in federal court.

Which of the following statements most accurately describes the constitutional status of the fare increase?

(A) The fare increase is unconstitutional because the Belching Rapids city council is composed solely of nonpoor and nonminority members who cannot adequately represent the interests of poor persons, who need low bus fares to survive.

(B) The fare increase is unconstitutional, because the city cannot show that the resulting disparate impact of the fare increase is necessary for a compelling state interest.

(C) The fare increase is constitutional, because there is no evidence that the Belching Rapids city council acted irrationally or was motivated by an intent to discriminate on the basis of race.

(D) The fare increase is constitutional, because a political question is involved and fares and fees may be increased if the city council deems such increases appropriate to cure deficits.

Question 198

On completion of a major expansion project, the Smallville Public Library Board adopted a usage policy for the new meeting room that was added to the facility. To alleviate the scheduling burden on the staff if the meeting room were open to all groups, the policy provided that the meeting room was to be used only for "library purposes" by the library staff, the library board, or groups affiliated with the library, such as the library's teen advisory group or volunteer "Friends of the Library" group. Dialog, a local organization that promoted the political interests of an ethnic minority in the Smallville area, requested use of the meeting room for an informational meeting that would be open to the public. Although no other event was scheduled for the meeting room at the time requested, the library director declined Dialog's request, citing the meeting room policy adopted by the library board.

Dialog filed suit in federal district court, challenging the library's policy and seeking access to the meeting room. How is the court likely to rule?

(A) The library's policy is valid, because limiting the meeting room's use to library purposes is reasonably related to a legitimate government purpose.

(B) The library's policy is valid, because limiting the meeting room's use to library purposes is narrowly tailored to serve a significant government interest.

(C) The library's policy is not valid, because limiting the meeting room's use to library purposes is restricting speech based on its content.

(D) The library's policy is not valid unless there are alternative facilities in the area available for groups to hold meetings.

Question 199

While checking her mail at the front desk of the hotel at which she was staying, Debby observed that Vicky, who had been wearing very expensive jewelry when she and her husband had checked in earlier in the evening, was no longer wearing any jewelry. After finding out Vicky's room number, Debby broke into a supply room and put on a bellhop's uniform. She then grabbed some flowers from a vase in the hall and knocked on the door to Vicky's room, announcing the delivery of a bouquet of flowers. After Vicky's husband, Vernon, let her in, Debby scanned the room for the jewelry while putting the flowers in a vase. When she did not see the jewelry, she pulled out a knife and forced Vernon to reveal the whereabouts of the jewelry. Since Vicky had stored the jewels in the hotel safe, Debby made Vernon call the front desk and ask that someone bring them up to the room. Debby then locked Vernon in the bathroom, changed out of the bellhop's uniform, and accepted the jewelry when it was brought to the room. She was apprehended a few days later trying to sell the jewelry.

Under these facts, what are the most serious crimes Debby can be convicted of?

(A) Burglary and larceny.

(B) Burglary and robbery.

(C) Larceny only.

(D) Robbery only.

Question 200

As a result of an automobile accident at the intersection of First and Main, Paul sued Dennis, claiming that Dennis's car was traveling at a high rate of speed and went through a red light just before the crash. Walter, a witness for Paul, testified that he observed the accident and that Paul's car was traveling at a low speed with a green light at the time of the accident.

Which of the following is the court ***least*** likely to allow to impeach the credibility of Walter?

(A) A certified copy of a certificate of conviction for felony assault and battery seven years ago.

(B) The testimony of Daisy that, last month, while having a drink at a bar, Walter told her that Paul's light was red.

(C) A record of an arrest one week ago for embezzlement.

(D) On cross-examination of Walter, the question "Isn't it a fact that you lied to your employer last year concerning your meal expenses on a business trip to Chicago?"

ANSWER SHEET

101. ________
102. ________
103. ________
104. ________
105. ________
106. ________
107. ________
108. ________
109. ________
110. ________
111. ________
112. ________
113. ________
114. ________
115. ________
116. ________
117. ________
118. ________
119. ________
120. ________
121. ________
122. ________
123. ________
124. ________
125. ________
126. ________
127. ________
128. ________
129. ________
130. ________
131. ________
132. ________
133. ________
134. ________
135. ________
136. ________
137. ________
138. ________
139. ________
140. ________
141. ________
142. ________
143. ________
144. ________
145. ________
146. ________
147. ________
148. ________
149. ________
150. ________
151. ________
152. ________
153. ________
154. ________
155. ________
156. ________
157. ________
158. ________
159. ________
160. ________
161. ________
162. ________
163. ________
164. ________
165. ________
166. ________
167. ________
168. ________
169. ________
170. ________
171. ________
172. ________
173. ________
174. ________
175. ________
176. ________
177. ________
178. ________
179. ________
180. ________
181. ________
182. ________
183. ________
184. ________
185. ________
186. ________
187. ________
188. ________
189. ________
190. ________
191. ________
192. ________
193. ________
194. ________
195. ________
196. ________
197. ________
198. ________
199. ________
200. ________

barbri BAR REVIEW

Multistate Exam Workshop

Explanatory Answers

ANSWER KEY AND SUBJECT MATTER KEY

	Answer	Subject Matter
1.	C	Criminal Law/Procedure—search and seizure
2.	C	Constitutional Law—spending power
3.	A	Contracts—promissory estoppel/third-party beneficiary
4.	B	Real Property—recording acts/priorities
5.	C	Evidence—vicarious admissions
6.	B	Criminal Law/Procedure—Fifth Amendment
7.	B	Torts—defense of property
8.	D	Constitutional Law—First Amendment
9.	A	Torts—conversion
10.	C	Constitutional Law—equal protection
11.	A	Torts—negligence
12.	D	Torts—negligence/violation of statute
13.	A	Real Property—marketable title/adverse possession
14.	B	Contracts—consideration
15.	A	Contracts—requirements contract
16.	D	Contracts/Sales—damages
17.	C	Contracts—impracticability
18.	A	Real Property—life estate/doctrine of waste
19.	C	Criminal Law—self-defense
20.	A	Constitutional Law—voting rights/equal protection
21.	A	Constitutional Law—equal protection
22.	D	Contracts/Sales—lost profits damages
23.	B	Criminal Law—homicide
24.	B	Contracts—Statute of Frauds
25.	A	Real Property—joint tenancy
26.	A	Real Property—mortgages
27.	D	Torts—invasion of privacy
28.	C	Contracts—unilateral contract
29.	C	Contracts—offer and acceptance
30.	A	Real Property—priority of security interests
31.	A	Constitutional Law—fundamental rights
32.	C	Evidence—impeachment
33.	A	Evidence—hearsay rule
34.	A	Contracts/Sales—risk of loss
35.	B	Contracts—assignment/damages
36.	A	Constitutional Law—preemption
37.	B	Real Property—equitable servitude/common development scheme
38.	B	Criminal Law—requisite mental state
39.	A	Criminal Law—requisite mental state
40.	C	Evidence—judicial notice
41.	D	Contracts—offer and acceptance
42.	C	Real Property—land sale contract
43.	B	Evidence—character evidence
44.	C	Evidence—settlement offers
45.	C	Torts—battery
46.	B	Real Property—easements
47.	C	Contracts—consideration

48.	C	Contracts—Statute of Frauds
49.	D	Criminal Law—attempt/requisite intent
50.	D	Evidence—recollection refreshed
51.	C	Real Property—easement
52.	B	Torts—defamation of public figure
53.	B	Criminal Law—conspiracy/solicitation
54.	C	Criminal Law—common law murder
55.	D	Real Property—transfer of security interests
56.	C	Real Property—priority of security interests
57.	A	Evidence—impeachment
58.	D	Evidence—hearsay
59.	B	Constitutional Law—ripeness
60.	C	Evidence—materiality of evidence
61.	C	Contracts—consideration
62.	A	Contracts—accord and satisfaction
63.	B	Criminal Law—conspiracy
64.	C	Torts—assault
65.	D	Torts—false imprisonment
66.	D	Real Property—riparian rights
67.	B	Criminal Law—accomplice liability
68.	C	Evidence—judge/jury responsibility
69.	C	Criminal Law/Procedure—burden of proof
70.	D	Constitutional Law—First Amendment Establishment Clause
71.	A	Torts—products liability based on strict liability
72.	C	Torts—strict liability for animals
73.	B	Constitutional Law—procedural due process
74.	C	Constitutional Law—First Amendment
75.	B	Criminal Law/Procedure—Sixth Amendment
76.	B	Evidence—hearsay
77.	B	Constitutional Law—First Amendment Free Exercise Clause
78.	D	Real Property—specific performance of land sale contract
79.	B	Torts—trespass to land
80.	C	Torts—nuisance
81.	B	Criminal Law/Procedure—Fifth Amendment
82.	C	Criminal Law/Procedure—Sixth Amendment
83.	C	Evidence—probativeness vs. prejudicial effect
84.	C	Torts—rescuer's liability
85.	B	Constitutional Law—taxing and spending power
86.	A	Torts—duty of care
87.	B	Contracts—rescission
88.	C	Contracts—mutual mistake
89.	B	Constitutional Law—state taxation of interstate commerce
90.	B	Constitutional Law—executive power
91.	C	Evidence—character evidence
92.	B	Torts—battery
93.	B	Criminal Law—accomplice liability
94.	B	Constitutional Law—Commerce Clause
95.	D	Torts—respondeat superior
96.	C	Evidence—impeachment
97.	C	Real Property—adverse possession
98.	D	Real Property—prescriptive easement

99.	B	Torts—products liability based on strict liability
100.	C	Evidence—character evidence
101.	A	Torts—breach of duty
102.	A	Contracts/Sales—offer and acceptance
103.	B	Evidence—character evidence
104.	A	Torts—physician's standard of care
105.	C	Contracts—anticipatory repudiation
106.	C	Contracts—material vs. minor breach
107.	D	Contracts—impossibility of performance
108.	B	Contracts—assignment/consideration
109.	A	Criminal Law—attempt
110.	C	Constitutional Law—case or controversy requirement
111.	C	Real Property—recording of deed
112.	C	Real Property—recording acts
113.	D	Evidence—impeachment
114.	D	Real Property—assignment of leasehold
115.	C	Torts—negligence/landowner's duties
116.	A	Constitutional Law—judicial review
117.	D	Constitutional Law—standing
118.	D	Criminal Law—murder/requisite intent
119.	A	Criminal Law/Procedure—grand jury/exclusionary rule
120.	B	Evidence—admission by silence
121.	C	Evidence—hearsay
122.	C	Evidence—hearsay
123.	B	Evidence—subsequent remedial measures
124.	B	Contracts—assignment and delegation
125.	A	Contracts—mistake
126.	A	Criminal Law—involuntary manslaughter
127.	B	Criminal Law/Procedure—search and seizure
128.	C	Criminal Law/Procedure—search and seizure
129.	D	Real Property—termination of tenancy
130.	C	Constitutional Law—advisory opinions
131.	B	Constitutional Law—standing
132.	B	Real Property—assignment of lease
133.	A	Torts—child's standard of care
134.	A	Criminal Law—conspiracy
135.	A	Criminal Law—attempt
136.	B	Contracts—modification
137.	D	Evidence—expert testimony
138.	B	Evidence—impeachment
139.	B	Real Property—future interests
140.	C	Evidence—character evidence
141.	B	Evidence—authentication/opinion testimony
142.	C	Contracts/Sales—merchant's firm offer
143.	A	Criminal Law/Procedure—search and seizure
144.	B	Criminal Law/Procedure—search and seizure
145.	D	Real Property—marketable title
146.	A	Constitutional Law—First Amendment/obscenity
147.	B	Contracts—"time of the essence"
148.	C	Contracts/Sales—shipment of nonconforming goods
149.	C	Real Property—future interests

150.	B	Real Property—fee simple determinable/Rule Against Perpetuities
151.	C	Constitutional Law—fundamental rights
152.	B	Torts—indemnity
153.	D	Torts—negligence
154.	B	Constitutional Law—executive power
155.	B	Constitutional Law—equal protection
156.	D	Torts—products liability based on negligence
157.	D	Torts—products liability/duty to inspect
158.	B	Constitutional Law—First Amendment Establishment Clause
159.	C	Real Property—fee simple determinable
160.	A	Evidence—spousal privilege
161.	D	Criminal Law—arson
162.	A	Evidence—relevancy/real evidence
163.	B	Constitutional Law—substantive due process
164.	B	Criminal Law—mens rea/kidnapping
165.	B	Torts—trespass to land/necessity
166.	B	Torts—parent duty of care
167.	C	Contracts—remedies
168.	D	Real Property—fixtures
169.	A	Real Property—joint tenancy
170.	C	Constitutional Law—Commerce Clause
171.	B	Contracts—parol evidence rule
172.	D	Contracts/Sales—seller's right to cure
173.	A	Criminal Law/Procedure—double jeopardy
174.	D	Constitutional Law—Commerce Clause
175.	B	Real Property—class gifts/Rule Against Perpetuities
176.	C	Real Property—foreclosure of mortgages
177.	A	Torts—strict liability
178.	A	Torts—strict products liability
179.	C	Evidence—lay opinion testimony
180.	D	Criminal Law—requisite mental state
181.	B	Evidence—habit evidence
182.	D	Real Property—doctrine of waste
183.	C	Real Property—future interests
184.	D	Constitutional Law—"Takings" Clause
185.	D	Real Property—description of deeds
186.	D	Criminal Law—mistake of law
187.	A	Evidence—powers of judge
188.	B	Torts—infliction of emotional distress
189.	D	Evidence—hearsay
190.	C	Torts—strict products liability
191.	C	Torts—negligence
192.	B	Torts—comparative contribution
193.	C	Criminal Law—larceny
194.	B	Constitutional Law—First Amendment
195.	A	Contracts—condition precedent
196.	C	Contracts—promise vs. condition
197.	C	Constitutional Law—equal protection
198.	A	Constitutional Law—First Amendment
199.	B	Criminal Law—burglary/robbery
200.	C	Evidence—impeachment

30

Answer to Question 1

(C) The use of night-vision binoculars to observe the marijuana where it could not be observed by simply using the naked eye renders the validity of the search in (C) doubtful. To be able to assert a Fourth Amendment right, a person must have a reasonable expectation of privacy with respect to the place searched or the item seized. There is no such expectation of privacy in objects or places held out to the public. Thus, the police may fly over a field to observe it with the naked eye, and even a low flyover by a helicopter to view inside a partially covered greenhouse is permissible. Also, the police may take aerial photographs of a particular site. In (C), the police have flown over the defendant's greenhouse at night and used a means of enhancing their vision that is not available to the general public. This enabled them to see what could not have been observed with the naked eye, which constitutes a search. [*See* Kyllo v. United States (2001)] Given that the defendant was replacing semi-opaque glass panes on his greenhouse in the middle of the night, he has an argument that he had a reasonable expectation of privacy in the greenhouse because it was not held open to public view, even by air. (D) simply describes a situation in which the police take aerial photographs of a particular site. As mentioned above, the photographs are permissible here because the fields could have been observed with the naked eye. (B) is incorrect. Pursuant to the "open fields" doctrine, areas outside the "curtilage" (*i.e.,* dwelling house and outbuildings) are subject to police entry and search because these areas are held out to the public and are not protected to the same extent under the Fourth Amendment. A barn may be considered to be outside the curtilage. Thus, looking into the defendant's barn 150 feet from the fence around his house, as described in (B), probably does not violate any Fourth Amendment protection. (A) describes a search incident to a lawful arrest. The arrest of the defendant for driving under the influence was lawful, because the weaving of the defendant's car and his disoriented appearance gave the police probable cause to arrest. The police may conduct a warrantless search incident to a lawful arrest, including a search of the person and areas into which he might reach to obtain weapons or destroy evidence (his wingspan). After arresting the occupant of an automobile, the police may conduct a warrantless search of the passenger compartment (including any containers therein), because the entire passenger compartment is within the arrestee's wingspan (regardless of whether the arrestee has already been removed from the automobile). In (A), having lawfully arrested the defendant, the police were entitled to search his car's glove compartment incident to the arrest. Thus, the search described in (A) was not unreasonable.

Answer to Question 2

(C) The court should uphold the federal provision because it is within Congress's power to spend for the general welfare. Article I, Section 8, provides that Congress may spend to "provide for the common defense and the general welfare." This spending may be for any public purpose—not merely the accomplishment of other enumerated powers. Under this power, Congress may "regulate states by imposing explicit conditions on the grant of money to state or local governments." Such conditions will not violate the Tenth Amendment merely because Congress lacked the power to directly regulate the activity that is the subject of the spending program. [South Dakota v. Dole (1987)] Here, Congress has attempted to address a national problem—minors embarking on a potentially addictive habit that has been shown to damage health—by restricting access to the product causing the problem. Even if Congress's enumerated powers would not permit it to directly require businesses to take the steps specified by the legislation, it may use its spending power to encourage states to impose these steps. (A) is incorrect. The fact that the businesses involved could not be regulated directly under Congress's power over interstate commerce is irrelevant. As long as Congress is not inducing the states to do something that would not be within their constitutional power (which is not the case here), Congress can indirectly "regulate" activities that it could not regulate directly by imposing conditions on the grant of money to states. (B) is incorrect because, as discussed above, making a grant of money to a state conditional on the state's taking governmental action does not violate the Tenth Amendment. (D) is incorrect because that is not the standard that the Court would use to test conditions on grants of federal funds. As long as the restrictions have some relevance to the federal interest involved, they will be upheld. Here, conditioning grants that the state will provide for businesses is relevant to the goal of getting businesses to restrict minors' access to cigarettes.

Answer to Question 3

(A) The church will be able to recover against the insurance company on a promissory estoppel theory because of the letter that the company sent to the church. Under the majority view, consideration is not necessary to make an agreement at least partially enforceable where the facts indicate that the promisor should be estopped from not performing. Under the Second Restatement, a promise is enforceable to the extent necessary to prevent injustice if the promisor should reasonably expect the promise to induce action or forbearance and such action or forbearance is in fact induced. Here, the insurance company sent a letter to the church informing it that the employee had named the church beneficiary under his employee benefits program. The company did not warn the church that the employee had the right to change his beneficiary and should have reasonably expected that the church would rely on the promise in some way; it is not necessary in charitable contribution cases that the promisor know of a specific expenditure that the recipient made or is going to make. Hence, the church can recover against the company because it installed the windows in reliance on the funds from the employee benefit program. (B) is incorrect because the employee's contractual right to change his beneficiary was not affected by any reliance on the part of the church. In the usual case, an intended third-party beneficiary can prevent the contracting parties from rescinding or modifying the contract once his rights have vested. Vesting occurs when the beneficiary (i) manifests assent to the promise in a manner invited or requested by the parties; (ii) brings suit to enforce the promise; or (iii) materially changes position in justifiable reliance on the promise. However, the parties may by agreement determine the issue of whether or when a third-party beneficiary's rights vest. This is commonly done in life insurance policies and employee benefit plans, such as the one in this case, by reserving to the policyholder or the employee the power to change the beneficiary at any time. The facts indicate that the employee retained an unrestricted right to change his beneficiary and that he exercised that right. The fact that the company contacted the church and the church detrimentally relied on the company's letter did not deprive the employee of the power to change the beneficiary of his benefit plan. The church's recovery will be on the basis of promissory estoppel against the company rather than as a third-party beneficiary of the agreement between the company and the employee. (C) is incorrect. As discussed above, the fact that the employee had the power to change the beneficiary of the benefit plan prevented the church's third-party beneficiary rights from vesting. However, it did not affect the liability the company incurred to the church under a promissory estoppel theory. (D) is incorrect for the same reason as (C): the company did have a duty to pay the new church because the employee had the power to change beneficiaries under the plan; however, the company also caused the first church to detrimentally rely on the statement in the letter that it was the beneficiary.

Answer to Question 4

(B) The investor has title to the back half subject to the bank's mortgage, and the investor has no rights in the front half. The recording statute in the question is a pure notice statute, which allows subsequent purchasers for value and without notice of a prior conveyance to prevail over the prior transferee, regardless of whether the subsequent purchaser records. In addition, the "shelter rule" allows a person who takes from a bona fide purchaser to prevail against any interest that the transferor-bona fide purchaser would have prevailed against, even if the transferee had actual knowledge of the prior unrecorded interest. Thus, the buyer would prevail over the investor even though the buyer was aware of the investor's interest in the parcel, because the buyer obtained title from the landowner's friend, a bona fide purchaser. Thus, the investor's rights in the front half of the parcel are extinguished. With regard to the back half, the investor has superior title to it over the landowner, but takes subject to the mortgage on it by the bank because mortgagees for value are treated as "purchasers" under recording statutes and because the bank had no notice of the investor's interest. (A) and (C) are wrong because the investor takes subject to the bank's mortgage, as discussed above. The fact that the bank did not record and the investor subsequently did record, while it would allow the investor to take free of the bank's mortgage under a ***race-notice*** statute, does not have this effect under the statute here, which is a ***notice*** statute. (A) and (D) are wrong because, as discussed above, the buyer prevails over the investor under the shelter rule despite her knowledge of the investor's interest in the property.

Answer to Question 5

(C) The helper's written statement is admissible if it qualifies as a vicarious admission. Federal Rule 801(c) defines hearsay as a statement, other than the statement made by the witness while testifying, offered into evidence to prove the truth of the matter asserted. The helper's written statement meets that definition. Therefore, it will be excluded by the hearsay rule unless the statement is removed from the definition of hearsay by 801(d) or is covered by one of the exceptions to the hearsay rule found in Rules 803 and 804. Federal Rule 801(d) provides that admissions by a party are not hearsay and, therefore, an admission will not be excluded by the hearsay rule. An admission is a statement by a party to the action offered by the opponent of the party. Admissions also include statements by a party's employees if made during and in the scope of the employment relationship. Thus, if it can be established that the helper is an employee of the moving company and that his statement was made in the scope of employment, the helper's statement will be admissible as an admission under 801(d). (A) is wrong because if the helper testifies, his written statement would be a prior consistent statement, which is generally only admissible to rebut a charge that the witness is lying or exaggerating because of some motive, and nothing of that nature is suggested by the facts. (B) is wrong. Even if the helper is unavailable to testify, his written statement meets the definition of hearsay under 801(c) and is neither removed from the definition by 801(d) nor qualifies as an exception (without the additional facts stated in choice (C) establishing it as a vicarious admission). (D) is too broad a statement. If the helper testifies in the current trial and contradicts his written statement, the prior inconsistent statement under oath would be removed from the definition of hearsay by 801(d). Alternatively, if the helper had testified in a previous trial and the motorist (or a predecessor in interest) had an opportunity to cross-examine the helper, his previous testimony would qualify under the former testimony exception to the hearsay rule. Neither situation is suggested by the facts presented.

Answer to Question 6

(B) The defendant's motion should be denied because his interrogation did not violate his Fifth Amendment right to counsel. At any time prior to or during interrogation, a suspect may invoke a *Miranda* (Fifth Amendment) right to counsel. However, the request must be unambiguous and specific. If the defendant agrees to answer questions orally, but requests the presence of counsel before making any written statements, the defendant's oral statements are admissible. The defendant's agreement to talk constitutes a voluntary and knowing waiver of the right to counsel, even if it could be argued that it indicates a misunderstanding of the evidentiary effect of oral statements. [Connecticut v. Barrett (1987)] Thus, (B) is correct and (D) is incorrect. (A) is incorrect because it is irrelevant to the defendant's Fifth Amendment right to counsel that the officers questioned him about a different crime. If the accused invokes his right to counsel under *Miranda*, all questioning must cease, even about a totally unrelated crime, because the Fifth Amendment right to counsel under *Miranda*, unlike the Sixth Amendment right to counsel, is not offense specific. Here, the statements are admissible because the defendant did not effectively invoke his right to counsel. (C) is incorrect because as long as *Miranda* warnings have been given and adversary judicial proceedings have not commenced, voluntary statements are admissible even if the police lie to the defendant's lawyer about their intent to question him and fail to inform the defendant that his lawyer is attempting to see him. [Moran v. Burbane (1986)]

Answer to Question 7

(B) The trespasser will prevail against the electric company because it did not have the right to use deadly force to protect its property. As a general rule, one may use reasonable force to prevent the commission of a tort against one's property. However, force that is likely to cause death or serious bodily harm is not permitted when the invasion is threatening property alone. Furthermore, one may not use indirect deadly force when such force could not lawfully be directly used. Because the trespasser was threatening only the property interest of the electric company, the use of deadly force would not be privileged against him. By leaving the power on to prevent theft, the electric company was using indirect deadly force to defend its property where such force could not lawfully be directly used. Hence, it will be liable to the trespasser for his injuries. (A) is incorrect because the electric company's status with respect to the land is irrelevant for the type of claim that the trespasser is asserting. In negligence actions, the limited duty to trespassers that a landowner has is not shared by persons with an easement or license to use the land; they owe a duty of reasonable care even to trespassers. Here, however, the theory of the trespasser's claim is not negligence but more likely battery, because the electric company intended to leave the power on to protect its property and will be deemed to have intended the consequences of that conduct. Even if the electric company had been the landowner, it would not have been privileged to leave the power on solely to protect its property from theft. (C) is incorrect because, as discussed above, the trespasser's status as a trespasser does not provide the electric company with a privilege to use deadly force against him. (D) is wrong because the fact that the trespasser was attempting to steal the electric company's property would not, standing alone, give the electric company the right to use deadly force, either directly or indirectly, to protect the property.

Answer to Question 8

(D) The court should rule in favor of the publisher because the tax exemption regulates speech based on its content in violation of the First Amendment. The freedom of the press is guaranteed by the First Amendment. As with other areas within the First Amendment, the freedom does not prohibit all government regulation of the press, but it does place limits on regulation. The press and broadcasting companies can be subject to general business regulations and taxes, but generally may not be singled out for a special tax. Moreover, a tax impacting on the press or a subpart of the press cannot be based on the content of the publication absent a compelling justification. Although the state tax here appears to be a general receipts tax, the exemption is based on content, which means that the tax also is based on content (*i.e.,* a publication is subject to the tax unless it contains . . .). As discussed below, a compelling interest is not presented here, so the exemption is invalid and the tax should fail. (A) is incorrect because the publisher would certainly have standing to litigate her tax bill. To have standing, a plaintiff must show that she has suffered an injury in fact, caused by the government, that can be remedied by a court decision in her favor. If the tax here is unconstitutional, the publisher has suffered an injury because she was required by the government to pay the tax, and a decision in her favor will remedy her injury. Therefore, the publisher has standing. The doctrine that taxpayers do not have standing applies to cases where the taxpayer is litigating the way her tax money is spent rather than whether she owes a particular tax. (B) and (C) are incorrect because the facts are insufficient to establish whether the state has a compelling interest here; and therefore, it cannot be determined whether the Equal Protection Clause has been violated. The Equal Protection Clause prohibits government discrimination absent a compelling interest, and laws that favor a minority are subject to the same strict scrutiny standard as laws that discriminate against a minority. However, the Supreme Court has found that remedying past discrimination against a minority—either by the government or by the public—is a compelling interest. Therefore, a government program favoring a minority will be upheld if it is narrowly drawn to remedy past discrimination. Here, we are not given any facts about past discrimination and so cannot decide whether the Equal Protection Clause has been violated. Therefore, neither (B) nor (C) is as good an answer as (D).

Answer to Question 9

(A) The neighbor is entitled to $300, but the homeowner will keep the leaf blower. If the plaintiff is successful in a conversion action, the measure of damages is the fair market value of the chattel converted. This value is generally computed as of the time and place of the conversion. The defendant is given title upon satisfaction of the judgment so that, in effect, there is a forced sale of the chattel. (Note that even if the defendant wishes to return the item, the plaintiff is not obligated to take it back once it has been converted.) Here, the value of the leaf blower at the time the homeowner took it was $300, so that is what the neighbor is entitled to. (B) is wrong because damages are measured not by the cost of replacing the converted chattel but by its fair market value at the time and place of conversion. (C) is wrong because damages based on the cost of repair of the motor are more appropriate as a measure of actual damages for a trespass to chattels action. For interferences with a chattel that are so serious as to constitute a conversion, the damages remedy is different. (D) is similarly wrong because it does not state the appropriate measure of damages for conversion.

Answer to Question 10

(C) If Lourdes prevails, it will be because the state has failed to show that the law is necessary to achieve a compelling state interest, as required by the Equal Protection Clause of the Fourteenth Amendment. Under that clause, a governmental action involving classification of persons will be subject to strict scrutiny if a suspect classification is involved. The law will be struck down unless the government proves that it is necessary to achieve a compelling interest. State and local laws that classify persons based on alienage are subject to strict scrutiny unless the law is discriminating against alien participation in the functioning of the state government. In that case, the law will be upheld as long as it is rationally related to a legitimate government interest. Thus, a state can validly refuse to hire aliens as teachers or police officers because these positions have a direct effect on the functioning of government. On the other hand, a state law requiring citizenship for all civil service positions was held to be invalid. Similarly, a state law requiring a notary public to be a citizen was struck down under the strict scrutiny standard because a notary's responsibilities are essentially clerical. Lourdes could argue that the civil engineer position involves engineering skills rather than the functioning of government. If she prevails it will most likely be because the court agreed with her position and the state failed to meet its difficult burden under the strict scrutiny test of proving that the ban was necessary to achieve a compelling government interest. (A) is wrong because when the strict scrutiny standard is applied, the burden of proof is on the government rather than on the challenger. (B) is incorrect. It is very unlikely that a court would decide that a civil engineer position has a direct effect on the functioning of government. If it were to decide this, it would require only that the law have a rational relationship to a legitimate government interest, and it would be very unlikely that Lourdes could prove that the ban does ***not*** have a rational basis. Thus, (B) does not state the most likely basis for Lourdes to prevail. (D) is incorrect because it states the standard for analyzing government actions based on quasi-suspect classifications such as gender and legitimacy. State law classifications based on alienage are subject to a different standard.

Answer to Question 11

(A) If it was reasonably foreseeable that Eddie's seizures might recur after Eddie was removed from the medication and create an unreasonable risk of harm to third parties, Dr. Dock's removal of Eddie from the medication was negligent, and Dr. Dock will be liable for the damages caused thereby. A prima facie case for negligence consists of: (i) a duty on the part of the defendant to conform to the standard of care of a reasonable person for the protection of the plaintiff against an unreasonable risk of injury; (ii) breach of that duty; (iii) that the breach was the actual and proximate cause of the plaintiff's injury; and (iv) damage to the plaintiff's person or property. If the recurrence of Eddie's seizures following removal from the medication was not reasonably foreseeable, then Dr. Dock breached no duty to anyone by taking Eddie off the medication. However, if the recurrence of seizures was reasonably foreseeable, then it was also reasonably foreseeable that Eddie might engage in some activity (*e.g.,* driving a car) that could cause harm to third parties in the event of a seizure. In this event, Dr. Dock breached a duty to foreseeable plaintiffs (*e.g.,* those driving cars near Eddie at the moment of a seizure) in removing Eddie from the medication, apparently without cautioning Eddie about driving. This breach actually and proximately caused Pompeia to suffer physical injuries and property damage, as well as to incur hospitalization costs. Thus, on the assumption stated in (A), Pompeia should be able to recover from Dr. Dock. (B) is incorrect because it only addresses the issue of causation (specifically, causation in fact). If the accident would not have occurred but for the removal of Eddie from medication, then the removal from medication is a cause in fact of the accident. However, causation is only one element of a prima facie case for negligence (and actual cause is only part of the element of causation). If Dr. Dock owed no duty to Pompeia, or breached no duty owed to her, then he is not liable to her solely by virtue of the fact that the removal of Eddie from medication was the cause in fact of the accident. (C) is incorrect because it implies that Dr. Dock could be liable even if it was not reasonably foreseeable that Eddie's seizures might recur and that harm to third persons might result. No duty is imposed upon a person to take precautions against events that cannot reasonably be foreseen. Thus, if the harm resulting from removal of Eddie from medication was not reasonably foreseeable, then Dr. Dock was under no duty to warn Eddie about driving without medication. Therefore, the imposition of liability based solely on a failure to warn, as suggested by (C), would be incorrect. The decision to suspend the medication may have been, as (D) suggests, a reasonable medical decision as it applied to Eddie (*i.e.,* the seizures had stopped, and the medication produced unpleasant side effects). However, the issue in the question relates to how the decision affected a third party (Pompeia). If the decision created an unreasonable risk of injury to persons such as Pompeia, and such risk was reasonably foreseeable, then Dr. Dock will not be insulated from liability for the resulting injury by the medical reasonableness of the decision for Eddie. Thus, (D) is incorrect.

Answer to Question 12

(D) If Eddie had reason to believe that he might lapse into unconsciousness, his act of driving a car created an unreasonable risk of injury to other persons. On the other hand, if Eddie had no reason to believe that he might lapse into unconsciousness, his operation of the car breached no duty and he will not be liable. The general negligence analysis in the preceding question applies here as well. When a person engages in an activity, he is under a legal duty to act as an ordinary, reasonable person. There is no duty to take precautions against events that cannot reasonably be foreseen. However, a person is expected to know his physical handicaps and is under a duty to exercise the care of a person with such knowledge. Here, Eddie sought medical treatment for his seizures. Eddie followed his doctor's prescribed course of treatment, and eventually the seizures stopped. Thus, at the time of the accident, Eddie had done all that could reasonably be done regarding the treatment of his condition, and apparently had no reason to think that the seizures might recur. In that event, Eddie was under no duty to refrain from driving. However, if Eddie had reason to believe that the seizures might recur, he was under a duty to refrain from driving so as not to create an unreasonable risk of injury to nearby pedestrians or motorists. Breach of this duty would be the actual and proximate cause of the physical injuries and property damage incurred by Pompeia, thus rendering Eddie liable to Pompeia. (B) is incorrect because any prior lapses into unconsciousness do not necessarily impose upon Eddie a duty to take precautions against future seizures. If Eddie reasonably believed that the condition giving rise to the seizures had been remedied through medical treatment, he breached no duty to Pompeia by driving the car. (C) is incorrect because Eddie's breach of duty occurred when he drove the car (if he had reason to believe that he might lapse into unconsciousness). Therefore, the conduct giving rise to the breach of duty occurred while Eddie was still conscious. (A) is incorrect even though the statute sets a specific standard of care to be followed. The statute here that makes it illegal to cross the double yellow line was intended to prevent collisions with oncoming traffic. Thus, Pompeia is in the class intended to be protected by the statute, and the harm she suffered is of the type that the statute was designed to prevent. Consequently, the duty imposed by the statute will replace the more general common law duty of due care. In most states, violation of such a statute establishes a conclusive presumption of duty and breach of duty. However, violation of a statute may be excused where compliance would be beyond the defendant's control. Although Eddie's car did cross a double yellow line, it did so after he lost consciousness (a circumstance that may not have been reasonably foreseeable). Consequently, compliance with the statute was beyond Eddie's control; his violation of it will be excused.

Answer to Question 13

(A) Absent a judgment in an action to quiet title or other tangible proof that title to the five-foot strip has actually been acquired, most jurisdictions would not consider the owner's title marketable. All contracts for the sale of land contain, unless the contract expressly provides otherwise, an implied warranty by the seller that she will deliver to the buyer a marketable title at the date of closing. Marketability refers to freedom from the possibility of litigation concerning the title; title is marketable if a reasonably prudent buyer, ready and able to purchase, will accept it in the exercise of ordinary prudence. At times, sellers will rely on adverse possession to show that defects in title have been cleared. However, courts generally will not permit such reliance when proof of adverse possession rests only on oral evidence that will not be available to the buyer in the future. Here, title to the property described in the contract is unmarketable because the five-foot strip was a private right-of-way and not part of the owner's record title. The owner's adverse possession of the strip will not be sufficient by itself to establish marketable title; there is no longer any physical evidence of the owner's possession. Thus, at the least the owner must offer the buyer additional proof that the buyer can use to defend any lawsuit challenging title. (B) is wrong because the owner removed the fence after she had acquired title by adverse possession. While that makes it more difficult for her to establish marketable title in selling the property, it does not affect the ownership rights she gained by adverse possession. (C) is a misstatement of law. Although government property, including public right-of-ways, is generally exempt from the operation of statutes of limitation, the facts of this question specifically state that this is a private right-of-way. (D) is wrong because, as discussed above, the fact that the owner has title to the strip does not mean that she has marketable title.

Answer to Question 14

(B) Nicelady will recover nothing because her finding the lost dog occurred prior to Dawglost's promise to pay the $200. An enforceable contract must be supported by consideration. Consideration consists of: (i) a bargained-for exchange between the parties; and (ii) an element of legal value to that which is bargained for. The majority rule is that legal value is present if the promisee has incurred a detriment (*i.e.,* has done something she is under no legal obligation to do or has refrained from doing something that she has a legal right to do). For the presence of "bargained-for exchange," the promise must induce the detriment, and the detriment must induce the promise. If something has already been given or performed before the promise is made, it will not satisfy the "bargain" requirement, because it was not given in exchange for the promise when made. Here, Nicelady was under no legal obligation to return the dog to its owner. Thus, in doing so, she incurred a detriment. However, Nicelady was not induced to so act by Dawglost's promise to pay $200. Because Nicelady's actions regarding the dog were performed before Dawglost's promise, those actions were not given in exchange for the promise when made. Thus, the "bargain" element is absent. (A) is incorrect because for a communication to constitute an offer, the acceptance of which results in a contract, it must express a promise to enter into a contract on the basis of terms that are certain and definite. Here, Dawglost simply offered to pay $200 in gratitude for an act already performed by Nicelady. This was not an expression of a commitment to enter into a contract. Thus, there was no "offer" that was capable of either acceptance or rejection. In addition, as detailed above, consideration was not present. Even if Nicelady had not declined Dawglost's promise, she could not have enforced its performance. (C) is incorrect for two reasons. First, the technical defense bar, to which it apparently refers, is inapplicable to these facts. If a past obligation (*e.g.,* a promise to pay money) would be enforceable but for the existence of a technical defense (*e.g.,* statute of limitations, discharge in bankruptcy), a new promise is enforceable if it is written or has been partially performed. Here, Dawglost owed no past obligation to Nicelady. Second, the Statute of Frauds is inapplicable here. The Statute of Frauds provides that certain agreements must be evidenced by a writing signed by the party sought to be charged. These agreements are: (i) a promise by an executor or administrator to pay the estate's debts out of his own funds; (ii) a promise to answer for the debt of another; (iii) a promise made in consideration of marriage; (iv) a promise creating an interest in land; (v) a promise that cannot be performed within one year; and (vi) a promise for the sale of goods for $500 or more. None of these types of promises is at issue here. Therefore, the Statute of Frauds does not come into play. (D) is incorrect for two reasons. First, as explained previously, consideration is not present on these facts. Consequently, Nicelady cannot enforce the promise to pay $200, regardless of any right of Dawglost to revoke his offer. Second, it is not true that Dawglost could not have revoked the offer until February 14. An offer not supported by consideration or detrimental reliance can be revoked at will by the offeror if revocation is communicated to the offeree prior to acceptance. Here, Nicelady gave no consideration, nor did she detrimentally rely, so Dawglost could have revoked his offer at any time.

Answer to Question 15

(A) The original agreement between the distiller and the club is a single bilateral contract because it is an exchange of mutual promises, supported by valuable consideration. The existence of a contract requires mutual assent, *i.e.,* an offer and an acceptance. An offer creates a power of acceptance in the offeree and a corresponding liability on the part of the offeror. To be an offer, a communication must create a reasonable expectation in the offeree that the offeror is willing to enter into a contract on the basis of the offered terms. Such a reasonable expectation depends on whether there was: (i) an expression of a promise or undertaking to enter into a contract; (ii) certainty and definiteness in the essential terms; and (iii) communication to the offeree. If an offeror promises contractual liability in exchange for a counterpromise by the offeree to do a stipulated act, the exchange of promises creates a bilateral contract. On the other hand, if an offer makes acceptance possible only by performing a stipulated act, a unilateral contract is contemplated. Any objective manifestation of the offeree's counterpromise, whether by words or acts, is usually sufficient for acceptance and the formation of a bilateral contract, *i.e.,* where the offeree knowingly takes steps that a reasonable person would consider an acceptance. The January 3 letter from the sales director (on behalf of the distiller) expressed an undertaking to supply all of the club's vodka requirements for the current calendar year. This letter contained the essential terms of the transaction: (i) identity of the offeree and subject matter; (ii) price; (iii) time of delivery; and (iv) quantity (an agreement to buy all of one's requirements is capable of being made certain by reference to objective, extrinsic facts). The definiteness and certainty of these terms made reasonable an expectation on the part of the club that the distiller had expressed an intention to contract, and also rendered the agreement capable of enforcement. Consequently, the communication of these terms to the club constituted an offer. This offer could be accepted by the club's counterpromise to purchase all of its vodka requirements for the current calendar year from the distiller. Thus, a bilateral contract was contemplated. The manager's letter objectively manifested the club's counterpromise to satisfy its vodka requirements for the current calendar year through purchases from the distiller, on the terms stated in the distiller's letter. This was an acceptance. Consideration is present because: (i) the distiller is doing something that it is under no legal obligation to do (supplying the club with its vodka requirements for the year); and (ii) the club is refraining from doing something that it has a legal right to do (purchasing its vodka for the year from a source other than the distiller). Consequently, there is an enforceable bilateral contract and (D) is incorrect. (B) is incorrect for two reasons: First, the agreement between the distiller and the club calls for the purchase and sale of a quantity of vodka sufficient to meet the needs of the club for the current calendar year. Thus, there is one contract, for the duration of one year. The fact that deliveries of varying size are made once a month does not convert this into a ***series*** of contracts. Second, the distiller's offer did not make acceptance possible only by performing a stipulated act; *i.e.,* the club could (and did) accept by making a counterpromise. Therefore, this was not a unilateral contract. Similarly, (C) is incorrect for two reasons: First, as explained in the analysis of (B), this is a single contract, not a series of contracts. Second, an option is a contract in which the offeree gives consideration for a promise by the offeror not to revoke an outstanding offer. The facts do not indicate the existence of such a contract.

Answer to Question 16

(D) The club is entitled to recover the difference between the price of the substitute vodka and the contract price, as well as damages for lost profits resulting from reduced sales of vodka drinks, *i.e.,* consequential damages of which the distiller had reason to know. The measure of damages for breach of a contract for the sale of goods is found in the Uniform Commercial Code ("U.C.C."). Where the seller fails to deliver or repudiates, the buyer may measure his damages by the difference between the contract price and the amount he actually has to pay for replacement goods ("cover"). If the buyer chooses to fix damages in this manner, he must make a reasonable contract for substitute goods in good faith and without unreasonable delay. [U.C.C. §2-712] In addition to such damages, the buyer is entitled to incidental and consequential damages (less expenses saved as a result of the seller's breach). Incidental damages include expenses reasonably incurred in inspection, receipt, transportation, care, and custody of goods rightfully rejected. Consequential damages include any loss resulting from the general or particular requirements and needs of which the seller had reason to know at the time of contracting, and which could not be prevented by purchasing substitute goods or otherwise. Where one party's words or actions make it clear that he is unwilling or unable to perform (*i.e.,* there has been an anticipatory repudiation), the aggrieved party may resort to any remedy for breach. [U.C.C. §2-610] The sales director's comments to the manager indicate unequivocally that the distiller will not sell any more vodka to the club at $120 per case, as it was required to do by its agreement with the club. Thus, the club can treat this as a repudiation by the distiller, and may resort to its remedies for breach. Upon learning of the repudiation, the club (through the manager) promptly and in good faith entered into a contract with a competitor for substitute vodka. The competitor's vodka cost $15 more per case than the distiller's vodka would have cost under the contract. Thus, because the club chose to cover, it can recover $15 (the difference between the contract price per case and the amount per case paid for replacement goods) times the number of cases composing that portion of its yearly requirements that the distiller failed to deliver (*i.e.,* the number of cases purchased from the competitor from April through December). The distiller knew at the time of contracting that the club sold alcoholic drinks (including vodka drinks) to its members. The distiller had reason to know that a breach on its part would result in the club's losing profits from reduced sales of vodka drinks to its members, due to the club's being compelled to serve a vodka brand with less appeal than the distiller's. Therefore, the club can recover these lost profits as consequential damages. (B) is incorrect because it does not allow for recovery of the lost profits which, as explained above, are recoverable as consequential damages. (C) is incorrect because it does not allow for recovery of the cost of cover. Nominal damages may be awarded where a breach is shown but no actual loss is proven. Here, the club has incurred lost profits as well as increased costs for the procurement of substitute vodka. Consequently, (A), which would restrict recovery to nominal damages, is incorrect.

Answer to Question 17

(C) The social upheaval in the distiller's country of origin, and the extreme increase in production and import costs resulting therefrom, may constitute circumstances of impracticability that will discharge the distiller's duty to perform. In contracts for the sale of goods, the U.C.C. provides that the seller's duty to perform may be discharged where performance would be impracticable. Conditions giving rise to impracticability must be such that their nonoccurrence was a basic assumption on which the contract was made. Such conditions would include, *e.g.,* embargoes, crop failure, currency devaluation, war, labor strikes, or the like that entail unforeseen cost increases. [U.C.C. §2-615] The social upheaval in the distiller's country of origin could well be such a condition. When the club and the distiller entered into their contract, the contractual terms (including the price) were based on an assumption that conditions of extraordinary social upheaval would not occur. When such conditions actually did occur, they resulted in an extreme increase in production and import costs for the distiller, which in turn necessitated an increase in the price of the distiller's vodka. This unforeseen cost increase could warrant the discharge of the distiller's contractual duties on the ground of impracticability. (A) is incorrect because a "requirements" contract is enforceable. In making its promise to buy all of its vodka requirements for the year from the distiller, the club relinquished its legal right to purchase the vodka it needs from another source. Thus, the club's promise was supported by consideration. The fact that no minimum or maximum quantities of vodka were stated does not make the promise illusory. Quantities subject to a requirements contract may not be unreasonably disproportionate to: (i) a stated estimate; or (ii) in the absence of such an estimate, to any normal or otherwise comparable prior requirements. [U.C.C. §2-306] The club's promise was tempered by a requirement of good faith, and was capable of being made certain by reference to objective, extrinsic facts (*i.e.,* the club's normal prior vodka requirements). Thus, the promise was not illusory. (B) is incorrect for two reasons: First, the agreement between the distiller and the club calls for the purchase and sale of a quantity of vodka sufficient to meet the needs of the club for the current calendar year. Thus, there is one contract for the duration of one year. The fact that deliveries of varying size are made once a month does not convert this into a series of monthly contracts. Second, the distiller's offer did not make acceptance possible only by performing a stipulated act; *i.e.,* the club could accept by making a counterpromise. Therefore, this was not a unilateral contract. (D) is incorrect because the January 3 letter from the sales director (on behalf of the distiller) expressed an undertaking to supply all of the club's vodka requirements for the current calendar year, and contained the essential terms of the transaction. The definiteness and certainty of these terms created a reasonable expectation on the part of the club that the distiller had expressed an intention to contract on the basis of such terms. Thus, there was an offer.

Answer to Question 18

(A) Wanda, as the life tenant, is obligated to pay all ordinary taxes on the land to the extent of income or profits from the land. Thus, since the income from Greenacres has exceeded the taxes due, Wanda is personally liable for the taxes. A tax sale, however, will cut off the rights of the remaindermen, Debi, Doreen, and Donna; so they definitely have an interest in paying the taxes. (B) misstates the law. The remaindermen are not liable in any way for these taxes. (C) is incorrect because Donna cannot be forced to pay one-third of the actual tax bill. Note, however, that if, to protect the property, Debi and Doreen pay the full amount of the taxes owing (rather than just two-thirds), they can then, as co-tenants, seek a contribution from Donna for her one-third share. (D) is incorrect because a tax sale cuts off the rights of remaindermen.

Answer to Question 19

(C) If Donald is found not guilty, it will be because he acted reasonably in self-defense. Under principles of self-defense, a person who is without fault may use such force as reasonably appears necessary to protect himself from the imminent use of unlawful force upon himself. If Donald is found not guilty, it will be because the jury determined that he was acting reasonably in self-defense. (A) is inaccurate. Common law battery can be established by showing that the defendant recklessly caused injury to the person of another. Therefore, Donald could have been found guilty even if he did not intend to injure Victor. (B) is wrong. While there may be consent to the contact incident to the game, hockey players do not consent to the type of action engaged in by Donald. (D) is wrong because it is too broad. Even though Victor was the original aggressor, Donald would be limited to the amount of force reasonably necessary to defend himself. He would be guilty of battery if the jury found that he acted unreasonably and with excessive force against Victor's aggression. Thus, (C) is a more accurate statement.

Answer to Question 20

(A) Because the Lilyville at-large election system appears to have been established and maintained for the purpose of suppressing the voting power of minority-race voters, the system violates the Equal Protection Clause. The Fourteenth Amendment Equal Protection Clause has been interpreted by the Supreme Court as prohibiting state dilution of the right to vote by malapportionment of electoral districts. In effect, this constitutes a ban on fewer representatives per voter in some districts than in others. This "one person-one vote" principle has also been applied to elections for local government bodies. Generally, an at-large system of election presents no one person-one vote problem, because such a system contains no electoral districts. However, where such a system has been established or maintained for the purpose of suppressing minority-race voting power, it has been found unconstitutional. Here, the Good Ole Boys Club, which dominates Lilyville's political life, has only slated one member of a minority race as a candidate for the city council (Bill Johnson). When Johnson, as a member of the council, raised issues of importance to the black community, the Good Ole Boys Club withdrew its support, resulting in his defeat. Johnson's receipt of 95% of the black vote indicates that he enjoyed considerable support among the black community, and that his actions as a member of the council reflected the concerns of that community. The Good Ole Boys' withdrawal of support from Johnson and subsequent failure to slate any other minority candidates suggests a pattern of discrimination against minorities and unresponsiveness to their needs, thus supporting an inference of purposeful discrimination against minorities to suppress their voting power. Therefore, the Lilyville voting system could most likely be invalidated by relying on the Equal Protection Clause. (B) is incorrect. The Due Process Clause prohibits arbitrary governmental action, and comes into play where a law limits the liberty of all persons to engage in some activity. However, where a law limits the liberty of some persons but not others, there is an equal protection problem. The Lilyville voting system does not limit the voting powers of all persons; rather, it limits the voting power of minority races. Consequently, this question is more appropriately resolved as an equal protection matter rather than one of due process. (C) is incorrect. The Fourteenth Amendment clause protecting privileges and immunities has been interpreted as protecting only against state infringement of rights peculiar to ***national*** citizenship, *e.g.,* the right to vote in national elections. At issue here is the right to vote in a ***local*** election, which is not protected by that clause. (D) is incorrect. Article I, Section 2, Clause 4 of the Constitution directs the governor of a state to issue writs of election to fill vacancies in the United States House of Representatives. Because this question does not involve a vacancy in the House of Representatives, (D) is totally inapplicable.

Answer to Question 21

(A) The court should find that the museum is a private entity and that it may constitutionally hire and fire as it pleases because its actions do not constitute state action. The Equal Protection Clause prohibits states from discriminating against persons on the basis of race, alienage, or national origin unless the discrimination is necessary to achieve a compelling state interest. The museum's policy here of not hiring persons of German descent clearly violates the Clause's prohibitions. However, there is no constitutional violation here because there is no state action. The Equal Protection Clause prohibits only ***government*** infringement. This does not mean that only direct government action is proscribed. Private action may constitute state action where the private actor is performing an exclusive state function or the government is significantly involved in the private actor's activities. The running of the museum here, however, is not an exclusive government function (*e.g.,* running elections), and the state's grant of the land for the museum does not constitute significant state involvement in the museum's affairs (*see* below). Thus, there is no state action here and no constitutional violation. (Note that the museum's actions probably violate several civil rights ***statutes*** that apply to private citizens.) (B) is incorrect because it reaches the proper result on a faulty rationale. If the museum's acts were state action, the excuse of remedying past discrimination would not validate the discrimination. Remedying past discrimination has never been used as a basis for explicit discrimination ***against*** a suspect class, but rather has only been used to justify action favoring a group in limited circumstances. As noted above, discrimination against a suspect class will be upheld only if it is necessary to a compelling interest, and only one case of explicit discrimination against a suspect class has been upheld—incarcerating United States citizens of Japanese ancestry during World War II. It is doubtful that the explicit discrimination would be upheld. (C) is incorrect because the grant of land simply does not constitute significant state involvement, which requires that the state affirmatively facilitate, encourage, or authorize the acts of discrimination. Merely granting land to an entity that then decides to adopt a discriminatory policy does not constitute the necessary affirmative action. (D) is incorrect for the reasons stated under (C)—there is no significant state involvement in the discrimination since the state is deriving no benefit from the discrimination and has not authorized or encouraged it. [*Compare* Burton v. Wilmington Parking Authority (1961)—state action found where city/landlord charged tenant high rent to operate a "whites only" restaurant in the city garage building]

Answer to Question 22

(D) The retailer will recover $1,000, which is the difference between its lost profits and the buyer's down payment. When the buyer repudiates or refuses to accept goods, the usual measure of the seller's damages is the difference between the contract price and the market price or the difference between the contract price and the resale price of the particular goods. However, neither of those measures of damages give adequate compensation for the buyer's breach where the seller has an unlimited supply of the goods and the demand is limited (*i.e.*, a lost volume seller), because, but for the buyer's breach, the seller would have made two sales instead of one. In this type of case, lost profit is measured by the contract price less the cost to the dealer. Here, the retailer could have made two sales of that model of watercraft because it could get as many as it needed from the manufacturer. Hence, it lost a profit of $3,000 as a result of the buyer's breach. This amount is offset against the amount of the down payment that the buyer made, resulting in a net recovery of $1,000 by the retailer. (A) is incorrect because the retailer did suffer damages as a result of the buyer's breach. (B) is wrong because it represents the difference between the contract price and the resale price for the goods, which does not adequately compensate the retailer for its damages from the buyer's breach. (C) is incorrect because $3,000 constitutes the retailer's lost profits from the buyer's breach, but it must be offset against the down payment that the retailer received from the buyer.

Answer to Question 23

(B) In forcing the principal to dress in the robber's clothing and to leave the school first, the robber exhibited extreme indifference to an unjustifiably high risk to human life; *i.e.,* the robber acted with malice aforethought. Murder is the unlawful killing of a human being with malice aforethought. Malice aforethought exists if the defendant has any of the following states of mind: (i) intent to kill; (ii) intent to inflict great bodily injury; (iii) awareness of an unjustifiably high risk to human life; or (iv) intent to commit a felony. When the robber forced the principal to dress in the robber's clothing and leave the school first, the robber knew that there was a high risk that the police would mistake the principal for the robber and shoot the principal, who could not raise his hands in the air. By compelling the principal to proceed into a situation that presented an unjustifiably high risk to the principal's life, the robber manifested extreme indifference to that risk. Thus, the robber acted with a state of mind that was sufficient to constitute malice aforethought. This state of mind, in conjunction with the robber's act of placing the principal in this position, makes the robber guilty of the murder of the principal. (C) is incorrect because, not only was it foreseeable that the police would use deadly force against what they perceived to be an armed and dangerous felon, but it was highly probable that they would do so. (D) is incorrect because, by consciously creating the appearance that the principal was actually the robber, an armed and dangerous felon, and compelling the principal to proceed out the door without his hands up, the robber is deemed to be responsible for the shooting of the principal. It may be true that, as (A) states, the police were justified in using deadly force under the circumstances. The police may use deadly force to apprehend an armed felon who poses a threat of serious bodily harm, and it appeared to the police that the principal was such a person. However, (A) is incorrect because it implies that the robber would not be guilty if the police were not justified in using deadly force. The robber's indifference to an unjustifiably high risk to human life does not depend on whether the police response was legally justified. In effect, (A) would make the robber's mental state dependent on his knowledge of the law regarding police use of deadly force. Even if the police response was not legally justified, there was still an unjustifiably high risk that the police would shoot under these circumstances. (B) addresses this risk, while (A) does not.

Answer to Question 24

(B) If the uncle's main purpose in making the agreement was to benefit himself rather than his nephew, the agreement is outside of the Statute of Frauds and is enforceable even though it was oral. Under the Statute of Frauds, certain agreements must be evidenced by a writing that contains: (i) the identity of the party sought to be charged; (ii) identification of the contract's subject matter; (iii) terms and conditions of the agreement; (iv) recital of consideration; and (v) signature of the party to be charged, or of his agent. One type of agreement that is covered by the Statute of Frauds is a promise to answer for the debt or default of another where the promise is collateral rather than primary. However, where the main purpose or leading object of the promisor is to secure an advantage or pecuniary benefit for himself, the contract is not within the Statute of Frauds, even if the effect is still to pay the debt of another. The uncle guaranteed the loan to his nephew, which means that the uncle agreed to repay the loan only if his nephew refused to do so. Therefore, the uncle made a collateral promise to answer for the debt or default of the nephew regarding the loan from the bank. However, if, as (B) states, the main purpose of the uncle's making the agreement was to benefit himself rather than his nephew (by, *e.g.,* being allowed to use the tractor rent-free), then the agreement is outside the scope of the Statute of Frauds and would be enforceable against the uncle even in the absence of a writing. (C) is incorrect because, although the lack of a writing would ordinarily render the agreement unenforceable, the additional statement of the uncle's purpose contained in (B) would result in the agreement's not falling within the Statute of Frauds. (A) is incorrect because, even if the agreement were supported by consideration, the bank could not win unless the main purpose rule caused the agreement to fall outside the Statute of Frauds. Furthermore, separate consideration need not flow between the bank and the uncle to support the suretyship agreement. The bank's agreeing to engage in the loan transaction is sufficient to support the uncle's promise even if the uncle received no benefit from it. (D) is incorrect because the uncle did not withdraw his promise until after his offer of guarantee had been accepted by the bank (through the loan officer). An offeror may terminate an offer by communicating revocation to the offeree prior to acceptance. Here, the loan officer communicated directly to the uncle an absolute and unequivocal acceptance of the uncle's offer of guarantee. Thus, the uncle's attempted withdrawal of his promise came too late to constitute an effective revocation. While it could be argued that the uncle's repudiation required the loan officer to mitigate damages by stopping the check from being issued, damages must be reasonably certain of being incurred for the requirement of mitigation to apply. Here, any damages are only speculative at this point because the nephew has the primary duty to pay off the new loan and the uncle may not be required to do anything. The duty to mitigate damages does not require that the creditor forgo, for the guarantor's sake, a potentially income-producing transaction merely to avoid a ***possibility*** of breach by the principal.

Answer to Question 25

(A) The conveyances of 20% of Blackacre to Donna and Dan sever the joint tenancy only as to that 20%, leaving Hal and Wallene with an 80% interest as joint tenants. Donna and Dan, by virtue of the separate conveyances to them, each have a 10% interest as tenants in common. Creation of a joint tenancy requires four unities: (i) time (interests must vest at the same time); (ii) title (interests must be acquired by the same instrument); (iii) interest (interests must be of the same type and duration); and (iv) possession (interests must give identical rights to enjoyment). Under modern law, a joint tenancy results only when an intention to create a right of survivorship is clearly expressed. When two or more persons take property by a single conveyance, a tenancy in common is presumed rather than a joint tenancy. An inter vivos conveyance by all joint tenants of a portion of the property held in joint tenancy severs the joint tenancy as to the portion that is conveyed. However, the joint tenancy is preserved as to the unconveyed portion of the property. The transferee takes as a tenant in common, because she does not share the unities of time or title with the joint tenants (*i.e.,* her interest vested at a different time and was acquired by a different instrument). Here, Hal and Wallene owned Blackacre as joint tenants. When they conveyed 10% of Blackacre to Donna, the joint tenancy was severed as to that 10%. At that point, Hal and Wallene held an interest in 90% of Blackacre as joint tenants because, as between themselves, the four unities were preserved as to that 90%. Donna did not share the unities of time or title with Hal and Wallene. Thus, Donna took a 10% interest as a tenant in common rather than as a joint tenant. When Hal and Wallene conveyed another 10% of Blackacre to Dan, the joint tenancy was further severed as to that 10%, leaving Hal and Wallene with an 80% interest as joint tenants. Dan, who did not share the unities of time or title with Hal and Wallene, took his 10% interest as a tenant in common. (B) is incorrect because it indicates that the joint tenancy of Hal and Wallene has been converted into a tenancy in common as to their 80% interest. As explained above, Hal and Wallene retain a joint tenancy as to this 80%. (C) and (D) are incorrect in stating that Donna and Dan have a 20% interest as joint tenants. Donna and Dan took their interests in Blackacre at different times. These interests were not conveyed to them together. Thus, Donna and Dan each hold a separate 10% interest rather than a single combined 20% interest. Even if Hal and Wallene had conveyed a 20% interest to Donna and Dan together (so that the four unities would exist as between them), a tenancy in common (rather than a joint tenancy) would be presumed under modern law absent a clear expression of intent to the contrary.

Answer to Question 26

(A) Both Blandings and Grant are personally liable for the deficiency. If a sale of foreclosed property does not bring enough to satisfy the mortgage debt, the mortgagee/lender can bring a personal action against the mortgagor/debtor for the deficiency (as long as the jurisdiction does not bar deficiency judgments). When the mortgagor sells the mortgaged property and gives a deed, the grantee takes subject to the mortgage, which remains on the land. If the grantee does not sign an agreement to assume the mortgage, he does not become personally liable on the loan, and the original mortgagor remains primarily and personally liable. If the grantee does sign an assumption agreement, however, the lender is considered a third-party beneficiary of the agreement, and hence may sue either the original mortgagor or the assuming grantee on the mortgage note. Here, Grant signed the recital providing for the assumption, so he will be personally liable on the loan; (B) is therefore incorrect. (C) is incorrect because Blandings, the original mortgagor, did not extinguish his own personal liability on the loan by obtaining the assumption agreement from Grant. He remains secondarily liable as a surety. Thus, Ace may sue Blandings on the original mortgage agreement. (Note that while Ace may obtain a judgment against both of them, its maximum recovery will be the $14,000 deficiency.) (D) is incorrect because the facts indicate that the jurisdiction does not bar deficiency judgments.

Answer to Question 27

(D) The patient's best argument would be that the psychiatrist has intruded into her physical seclusion.

One of the four branches of the tort of invasion of privacy is intrusion upon a person's seclusion, which can be proved by showing an act of intrusion upon the seclusion of the plaintiff that would be objectionable to a reasonable person, where the thing intruded upon is private. A person's body language while revealing inner secrets to a psychiatrist is probably sufficiently private to be the subject of such an action. The fact that the patient permitted the psychiatrist to observe her does not preclude her activity from being "private"; she did not consent to a permanent record being made of it. Therefore, (D) is correct. (A) is incorrect because "false light" requires revelation of facts that attribute to the plaintiff views she does not hold or action she did not take. Here, the psychiatrist would not be revealing anything untrue about the patient. She actually made whatever gestures the tape recorded. (B) is incorrect because public disclosure of private facts requires some publication or publicity concerning the private facts. Nothing in the facts indicates that the psychiatrist has shown the tapes to anyone yet, so they were not publicly displayed. If the psychiatrist had shown the tapes publicly, the prima facie tort would be present. (C) is incorrect because misappropriation of a person's likeness requires use of the likeness for commercial advantage, and the psychiatrist has not yet published the videotapes or gained any commercial advantage from them.

Answer to Question 28

(C) An offer for a unilateral contract best describes Ken and George's agreement. An offer for a unilateral contract is a promise to perform in exchange for a requested performance. Here, all that Ken promised was to sell the car to George if George performed by tendering $12,000. The contract would be unilateral because Ken was requiring acceptance by completion of performance rather than by a return promise. Thus, (C) is correct. (A) is incorrect because grounds for promissory estoppel are not present. Promissory estoppel will arise where a promisee detrimentally relies on a promise that the promisor should foresee will cause such reliance. Here, George did nothing to detrimentally rely on Ken's promise; in fact, there is no indication that George took any action whatsoever. (B) is incorrect because quasi-contract is a remedy to disgorge unjust enrichment and is not a description of an actual agreement. Quasi-contract is a legal fiction imposed to force one who has been unjustly enriched to return the unjust benefit to the person it should belong to where that person had a reasonable expectation of being compensated. Here, Ken was not unjustly enriched. (D) is incorrect because George did not receive an option. An option is a promise to keep an offer open for an agreed-upon time in exchange for consideration; it is itself a contract and must meet the requirements of contracts to be enforceable. Here, there was no consideration given for Ken's promise to keep the offer open, so Ken had the right to revoke the offer at any time until George began performance. Thus, there was no option contract here. (Note that if George had begun performance, the offer would become irrevocable and, under the Second Restatement, an option contract would be implied, but here there is no indication that George did anything; hence, no option contract was created.)

Answer to Question 29

(C) Lester will recover the $1,600 because he obtained a buyer for more than $15,000. Whether Lester can recover depends on whether there is a contract between Lester and Ken. Lester's statement that he could find a buyer for 10% of the price of no less than $15,000 was sufficiently definite to be an offer. While Ken did not accept the offer immediately, when Lester informed Ken that he had found a buyer, Ken asked for the buyer's telephone number. This was a sufficient acceptance even though Ken did not explicitly state that he was accepting, since acceptances are tested by an objective standard, and a reasonable person would presume that Ken's statement was an acceptance—given that Ken knew that the information was being supplied under the terms of

Lester's offer. Thus, (C) is correct. (A) is incorrect because there is nothing in the facts that indicates that a 10% finder's fee is unconscionable. Unconscionability is tested at the time a contract is formed. A contract will be found to be unconscionable where the court finds that the terms are extremely one-sided. Such contracts are often found where the parties are of unequal bargaining positions. Here, the parties appear to be in equal bargaining positions; indeed, Ken did not need Lester's services at all. Neither do the terms of the contract appear to be one-sided, since Lester offered to obtain a better price for Ken than Ken had obtained himself. Thus, the contract was not unconscionable. (B) is incorrect because Ken did receive consideration. Consideration is something of legal value given in exchange for a promise or performance. Here, Lester was under no obligation to tell Ken the identity of the prospective purchaser, and his doing so was of legal value; thus, there was consideration for Ken's promise to pay. (D) is incorrect because it is irrelevant. Lester discharged the only condition precedent to Ken's duty to pay under the terms of the contract—providing a buyer for more than $15,000. It does not matter that Ken could have found a buyer on his own.

Answer to Question 30

(A) Jones holds Midacre subject to both mortgages, and the Senior Bank mortgage is subordinate to the Junior Bank mortgage. Central's recording act is a race-notice statute. Under this statute, a bona fide purchaser is protected only if he records before the prior transferee or mortgagee records. Here, Jones had record notice of the Junior Bank mortgage, so he was not a bona fide purchaser protected by the recording statute as to that mortgage. As to the Senior Bank mortgage, he was a bona fide purchaser because he had no notice of that mortgage executed by Smith, but Jones did not record until after that mortgage was recorded. Hence, he holds Midacre subject to both mortgages. The Senior Bank mortgage is subordinate to the Junior Bank mortgage because mortgagees for value are treated as "purchasers" under the recording statutes, and Junior Bank executed its mortgage without notice of the prior Senior Bank mortgage and recorded it before Senior Bank recorded its mortgage. Thus, Junior Bank's mortgage has priority over Senior Bank's mortgage, and (B) is incorrect. (C) is incorrect because Midacre is subject to Senior Bank's mortgage also. Unlike in a notice jurisdiction, in a race-notice jurisdiction the fact that Jones was a subsequent bona fide purchaser without notice of the Senior Bank mortgage is irrelevant because Senior Bank recorded before Jones did. (D) is incorrect because Midacre is subject to Junior Bank's mortgage also. At the time of the conveyance of Midacre to Jones on April 1, Jones had record notice of the Junior Bank mortgage because it was recorded in February, so Jones takes subject to it.

Answer to Question 31

(A) The court should require the woman to show that the legislation is not rationally related to any legitimate state interest. The Supreme Court has held that the right of privacy includes the right of a woman to have an abortion under certain circumstances without undue interference from the government. However, neither federal nor state government is required to grant medical benefit payments for abortions, even if it grants benefits for childbirth services. The Court has held that a state's failure to provide funding for a woman's abortion decision does not constitute interference with her constitutional right to make that decision; hence, such legislation is valid unless the plaintiff can show that it is not rationally related to a legitimate state interest. [*See* Maher v. Roe (1977)] (B) is incorrect because the legislation does not create a gender-based classification that would require application of an intermediate scrutiny standard. The fact that the restriction applies to a drug prescribed only to women does not establish gender-based discrimination. [*See* Geduldig v. Aiello (1974)] (C) is wrong because, as discussed above, legislation excluding abortion-related expenses from government funding has been held not to constitute interference with a woman's constitutional right to choose to have an abortion. Therefore, the undue burden test does not apply. (D) is incorrect for the same reason as in (C), and also because it does not state the standard that the Court uses to evaluate abortion regulations. Regulations restricting pre-viability abortions will be invalidated if they constitute an "undue burden" on a woman's right to have an abortion. [Planned Parenthood of Southeastern Pennsylvania v. Casey (1992)]

Answer to Question 32

(C) Margaret's testimony is admissible to show bias. A witness can be impeached, either in cross-examination or by extrinsic evidence, with evidence that suggests a bias on the part of the witness, because it tends to show that the witness has a motive to lie. Evidence that the witness disliked the party he is testifying against would qualify as evidence of bias. Margaret could testify that she saw Walter throw the rock through the window of Good Eats, because such evidence would help establish Walter's bias against Good Eats. (A) is incorrect for two reasons. Federal Rule 608 provides that evidence of prior bad acts, if offered to impeach, may not be proved through other extrinsic evidence, but may be inquired into during cross-examination. Furthermore, if the prior bad act also helps establish bias, the courts have held that extrinsic evidence will be admissible. (B) is wrong as well for this latter reason. (D) is too broad a statement. In a broad sense, the evidence is offered to impeach the credibility of Walter and to suggest to the jury that he may be lying under oath. However, the reason it is relevant and does not constitute impeachment on a collateral matter is because it is offered to show bias, making (C) the better answer.

Answer to Question 33

(A) The court should rule that Willis's testimony is admissible nonhearsay for the limited purpose of showing that Dean knew that the mudflap assembly was loose. Hearsay is a statement, other than one made by the declarant while testifying at trial, offered in evidence to prove the truth of the matter asserted. When the out-of-court statement is introduced for any other purpose, the statement is not hearsay. Thus, in a negligence case when knowledge of a danger is an issue, the third person's statement of warning is admissible for the limited purpose of showing knowledge or notice on the part of the listener. Here, the statement of the third person over the CB radio can be testified to by Willis to show that Dean was notified of the loose mudflap assembly. (B) is incorrect because the testimony would not be admissible as substantive evidence that the assembly was loose. In that case, the statement would be inadmissible hearsay because it was made by an out-of-court declarant and offered to prove the truth of what the declarant stated. (C) is incorrect because it is not necessary that the out-of-court declarant be identified. Since the statement is being offered only to show that Dean had notice of the loose mudflap assembly, it does not matter that Willis does not know who made the statement; he can still testify to what he heard spoken to Dean. (D) is wrong because, as stated above, the statement is admissible nonhearsay for the limited purpose of proving that Dean had notice that the mudflap assembly was loose.

Answer to Question 34

(A) Pucker will lose since it had the risk of loss at the time the grain was destroyed. Since crops such as wheat are goods, this contract will be governed by the Uniform Commercial Code (U.C.C.). The U.C.C. modifies the common law rule that destruction of the subject matter without fault of either party discharges both parties of their obligations under the contract. Under the U.C.C., the risk of loss falls on the buyer or seller according to the terms of their contract. Here, the contract called for Agrigiant, Pucker's assignor, to deliver the wheat "F.O.B." (free on board) St. Louis.

When a contract has an F.O.B. delivery term, the seller is obligated to get the goods to the destination indicated and make a reasonable contract for freight if the destination indicated is not the buyer's place of business. The seller has the risk of loss until the goods make it to the F.O.B. destination, and thereafter the buyer has the risk. Here, the destruction occurred before the seller got the goods to the F.O.B. destination (St. Louis), so the risk of loss was on the seller (Pucker), who is in breach for nondelivery. Thus, Pucker will lose. (B) would be incorrect even if Pucker did not have the risk of loss. A seller's remedy if the goods are destroyed when the risk of loss is on the buyer would be the contract price. If the seller were given the value of the destroyed goods, he might recover more or less than the contract price (depending on the price agreed upon by the parties), whereas the aim of the U.C.C. is to put a nonbreaching party in as good a position as he would have been had there not been a breach. (C) would be correct if Pucker did not have the risk of loss—as indicated above, the nonbreaching seller's remedy for destroyed goods is the contract price. (D) would be incorrect even if Pucker did not have the risk of loss, because merely awarding a nonbreaching seller the profits on a contract where the goods are destroyed rather than the full contract price will cause him a loss, since he had to pay for the manufacture or purchase of the goods and would not be recovering those costs.

Answer to Question 35

(B) If WBC brings an action against Agrigiant, WBC will be able to recover the costs of replacing the destroyed wheat, since Agrigiant remained liable on the assigned contract and it had the risk of loss. Although most contractual duties may be assigned—unless they are personal—and the obligee must accept performance from the delegate, the delegating party (delegator) remains liable on his obligation. Thus, an assignment of a contract that includes a delegation of duties does not relieve the assignor from its duty to perform. Here, WBC did not receive the performance that was due (the wheat), so it could sue Agrigiant to recover for the breach. When a nonbreaching buyer does not receive the contracted goods, it has several options: it can cancel the contract and recover any incidental damages, or it can purchase replacement goods and sue for the cost of replacement—"cover." Damages under the latter option are measured by the difference between the contract price and the amount the buyer actually has to pay for the replacement goods. Thus, (B) is correct and (A) is incorrect. Note that (A) would have been correct if U.C.C. section 2-613 were applicable, because it provides for avoidance of the contract when goods are destroyed without fault of either party before risk of loss passes to the buyer. However, that section applies only when particular goods are identified to the contract ***when the contract was made***; here, there is no designation of specific bushels of wheat until shipment. (C) is not a proper measure of damages unless WBC has already paid for the wheat and wishes to cancel (and the facts do not indicate this to be the case), since the contract price may not be enough to purchase replacement goods if the price of wheat has risen, and would be too much if the price has dropped. (D) is incorrect because specific performance is usually not available for goods unless the circumstances call for it—for example, if replacement goods could not be obtained or the goods are unique. Here, the goods are not unique and there is no indication that replacement wheat is not available.

Answer to Question 36

(A) The court should rule for the state because the purpose of the federal law is different from the purpose of the state law. The question here is whether the state law is preempted by the federal law. Preemption will be found where it was the intent of the federal government to occupy the entire field with its regulation or where the state law is found to interfere with the federal scheme of regulation. Since the federal law here is aimed only at occupational safety, no conclusion can be drawn that the federal government intended to occupy the entire field of regulation of pesticides, and the state law does not interfere with the federal law. Hence, the state law is not preempted, and (A) is correct and (D) is incorrect. (B) is incorrect because the Tenth Amendment reserves to the states only those powers not granted to the federal government by the Constitution, and the federal government has the power to regulate pesticides under the Commerce Clause, which gives Congress plenary power to regulate any activity that, either in itself or in combination with other activities, has a substantial economic effect on, or effect on movement in, interstate commerce. The production and distribution of food products containing pesticides would be such an activity. (C) is incorrect because there need be no specific authorization for a state to regulate, as long as federal preemption does not apply. While congressional power over interstate commerce is plenary, it is not exclusive—states may regulate local aspects of interstate commerce under certain conditions.

Answer to Question 37

(B) The shopkeeper will win if she can establish a common development scheme for the entire subdivision and that the subdivision appeared to conform to the scheme. An injunction against breaching a covenant may be obtained by enforcing the covenant as an equitable servitude. An equitable servitude can be created by a writing complying with the Statute of Frauds concerning a promise that touches and concerns the land and indicates that the servitude exists, as long as notice is given to the future owners of the burdened land. Here, there was a promise that touched and concerned the land and indicated that a servitude existed (the deed restrictions), but the promise was not contained in the supermarket's deed. Nevertheless, the court will imply the covenant here. A court will imply a covenant—known as a reciprocal negative servitude—where evidence shows that the developer had a scheme for development when sales began and the grantee in question had notice of the plan. The covenant protects the parties who purchased in reliance on the scheme. Evidence of the scheme can be obtained from the general pattern of other restrictions, and notice can be from actual notice, record notice, or inquiry notice. Here, the supermarket had inquiry notice of the restriction regarding industrial use because of the uniform residential and commercial character of the other lots in the development. Thus, the covenant will be implied and (B) is correct. (A) is incorrect because actual awareness of the restriction on the part of the firm and the supermarket is not essential; they have inquiry notice (which is a type of constructive notice). On the other hand, mere notice of the restriction would not be enough if the other elements for an implied negative servitude (common scheme when sales began) are not present. (C) and (D) are incorrect because an implied negative servitude would bind subsequent purchasers whether or not the restriction appeared in their deeds, and despite the fact that the restrictive language in the shopkeeper's deed purported to bind only the buyer and her successors. Based on the developer's representations, the shopkeeper was entitled to rely on the fact that similar restrictions would be imposed on all other purchasers of the lots.

Answer to Question 38

(B) Howard should be convicted because he was intoxicated when he damaged Webster's property. Howard is being charged with reckless damage to property. A person acts recklessly when he consciously disregards a substantial or unjustifiable risk that a prohibited result will follow and this disregard constitutes a gross deviation from the standard of reasonable care. Driving earth-moving equipment while intoxicated would be considered to be reckless because of the great potential for destruction arising from the huge size and power of the equipment. Therefore, (B) is correct. (A) is incorrect because merely driving the equipment in violation of statute would not necessarily be reckless. For instance, here, the statute likely was enacted to prevent untrained persons from driving dangerous equipment, but Howard was trained to operate the heavy equipment in question; thus, if not for the fact that he was drunk, his action would not necessarily have been reckless.

Violating the statute may be evidence of negligence, but negligence is insufficient to establish recklessness. (C) is incorrect for the same reason that (B) is correct—driving the equipment while intoxicated constitutes reckless conduct. While voluntary intoxication is a defense to a crime that requires purpose or knowledge, it is no defense to crimes involving recklessness. Even though the defendant's condition may in fact have precluded him from being consciously aware of the risk, his initial act of becoming voluntarily intoxicated was sufficiently reckless to justify holding him liable for his conduct while intoxicated. (D) is incorrect because it states the mental state for knowing conduct—if the defendant is aware that his conduct will necessarily or very likely cause a certain result, he acts knowingly with respect to that result. Recklessness is a lesser standard of fault.

Answer to Question 39

(A) Dudley cannot be found guilty of violating the statute because he did not know that his act would cause the damage to Harry's computer that it did. Under the Model Penal Code fault standards adopted by modern criminal codes, a person acts "knowingly" with respect to the nature of his conduct when he is aware that his conduct is of that nature or that certain circumstances exist. He acts knowingly with respect to the result of his conduct when he knows that his conduct will necessarily or very likely cause such a result. When a statute establishes a culpable state of mind without indicating to which material elements of the offense it is to apply, the statute will be interpreted as requiring that state of mind for every material element of the offense. In this case, the statute requires that the defendant "knowingly cause over $200 in damage to another's property." The requirement that the damage caused be over $200 is a material element of the offense because it defines the harmful result that will trigger criminal liability under the statute. Thus, Dudley must have known that his act of sending the computer virus would necessarily or very likely cause over $200 in damage to Harry's computer to be liable under the statute in this case. (B) is incorrect because intent is not required by the statute for Dudley to be liable. Under modern criminal codes, intent is equated with purpose, which is defined as having a conscious object to engage in certain conduct or cause a certain result. Here, Dudley could be guilty under the statute even if he did not have the objective of causing that damage to Harry's computer, as long as he knew that it was at least very likely to occur. (C) is incorrect because the fact that Dudley knew that he was sending a virus is not enough to establish guilt. As discussed above, the statute also requires that he know that his conduct will or is very likely to cause over $200 in damage to Harry's computer. (D) is incorrect because, even if Dudley knew that there was a small chance that this damage ***might*** occur, he has not acted with the required degree of culpability under the statute. Dudley must have known, at a minimum, that his conduct was very likely to cause the damage to Harry's computer. Being aware that such damage could occur in a very small percentage of cases may establish that Dudley acted recklessly, but it does not establish that he acted knowingly.

Answer to Question 40

(C) Judicial notice operates as a substitute for proof as to facts that are matters of common knowledge in the community or are capable of certain verification through easily accessible, well-established sources. When a court takes judicial notice of a fact under the federal rules in a criminal case, the jury may, but is not required to, accept the fact noticed; thus, its effect is only to relieve the prosecutor of her burden of producing evidence on that fact. (A) is incorrect because taking judicial notice does not affect the burden of persuasion, which is the burden of one litigant to overcome the case of the opposing litigant. (B) is incorrect because judicial notice of a fact does not establish proof of the fact beyond a reasonable doubt; as discussed above, the jury is not required to accept the fact noticed. (D) is incorrect because it is the rule for civil cases; in criminal cases, the jury is instructed that it may, but is not required to, accept as conclusive any fact judicially noticed.

Answer to Question 41

(D) The homeowner will likely prevail on the contract claim because he did not enter into a contract with the roofer. To form a contract, there must be a valid offer and acceptance. The homeowner made an offer, but the roofer rejected the offer the next day with his first phone call. Once an offer is rejected, the offeree's power of acceptance is destroyed. Thus, the roofer's second call was not an acceptance, but rather an offer. The homeowner did nothing to accept the roofer's offer, and this is not the type of case where silence will be deemed to be an acceptance (*e.g.,* where the parties have so agreed or where that has been their course of dealing). Thus, there was no acceptance and no contract. Therefore, (D) is correct and (A) is incorrect. (B) is incorrect because it suggests a remedy of quasi-contract (which allows a party to recover the value of his services under some circumstances even if a contract cannot be established), and the question specifically states that the roofer's action is limited to a breach of contract claim. (C) is incorrect because whether the homeowner was bound depends on whether there was a valid offer and acceptance, not on whether he was aware of the performance. If the homeowner had accepted and did not know of the performance until he returned, there would still be an enforceable contract.

Answer to Question 42

(C) The court will use the doctrines of part performance and equitable conversion to grant full title to Pineacre to Rhonda in fee simple. Under the doctrine of part performance, a court may order specific performance of a land sale contract despite the absence of a writing if additional facts are present. In most jurisdictions, part performance can be established by two of the following: (i) possession of the land by the purchaser; (ii) making of substantial improvements; and/or (iii) payment of all or part of the purchase price. Here, for Burton's estate to be entitled to specific performance of the contract by paying the full balance as permitted by the statute, the court will have to find that Burton has satisfied the requirements for part performance. Thus, (B) is incorrect. Under the doctrine of equitable conversion, once a contract is made and each party is entitled to specific performance, equity regards the purchaser as the owner of the real property. If the purchaser dies before title has passed, his interest is characterized as real property in his estate and will go to the takers of the estate's real property at the closing of the contract. Furthermore, they are entitled to payment of the lien or encumbrance from the personal property estate and take the land free of any encumbrances. Thus, the court will apply the equitable conversion doctrine to provide Rhonda with the fee simple rights to Pineacre. (A) and (D) are incorrect because the equitable mortgage doctrine is not applicable. A landowner needing cash may "sell" the land to a person who will pay cash, with the landowner giving the "purchaser" an absolute deed rather than a mortgage, and the landowner may remain on the land and make monthly payments to the lender. If the court concludes that the deed was really given for security purposes, it will treat the deed as an "equitable" mortgage and require that the lender foreclose it by judicial action, like any other mortgage. Here, there was no such security arrangement between Ogden and Burton. Thus, the doctrine of equitable mortgage does not apply.

Answer to Question 43

(B) It was error to admit the reputation evidence from Herman's co-worker because, in civil trials, character evidence is inadmissible to prove that the litigant acted in conformity with that character. An exception exists when the litigant's character is directly in issue (*e.g.,* in a defamation action), but that is not the case here. (A) is incorrect because it is not the rule in civil trials; it is, however, the rule for criminal trials—evidence of character is admissible only if the party puts his character in issue. (C) is incorrect because character evidence generally is inadmissible in civil cases whether or not the witness had personal knowledge of specific conduct of the litigant.

Moreover, when character evidence is admissible, it is permissible to testify to the litigant's reputation in the community; knowledge of specific acts is not required. (D) is incorrect because there is no exception to the rule against reputation evidence in civil cases that would allow character evidence that can be verified by an unbiased witness. It would, however, be proper to call the unbiased witness to testify as to how much Herman drank the night of the accident.

Answer to Question 44

(C) Witness can testify to one of Dane's statements but not the other. An admission is a statement made by a party offered by the opponent of that party that is relevant to an issue in the case. If an out-of-court statement qualifies as an admission, it will not be excluded by the hearsay rule. However, it will be excluded if there is a specific rule excluding the admission. Federal Rule 408 provides that settlement offers and factual statements made during settlement negotiations are inadmissible if offered to prove liability, invalidity of the claim, or to establish the amount of damage. Rule 408 only applies, however, when there is a dispute between the parties. A statement made at the scene of an accident would rarely qualify. Federal Rule 409 excludes evidence of the payment or offer to pay medical expenses if offered to help establish liability for an injury. Rule 409, however, does not exclude factual statements made in conjunction with the payment or offer. Such factual statements would be admissible as an admission by a party. Hence, Dane's statement would not qualify as a settlement offer. His statement "I'll take care of your medical bills" would be excluded under Rule 409. His statement "I was not paying attention" would not be excluded by Rule 409 and would be admissible as an admission. (A) is wrong because Dane's statement is not a settlement offer. (B) is too broad a statement. As discussed above, Dane's statement "I'll take care of your medical bills" would be excluded. (D) is tempting but wrong. Even if Port was negligent per se, Dane's statement would probably be admissible on the issue of contributory negligence or, in a comparative negligence jurisdiction, on the issue of damages.

Answer to Question 45

(C) Chloe will recover because Chuck intended to frighten her. To make out a prima facie case for battery, a plaintiff must show that the defendant intended to bring about a harmful or offensive contact to the plaintiff, that defendant's act did so, and that defendant caused the result that occurred. Here, there was definitely a harmful contact, but Chuck did not have the intent to cause the contact. Nevertheless, he will be liable for battery because he did have the intent to assault Chloe (*i.e.,* he intended to cause Chloe apprehension of immediate harmful or offensive contact). Under the doctrine of transferred intent, his intent to commit the assault will be transferred to the battery action to complete the prima facie case. Thus, (C) is correct. (A) is incorrect because provocation is not a defense to battery. If Chloe's remarks had caused Chuck to reasonably believe that he was in danger, he would have had the defense of self-defense, but Chloe's words were not sufficient to make such a claim here. (B) is incorrect because although the defective axe may have been a cause in fact (*i.e.,* "but for" cause) of Chloe's injury, it did not break the causal connection between the defendant's act and the plaintiff's injury. As established above, Chuck's act was also a cause in fact of Chloe's injury and a substantial factor in bringing it about. Hence, he will be held liable for the unintended consequences of his act. (D) is incorrect because, as discussed above with regard to choice (A), provocation is not a defense to battery.

Answer to Question 46

(B) The nephew should prevail because his interest is a legal interest in the property and could have been discovered by the developer in the grantor-grantee index. The owner granted the buyer an easement by express grant. The easement was properly recorded with the buyer's deed, and since it contained no limitation, it is perpetual. The easement here is appurtenant (*i.e.,* one benefiting the holder of the easement), since it benefits the buyer's land (the dominant tenement) and burdens the owner's land (the servient tenement). Where there is an easement appurtenant, it passes with a transfer of the dominant tenement, even though it is an interest in the servient tenement. Thus, the buyer's easement passed to his nephew. Since the easement is perpetual, it is binding on all of the owner's subsequent transferees regardless of whether the conveyance refers to the easement, as long as the transferees have notice of it. Many courts will find record or constructive notice here because the nephew's property is adjacent to the developer's property, is deeded from a common grantor (the owner), and includes the easement in the original deed from the owner. Thus, (B) is correct because it best describes the legal effect of the easement for the nephew to prevail. (A) is incorrect because the parties did not create a covenant to allow access to the lake (*i.e.,* a promise that is something less than an interest in land); rather, the owner expressly granted the buyer an easement, which is an actual interest in the land that is a legal incident of the property owned by the developer. Thus, the nephew need not resort to an estoppel argument to obtain the injunction. (C) is incorrect because it is untrue. Purchasers of land are subject to easements in their chains of title regardless of the type of recording index, since they are deemed to have constructive notice of any easement that was recorded. There is no independent duty to discover riparian rights when there is no tract index. The nephew can enforce the easement here only because it was in the chain of title of the developer's property. (D) is incorrect because it is too broad. An easement must comply with all formal requisites of a deed, and deeds are valid only as to those who have notice of them (actual, constructive, or inquiry). Hence, the easement must be recorded in the chain of title; if the easement is not properly recorded, it might not be binding on all successive owners.

Answer to Question 47

(C) Sheila will prevail because she has performed under a valid contract. Sheila entered into and performed a valid unilateral contract with her father: He offered to give her $10,000 if she quit smoking, and she accepted by fully performing; her giving up the right to do something that she had a legal right to do constitutes valid consideration. Since Sheila fully performed her duties under the contract, Gordon's estate is bound to perform his duties and must now pay Sheila. Therefore, (C) is correct. (A) is incorrect. An oral contract is valid and enforceable unless it falls within the Statute of Frauds; this contract does not. To prove the contract, Sheila could have a witness from the party testify as to the oral contract; that testimony would be sufficient to prove the terms of the contract. (B) is incorrect because an offer will not be terminated by the death of the offeror if the offeror's power to revoke is limited by law, such as in the case of a valid unilateral contract. Here, Sheila has begun performance, making the offer irrevocable during the time she was given to complete performance. (D) is incorrect because it contemplates promissory estoppel, which is a remedy that makes a promise enforceable when there is insufficient consideration to enforce the contract. It is not necessary to rely on promissory estoppel here because there is an enforceable contract, as discussed above.

Answer to Question 48

(C) The estate's best defense is that the contract was oral. Generally, contracts need not be in writing to be enforceable; however, under the Statute of Frauds, certain contracts must be evidenced by a writing signed by the party to be charged to be enforceable. One such contract is to pay the debt of another, such as Nancy's promise here to pay Gordon's debt if he does not pay. Therefore, (C) is correct. (A) is incorrect because the promise was not illusory. A promise is illusory when there is not consideration on both sides of the contract. Here, Sheila will receive $10,000 if she performs, and Nancy will receive Sheila's detriment of not doing something that she has a right to do, which is valid consideration (the benefit to the promisor need not have economic value). Sheila's performance is valid consideration even though she has already promised Gordon to refrain from smoking (*i.e.,* it is not a preexisting duty), because Sheila was not bound by her promise to Gordon. Gordon's offer was for a unilateral contract (*i.e.,* one seeking performance rather than a promise to perform), and so could be accepted only by performance. Sheila had not yet performed when Nancy made her promise, so she had not yet accepted Gordon's contract and was not bound by her promise to refrain from smoking. Therefore, she was not under a preexisting duty, and Nancy's promise served as additional consideration for Sheila's performance. Note also that a surety such as Nancy will be bound by her promise to pay another's debt as long as she makes her promise before the creditor (Sheila) performs or promises to perform; the surety need not receive any separate consideration. (B) is incorrect because Sheila's giving up what she had a legal right to do—even if harmful—is sufficient consideration to support a contract, so Nancy could be bound to pay even though the contract was beneficial to Sheila. (D) is incorrect because Sheila's quitting smoking was the consideration that Nancy received. Moreover, as explained above, a surety need not receive consideration separate from the consideration of the person whose debt she is back-stopping.

Answer to Question 49

(D) Max may not be convicted of attempted murder because he lacked the necessary intent. A criminal attempt consists of (i) conduct that brings the defendant in close proximity to the completed offense, and (ii) intent to commit the completed crime. In other words, the defendant must have the intent to perform an act and obtain a result that would constitute the crime charged if achieved. Regardless of the intent required for the completed offense, an attempt always requires a specific intent. Thus, attempted murder requires the specific intent to kill another person, even though the mens rea for murder itself does not require a specific intent—had Marcia died, Max could be convicted of murder because malice aforethought can be established here by awareness of an unjustifiably high risk to human life (*i.e.,* "abandoned and malignant heart"). However, Max did not have the intent to kill either victim, so he lacked the intent necessary for attempt. (D) is therefore correct, and (A), (B), and (C) are incorrect. In answering questions such as this, remember to be objective and answer the question asked. While Max is surely guilty of some crimes (*e.g.,* assault and battery), he is not guilty of the crime charged.

Answer to Question 50

(D) The objection should be overruled because the accountant's testimony is admissible. As the plaintiff's accountant, he has personal knowledge of the relevant financial information, and so may testify. Although the accountant indicated that he could not remember the plaintiff's income, the rules of evidence allow a witness's recollection to be refreshed by just about anything. The witness may not read from the writing while he testifies; it is used solely to jog his memory. While the opposing counsel is allowed to examine the item being used to refresh the witness's testimony and may cross-examine the witness about it, he may not object to it. Therefore, (D) is correct. (A) is incorrect because the item used to refresh a witness's memory is not admitted into evidence, so it is not offered for the truth of the matter it asserts. Therefore, it cannot violate the hearsay rule. (B) is incorrect because the best evidence rule requires only that when the contents of a writing are sought to be proved, the writing itself should be entered into evidence, if it is available. Here, the contents of the tax return are not being entered into evidence; rather, the accountant is merely using the tax return to refresh his memory. Therefore, the best evidence rule does not apply. (C) is incorrect because the tax return is not being offered as a past recollection recorded. If a witness cannot remember a fact while testifying, counsel may attempt to refresh his memory, as counsel has done here. If, unlike the facts here, the witness still cannot remember, the thing used to refresh the witness's recollection can be read into evidence if a proper foundation is laid for its admissibility. In such a case, the "thing" must be a writing made by the witness at a time when the facts were known to him, and this is known as a past recollection recorded. The device was not needed here since the accountant was able to recall the facts requested after he saw the tax return.

Answer to Question 51

(C) The best way for Edward to accomplish his goals is to grant the city an easement for recreational use for two years. An easement would allow the city to use the land only for the purposes provided for in the easement, and Edward could limit the purposes to recreational uses. Thus, (C) is the best answer. (A) would not be a good choice because if Edward dedicated the land to public use, he would be giving title to the land to the government, so he would not be able to reclaim the land and build his stadium in the future. (B) would not be a good choice because a lease would give the city more control over the land than an easement, and would be more complicated to create. A lease grants the lessee the exclusive right to possess the premises, and broad rights to use them in any manner, unless specifically restricted. Thus, if Edward leases the land to the city, he would not have access to the land, and if he wanted it used only for recreational purposes, he would have to specifically restrict any undesired uses. Any restriction not included in the lease will be unenforceable. An easement, on the other hand, grants only a limited interest in the land—to use it for only those purposes stated in the easement; thus, it would be better than a lease. (D) is not a good choice because covenants usually are made in conjunction with a lease, deed, or other instrument; they promise some act or forbearance with respect to property and are generally not used to grant rights for access to property.

Answer to Question 52

(B) Burger could recover if Douglas made the statements knowing that they were false. To make out a case for defamation, a plaintiff must show that the defendant published a defamatory statement of or concerning the plaintiff that damaged his reputation. If the plaintiff is a public figure (or public official) or a matter of public concern is involved, the plaintiff must also prove falsity and fault on the defendant's part. The type of fault required when a public figure or public official is involved is "actual malice," defined as knowledge that the statement was false or reckless disregard as to its truth or falsity. Here, Judge Burger is a public official. Thus, he would be able to recover if Douglas made the statement knowing that it was false, since all of the required elements would be present: (i) the statement was defamatory of Burger and communicated to a third person; (ii) damage to reputation is presumed because it was slander per se (it adversely reflected on his abilities in his profession); and (iii) if Douglas knew that the statement was false, there is fault and falsity. Thus, (B) is correct. (A) is incorrect because negligence and actual injury would not be sufficient to establish the prima facie case. Since the judge is a public official, malice must be proved, and malice can be shown only if the defendant made the statement knowing that it was false or in reckless disregard as to its truth; negligence is not enough. Once malice is established, actual injury is not required. (C) is incorrect because, even if Douglas hated Burger and wanted to harm him, he would not be liable for defamation if the statements were true, since a public official such as Burger must prove that the statement was false. ("Malice" in the constitutional sense is different from malice in the sense of ill will.) Thus, it would not be enough merely to show that Douglas had bad motives. (D) is essentially the same answer as (C) and is incorrect for similar reasons.

Answer to Question 53

(B) The husband can be convicted of attempted murder and conspiracy to commit murder. The husband is liable for attempted murder under principles of accomplice liability because he solicited the ex-convict to commit murder with the intent that his wife be murdered. Where the person solicited proceeds far enough to be liable for attempt, the solicitor will be a party to that attempt. Here, the ex-convict's conduct satisfies the act requirement for attempted murder; therefore, the husband is liable as an accomplice to attempted murder. The husband is also liable for conspiracy to commit murder because, acting with the intent to kill his wife, he entered into an agreement with the ex-convict to kill her. Under the majority rule, conspirators can be convicted of both criminal conspiracy and the crime they committed pursuant to the conspiracy; *i.e.*, there is no merger. (A) and (C) are incorrect because, unlike conspiracy, solicitation merges into the principal offense. Thus, the husband cannot be convicted of both solicitation and attempted murder, as those choices state. (D) is incorrect because, as discussed above, conspiracy does not merge into the completed crime. Also, the fact that the charge of conspiracy was dropped against the ex-convict does not preclude a conviction of conspiracy against the husband. While an ***acquittal*** of the other party to a conspiracy precludes conviction of the remaining defendant, this rule does not apply where the other party is charged with a lesser offense or is no longer being prosecuted.

Answer to Question 54

(C) The defendant in (C) would be most likely to be convicted of common law murder. The common law defines murder as the killing of another human being with malice aforethought. Malice can come from an intent to kill, an intent to inflict great bodily injury, an intent to commit a felony, or an awareness that one's actions pose an unjustifiably high risk to human life. Here, the defendant did not intend to kill or injure, and driving while intoxicated is not a common law felony. But driving to a bar when one knows from past experiences that he is likely to become intoxicated and drive home in his impaired condition shows an awareness of high risk to human life, which is sufficient to show malice aforethought. Thus, (C) is correct. (A) is not a good choice because if it is true that the defendant fired the gun while unconscious, there is no voluntary act. Defendants are liable only for voluntary acts that are triggered by a conscious exercise of the will, and acts performed while the defendant was either unconscious or asleep are not voluntary. (Note that while it is unlikely that a person could fire a gun while unconscious, this question requires you to make that assumption; don't ever fight the facts that the question gives you.) (B) is not a good choice because Louie lacks the necessary intent for murder. Louie had no intent to kill anything but the rats here, and intent to kill a rat will not constitute an intent to kill or injure a person. Moreover, Louie did not have any reason to know that anyone else was in his basement, so he was not acting with an awareness of a high risk of danger to human life (his actions may have been negligent, but that is not enough to establish malice aforethought). (D) is not a good choice for similar reasons: Mickey had no intent to kill or injure, and shooting while others are around but not in the line of fire, while it may be negligent, does not amount to an awareness of an unjustifiably high risk to human life.

Answer to Question 55

(D) Darwin has an enforceable mortgage for $30,000, and can enforce the promissory note against Barton for any deficiency. All parties to a mortgage can transfer their interests. When a note is properly transferred, a mortgage will automatically follow it as a general rule; no special written assignment is necessary. If the note is negotiable, it is considered to embody the obligation, and payment will count only if made to the holder of the note. Any payment made by the mortgagor to the original mortgagee after a transfer of the note has taken place will not be binding on the holder, even if the mortgagor had no notice of the transfer. Here, the promissory note given to Currier by Barton was properly negotiated to Darwin, and the mortgage on Texacre automatically follows it; (A) is therefore incorrect. (B) is incorrect because the jurisdiction specifically allows for a deficiency judgment against the mortgagor. As holder of the note, Darwin can recover against Barton personally if the proceeds of the foreclosure action are insufficient to satisfy the mortgage debt. (C) is incorrect because Darwin is the holder of the note; even though he did not pay its face value, he can enforce it for that amount. Thus, as (D) states, Darwin's mortgage interest is $30,000, and he can enforce the note against Barton for that amount less the proceeds of the foreclosure sale.

Answer to Question 56

(C) Darwin's interest is superior to Arco's interest because Darwin is treated as a subsequent bona fide purchaser without notice under the recording statute. The statute quoted in the question is a notice statute, under which a subsequent bona fide purchaser (including a mortgagee) prevails over a prior grantee who failed to record by the time of the subsequent conveyance. The fact that Arco ultimately did record and neither Currier nor Darwin apparently recorded will not change the result. Under a notice statute (unlike a race-notice statute), the subsequent purchaser is protected against the prior purchaser who does not record. Thus, (C) is correct and (A) is incorrect. (B) is incorrect because the fact that Arco's interest is a purchase money mortgage does not establish Arco's priority. A purchase money mortgage, given when the mortgagor buys the property, is considered to have priority over non-purchase money mortgages executed at about the same time, even if the other mortgages are recorded first. As between two purchase money mortgages, the priority rules are designed for the typical situation where each mortgagee knows of the other's interest and the recording statute does not come into play. Here, Darwin's interest is also a purchase money mortgage that was created by the vendor of the property, Currier, and neither mortgagee had notice of the other. Thus, the recording statute would apply and provide the subsequent purchaser, Darwin, with priority. (D) is incorrect because, even if the purchase money priority rules were applicable, Darwin's interest would have priority because it was a purchase money mortgage given to the vendor of the property and the other purchase money mortgage was given to a third-party lender, Arco. In any case, as discussed above, the recording statute is applicable here and provides Darwin with priority.

Answer to Question 57

(A) Walker's testimony is admissible, but only for impeachment purposes. For the purpose of impeaching the credibility of a witness, a party may show that the witness has, on another occasion, made statements that are inconsistent with some material part of her present testimony. Here, Walker is prepared to testify that Glenda stated that she had been unable to get out of bed because of severe back pain at the time that she testified that she was with Driver and had taken over the driving, a fact that would be material to the allegations in the lawsuit. Thus, Walker's testimony is properly admissible for purposes of impeachment. (C) is incorrect because, under the Federal Rules, an inconsistent statement may be proved by either cross-examination or extrinsic evidence. (D) is incorrect because, while extrinsic evidence is admissible only if the witness is, at some point, given an opportunity to explain or deny the allegedly inconsistent statement, the opportunity need not come before the introduction of the statement under the Federal Rules; Walker's testimony may be admitted now and Glenda subsequently be given an opportunity to explain or deny it. (B) is incorrect because Walker's testimony is hearsay that is not admissible for substantive purposes because it does not fall under the exception for declarations of physical condition. Under the Federal Rules, declarations of present bodily condition are admissible as an exception to the hearsay rule when made to anyone, not just a physician, whereas declarations of past physical condition are admissible as a hearsay exception only if made to medical personnel to assist in diagnosing or treating the condition. Here, Glenda's statement to Walker pertained to her past physical condition, and there is no indication that Walker is her doctor. Hence, Glenda's statement does not fall within these or any other exceptions to the hearsay rule, and is admissible for impeachment purposes only.

Answer to Question 58

(D) The evidence is admissible because it is a declaration of Robert's present state of mind, offered as circumstantial evidence that Robert carried out his intent to go to his mother-in-law's house. Hearsay is a statement, other than one made by the declarant while testifying at the trial or hearing, offered in evidence to prove the truth of the matter asserted. One exception to the hearsay rule is for statements of present state of mind. Declarations of existing state of mind are admissible not only when the declarant's state of mind is directly in issue and material to the controversy, but also when the declarant's state of mind is not directly in issue, but the declarations of intent are offered to show subsequent acts of the declarant; *i.e.,* a declaration of intent to do something in the future is offered as circumstantial evidence tending to show that the intent was carried out. Robert's statement that he was going to his mother-in-law's house is a statement made by the declarant out of court. This statement is offered to prove the truth of the matter asserted therein: that on the day of the alleged armed robbery, Robert intended to go to his mother-in-law's house. This is being offered as circumstantial evidence that Robert did go to his mother-in-law's house. Thus, the statement is hearsay. However, the statement does come within the present state of mind exception. Although Robert's state of mind is not directly in issue, his statement is a declaration of intent to do something offered to show that such intent was in fact carried out. Therefore, the statement is admissible under the present state of mind exception to the hearsay rule. [*See* Mutual Life Insurance Co. v. Hillmon (1892)] (A) incorrectly states that the evidence is not within any hearsay exception. As stated above, the evidence is within the present state of mind exception. (C) is incorrect because the evidence is being offered to prove the truth of the matter stated, that Robert intended to go to his mother-in-law's house on December 16, because his intent provides circumstantial evidence that he did in fact do so. Thus, the statement is hearsay. (B) is incorrect because the evidence tends to make Robert's absence at the time and place of the alleged crime more probable than it would be without the evidence. This fact is of consequence to the determination of Robert's guilt of the crime charged. Thus, the evidence is relevant.

Answer to Question 59

(B) The Constitution gives the federal courts power to hear cases and controversies, and the Supreme Court has interpreted this to mean that the federal courts should hear a case only when there is some real harm or immediate threat of harm involved. There is no immediate threat of harm under the facts here because Ben's action is only in the planning stage—he is not yet married and has not yet fathered a child. Thus, his case is not ripe and (B) is correct. (A) is not a good defense because the question presented is not a political question; it involves Ben's constitutional rights. Political questions involve issues committed by the Constitution to other branches of the government and issues inherently incapable of judgment and enforcement by the courts. (C) is incorrect because the statute imposes on a woman's right to decide whether to have an abortion as well as on the right of a married couple to procreate, which are within the right of privacy protected by the Fourteenth Amendment. Therefore, a substantial federal question is involved. (D) is incorrect because it is not as precise a justification for dismissal as (B). A person has standing to challenge the constitutionality of a government action only if he can demonstrate a concrete stake in the outcome of the controversy and that the government law at issue impairs his own rights, such as by threatening some injury to him if he fails to comply with the law. Here, assuming the truth of Ben's allegations, he has a personal stake in the outcome of the action because he wants to have children before he is 25 and the law may deter him from doing so. At this point, however, his claim is not yet ripe for adjudication.

Answer to Question 60

(C) Wilma's testimony is admissible because it is evidence of a matter in issue. Generally, evidence is admissible if it is relevant. The Federal Rules define relevant evidence as any evidence tending to make the existence of any fact of consequence to the determination of the action (materiality) more or less probable than it would be without the evidence (probativeness). Whether the paper received the request for the retraction governs whether the statutory prerequisite for the defamation action here was met, so the testimony is material. The testimony is also probative because, if the paper received a letter from Rupert on the day in question, it is likely that it was the request for retraction; thus, the testimony makes it more likely that the fact sought to be proved (that Rupert requested a retraction) was true. Furthermore, Wilma is competent to testify about receipt of the letter because people are competent to testify to facts within their personal knowledge, and whether Wilma remembered receiving a letter from Rupert on the day in question is certainly within her personal knowledge. Thus, (C) is correct. (A) is incorrect because Wilma's competency to testify as to whether she received a letter on a particular day is unaffected by her employment status. Her employment status may be relevant to other evidentiary issues (such as whether she may be treated as a hostile witness and whether her statement can be deemed to be an admission), but it is irrelevant here. (B) is incorrect because the best evidence rule is not relevant here. That rule provides that when the contents of a writing are sought to be proved at trial, the writing itself should be introduced if it is available. Here, Wilma is not testifying as to the contents of the writing, but only to the fact that the paper received a letter from Rupert on the day in question. (Rupert is relying on his own testimony to create an inference that the letter was a request for retraction.) (D) is incorrect because Wilma is not seeking to testify to an admission, which is a prior statement made or act done by a party. She is merely testifying to an event that she recalled: the receipt of a letter from Rupert. Hence, the testimony does not even raise a hearsay issue.

Answer to Question 61

(C) The new agreement between the two parties is enforceable as an accord. An accord is an agreement in which one party to an existing contract agrees to accept, in lieu of the performance that she is supposed to receive from the other party, some other, different performance. Generally, an accord must be supported by consideration, but the consideration may be of a lesser value than the originally bargained-for consideration in the prior contract, as long as it is of a different type or the claim is to be paid to a third party. Here, Decker's obligation to provide Crieder's girlfriend with a new entertainment system was a sufficient new consideration to form a valid accord. (A) is incorrect because the preexisting legal duty rule does not apply when the party's duty is varied in some way, as Decker's duty was here. (B) is incorrect because it is not necessary that the benefit to Crieder in the accord agreement have the same value as the original debt here. While generally the preexisting duty rule does not allow payment of a smaller sum than due on an existing debt to be sufficient consideration for a promise by the creditor to discharge the debt, courts will find sufficient consideration as long as the consideration is in any way new or different. Here, regardless of how much the entertainment system would have cost Crieder, the variance in Decker's duty is sufficient to support the accord agreement. (D) is incorrect because the original agreement was not a sale of goods contract under the U.C.C., which provides that an agreement modifying a contract subject to Article 2 needs no consideration to be binding, as long as the parties were acting in good faith. Here, however, the original obligation was to pay a debt on a promissory note, so this provision does not apply.

Answer to Question 62

(A) Decker may enjoin Crieder's action because Crieder currently does not have the right to enforce the promissory note. A valid accord, taken alone, does not discharge the prior contract. It merely suspends the right to enforce it in accordance with the terms of the accord contract. The performance of the accord agreement, which is called satisfaction, discharges not only the accord agreement but the original contract as well. Where the accord agreement is breached by the creditor by suing on the original contract, as is the case here, the debtor may seek to have the action enjoined by raising the accord agreement as an equitable defense. (B) is incorrect because the accord agreement does not discharge the original obligation, it only suspends it. Hence, if Decker were to breach the accord agreement, Crieder could sue on either the original promissory note obligation or the accord agreement. (C) is incorrect because Decker does not need to establish promissory estoppel or detrimental reliance to enforce the accord agreement. Even if Decker has not yet relied to his detriment on Crieder's promise, Decker can enforce the accord agreement, which suspends his obligation on the original debt. (D) is incorrect because, while Decker may wait until he is damaged by Crieder's lawsuit and then sue for breach of the accord agreement, he is not limited to that remedy. As discussed above, he may enjoin Crieder's action by raising the accord agreement as an equitable defense.

Answer to Question 63

(B) Ron's withdrawal from the conspiracy absolves him of liability for the subsequent murder committed by Mike, but does not provide a defense to the crime of conspiracy. Conspiracy consists of: (i) an agreement between two or more persons; (ii) an intent to enter into an agreement; and (iii) an intent to achieve the objective of the agreement. In addition, most states require an overt act in furtherance of the conspiracy (although an act of mere preparation will suffice). Each conspirator is liable for the crimes of all other conspirators if such crimes were committed in furtherance of the objectives of the conspiracy and they were a natural and probable consequence of the conspiracy, *i.e.,* foreseeable. However, if a conspirator has made a legally effective withdrawal from the conspiracy at the time of commission of such a crime, he will not be liable for that crime. Withdrawal requires an affirmative act that notifies all members of the conspiracy and is done in time for them to have the opportunity to abandon their plans. Withdrawal, however, will not be a defense to the conspiracy charge itself. Ron, Mike, and Dick agreed to rob elderly women whom they followed home from the shopping center. They intended to enter into this agreement and to achieve its objective (to rob the women). Coming to the shopping center at the agreed-upon time, armed with a gun or a knife, constitutes a sufficient act in furtherance of the conspiracy. Consequently, Ron has satisfied all of the elements of conspiracy. Because he cannot use withdrawal from the conspiracy as a defense to that charge, he will be convicted of conspiracy. (A) is therefore wrong. Ordinarily, Ron would also be guilty of the woman's murder. The killing resulted from a beating administered during the course of the robbery; thus, it was committed in furtherance of the conspiracy's objective. Also, it was foreseeable that death might result where all of the intended victims were elderly women. However, Ron had withdrawn from the conspiracy prior to the time the killing was committed. Ron made an effective withdrawal when he explicitly told Mike and Dick that he no longer wanted any part of their plan at a time when there was still an opportunity to abandon the plan. Thus, criminal liability for the killing will not attach to Ron, and (C) and (D) are therefore incorrect.

Answer to Question 64

(C) If the customer brings an action for assault against the store, he will recover if the security guard was unreasonable in suspecting him, because the guard's actions will not have been privileged. To make out a prima facie case for assault, the plaintiff must prove that the defendant's actions caused the plaintiff to be in reasonable apprehension of immediate harmful or offensive contact, and that the defendant intended to cause this reaction. The customer can establish a prima facie case because the guard's pulling out the handcuffs and reaching for the customer's arm created a reasonable apprehension of immediate offensive contact, and the guard intended to create this apprehension so that the customer would go willingly to the manager's office. However, the store could raise the defense of recapture of chattels if the guard reasonably believed that the customer was a shoplifter. This defense, which allows the property owner (or his agent) to use reasonable force or the threat of force to recapture his chattels from a tortfeasor who has stolen them, has a specialized application in the shopkeepers' privilege to reasonably detain individuals whom they reasonably believe to be in possession of shoplifted goods. Although the privilege usually applies as a defense to a false imprisonment action, it is equally applicable as a defense to other intentional torts. However, if the security guard's belief that the customer was a shoplifter was unreasonable, the defense would not be available and the supermarket would be liable for the assault. (A) is incorrect because assault is actionable without alleging a specific injury or damages. Moreover, the customer has suffered the injury of having friends and neighbors witness his detention. (B) is incorrect because the only intent required for assault is the intent to place someone in apprehension of harmful or offensive contact, and the guard had the requisite intent here. The plaintiff does not have to show that the defendant intended to harm him. (D) would be the best answer if (C) were not available, because it mentions one of the elements of assault, but it is not as good an answer as (C) because even if the customer made out a prima facie case, he would lose if the guard's actions were prompted by a reasonable suspicion that the customer was a shoplifter, and (C) negates this possibility.

Answer to Question 65

(D) The customer will be able to recover for his humiliation because he was falsely imprisoned. All of the elements of a prima facie case for false imprisonment are present in these facts: an act or omission by defendant that confined or restrained plaintiff to a bounded area, intent by defendant to do so, and causation. Here, the confinement was brought about by the invalid use of legal authority by the security guard. The supermarket cannot avail itself of the shopkeepers' privilege for detaining a suspected shoplifter because the detention must be for only a reasonable period of time for the purpose of making an investigation, and here the hour-long detention clearly was unreasonable under the circumstances. On proof of the prima facie case, the plaintiff can recover all foreseeable damages that arise from the tort. Humiliation is a foreseeable consequence of a false arrest, so the customer will be able to recover. (A) is incorrect. While humiliation is not an actionable tort in and of itself, humiliation is a recognized element of damages from the commission of an intentional tort. (B) is incorrect because it relies on the shopkeepers' privilege to detain, and the privilege was not available here even if the guard and employee were reasonable in suspecting that the customer was a shoplifter. The manner and length of detention must also be reasonable for the privilege to apply, and here the detention was for an unreasonable length of time. (C) is incorrect because the store's action need not amount to extremely outrageous conduct to make it liable for false imprisonment; it is sufficient that the guard intentionally detained the customer without a right to do so.

Answer to Question 66

(D) Uri will prevail because Dmitri's use of the water is not a natural use under the riparian doctrine. In jurisdictions following the riparian doctrine for allocation of water in watercourses, the reasonable use theory permits each riparian owner (*i.e.*, owner of land bordering the watercourse) a reasonable use of the water, and a downstream owner cannot enjoin the reasonable use by an upstream riparian owner unless it substantially interferes with the downstream owner's comparable use. Under this doctrine, uses are categorized as natural or artificial. Natural uses (*e.g.*, household consumption, gardening, limited grazing) prevail over artificial uses (*e.g.*, irrigation, manufacturing); riparian owners can take all the water they need for natural uses, but cannot take water for artificial uses unless there is enough water for the domestic needs of all other riparian owners. Here, Dmitri's use of Timur Creek for irrigation is an artificial use, so Uri's use of the water for domestic purposes takes priority over Dmitri's use, even though Uri's use may substantially interfere with Dmitri's use. (A) is incorrect because the fact that Dmitri's use was prior to Uri's is determinative in a state following the prior appropriation doctrine, but not in a riparian doctrine state. (B) is wrong because water rights cannot be acquired by prescription. (C) is incorrect because the fact that Uri's use allows partial satisfaction of Dmitri's needs is not controlling. Because Uri's use is a natural use and Dmitri's is an artificial use, Uri would prevail even if his use totally deprived Dmitri of his water needs.

Answer to Question 67

(B) One who aids, counsels, commands, or encourages another in the commission of a crime and who is present when the crime is committed is generally guilty of aiding and abetting (under the common law, a principal in the second degree). Because the statute makes furnishing alcohol to a minor illegal and a minor requested the patron to furnish him with alcohol, which the patron did, the minor could be found guilty of aiding and abetting under the general rule. However, there are exceptions to the general rule, including an exception for members of the class sought to be protected by the statute that has been violated. Because the statute speaks in terms of selling or furnishing to a minor, without creating any punishment for the minor to whom the alcohol is furnished, it probably was intended for the protection of minors, and a legislative exemption for those same minors can be presumed that overrides principles of aiding and abetting. (A) is incorrect because in most jurisdictions an aider and abettor can be convicted even if the principal cannot be convicted, and this was true even under the common law as to principals in the second degree (aiders and abettors), such as the minor. (C) is an incorrect statement of law; there is no aiding and abetting exception for minors in general, and minors over age 14 can generally be found guilty of committing a crime. (Minors under age 14 may have the benefit of a presumption that they lack the necessary mental state.) (D) is an incorrect statement of law, and closely akin to (A); the patron violated the law and the minor can be convicted as an aider and abettor even though the patron is never apprehended or convicted, unless some superseding principle intervenes, as in (B).

Answer to Question 68

(C) Defendant's objection to the contract negotiations is not appropriate because whether an agency relationship existed is determined by the jury. The Federal Rules of Evidence distinguish preliminary facts to be decided by the jury, which determine whether the offered evidence is relevant to the issues in the case, from preliminary facts to be decided by the judge, which determines whether the offered evidence is competent to be admitted at all. Whether an agency relationship existed between the defendant and a third party is a question of fact to be decided by the jury; if the jury decides that thc third party was not defendant's agent, it will disregard as irrelevant the evidence of contract negotiations undertaken by the third party. While the judge must find that the proponent of the contract negotiations has introduced enough evidence to allow the jury to find that an agency relationship existed, the ultimate determination of agency rests with the jury. (A) is incorrect because the judge must determine the qualifications of a witness called as an expert before permitting the witness to offer an opinion or conclusion on a matter appropriate for expert testimony. If the judge decides that the engineer does not qualify as an expert, he will not be permitted to testify on the structural integrity of the building. (B) and (D) are incorrect because all preliminary fact questions involving the standards of trustworthiness of exceptions to the hearsay rule must be determined by the court. Thus, the court must decide whether a purported business record was made in the regular course of business, and whether a statement offered as a dying declaration was made under a sense of impending death.

Answer to Question 69

(C) The appellate court should rule that only Instruction II was constitutional. Due process of law requires a state to prove each element of the crime charged beyond a reasonable doubt. However, as to affirmative defenses to the criminal charge, the Supreme Court has held that the state can place the burden of proof on the defendant without violating the defendant's constitutional rights. [Leland v. Oregon (1952)] Common law larceny is the taking and carrying away of property in the possession of another with the intent to permanently deprive the other of the property. Since the intent to permanently deprive is an element of the crime, the state cannot require the defendant to prove that he intended to return the car, which would negate the required intent for larceny. The state must prove beyond a reasonable doubt that he intended to permanently deprive. Hence, Instruction I is unconstitutional, making (A) and (D) wrong. Instruction II is constitutional. As to the defense of mental illness, the Supreme Court has held that the state can require (as federal courts do) that the defendant prove the defense by clear and convincing evidence. The state also can place the burden on the defendant to prove the defense of mental illness by a preponderance of the evidence, which is a lesser burden of proof. The fact that the instruction placed a lighter burden on the defendant than the statute specified would not make the instruction a violation of the defendant's constitutional rights. Thus, choices (B) and (D) are incorrect.

Answer to Question 70

(D) The facts in I., II., and IV. would make the program unconstitutional under the Establishment Clause of the First Amendment. A state law may not respect the establishment of a religion. Unless a law prefers one religious sect over another, which is not the case here, it is unconstitutional if it fails to pass any of the three following tests: (i) it has a secular purpose; (ii) its primary effect neither advances nor inhibits religion; and (iii) it does not produce excessive government entanglement with religion. [Lemon v. Kurtzman (1971)] Here, statement I. is relevant to test (ii); statement II. is relevant to test (i); and statement IV. is relevant to test (iii). Statement III. is irrelevant; the fact that no compelling interest exists would not make the program unconstitutional if it satisfied the three-part *Lemon* test. Whether a compelling state interest exists would be relevant only if the state program had discriminated among religious sects. Thus, choice (D), containing statements I., II., and IV., is correct.

Answer to Question 71

(A) The motorist will prevail because the dealer sold defective tires to him. In a strict liability action based on a defective product, a commercial supplier of a product who sells the product in a defective condition unreasonably dangerous to consumers will be held strictly liable for the damage caused by the defective product. The dealer was a commercial supplier of the product; the tires were in a dangerous condition when the dealer put the tires on the car and sold the car to the motorist. Thus, the motorist will likely prevail. (B) is wrong because the dealer would be liable on a strict liability theory regardless of whether the manufacturer was negligent, and also because the dealer's liability arises when it sells the car to the consumer, not when it "uses" the tires. (C) is incorrect because there is nothing in the facts to suggest that the motorist knew of the risk that the tires were defective; the discount price is not sufficient. (D) is wrong. Misuse of a product is a defense to a strict liability claim only if the misuse was not foreseeable by the defendant. It would certainly be foreseeable that a new car owner might occasionally drive 80 m.p.h.

Answer to Question 72

(C) Victoria will prevail because Horace is classified as a wild animal. An owner of a wild (*i.e.*, nondomestic) animal will be strictly liable for the damage caused by the animal. A bear, even a very tame one, will be classified as a wild animal. Therefore (C) is correct and (A) is wrong. (B) is wrong because the injury Victoria suffered was within the "normal dangerous propensity" of the animal. Strict liability for wild animals includes liability for the harm that results when a person is attempting to flee from what is perceived to be a dangerous animal. (D) is incorrect. The fact that the activity was uncommon in the locale would have some relevance if the lawsuit were based on a theory of strict liability for an ultrahazardous activity. It has nothing to do with strict liability for damage caused by animals.

Answer to Question 73

(B) The state law is valid because the prior judicial determinations that Donna violated the speeding laws satisfy the procedural due process requirements of the Fourteenth Amendment. Under the Due Process Clause of the Fourteenth Amendment, the state must provide some fair process or procedure before it may deprive a person of "life, liberty, or property." Fair procedure at a minimum requires an opportunity to present objections to the proposed action to a fair, neutral decision-maker. Whether a prior evidentiary hearing is required and the extent of procedural requirements is determined by ***weighing*** (i) the importance of the individual interest involved, (ii) the value of specific procedural safeguards to that interest, and (iii) the governmental interest in fiscal and administrative efficiency. [Mathews v. Eldridge (1976)]

Because the government has taken control of who may drive automobiles on public roads, which is a sufficiently important area of human activity that persons have a liberty interest in it, the government must provide fair procedure to those who are specifically barred from engaging in the activity. In applying the *Mathews v. Eldridge* balancing test, the Court has held that the state generally must afford a prior hearing before a driver's license is suspended or terminated. However, where the suspension is based on prior judicial determinations that traffic laws were violated, the driver has already had prior evidentiary hearings before unbiased decisionmakers on the significant factual issues involved. The governmental interest in keeping unsafe drivers off public roads and in not relitigating issues already fairly decided outweighs Donna's interest in keeping her driver's license. The procedural safeguards in the judicial proceedings in which she was convicted were sufficiently broad so that no additional prior hearing is necessary. Thus, the court should rule that the state law satisfies procedural due process requirements. (A) is incorrect because the liberty and property interests that a person cannot be deprived of without procedural due process do not turn on whether the interest involved is a "right" rather than a "privilege." That distinction has been rejected by the Supreme Court. (C) is incorrect because the presumption created by the law is rationally related to a legitimate state goal. If the government "presumes facts" against a person so that she cannot demonstrate that she is qualified for some important benefit or right, the "irrebutable presumption" may be unconstitutional. If the presumption involves a fundamental right or a suspect or quasi-suspect classification, it will likely be held invalid under a strict scrutiny or intermediate scrutiny analysis. If some other right or class is involved, it will likely be upheld under the rational basis standard. Here, no suspect or quasi-suspect class is involved, and driving is not a fundamental right. Thus, the action will be upheld because suspending licenses of drivers convicted of speeding is rationally related to the legislature's goal of reducing the death toll on the state's highways. (D) is incorrect because, as discussed above, the prior judicial proceedings in which she was convicted provide sufficient due process; no additional prior hearing is necessary before her license is suspended.

Answer to Question 74

(C) Delbert's strongest argument is his right to freedom of speech. The First Amendment forbids Congress from abridging the freedom of speech or of the press. While there are numerous exceptions and qualifications to this right (and Delbert might not ultimately succeed), this is Delbert's strongest argument, because the statute purports to punish him for publishing information even though he is motivated only by political reasons (he disagrees with the price support program). (A) is incorrect because the Equal Protection Clause of the Fourteenth Amendment applies to state governments and the law here is federal. Additionally, equal protection only prevents states from treating classes of people differently, and here no classification is made. (B) is incorrect because nothing in the statute indicates that punishment will be imposed without a hearing, so Delbert will not be deprived of liberty without due process of law (*i.e.*, procedural due process). Nor does the statute violate substantive due process, because it does not affect any of Delbert's fundamental rights. (D) is incorrect because Congress has plenary power over interstate commerce and may adopt laws controlling interstate commerce—even ones burdening interstate commerce—as long as the laws do not otherwise violate the Constitution.

Answer to Question 75

(B) Cheryl may be fined under the statute but not imprisoned. The right to counsel under the Sixth Amendment gives the defendant the right to be represented by privately retained counsel or to have counsel appointed for her by the state if she is indigent. However, the right to counsel applies to misdemeanor trials only when a sentence of imprisonment is ***actually*** imposed (including a suspended sentence). Thus, even though the misdemeanor statute permits a potential jail term, its alternative penalty of a fine may constitutionally be imposed on the defendant despite the refusal to provide her with counsel. (A) and (C) are incorrect because the right to counsel would apply to any misdemeanor trial in which imprisonment is actually imposed. The failure to provide Cheryl with counsel would preclude the imprisonment sentence. (D) is incorrect because, as discussed above, the misdemeanor's alternative penalty of a fine may be imposed without violating the constitutional right to counsel at trial.

Answer to Question 76

(B) The ledger is admissible under the business records exception to the hearsay rule. Any writing or record of any act or transaction is admissible as proof of that act or transaction if the record was made in the regular course of a business and if it was customary to make the type of record involved (*i.e.*, the entrant was under a business duty to make the entry). Here, testimony has established that it was Data Exchange's customary practice to have one clerk identify the type of computer and its components and have the other clerk record the information. Thus, the authenticated record showing that no CD-ROM drive was indicated for Porter's computer is admissible as a business record. (A) is incorrect because the ledger entry is not being used as evidence of a past recollection by a witness testifying. That exception to the hearsay rule allows a writing to be read into evidence when a witness has insufficient recollection of the event to enable him to testify accurately, even after consulting the writing to refresh his recollection. Here, the entry is being offered into evidence standing alone as a business record, rather than as the recollection of a witness on the stand. (C) is incorrect because most business record statutes do not require that the person making the entries have personal knowledge of the event. As long as the one with personal knowledge and the one making the record are both employees of the business with a duty to report and record the information accurately, the business records exception applies to both hearsay statements—the statement by the first clerk and the record made by the second clerk. (D) is incorrect. While the absence of the notation ***is*** being offered as an implied statement that no CD-ROM was returned, such a statement falls within the business record exception. Modern business record statutes, including Federal Rule of Evidence 803(7), permit a record to be used to prove the nonoccurrence of a matter if it was the regular practice of the business to record all such matters.

Answer to Question 77

(B) The law will be upheld because it is a neutral law that is applicable to all drivers in the state. The Free Exercise Clause does not require exemptions from government regulations for a person whose religious beliefs prevent him from conforming his behavior to the requirements of the law. Unless the law was motivated by a desire to interfere with religion, it can be applied to regulate the conduct of one whose religious beliefs conflict with the law. Here, the Flemarite must allow his photograph to be taken if he wants to obtain a driver's license; the state is entitled to enforce this regulation because it is a neutral law of general applicability. (A) is incorrect because it may be possible for a state to make accommodations for groups objecting to a particular state regulation without violating the Establishment Clause, even though it is not ***required*** to do so under the Free Exercise Clause. The state here could permit an exemption from the photograph requirement for persons who present legitimate reasons for it; such an accommodation would not be an impermissible advancement of religion. (C) is incorrect because the "compelling interest" test is not currently used to judge the validity of neutral laws that happen to interfere with a person's religious practices. (D) is incorrect because the sincerity of the Flemarites' beliefs does not provide a basis for avoiding application of the law to them.

Answer to Question 78

(D) This answer states the traditional rule where the amount of land in a land sale contract is less than as agreed. When a buyer has a remedy of specific performance in a land sale contract, a court of equity will order a seller to convey the title if the buyer tenders the purchase price. If the seller cannot provide marketable title under the terms of the contract, but the buyer wishes to proceed with the transaction, the buyer can usually get specific performance with an abatement of the purchase price in an amount reflecting the title defect. A defect as to the quantity of land conveyed is usually corrected by a pro rata abatement of the price. Choice (D) states the factors that a court of equity will look for when deciding whether to grant specific performance with abatement. (A) is incorrect because the parties' contract did not merely refer to the farm as a named parcel of land; it recited that it contained 250 acres of prime farmland. Based on this recital, a court could readily conclude that the difference of two acres is a material change in the terms of the contract and that Sherm's tender of 248 acres was not substantial performance. (B) is incorrect because viewing the property did not put Billy on notice as to the discrepancy; the buyer is not required to visually calculate the amount of acreage a parcel of land contains. (C) is not as good an answer as (D) even though it is probably a true statement. Not only must the defect as to quantity be material, so that the buyer is not receiving what he bargained for, but the abatement amount must be appropriate and not an excessive variance from the parties' agreement.

Answer to Question 79

(B) Pinkerton can recover damages for trespass to land because Dalton intended to conduct the activities that caused the trespass. To establish a prima facie case for trespass to land, plaintiff must prove (i) an act of physical invasion of plaintiff's real property by defendant, (ii) intent on defendant's part to bring about the physical invasion, and (iii) causation. Here, flakes of the chemical byproduct of Dalton's soap factory physically invaded Pinkerton's property when the wind blew. Dalton intended to bring about the trespass because, after Pinkerton had complained, Dalton ***knew with substantial certainty*** that the flakes would continue to fall on the farm whenever the wind was right. Finally, Dalton's operation of the soap factory was the cause of the flakes settling on Pinkerton's strawberries, completing the prima facie case of trespass to land. (A) is incorrect because the fact that Dalton's discharge entered Pinkerton's land is not enough to establish liability. Dalton is not engaged in an ultrahazardous or abnormally dangerous activity, for which strict liability would apply. If the discharge had been a single accidental occurrence, Dalton would not have had the intent for trespass to land. (C) is incorrect because an intent to harm or to cause injury is not necessary for liability; only an intent to enter on the land is required. (D) is incorrect because mistake as to the lawfulness of the entry is no defense, even if reasonable. Because Dalton knew that the particles would enter the land when the factory continued to operate, he had the "intent" to bring about the physical invasion of property owned by Pinkerton.

Answer to Question 80

(C) Paul will not prevail if the smoke would not disturb a person of ordinary sensibilities. For a private nuisance action to lie, the interference with the plaintiff's use or enjoyment of his land must be substantial. This means that it must be offensive, inconvenient, or annoying to an average person in the community. It will not be characterized as substantial if it is merely the result of plaintiff's hypersensitivity. Here, if Paul is unable to use his yard when the smoke blows into it only because of his extremely sensitive eyes, the interference will not be characterized as substantial. Hence, Paul will not prevail given the condition stated in choice (C). (A) is incorrect because it is not sufficient that Donald's conduct interfered with Paul's use and enjoyment of his yard; the interference must be both substantial and unreasonable for Paul to prevail. (B) is incorrect because Donald's violation of a health code regulation does not establish that an actionable nuisance is present. While violation of a zoning ordinance or regulation may be a factor in balancing whether the severity of the injury outweighs the utility of the defendant's conduct and is therefore unreasonable, it is not determinative. (D) is incorrect for the opposite reason. The fact that the health code regulation was not designed to protect against the harm suffered by Paul does not establish that Donald's activity was not a nuisance; it could constitute a nuisance even if it complied with the regulation.

Answer to Question 81

(B) These two "best of the lot" questions highlight the approaches for evaluating the admissibility of self-incriminating statements at various stages in the criminal procedure process. Prior to a suspect's being charged with a crime, the Fifth Amendment privilege against compelled self-incrimination is the usual basis for ruling on the admissibility of a confession. [Miranda v. Arizona (1966)] Under *Miranda,* statements made during custodial interrogations are inadmissible unless the defendant is first warned of his right to remain silent and his right to an attorney. Thus, *Miranda* applies only when the defendant is in custody and only when the defendant's statements are the result of interrogation. While almost ***any*** words or actions on the part of the police that they should know are reasonably likely to elicit an incriminating response qualify as interrogation, *Miranda* does not apply to spontaneous statements not made in response to interrogation. Here, the police did nothing to solicit the statement from Jorge; it was spontaneous. Thus, (B) is correct. (A) is incorrect because the defendant need not yet be charged for *Miranda* rights to apply as long as he is in custody (*i.e.,* not free to leave). Being in jail on another charge (as Jorge was) satisfies the custody requirement. (C) is incorrect because the fact that the officer who took Jorge's admission had nothing to do with Jorge's burglary investigation does not alter the rules of *Miranda*—questioning that is totally unrelated to the matter for which the accused is in custody may still violate the accused's *Miranda* rights. (D) is incorrect. Due process requires that a confession be voluntary (*i.e.,* not the product of police coercion). The *Miranda* rule, however, goes beyond voluntariness. It makes inadmissible all statements obtained without *Miranda* warnings or without a valid waiver of *Miranda* rights, not just statements actually coerced by the police.

Answer to Question 82

(C) This question illustrates the operation of the Sixth Amendment right to counsel approach, which you should use to evaluate the admissibility of any statements made after the defendant has been charged with the relevant crime. The Sixth Amendment provides defendants with a right to counsel at any post-indictment interrogation. Since Jorge was on trial for murder, any interrogation relating to those charges must take place, if at all, in the presence of Jorge's counsel unless the defendant has knowingly and intelligently waived the right. Nothing indicates that Jorge knowingly waived his right to counsel, so (C) is correct. (A) is incorrect because the failure to give *Miranda* warnings, which may violate the Fifth Amendment privilege against self-incrimination, does not prevent use of otherwise voluntary statements for impeachment purposes, as in this case. In contrast, evidence obtained from a direct violation of the Sixth Amendment right to counsel (the bailiff's questioning of Jorge in the absence of his counsel) has not been held to be admissible, even for only impeachment purposes. [*See* Michigan v. Harvey (1990)] (B) is not the best answer because the Sixth Amendment right to counsel is the right of the defendant rather than the attorney; Jorge could have waived his right without the knowledge or consent of the attorney. The failure to inform Jorge's attorney does not by itself establish that Jorge's right to counsel was violated. [*See* Moran v. Burbine (1986)] (D) is not the strongest argument because the bailiff's status as a law enforcement officer does not, by itself, make the statements involuntary or otherwise inadmissible; the critical issue in this question is whether the bailiff obtained the statements in violation of Jorge's right to counsel.

Answer to Question 83

(C) This choice states the critical factor for admitting evidence of other crimes or misconduct to show motive, while the other choices raise issues that are relevant only when other crimes evidence is being offered for impeachment purposes. It is essential that you keep the impeachment rules distinct from the rules for admitting other crimes evidence when the evidence is independently relevant—the bar examiners will often mix these issues in the answer choices for this type of question.

One of the most important areas where recurring relevance questions have developed into established rules is the use of character evidence. The well-settled rule is that extrinsic evidence of other crimes is not admissible to show a criminal disposition or conduct in conformity with the other crimes. On the other hand, Federal Rule 404(b) permits this evidence to be introduced for other purposes, such as to show motive, opportunity, intent, or identity, whenever these issues are relevant in the case. Because of the potential for unfair prejudice of this type of evidence, the balancing test of Federal Rule 403 (paraphrased in choice (C)) is particularly important. Even though evidence of the other robberies is relevant to show motive, the court may very well find that its probative value is substantially outweighed by the danger of unfair prejudice, especially because the other crimes are of the same type as the crime charged. (A) is incorrect because a conviction is not required for other crimes evidence used for this purpose. Only when extrinsic evidence of another crime is being used to impeach a testifying defendant is an actual conviction required. (B) is incorrect because whether Jason has testified is only relevant when the other crimes evidence is being used for impeachment, since a defendant only puts his credibility at issue if he takes the witness stand; it is irrelevant when the other crimes evidence is used to show motive. (D) is incorrect. For independently relevant uncharged misconduct by the defendant to be admissible, there need only be sufficient evidence to support a jury finding that the defendant committed the prior act; clear and convincing evidence is not required.

Answer to Question 84

(C) If Darrel undertakes to rescue the hiker, he must be reasonably prudent in doing so. The general rule in tort law is that no legal duty is imposed on any person to affirmatively act for the benefit of others. However, one who gratuitously acts for the benefit of another is then under a duty to act reasonably. If he acts negligently, he will be liable for damage caused thereby. (A) is an incorrect statement of the law—a rescuer is not strictly liable for a victim's injuries, but rather is liable only for negligent acts. (B) is an accurate statement of the law but does not take into account that Darrel must be negligent to be liable at all. (D) is incorrect because it is not necessarily true. A violation of a statute will not be negligence per se where compliance would cause greater risk of harm than violation, such as in an emergency. If it was necessary to speed to get the hiker to the hospital for treatment of the snakebite, it may have been excusable to exceed the posted speed limit. If Darrel was not otherwise negligent, this would not establish negligence at all.

Answer to Question 85

(B) The statute is authorized by Congress's spending power. Article I, Section 8 gives Congress the power to spend "to provide for the common defense and general welfare." This power allows Congress to spend for any public purpose as long as it does not infringe on other specific constitutional restrictions (such as the Bill of Rights). The statute here is clearly for a public purpose and is not otherwise unconstitutional; it is therefore within Congress's spending power. (A) is not as good a choice as (B). The statute arguably does involve the commerce power, because Congress has plenary power to regulate interstate commerce, including any kind of commerce or transportation within a state that has a substantial economic effect on interstate commerce. However, that power is generally invoked for federal legislation that directly regulates the state activity. Here, no government action is involved except for the grant of money, which more closely implicates the spending power. (C) is incorrect because the Necessary and Proper Clause is not by itself a basis of power; it merely gives Congress power to execute specifically granted powers. The grant of money falls within a specific enumerated power of Congress; the Necessary and Proper Clause is not the primary source of authority here. (D) is incorrect because the power to conduct foreign relations is vested in the President. Congress shares some of this power in such cases as approval of treaties, but the President's power to act for the United States in day-to-day foreign relations is paramount.

Answer to Question 86

(A) The court should grant Northeast's motion because Peron has not established a prima facie case of negligence against Northeast. To establish a prima facie case for negligence, a plaintiff must show (i) a duty of care, (ii) breach of that duty, (iii) actual and proximate cause, and (iv) damages. As a common carrier, Northeast owed Peron a high duty of care, and therefore would be liable for slight negligence. However, Peron has offered no evidence to establish that Northeast breached its duty, and res ipsa loquitur is not applicable to these facts because the rocking motion of a train is not the type of event that would occur only as a result of negligence. Because Peron failed to establish breach of duty, the court should grant Northeast a directed verdict. (B) is incorrect because Northeast does not need to introduce that evidence to prevail. While evidence that a person in normal health would not have been injured by the bump may support Northeast's other evidence that it exercised due care, it is not necessary because Peron has failed to offer evidence that Northeast breached its duty. On the other hand, if Northeast had breached its duty of care to its passengers, the fact that a person in normal health would not have been injured by the bump on the knee would not be a defense to liability. Where a defendant's negligence causes an aggravation of plaintiff's existing physical illness, defendant is liable for the damages caused by the aggravation. (C) is incorrect because, as discussed above, Peron has failed to present evidence that Northeast breached the high duty of care that it owed to its passengers. (D) is incorrect even though it is a true statement of law, as discussed above. The reason Northeast prevails is because Peron has failed to establish a prima facie case.

Answer to Question 87

(B) Yogi must agree to a rescission of the agreement. A party to a contract may not unilaterally rescind it if the contract is valid (*i.e.,* in the absence of mistake, misrepresentation, etc.). However, both parties to a contract may agree to rescind and discharge their contractual duties as long as the duties are still executory on both sides. Here, neither party has performed under the contract, so the contract will be mutually rescinded if Yogi gives his assent to Walter. (A) is incorrect because Casey's rights as a third-party beneficiary of the contract have not yet vested; thus, his consent to the rescission is not needed. An intended beneficiary such as Casey can enforce a contract only after his rights have vested, which will occur when he (i) manifests assent to the promise in a manner invited or requested by the parties, (ii) brings suit to enforce the promise, or (iii) materially changes his position in justifiable reliance on the promise. Here, Casey has not even become aware of the agreement between Walter and Yogi, so his rights cannot have vested. (C) is incorrect because conditional promises are not illusory. They are enforceable, no matter how remote the contingency, unless the "condition" is entirely within the promisor's control. Here, the fact that both parties' performance is conditioned on the Seals' winning the pennant does not make the contract illusory because neither party (presumably) can control the occurrence or nonoccurrence of the condition. (D) is incorrect because an offer can only be revoked before it has been accepted, and here the offer has already been accepted and a contract formed. Whether the Seals win the pennant is merely a condition precedent to the parties' duty of performance.

Answer to Question 88

(C) Both of the listed occurrences would provide Yogi with a partial defense in the litigation. The promisee and promisor in a third-party beneficiary contract are free to modify their contract until the third party's rights have vested. As discussed in the previous question, a third-party beneficiary's rights cannot vest before he has knowledge of the contract. If Casey did not learn of the contract until September 5, the parties were free to modify the price under the contract on September 1. Assuming Walter has performed and Yogi's duty to perform is now absolute, Yogi would be liable to Casey for only $300 under the contract as modified. Therefore, I. is a partial defense. II. is also a partial defense. When a third-party beneficiary sues the promisor on the contract, the promisor may raise any defense he would have had against the promisee. Under the doctrine of reformation, either of the parties to the contract may ask a court in equity to modify the terms of the contract where the writing, through mistake or misrepresentation, does not incorporate the terms orally agreed upon. Here, the parties' mistake in memorializing the contract permits Yogi to have the contract reformed to show the parties' original agreement. This provides a partial defense that Yogi can use against Casey; Yogi is liable at most for $225 rather than $375. Therefore, (C) is correct and (A), (B), and (D) are incorrect.

Answer to Question 89

(B) Westco's strongest argument is that Northern's application of the tax to all of Westco's manufacturing plants violates the Commerce Clause. States may impose "doing business" taxes, such as a gross receipts tax, on companies engaged in interstate commerce as long as the tax does not discriminate against or unfairly burden interstate commerce. A tax will impose an unfair burden unless (i) the activity taxed has a substantial nexus to the taxing state, (ii) the tax is fairly apportioned, and (iii) the tax fairly relates to the services provided by the state. Here, the fact that the tax applies to revenue derived from Westco's plants located in other states strongly suggests that it imposes an unfair burden, because those plants may be potentially subject to a similar tax in those states, and the relationship between the tax and services provided by Northern is very tenuous with regard to the out-of-state plants. (A) is not as strong an argument because the tax is not levied directly against federal government property. Nondiscriminatory, indirect taxes levied by a state on the federal government or its property are permissible if they do not unreasonably burden the federal government. Here, the tax is not even on the products purchased by the federal government, but only on the company doing business with it. The fact that the costs of the tax may be passed on to the government through the price of the products does not impose an unreasonable burden. (C) is wrong because the use tax is a different type of tax than the gross receipts tax, and does not appear to be invalid. A use tax on users of goods purchased out of state is permissible as long as it is nondiscriminatory and otherwise does not unfairly burden interstate commerce. Although a use tax is directed at goods passing through interstate commerce, it is permissible if the use tax burden on the goods purchased out of state is equivalent to the sales tax burden on goods purchased within the state, as suggested by choice (C). (D) is incorrect because the fact that sales taxes are imposed on Westco's products in other states does not by itself suggest the invalidity of Northern's gross receipts tax, which is a different type of tax that is not being imposed directly on the transactions that other states are taxing. Hence, the argument that it constitutes an unfair burden on interstate commerce is not as strong.

Answer to Question 90

(B) Although the President has no power to declare war, Article II, Section 2 makes the President Commander in Chief of the military, which affords the President extensive power to deploy military forces against any enemy, foreign or domestic. Congress lacks such power. Therefore, (B) is correct; this statute directly infringes upon the President's authority as Commander in Chief to make such orders as he deems proper with respect to the armed forces, and thus violates the doctrine of separation of powers. (A) is incorrect because the duty to execute the laws of the United States is an obligation, not a grant of authority. (C) is incorrect because even if the measure has some effect upon interstate commerce, it is still a violation of the separation of powers doctrine. Congress's power under the Commerce Clause does not supersede other powers that the Constitution has specifically bestowed on another branch of government. (D) is incorrect because the enactment does not appropriate money to support the armed forces, but seeks to control their activities.

Answer to Question 91

(C) Evidence of defendant's prior misrepresentations is probably admissible to show intent. In both civil and criminal cases, evidence of other crimes or misconduct is admissible if these acts are relevant to some issue other than defendant's character or disposition to commit the act charged. In cases such as fraud, where the intent of the defendant is typically a key issue, evidence that defendant committed prior similar intentional misrepresentations is admissible in such a case to establish fraudulent intent (*i.e.,* absence of mistake) and negate good faith. Hence, the evidence in choice (C) is probably going to be relevant in the fraud claim against defendant and is therefore the evidence most likely to be admissible. (A) is incorrect because the school board president's charitable nature is not at issue. Character evidence is admissible in civil cases when a person's character itself is one of the issues in the case, such as in a defamation case. However, the character evidence must be relevant to the particular trait of character impugned by the defamation. Here, the allegation that the president embezzled funds does not call into question her generosity to charitable causes; thus, the fact that she donated services to a homeless shelter is inadmissible because it is not relevant. (B) is incorrect. If the defendant puts his character in issue by having a character witness testify as to the defendant's good character or reputation, the prosecution may rebut on cross-examination by inquiring into relevant specific instances of conduct. However, the prosecution may not establish specific instances of conduct by extrinsic evidence, such as offering a certified copy of a felony conviction. Furthermore, since the defendant is not testifying and thereby putting his credibility in issue, the conviction is not admissible against the defendant for impeachment purposes either. (D) is incorrect because, while a defendant may offer evidence of her good character in a criminal case, such evidence may only be in the form of reputation or opinion testimony. Evidence of specific acts of the person in question as demonstrating that person's character is permitted only in the few instances when character is itself one of the ultimate issues in the case.

Answer to Question 92

(B) Abigail can establish a prima facie case for battery regardless of whether the operation improved her physical well-being. The prima facie case for battery requires an act by defendant that will bring about a harmful or offensive contact to plaintiff, intent on the part of defendant to do the act, and causation. Here, Dr. Michaels's performing the operation would be offensive contact because it was unconsented to: Abigail had selected Dr. Smith to perform the operation and did not consent to Dr. Michaels's participating in the procedure. (A) is incorrect because damages is not an element of the prima facie case for battery. Even if Abigail cannot establish that the operation did not improve her physical well-being, she can obtain judgment in her favor and at least nominal damages. (C) is incorrect because the fact that Dr. Michaels is considered an expert in this type of operation is irrelevant; Abigail did not consent to his involvement. (D) is incorrect because Dr. Smith had no authority to approve the substitution of Dr. Michaels. Since no emergency existed, there was no justification for not obtaining Abigail's consent to the substitution.

Answer to Question 93

(B) Beavis will be found not guilty if he did not have the required state of mind for liability. If a defendant is charged under a theory of accomplice liability, the prosecution must establish that the defendant encouraged or helped another person to commit a crime and had a culpable mental state. When the target offense requires a mental state of "intent," all courts hold that the accomplice must have intended for the crime to have occurred. When the target offense requires a mental state of "recklessness," some courts still require a showing of an actual intent on the part of the accomplice to have the crime occur, while other courts hold that the accomplice can be found guilty if he had a mental state of recklessness with respect to the crime committed. Regardless of the jurisdiction, Beavis would be found not guilty if he did not intend to cause Ashley bodily harm and was not reckless with respect to her injury. (A) is wrong because a person who encourages a crime with the culpable mental state will be guilty as an accomplice even if he did not personally engage in the behavior prohibited by the criminal statute. (C) is wrong. Even if Beavis intended to encourage Butthead, he would not be guilty unless he intended to cause Ashley bodily injury or was reckless with respect to the injury. While the trier of fact ***might*** find that Beavis was reckless with respect to the injury, choice (B) specifically negates that element of the crime. (D) is wrong. To be liable as an accomplice, a person must encourage or help ***and*** have the culpable mental state. The act of encouragement alone does not suffice to establish the required intent.

Answer to Question 94

(B) The state will prevail because Congress has consented to the state regulation of interstate commerce. A state may regulate local aspects of commerce (*i.e.*, ***intrastate*** commerce), but state regulation that discriminates against or substantially burdens ***interstate*** commerce may be held invalid under the Supremacy Clause, because of Congress's plenary power to regulate interstate commerce under the Commerce Clause. Here, the state statute, standing alone, might have been held invalid because its substantial burden on interstate commerce could have been found to outweigh any legitimate local interest in reducing eyestrain. However, the federal statute changes the equation. Because Congress's power over interstate commerce is plenary, Congress may allow a state to adopt legislation that would otherwise be invalid as an unconstitutional burden on interstate commerce; this is what Congress did here. By allowing the state regulation, it is actually exercising the federal commerce power—it simply allows for nonuniform (state-by-state) rules. Therefore, (B) is correct and (C) is incorrect. (A) is incorrect because the Tenth Amendment merely reserves to the states the powers not delegated to the federal government, and the power to regulate interstate commerce—the power in question here—was not reserved to the states because it was granted to Congress by the Constitution. (D) is incorrect because the statute, as far as described in the problem, appears to be exactly what Congress authorized. There is no information indicating that the statute is overbroad or exceeds the authorization, which apparently allows a broad range of regulation beyond just location and hours of operation.

Answer to Question 95

(D) Jones is likely to be liable if it knew or should have known of Lamont's prior convictions. Under the doctrine of respondeat superior, an employer is not vicariously liable for the acts of an employee outside the scope of his employment. However, the employer may be liable for its own negligent selection if it has some reason to be on notice that the actions that resulted in harm were likely to occur. Thus, if plaintiffs can show that a reasonable employer could have learned of Lamont's violent criminal record, by definition Jones did not act with reasonable care in not discovering it (and likely was negligent in hiring someone as an armed guard whom it should have known had violent propensities). (A) is incorrect because the rule it states is only for an employer's vicarious liability, and negligent selection of an employee is not vicarious liability; it is independent negligence on the part of the employer. (B) is incorrect because a duty can arise in circumstances such as those stated in (D). (C) is incorrect because merely giving Lamont the pistol does not breach Jones's duty—Jones must have had some reason to know of Lamont's dangerous propensities.

Answer to Question 96

(C) Walden's prior inconsistent statement is admissible both for impeachment and as substantive evidence. One of the most common means of impeaching the credibility of a witness is by showing that the witness has, on another occasion, made statements that are inconsistent with some material part of his present testimony. While the witness is still on the stand, he may be questioned as to the prior statement and given an opportunity to explain or deny it. [*See* Fed. R. Evid. 613(b)] Furthermore, the prior statement may be considered by the jury as substantive proof of the facts stated if the statement was given under oath at a prior trial or a deposition. [Fed. R. Evid. 801(d)(1)] Here, Walden's prior statement is inconsistent with his in-court statement and was made at a deposition; hence, it is admissible as substantive evidence as well as for impeachment. (A) is incorrect because Walden's prior statement can be used for more than just refreshing his present recollection. Present recollection revived applies where a testifying witness uses a writing or thing to refresh her present recollection. The witness may not read from the writing, and the writing is not admitted into evidence; it may be used only to refresh her recollection, and her subsequent testimony must demonstrate a ***present*** recollection. While the deposition statement could be used this way, it is much more effective to offer it as substantive evidence, particularly if the witness does not recall it or denies making it. (B) is incorrect because the Federal Rules admit prior inconsistent statements not only for impeachment purposes but also as substantive evidence when made under oath at a prior trial or a deposition. Although it would ordinarily be hearsay when used as substantive evidence (because it is being offered for the truth of the matter asserted), the Federal Rules specifically categorize such statements as nonhearsay. [Fed. R. Evid. 801(d)(1)(A)] (D) is incorrect because Federal Rule 607 provides that the credibility of a witness may be attacked (such as through a prior inconsistent statement) by ***any*** party, including the party that called him.

Answer to Question 97

(C) One may obtain title to land by taking and maintaining possession of it for the statutory period provided by the jurisdiction. The possession must be actual, open and notorious (sufficient to put the true owner or the community on notice of the fact of possession), continuous (used in a way that the actual owner would use it), exclusive, and hostile (without the true owner's permission). Here, Proctor's installation and maintenance of the generator for more than the 20 years provided by the statute of limitations for ejectment satisfies the requirements for him to acquire title by adverse possession. (A) is incorrect because the statute of limitations is not tolled by an ***intervening*** disability. Gamble's mental incompetence would have benefited him against Proctor only if he was suffering from it at the ***inception*** of the adverse possession. (B) is incorrect because claim of right is not an essential element of adverse possession under the majority view. It does not matter whether the possessor believes he is on his own land, knows he is trespassing on someone else's land, or has no idea who owns the land. (D) is incorrect because a prescriptive easement, like easements generally, is a nonexclusive right to use the land rather than an exclusive right to possess and enjoy the land. The typical easement gives its holder the right of access across a tract of land (*e.g.,* a utility line or road) without precluding the owner of the land from also using it; here, Proctor's installation and enclosure of the generator amounted to a permanent and exclusive possession of the land on which the generator rested.

Answer to Question 98

(D) Proctor has not acquired a prescriptive easement because Gamble consented to the wiring crossing his land. The holder of an easement has the right to use a tract of land for a special purpose, but has no right to possess and enjoy the tract of land. Gamble's oral consent to the wiring's crossing his land was not effective to create an easement: the Statute of Frauds requires that any conveyance of an easement interest of greater than one year in duration must be in writing to be enforceable; an oral attempt to create an easement results in a revocable license. What Gamble's consent did, however, was to make it impossible for Proctor to acquire an easement by prescription. As with adverse possession, an easement by prescription requires that the use be adverse or hostile. Because Gamble consented to Proctor's running of the wires, Proctor's use of the land will never ripen into a prescriptive easement; (B) is therefore incorrect. (A) is incorrect because, as discussed in the previous question, acquiring title by adverse possession requires that the possessor's actions amount to exclusive possession of the land, rather than a use of the land that does not exclude other uses. Running electrical wires across land could at most create a prescriptive easement. (C) is incorrect because the continuous use requirement does not require a constant use; it merely precludes sporadic and occasional trespasses from ripening into prescriptive easements. As with the continuous possession requirement for adverse possession, a seasonal use is sufficient if it is a use that the owner might make of the property under the circumstances.

Answer to Question 99

(B) Douglas's best defense is that it did not breach a duty to Paul because it did not place the parachutes in the stream of commerce. To establish liability in a strict liability action based on a defective product, plaintiff must prove that defendant is a commercial supplier of the product in question and that the product is expected to be supplied to the consumer without substantial change in the condition in which it is supplied. To establish breach of duty, the plaintiff need not prove that the defendant was at fault in supplying a defective product, just that it supplied the defective product, either by selling it or producing it and placing it into the stream of commerce. Here, Douglas produced the defective parachutes but did not place them into the stream of commerce and did not intend to do so. Thus, it did not breach a duty to Paul with regard to the defective parachutes. (A) is incorrect because it is not a defense in a strict liability action that the defendant acted reasonably (*i.e.*, without fault). The element of negligence need not be proved in a strict liability case. (C) is incorrect because the fact that Paul was not in privity of contract with Douglas is not a defense. A strict liability action may be maintained against a commercial supplier not only by the buyer but also by the buyer's family, friends, and employees, and by foreseeable bystanders. (D) is incorrect because ordinary contributory negligence is not a defense in a strict liability action where the plaintiff failed to discover the defect or guard against its existence. While voluntarily and unreasonably encountering a ***known*** risk is a defense, there is no indication that Paul knew that the parachutes might be defective just because they were sold on the black market.

Answer to Question 100

(C) Warren's testimony is admissible character evidence. Under Federal Rule 404, in a civil case, evidence of the character of a person generally is inadmissible if offered to prove that the person may have acted in conformity with his character on a particular occasion. If, however, the character evidence is offered for some other purpose, such as where a person's character itself is one of the issues in the case, Rule 404 will not exclude the evidence. Warren's testimony is evidence of John's character but, if offered against First Bank, it would be offered to show that First Bank may have been negligent when it entrusted the gun to John. Thus, the evidence would not be excluded by Rule 404. In addition, the evidence would be relevant even if First Bank did not know of John's reputation, because the jury could find that a reasonable investigation by First Bank would have uncovered the information and First Bank should have known of John's reputation. (A) is too broad a statement. In a civil case, character evidence is not admissible to help prove that a person acted in conformity with their character, but it may be admissible for the purpose it is offered here. (B) is too narrow a statement. The evidence clearly would be admissible if First Bank knew of John's reputation. Thus, (B) is technically a correct statement. However, since the theory of the case against First Bank is "negligent entrustment," the evidence could be admitted even if First Bank did not know of John's reputation but should have known. Thus, (C) is a more complete statement than (B). (D) is wrong. Under Rule 404, the evidence is not admissible to help establish that John may have acted negligently.

Answer to Question 101

(A) The court should grant the petroleum company's motion for a directed verdict in its favor because the employee has not established a prima facie case against the petroleum company. The question does not indicate the theory of liability for the employee's lawsuit; however, because strict liability is not applicable against the petroleum company for operation of the refinery (as discussed below) and because there is no evidence to establish that the petroleum company is vicariously liable for another party's negligence here, the employee's only feasible theory of liability is that the petroleum company itself was negligent. While the employee has established the negligence elements of duty, causation, and damages, he has not established the element of breach of duty. While breach of duty is ordinarily a question for the trier of fact, plaintiff's failure to offer ***any evidence*** on that element of the prima facie case will permit a directed verdict for defendant. Under certain circumstances, the fact that a particular injury occurred may itself establish or tend to establish a breach of duty owed, permitting the trier of fact to infer defendant's liability. This is the doctrine of res ipsa loquitur. However, for the doctrine to apply, plaintiff must show that (i) the accident causing his injury is the type that would not normally occur unless someone was negligent; (ii) the negligence was attributable to defendant; and (iii) the injury was not attributable to plaintiff. For the second requirement, plaintiff must establish that this type of accident ordinarily happens because of the negligence of someone in defendant's position. This can often be done by showing that the instrumentality causing the injury was in the exclusive control of the defendant. Here, however, the crane that caused the injury was designed and constructed by a company other than the petroleum company and was serviced and maintained by still another company not selected by the petroluem company. Even assuming that the collapse of the crane was the type of accident that does not normally occur unless someone was negligent, there is no evidence that the petroleum company was the source of that negligence. The accident could well be attributable to negligence on the part of the manufacturer or the company hired by the manufacturer to service the crane, or simply to a defect in the materials used to construct the crane, and there is no basis for the petroluem company being vicariously liable for the actions of either company, since the exceptions that impose vicarious liability for the conduct of an independent contractor do not apply. Since no other evidence of breach of duty was established, the petroleum company's motion for a directed verdict should be granted. (B) is incorrect because the petroleum company owed a duty to the employee, since the employee was an invitee on the petroleum company's property. An invitee is one who enters on the premises in response to an express or implied invitation of the landowner or occupier, including those who enter for a purpose connected with the business interests of the landowner. Here, even though the employee was an employee of an independent contractor, he was on the premises for the benefit of the petroleum's company refinery operations and at its invitation. Thus, he is an invitee to whom thc petroleum company owed a duty of reasonable care. (C) is incorrect because the refinery operation is not an ultrahazardous or abnormally dangerous activity. For strict liability to apply to an activity, the activity (i) must involve a risk of serious harm to persons or property, (ii) must be one that cannot be performed without a risk of serious harm no matter how much care is taken, and (iii) must not be a commonly engaged-in activity in the community. Because an oil refinery can be operated in many locations without the risk of serious harm as long as due care is exercised, a court probably would not find it to be an ultrahazardous or abnormally dangerous activity; hence, the petroleum company would not be strictly liable to the employee. (D) is incorrect because, as discussed above, the employee has presented no evidence of the petroleum company's negligence and has therefore failed to establish his prima facie case.

Answer to Question 102

(A) The manufacturer and the retailer have a contract without the arbitration clause. In contracts for the sale of goods a definite expression of acceptance operates as an acceptance even if it states additional terms. Between merchants, additional terms proposed by the offeree in an acceptance automatically become part of the contract unless (i) they ***materially*** alter the original terms of the offer (*e.g.*, they change a party's risk or the remedies available); (ii) the offer expressly limits acceptance to the terms of the offer; or (iii) the offeror objects to the additional terms within a reasonable time. Most courts consider a clause requiring that disagreements be subject to arbitration to be a material alteration because such a clause affects the remedies that the parties can pursue. Hence, the acceptance is effective to create a contract but the arbitration clause would not become part of the contract. (B) is therefore incorrect. (C) is incorrect because it reflects the common law "mirror image" rule, which the U.C.C. has rejected in sale of goods cases. (D) is incorrect because under the U.C.C. rule, the inclusion of a material additional term does not prevent formation of a contract; instead, a contract is formed without the inclusion of that additional term.

Answer to Question 103

(B) The witness's testimony is admissible. Under Federal Rule 404(a), a criminal defendant is allowed to present relevant character evidence to help establish that he may not have committed the crime charged. Thus, evidence that the defendant had a reputation for being an honest person would be admissible to show that he might not have embezzled funds because embezzlement is a crime of dishonesty. (A) is too broad a statement. While as a general matter, a defendant does have a constitutional right to call witnesses, the testimony of the witnesses must comport with the rules of evidence (unless the rule itself is declared unconstitutional), including the requirement that character evidence must be relevant to the crime charged. (C) is wrong because, as discussed above, Federal Rule 404 specifically allows such evidence. (D) is wrong. It is true that a party may not present evidence to bolster the credibility of his own witness until the witness has been impeached. However, if the evidence of good character is offered for any other legitimate purpose, the fact that it also helps bolster the credibility of the witness will never result in the exclusion of the evidence. Here the evidence is admissible to show that the defendant may not have embezzled funds; hence, the rule excluding evidence offered to bolster credibility would not apply.

Answer to Question 104

(A) Prex will not prevail if a reasonable person in Prex's position would have used the cream even after being told of the potential side effects. A person who is a professional or has special skills (*e.g.*, a doctor) is required to possess and exercise the knowledge and skill of a member of the profession or occupation in good standing in similar communities. Further, for medical specialists, most courts apply a "national" standard of care. As part of this standard of conduct, a doctor proposing a course of treatment has a duty to provide the patient with enough information about its risks to enable the patient to make an informed consent to the treatment. If an undisclosed risk was serious enough that a reasonable person in the patient's position would have withheld consent to the treatment, the doctor has breached her duty. Here, whether Doctor Dillamond breached her duty to Prex by not warning him of possible side effects would be determined ultimately by the trier of fact. However, if, as (A) states, a reasonable person in Prex's position would have consented to using the cream even after being informed of the potential side effects, Prex likely will not be able to show a breach of duty by Doctor Dillamond under these facts. (B) is incorrect because the listing of side effects on a printed insert does not necessarily satisfy Doctor Dillamond's duty to provide enough information for Prex to make an informed consent. If the information was buried in a lengthy insert that a reasonable person was not likely to read through, Doctor Dillamond may have had a duty to verbally disclose side effects, and she will have breached that duty if a reasonable person in the patient's position would have withheld consent to the treatment if given the information. (C) is wrong because Doctor Dillamond could be liable regardless of the severity of the reaction Prex experienced. If she should have warned about the particular side effects Prex experienced even though they are ordinarily less severe, the fact that Prex suffered an unforeseeably severe reaction to the medicine does not relieve her from liability. (D) is incorrect. While Doctor Dillamond, as a specialist, may be held to a higher level of knowledge and skill than a general practitioner, that does not mean that she is automatically liable for slight negligence or even that her conduct here was negligent. The only apparent duty issue here is whether she provided Prex with enough information to allow him to make an informed consent, as discussed above.

Answer to Question 105

(C) Because Farnsworth's statement did not amount to an anticipatory repudiation of the contract, Jones may not bring an immediate suit for breach of contract. Anticipatory repudiation requires that the promisor unequivocally indicate that he cannot or will not perform when the time comes, or act in a manner rendering him unable to perform. When this happens, the nonrepudiating party may treat the anticipatory repudiation as a total breach and sue immediately. Here, Farnsworth merely expressed doubt that he would be able to perform. An expression of doubt does not constitute an anticipatory repudiation. (A) is therefore wrong. (B) is wrong because Jones would have no right to rely on Farnsworth's telephone call because it was not a repudiation. However, the call did indicate a prospective inability to perform on Farnsworth's part, which would allow Jones to demand adequate assurances of performance from Farnsworth. Only after Farnsworth's noncompliance with such a demand could Jones safely change his position (*e.g.,* by hiring a substitute performer), because the failure to give assurances may be treated as a total repudiation. (D) states incorrect law. A repudiation also may be oral or by conduct, as long as it is unequivocal.

Answer to Question 106

(C) While Farnsworth clearly breached the contract, because he was under an absolute duty to perform and failed to do so, Jones would only be entitled to cancel the contract if the breach is material (*i.e.,* if the nonbreaching party did not receive the substantial benefit of his bargain). If the breach is only minor, the nonbreaching party is not entitled to cancel the contract (although he will have an action for any damages suffered). Six factors that courts look at to determine materiality of breach are: (i) amount of benefit nonbreaching party received, (ii) adequacy of damages remedy, (iii) extent of part performance by breaching party, (iv) hardship to breaching party, (v) whether breaching party's behavior was negligent or willful, and (vi) likelihood of breaching party completing performance. Although Farnsworth has not yet begun performance, his delay was only for 10 days and the contract was for a period of two years; also, Jones has an adequate remedy for damages for the 10-day period. Farnsworth's conduct does not appear to be negligent or willful, and he appears ready to perform the remainder of his contract. Thus, in the absence of facts indicating that Jones was materially prejudiced by Farnsworth's delay, the breach would be minor and Jones could not cancel the contract. (A) is incorrect because it just establishes that a breach occurred. Whether Jones may cancel depends on whether the breach is material or minor. (B) is incorrect because it goes too far. In the absence of the additional circumstance in choice (C), it appears that the breach was not material. (D) is incorrect not only because it is not entirely true (*i.e.,* notification on the same day performance was to begin probably did not give Jones time to procure a substitute performance), but also because notification of delay, while perhaps indicating absence of willful behavior, is not itself one of the factors courts consider in determining materiality of breach.

Answer to Question 107

(D) Farnsworth is excused from performance under the contract under the doctrine of impossibility.

An absolute duty to perform will be discharged where it has become impossible to do so. (If the impossibility is only temporary, the duty is only suspended; it "springs back" into existence when performance once more becomes possible.) In most cases the impossibility must be objective (*i.e.*, the duties could not be performed by anyone) rather than subjective, but in the case of a personal service contract such as the one in the question, the duty cannot be delegated to a third party by an obligor unable to perform because services such as singing are considered unique. Hence, Farnsworth's incapacity discharged his duty to sing during the two months, and he will not be liable for the additional costs that Jones incurred procuring a replacement. (A) is incorrect because notice is not required before duties are discharged on the basis of impossibility. (B) is incorrect because it has no bearing on whether the impossibility doctrine will apply. (C) is incorrect because fault is not relevant for purposes of impossibility. Even if Farnsworth did cause the accident, he will be discharged of his duty if his injuries make it impossible for him to perform.

Answer to Question 108

(B) The creditor will prevail because the debtor has made an effective assignment of his right to collect the debt from the third party. The general rule is that a writing is not required to have an effective assignment. Here, the oral assignment to the creditor of the debtor's right to the $4,000 was effective and enforceable by the creditor. (A) is incorrect for two reasons: The creditor's agreement to accept $4,000 did not constitute consideration because he no longer had a right to enforce the original debt. Furthermore, consideration is not required for an assignment; a gratuitous assignment is effective. The absence of a writing or consideration may allow the assignor (the debtor) to revoke an assignment, but will not prevent the assignee from enforcing it against the obligor. (C) is incorrect. While the obligor may raise contract defenses on the obligation he owes to the assignor (the debtor), he may not raise defenses that the assignor might have had against the assignee (the creditor) on a different obligation as a means of avoiding his own obligation. Here, there are no apparent defenses to the third party's liability to the debtor for the $4,000 debt, and the third party is not entitled to assert the debtor's statute of limitations defense to the debt that the debtor owed to the creditor. (D) is incorrect for a similar reason. The general rule is that a new promise to pay a legal obligation barred by law must be in writing to be enforceable; hence, if the debtor had made an oral promise to the creditor to pay him $4,000, the creditor may have had difficulty enforcing it against the debtor. However, the third party has a separate obligation to the debtor that is not barred by any defense; the debtor's gratuitous assignment to the creditor of his right to the $4,000 does not allow the third party to raise a defense that the debtor may have had against the creditor.

Answer to Question 109

(A) The homeowner will be found not guilty because he did not have the requisite mental state. To convict a person for an attempted crime, the prosecution must establish that the defendant had an actual specific intent to cause the harm prohibited by the statute and committed an act beyond mere preparation in furtherance of that intent. Those elements—specific intent and act—are required regardless of the mental state required by the target offense. A person who took a substantial step towards commission of the crime but was only reckless with respect to the target offense could not be found guilty of attempt. The homeowner did not intend to burn the neighbor's home. Therefore, he cannot be guilty of attempted arson of the neighbor's home. (B) is wrong. The fact that the fire was put out before it burned any of the neighbor's home would not preclude a conviction of attempted arson if the elements of attempted arson were otherwise established. (C) is wrong. To be guilty of attempted arson of the neighbor's home, the homeowner must have intended to burn the neighbor's home. The doctrine of transferred intent does not apply to attempt. (D) is wrong. A specific intent to burn the home is required for attempted arson. While malice satisfies the state of mind requirement for the completed crime of arson, it will not suffice for attempt.

Answer to Question 110

(C) The state's challenge to the decision of the state supreme court presents no substantial federal question and will be denied. The Supreme Court's appellate jurisdiction under 28 U.S.C. section 1257 extends to reviewing the decision of the highest court of a state where the validity of state legislation is called into question on the ground that it is unconstitutional or contrary to federal statutes. However, the Supreme Court will hear a case from a state court only if the state court judgment turned on federal grounds. The Court will refuse jurisdiction if it finds adequate and independent nonfederal grounds to support the state decision, because a different interpretation of the federal statutes would have no effect on the judgment rendered by the state court, so that the Supreme Court, in effect, would be rendering an advisory opinion. Here, even if the state court was incorrect in holding that federal statutes preempted the state legislation, it also held that the state constitution prohibited the state legislation. Hence, a different interpretation of the federal preemption issue would have no effect on the outcome of the case. (A) is incorrect because, as discussed above, the nonfederal grounds are fully dispositive of the case. Even if the federal grounds were wrongly decided, it would not affect the outcome of the case. (B) is incorrect because the state court has interpreted its legislation so that it also conflicts with its state constitution. Thus, its determination of whether its legislation conflicts with federal law has no effect. (D) is wrong because the Supreme Court has complete discretion under its appellate jurisdiction to review cases from the highest state court where a state statute allegedly violates state law; it is irrelevant that the state is challenging its state court decision.

Answer to Question 111

(C) Rupert's express rejection of the deed was sufficient to rebut any presumption of acceptance. As a general rule, delivery of the deed is the final operative act to complete a conveyance of title to the grantee, because courts will infer the grantee's acceptance if the conveyance is beneficial to him. However, all courts will consider evidence that is contrary to the presumption or inference. Hence, Rupert's express rejection of the gift is sufficient to establish that no conveyance of the property took place. (A) is an incorrect statement of law. If the grantor intends the recording of the deed to be the final act in vesting title in the grantee, then such recording creates a presumption of delivery even where the grantee did not know of the recordation. (B) is wrong because there is no such thing as a constructive reconveyance. Had Rupert accepted the gift (completing the conveyance) and later changed his mind, Rupert would have had to execute a new deed to convey the property back to his uncle. (D) is wrong because knowledge or permission of the grantee has no effect on the validity of the recordation; rather, it determines whether there has been an effective acceptance.

Answer to Question 112

(C) The home is not subject to the judgment lien even though the niece never recorded the conveyance. Under the recording acts, a subsequent mortgagee or bona fide purchaser for value generally prevails over the grantee of a prior unrecorded conveyance. However, most recording statutes do not protect subsequent judgment creditors on the theory that the creditor is not offering consideration at the time his lien is created, and the language of the recording statute generally extends protection to "purchasers," defined as those obtaining an interest in exchange for consideration. Also, courts generally interpret a judgment lien statute like the one in the question to apply to "any land" ***actually owned*** by the judgment debtor rather than any land for which the judgment debtor has record title. Hence, (C) is correct and (A) is incorrect; the home was validly conveyed to the niece and is not subject to the claim of the lien creditor. (B) is incorrect because if the home were part of the estate, it would be subject to any claim against the testator. (D) is incorrect because the insurance company's lien only applies against the judgment debtor or her estate. Even though the niece is sole beneficiary and executrix, she has no responsibility to pay charges against the estate out of what she already owns.

Answer to Question 113

(D) The evidence is admissible for impeachment purposes as an inconsistent statement of a hearsay declarant. Because the credibility of a hearsay declarant is as much at issue as the credibility of an in-court witness, Federal Rule 806 allows statements of a hearsay declarant to be impeached to the same extent as those of an in-court witness. Thus, a statement of the declarant made at any time that is inconsistent with his hearsay statement may be offered into evidence for impeachment purposes. Here, Oscar's hearsay statement (which probably qualified as an excited utterance) was testified to by Bill. Oscar's subsequent statement to Arthur is inconsistent with his hearsay statement and is therefore admissible to discredit that statement. (A) is wrong because the general requirement that an impeached witness be given an opportunity to explain or deny an apparently inconsistent statement does not apply to hearsay declarants. Because hearsay statements are often admissible at trial after the declarant has died or is otherwise unavailable, Rule 806 provides that the declarant need not be given an opportunity to explain or deny statements that are inconsistent with the declarant's hearsay statement. (B) is wrong because the statement is admissible for purposes of impeachment; hence, it does not fall within the definition of hearsay. (C) is wrong because the statement would be hearsay not within any exception if it were offered as substantive evidence as well as for impeachment. Under Federal Rule 801(d)(1), prior inconsistent statements are not admissible as substantive evidence unless made under oath at a prior trial or deposition.

Answer to Question 114

(D) The auctioneer may recover the cost of repair from either the developer or the buyer. A landlord's promise in a lease to maintain the property does not terminate because the property is sold. Although no longer in privity of estate, the original landlord and tenant remain in privity of contract, and the original landlord remains liable on the covenant unless there is a novation. A novation substitutes a new party for an original party to the contract. It requires the assent of all parties, and completely releases the original party. Since neither the auctioneer nor the buyer has agreed to a novation, the developer remains liable for the covenant because he and the auctioneer remain in privity of contract even after the sale. Thus, the promise to repair can be enforced against the developer. When leased property is sold, the purchaser may be liable for his predecessor's promises if the promise runs with the land. A covenant in a lease runs with the land if the parties to the lease so intend and the covenant touches and concerns the land. Generally, promises to do a physical act, such as maintain or repair the property, are considered to run with the land. Thus, the buyer is liable because he is in privity of estate with the auctioneer and the covenant to repair runs with the land. Consequently, both the developer and the buyer are potentially liable to the auctioneer for the repairs. While it is true that the sale/assignment to the buyer did not sever the developer's obligation to the auctioneer, as explained above, the developer is not the only person who is liable to the auctioneer. Since both the developer and the buyer are potentially liable for the repairs, (A) is incorrect. (B) is incorrect because although it is true that a covenant to repair touches and concerns the land and runs with it upon assignment, the developer as well as the buyer can be held liable. (C) is incorrect because the auctioneer may recover the ***full amount*** from either the developer or the buyer.

Answer to Question 115

(C) Eaton is not likely to recover unless Dinah's welcomed patrons into the kitchen to compliment the chef, which would allow him to claim invitee status while in the kitchen. The duty owed by an owner or occupier of land to those entering the land depends in most jurisdictions on whether the entrant is characterized as a trespasser, licensee, or invitee. A trespasser is one who comes onto the land without permission or privilege. A licensee is one who enters on the land with the landowner's permission, express or implied, for his own purpose or business rather than the landowner's benefit. An invitee is one who enters onto the premises in response to an express or implied invitation of the landowner. Here, Eaton was an invitee of Dinah's while he was dining at the restaurant and while exiting. However, a person loses his status as an invitee if he exceeds the scope of the invitation—if he goes into a portion of the premises where his invitation cannot reasonably be said to extend. Without any additional facts, Eaton lost the status of an invitee when he entered the kitchen; he became at best a licensee, even a trespasser if patrons were not permitted in the kitchen. While a landowner owes no duty to an undiscovered trespasser, he owes a discovered trespasser the duty to warn of artificial conditions known to the landowner that involve a risk of death or serious bodily harm and that the trespasser is unlikely to discover; for a licensee the duty extends to ***all*** dangerous conditions that create an unreasonable risk of ***any*** harm to the licensee. Here, there are no facts to suggest that anyone in the kitchen knew of Eaton's presence or the puddle of grease, even though it had congealed; hence, the facts do not establish a breach of the duty to warn discovered trespassers or licensees of dangerous conditions. On the other hand, if Dinah's policy was to welcome patrons into the kitchen to compliment the chefs, Eaton could claim that he was an invitee. The duty to invitees includes the duties owed to a licensee (stated above) and the duty to make ***reasonable inspections*** to discover dangerous conditions and, thereafter, make them safe. Eaton has a strong argument that a restaurant inviting patrons into its kitchen while the kitchen is in use has a duty to make frequent inspections to discover dangers, such as a greasy floor. Under this standard, a puddle of grease that had time to congeal should have been discovered and cleaned up, or at least been the subject of a warning. Hence, if Eaton has invitee status, he can probably show that Dinah's breached the duty it owed to him. (A) is incorrect. While places of public accommodation have an affirmative duty to use reasonable care to aid or assist their patrons, that duty rule does not alter the duty rules pertaining to the condition of the land, which are based on the status of the person on the premises (as discussed above). (B) is incorrect because the failure to exercise reasonable care to discover a dangerous condition breaches a duty owed only to invitees, as discussed above. However, without the additional facts stated in choice (C), Eaton was no longer an invitee when he entered the kitchen area. He was at most a licensee, for whom the duty to make reasonable inspections does not apply. (D) is incorrect. While a duty to warn does not exist where the dangerous condition is so obvious that the invitee should reasonably have been aware of it, just the fact that the grease was visible on the floor does not establish this. "Obviousness" is determined by all of the surrounding circumstances; *e.g.*, one whose attention may have been directed elsewhere may recover even though the condition was visible. In any case, even if the puddle were not visible Eaton would not be able to recover without the additional facts in (C), because he did not have invitee status when he entered the kitchen.

Answer to Question 116

(A) A plaintiff bringing an action in a state trial court is required to exhaust its state appellate remedies before seeking review in federal courts, even where federal issues are involved. (B) is incorrect because only a defendant may petition for removal under 28 U.S.C. section 1441 when the action could have been brought in the federal district court. The plaintiff, having initially selected the state court to file its suit, must pursue its state appellate remedies before seeking review in the federal courts. (C) is incorrect because a federal court of appeals never hears appeals from a state trial court. (D) is incorrect because a party may file a petition of certiorari only from a decision of the ***highest*** court of the state where a state statute allegedly violates the United States Constitution. [28 U.S.C. §1257]

Answer to Question 117

(D) NatureFoods has standing to sue because it can demonstrate a concrete stake in the outcome of the controversy and an impairment of its rights by the Oro statute. Courts will not consider a constitutional challenge to government action unless the person challenging the action has "standing" to raise the constitutional issue. Under the Supreme Court test, the person must have "such a personal stake in the outcome of the controversy as to ensure the concrete adverseness which sharpens the presentation of issues." Here, NatureFoods has taken substantial steps to open outlets in the state of Oro by contracting with landowners and construction firms in that state, but cannot begin to operate these outlets without violating the Oro statutes; obtaining the injunction against enforcement will eliminate the problem. The court will therefore hear the suit. (A) is incorrect even though NatureFoods has not yet been prosecuted for violating the statute. A person challenging the constitutionality of a statute does not need to violate it and await prosecution as the sole means of seeking relief. Where there exists a clear threat of prosecution if the person fails to comply with the statute (such as previous prosecutions of others), injury in fact is established. (B) is incorrect because threatened economic injury as well as threatened injury to civil liberties will create standing. (C) is incorrect even though a federal question is involved. If the court accepts the state official's claim that NatureFoods lacked standing to sue, it would dismiss the suit regardless of the issues involved.

Answer to Question 118

(D) The defendant who set fire to his rival's warehouse did not have the degree of recklessness necessary to support a finding of malice aforethought for murder. Murder is the unlawful killing of a human being with malice aforethought. Aside from the felony murder doctrine, which the question asks us to ignore, malice aforethought exists where defendant had (i) intent to kill, (ii) intent to inflict great bodily injury, or (iii) awareness of an unjustifiably high risk to human life ("abandoned and malignant heart"). In (D), the rival's warehouse was in a deserted commercial district and defendant did not know that anyone was in the building. Hence, he was not aware of any risk to human life when he set the fire. In (A), the defendant had the intent to kill but inadvertently killed the wrong victim. His intent to kill his girlfriend will be transferred to the killing of the neighbor and his wife, making him liable for murder. In (B), the defendant did not have an intent to kill, but his conduct is so recklessly indifferent to the high risk of harm to the women in the sorority house that it evidences an "abandoned and malignant heart" for purposes of implying malice aforethought for murder. In (C), defendant's conduct is not as reckless and wanton as in (B), because the shed itself is uninhabited, but its proximity to the victim's home makes the conduct substantially more reckless than the conduct in (D).

Answer to Question 119

(A) Oscar will not succeed in quashing the indictment even though it may be based on illegally obtained evidence. A grand jury may consider any evidence available to it in determining whether probable cause exists to return an indictment against the defendant. Because the exclusionary rule does not apply, a grand jury may base its indictment on evidence that would not be admissible at trial. Thus, even if the pistol was the product of an illegal search and seizure, and the grand jury based its indictment on this evidence, Oscar will not prevail in his attempt to quash the indictment. (B) is incorrect because it is irrelevant. If Henry's housekeeper could be characterized as an "agent" of the police because she was acting at their request, the search may have been illegal, but the evidence would still be admissible at the grand jury proceeding. (C) is incorrect. In addition to the fact that the grand jury may consider evidence obtained without probable cause, it does not appear that Oscar has a sufficient reasonable expectation of privacy as to items in Henry's bedroom that would allow him to claim that the potentially unlawful search violated his Fourth Amendment rights. (D) is incorrect regardless of whether Henry's housekeeper could be characterized as an agent of the police. As discussed above, even if the search is treated as a police search, the evidence can be considered by the grand jury.

Answer to Question 120

(B) Linda's silence cannot constitute an implied admission if Linda reasonably did not respond to Libby's statement. An admission is a statement or act done that amounts to a prior acknowledgment by one of the parties of one of the relevant facts. An admission can be express or it can be inferred from conduct, including silence in response to another person's statement. However, for silence to constitute an adoptive admission of the other person's statement, the circumstances must establish that the party would naturally have responded to it were it untrue. Here the prosecution is offering Libby's testimony to show that Linda impliedly admitted Libby's charge by not replying to it. However, if the court determines that Linda would not reasonably deny the statement under these circumstances (because it apparently was made in jest), it will not qualify as an implied admission and the court will not admit the evidence. (A) is not correct. To the extent that the evidence is being offered to prove the matter asserted, it would be admissible as an admission, which is not hearsay under the Federal Rules. The court's refusal to accept the evidence as an implied admission would be because it is not probative evidence on the matter asserted (it does not tend to establish anything as to Linda). (C) is incorrect because, as explained above, an admission by silence requires a statement or charge to which one would naturally respond were it untrue. (D) is incorrect because declarations against interest only apply to a person unavailable as a witness. A statement by a defendant qualifies as an admission by a party regardless of whether it is against his interest.

Answer to Question 121

(C) Officer Brown's testimony is being offered to prove the truth of the matter asserted: that the witness saw Linda commit the arson and run from the scene. Thus, the testimony is hearsay and, not being within any exception, is inadmissible. Hearsay is a statement, other than one made by the declarant while testifying at the trial or hearing, offered in evidence to prove the truth of the matter asserted. [Fed. R. Evid. 801(c)] Officer Brown is attempting to testify to the statement of the witness (an out-of-court declarant) that Linda was the arsonist the witness saw running from the scene. This statement is being offered to prove the truth of the matter asserted therein, namely, that Linda committed the crime. Consequently, the testimony is hearsay. Because the testimony does not come within any of the hearsay exceptions, it should not be admitted. (A) is incorrect because past recollection recorded is an exception to the hearsay rule that allows the introduction into evidence of a writing made by or under the direction of a witness at or near the time of an event, where the witness is presently unable to remember the facts. [Fed. R. Evid. 803(5)] Here, there is no attempt to introduce into evidence a writing prepared by Officer Brown, nor is Officer Brown unable to remember the facts. Therefore, past recollection recorded is inapplicable. (B) is incorrect. A statement of prior identification of a person made after perceiving her is not hearsay only if such prior statement was made by a testifying witness who is subject to cross-examination. [Fed. R. Evid. 801(d)(1)(C)] Here, the witness who made the prior identification is not testifying.

Thus, the statement of identification remains hearsay. (D) is incorrect because the picture of Linda is not even being offered into evidence. Generally, a photograph is admissible only if it is identified by a witness as a portrayal of certain relevant facts and verified by the witness as a correct representation of those facts. The evidence sought to be admitted is not the photograph, but rather a statement concerning the identification of the arsonist. Thus, the photograph need not be authenticated.

Answer to Question 122

(C) This question illustrates that a hearsay problem can arise even when the out-of-court declarant and the in-court witness are the same person. Linda is attempting to testify as to a statement made by her out of court, and this statement is being offered to prove the truth of the matter asserted. Thus, the statement is hearsay. Because it is not within any exception to the hearsay rule, it must be excluded. Hearsay is a statement, other than one made by the declarant while testifying at the trial or hearing, offered in evidence to prove the truth of the matter asserted. [Fed. R. Evid. 801(c)] Linda's out-of-court statement is being offered to prove the truth of the matter asserted therein, *i.e.,* that Linda used the turpentine to clean her paint brushes rather than to start fires. Linda is free to make that assertion as part of her in-court testimony, but cannot use her out-of-court statement for that purpose. Thus, the statement is hearsay. (A) would be correct if the prosecution had made a charge that Linda is lying or exaggerating about her explanation for the turpentine. A prior statement by a testifying witness is not hearsay if it is consistent with the declarant's in-court testimony and is offered to rebut a charge that the witness is lying or exaggerating because of some motive. Here, the prosecution has not charged that Linda has fabricated her explanation for the turpentine. Thus, Linda's out-of-court statement is not admissible as a prior consistent statement. It is true that, as (B) states, Linda's testimony tends to explain prosecution evidence. However, this does not provide a ground for the admission of hearsay. Thus, (B) is incorrect. (D) is incorrect because the fact that a statement is self-serving is not grounds for its exclusion. All of a criminal defendant's evidence can be considered self-serving in the sense that it furthers her claim of innocence.

Answer to Question 123

(B) Wally's testimony is admissible to help prove that Don owned the lot. Under Federal Rule 407, subsequent repairs or precautionary measures following an injury (such as cutting down rotten limbs after one fell) are not admissible if offered to prove that the defendant was negligent (*e.g.,* in not cutting down the limbs sooner). This rule of exclusion is to encourage people to make such repairs. The evidence may be admissible, however, if it is relevant to some other issue in the case, such as ownership or control. Since Don's defense is that he did not own the property, the evidence would help establish ownership. People do not usually make repairs to property for which they have no responsibility. (A) is wrong because, as discussed above, the evidence would be inadmissible to help establish negligence. (C) is incorrect because the evidence is not being offered to establish negligence; since it is offered only to show proof of ownership, it is admissible. (D) is wrong because it is not necessary that the evidence ***prove*** ownership. If the evidence ***would help establish*** ownership, it will be relevant.

Answer to Question 124

(B) Cyndy validly assigned her right to receive the money to Francis. However, this assignment was revocable, and it was revoked when Cyndy accepted the money from Debbie. Cyndy's right to receive the money from Debbie was a right that could be assigned. By telling Debbie to pay the money to Francis, Cyndy manifested an intent to transfer her rights completely and immediately to Francis. Neither a writing nor consideration was required for this assignment to be valid. However, these factors do affect revocability. This assignment was not given for consideration. Such a gratuitous assignment is generally revocable. Among the exceptions to this rule are situations where the obligor has already performed, or where the assignor is estopped from revoking by virtue of the fact that she should reasonably foresee that the assignee will change his position in reliance on the assignment and such detrimental reliance occurs. Here, Debbie (the obligor) has not already performed the terms of the assignment. On the contrary, Debbie tendered performance directly to the original obligee. Also, there is no indication that Francis in fact changed his position detrimentally in reliance on the assignment. Consequently, the general rule of revocability of a gratuitous assignment applies. One way in which a gratuitous revocable assignment may be terminated is by the assignor taking performance directly from the obligor. By accepting the money from Debbie, Cyndy (the assignor) took direct performance from the obligor, thereby revoking the assignment. As a result, Francis has no right to the money. (A) incorrectly fails to account for the fact that, although Cyndy effectively assigned her right, she later revoked this assignment. (C) is incorrect because Debbie was indebted to Francis while the assignment was in effect. Although Debbie did not herself incur the debt with Francis, a valid assignment that was not revoked would have obligated Debbie to pay Francis. (D) is incorrect because these facts do not indicate that there has been a novation. There is a novation where a new contract substitutes a new party to receive benefits and assume duties that had originally belonged to one of the original parties under the terms of the old contract. Here, the original agreement was between Debbie and Cyndy. Debbie's payment of the money to Cyndy and Cyndy's acceptance thereof did not substitute any new parties or extinguish contractual duties as between the original contracting parties. Thus, there was no novation.

Answer to Question 125

(A) Alan cannot enforce the contract for $4,000 if he had reason to know that $4,000 was too low a bid. When only one of the parties entering into a contract is mistaken about facts relating to the agreement, the nonmistaken party cannot "snap up" the offer if he knew or had reason to know of the mistake. Here, only Bert was mistaken as to the cost of the work; thus, there is a unilateral mistake. If Alan knew or had reason to know of the mistake, then he cannot enforce the contract under the erroneous price. (C) and (D) are incorrect because material effect and assumption of risk are elements of mutual mistake, where both parties entering into a contract are mistaken about the facts. That is not the case here. (B) is wrong because it is too broad. A unilateral mistake such as Bert's will not prevent formation of the contract if Alan had no reason to know that Bert had made an error.

Answer to Question 126

(A) Even if the jury believes that Darryl did not intend to hit George with the boomerang, Darryl can be found guilty of murder. Murder is the unlawful killing of a human being with malice aforethought. Malice aforethought exists if the defendant has any of the following states of mind: (i) intent to kill; (ii) intent to inflict great bodily injury; (iii) reckless indifference to an unjustifiably high risk to human life; or (iv) intent to commit a felony. Here, a jury could find that the act of throwing a heavy hunting boomerang at another person in a public park by someone unskilled in its use constituted a reckless disregard of a high risk of serious injury or death (*i.e.*, an "abandoned and malignant" heart). (B) is wrong because the facts do not support a conviction for voluntary manslaughter. An intentional killing is reduced from murder to voluntary manslaughter if it is committed under a provocation that would arouse sudden and intense passion in the mind of an ordinary person such as to cause him to lose self-control. Here, George merely yelled offensive words at Darryl. This will not be deemed to be adequate provocation so as to reduce an intentional killing to voluntary manslaughter. (C) is incorrect because it is possible for Darryl to be convicted of a more serious crime than involuntary manslaughter based on criminal negligence. Criminal negligence requires a substantial deviation from the standard of care that a reasonable person would exercise under the circumstances. While a jury could readily find that Darryl was guilty of involuntary manslaughter, it is not the ***most serious*** crime for which Darryl might be liable; a jury could also find that he had a sufficiently reckless indifference to a high risk to human life to make him liable for murder. (D) is incorrect because, as discussed above, Darryl could be found guilty of either murder or involuntary manslaughter. There are no causation issues regarding the death that would allow Darryl to avoid liability for the homicide.

Answer to Question 127

(B) The client's motion should be denied because the seizure of the marijuana was properly within the scope of the stop and frisk. A police officer may stop a person without probable cause for arrest if she has an articulable and reasonable suspicion of criminal activity. [Terry v. Ohio (1968)] In such circumstances, if the officer reasonably believes that the person may be armed and dangerous, she may conduct a protective frisk. The scope of the frisk is limited to a patdown of the outer clothing for concealed instruments of assault, but the officer may reach into the suspect's clothing and seize any item that the officer reasonably believes, based on its "plain feel," is a weapon ***or contraband.*** [Minnesota v. Dickerson (1993)] Here, the officer believed that the client put a weapon in his jacket as he was leaving a place where weapons and ammunition were being sold illegally; thus, she had reasonable grounds to conduct both a stop and a frisk. If the court accepts the officer's testimony that she instantly recognized the marijuana cigarettes ***based on the patdown only*** without any further conduct, they were properly seized and can be admitted into evidence. (A) is incorrect because the client was not under arrest at the time the patdown disclosed the marijuana. While the police may conduct a full search incident to a lawful arrest, they had only detained the client for purposes of an investigatory detention at the time of the seizure. (C) is incorrect because, as discussed above, a frisk for weapons also allows an officer to seize contraband if she immediately recognizes it as such. (D) is incorrect because the police did not need to rely on the search warrant to search the client; for the limited stop and frisk that occurred here, the police need only a reasonable suspicion of criminal activity and a reasonable belief that the suspect is armed and dangerous.

Answer to Question 128

(C) The client's motion should be denied because his constitutional rights were not violated by the search and seizure of the attorney's office based on an invalid warrant. To have a Fourth Amendment right to be free from unreasonable search and seizure, a person must have a reasonable expectation of privacy in the place searched or the item seized. Standing to challenge a search on Fourth Amendment grounds does not exist merely because a person will be harmed by introduction of evidence seized during an illegal search of a third person's property; the defendant's ***own*** expectation of privacy must be violated. Here, the client had no right of possession of the place searched and no property interest in the items seized; thus, he had no standing to object to the search of the attorney's office and the seizure of the records and money. (A) is incorrect because the client's motion should be denied regardless of the reasonableness of the police reliance on the search warrant. Under *United States v. Leon* (1984), a finding that a warrant was invalid because it was not supported by probable cause will not entitle a defendant to exclude the evidence obtained thereby if the police reasonably relied on a facially valid warrant. However, that determination does not need to be made with regard to the client because his constitutional rights were not violated by the defective warrant. (B) is incorrect because, as discussed above, the search was unlawful only with regard to the attorney's rights; the evidence may be used against the client because he had no expectation of privacy in the place searched. (D) is incorrect. While an exception to the exclusionary rule permits the admissibility of tainted evidence if the prosecution can show that the police would have inevitably discovered the evidence properly, there is nothing in the facts to support this exception. In any case, as discussed above, the exclusionary rule is not applicable because the client's Fourth Amendment rights were not violated by the search.

Answer to Question 129

(D) Turbo is bound to a year-to-year tenancy at $600 per month, which, absent six months' notice to terminate, will automatically renew on the following September 30. When a tenant continues in possession after the termination of his right to possession, the landlord may evict him or bind him to a new ***periodic*** tenancy. In a commercial lease, if the original lease term was for a year or more, a year-to-year tenancy results. If, prior to the termination of the original tenancy, the landlord notifies the tenant that occupancy after termination will be at increased rent, the tenant will be held to have acquiesced to the new terms if he does not surrender. A periodic tenancy is automatically renewed until proper notice is given. Proper notice for a year-to-year tenancy is six months' notice. In this case, Turbo's lease expired on September 30. Prior to that expiration, Blaze notified him that any continued tenancy would be at $600 per month. Thus, when Turbo remained in possession after September 30, Blaze could choose to hold him to a year-to-year tenancy (since the original term was five years) at $600 per month. Since the new tenancy is a periodic tenancy, it will be automatically renewed on the following September 30 unless one of the parties gives six months' notice of termination. (A) is wrong for two reasons: (i) the new tenancy is year-to-year, and (ii) the rent is $600 per month. (B) is wrong because the new tenancy is year-to-year, not month-to-month. (C) is wrong because Turbo had notice that if he stayed beyond September 30, the rent would be $600. Thus, Turbo is bound to the $600 rent. Note that Blaze's depositing of Turbo's check would not create an accord and satisfaction even though it was marked as rent payment. In addition to the requirement that a bona fide dispute must exist as to the amount owed, the check must conspicuously state that it is in full satisfaction of the debt before an accord and satisfaction can occur.

Answer to Question 130

(C) Because the federal legislation merely allows the district court to issue a "recommendation," the legislation permits the rendition of advisory opinions. Article III of the United States Constitution establishes the basis for the judicial power of federal courts. It provides that the judicial power extends to "cases and controversies." Although Congress has plenary power to delineate the jurisdictional limits of Article III courts, it is bound by the standards of judicial power set forth in Article III as to subject matter, parties, and the requirement of "case or controversy." Thus, Congress cannot require these courts to render advisory opinions or perform administrative or nonjudicial functions. The federal orange-marketing legislation at issue here does not give federal district courts the authority to render binding decisions in final resolution of a controversy. Rather, the legislation simply allows the courts to make a recommendation as to confirmation, modification, or rescission of a challenged marketing order. This recommendation is apparently nonbinding on the parties and is followed by a re-vote of the marketing council. These circumstances indicate that, under this federal legislation, an Article III federal court would be rendering an advisory opinion in violation of the Constitution. It is true that, as (A) states, the federal government may properly regulate items in interstate commerce. This commerce power permits congressional regulation of any activity, local or interstate, that either in itself or in combination with other activities has a substantial economic effect upon interstate commerce. This power would permit federal legislation of the marketing and sale of oranges. However, the validity of the legislation under the commerce power does not make it immune from constitutional challenge on other grounds. Because the legislation calls for the rendition of advisory opinions, it is unconstitutional. (B) is likewise incorrect, although it states a valid general proposition of law. Congress does possess auxiliary powers that are "necessary and proper" to carrying out all powers vested in the federal government. "Necessary and proper" includes anything that is appropriate to achieve a legitimate end, but a provision that violates a specific constitutional provision is not an "appropriate" means of achieving the end. Hence, the marketing order system is not valid under the Necessary and Proper Clause because it provides for advisory opinions. (D) is incorrect because Walter is not being deprived of property without due process. The facts do not indicate that Walter is without sufficient procedural safeguards to afford him protection against arbitrary governmental deprivation of his property. Fair procedure requires at least an opportunity to present objections to the proposed action to a fair, neutral decisionmaker. Walter could argue that he does not have the opportunity to object to a neutral decisionmaker, because the district court will not be rendering a "decision." However, this is a debatable proposition, whereas it is clear that the legislation allows for impermissible advisory opinions. Therefore, (C) is a better answer than (D).

Answer to Question 131

(B) Richard has standing to challenge the ordinance because his business will be harmed by the ordinance, and this will adversely affect his relationship with those who would buy and rent his equipment, resulting in an indirect violation of their rights. A person who challenges a government action must have standing to raise the constitutional issue. A person has standing only if he can demonstrate a concrete stake in the outcome of a controversy and that the governmental action at issue impairs his own rights. A plaintiff may assert third-party rights if he has suffered injury and that injury adversely affects his relationship with third parties, resulting in an indirect violation of their rights. Enforcement of the ordinance at issue will effectively destroy 70% of Richard's business. Thus, Richard is faced with an immediate and direct threat of injury to his livelihood as a result of the ordinance. This injury will adversely affect his relationship with those persons at the beach areas of Beachfront who would normally buy and rent his equipment, because they will now be prohibited from roller skating on the beaches between the hours of 7 a.m. and 9 p.m. This will, in turn, cause a potential violation of the rights of such third parties (*e.g.,* the law might violate their First Amendment right to join with other persons for expressive activity). Consequently, Richard is deemed to have standing to challenge the ordinance, and the court will reach the merits of the challenge. (A) is incorrect. The right to associate for expressive purposes is not absolute and generally does not encompass the right to secure patrons for one's business. Also, to the extent that the ordinance might interfere with the ***skaters'*** right of free association, that is an issue going to the merits of the challenge, which will not be reached until the matter of Richard's standing is resolved. (C) is incorrect because, although the ordinance does not prohibit Richard from renting skating equipment, it immediately and directly threatens his livelihood by prohibiting people who comprise 70% of his business from skating on public property during daytime hours. Hence, he will have standing to bring the challenge. (D) is incorrect because the facts stated in that choice are relevant only as a defense on the merits of the ordinance, rather than as factors on the issue of Richard's standing; they would not constitute grounds for the court to decline to hear the case.

Answer to Question 132

(B) The landowner can recover against the grocer and the florist jointly and severally for $10,000 and against the grocer and the barber jointly and severally for $10,000. If a tenant makes a complete transfer of the entire remaining term of his leasehold interest, he has made an assignment. In an assignment, the assignee and the landlord are in privity of estate, and each is liable to the other on all covenants in the lease that run with the land. Since the covenant to pay rent runs with the land, an assignee owes the rent directly to the landlord during the time that she is in privity of estate with the landlord. If the assignee reassigns the leasehold interest, her privity of estate with the landlord ends, and she is not liable for the subsequent assignee's failure to pay rent. Hence, the florist is liable to the landowner for the one year of rent while she was in privity of estate with her, but not for the year that the barber did not pay rent. The barber is liable for the one year of rent while he was in privity of estate with the landowner. The grocer continues to be liable for rent, even though he is no longer in privity of estate with the landowner, based on the contractual obligation in the lease to pay rent, *i.e.*, on privity of contract grounds. For each of the two years of rent, the two liable parties are jointly and severally liable for the rent because the landowner can choose to collect all of it from one party or some of it from one party and some from the other party. (A) is wrong because, as discussed above, the barber also is liable for the final year of rent payments because he was in privity of estate with the landowner. (C) is wrong because there is no basis for holding the florist liable for the second year that rent was not paid. She was not in privity of estate with the landowner at that time, and there is no indication that the florist specifically promised the landowner that she would be liable for the rent for the remainder of the lease term (which would have given the landowner a privity of contract basis for holding the florist liable). Also, the facts indicate that there was no specific promise in the agreement between the grocer and the florist regarding payment of rent, so the landowner has no third-party beneficiary grounds to sue the florist for the second year of rent. (D) is wrong because it states the result if the barber had only obtained a sublease from the florist rather than an assignment. If that were the case, the florist rather than the barber would be liable for the second year of rent because the barber would be in neither privity of contract nor privity of estate with the landowner. However, since the florist retained no part of the remaining term when she transferred her interest to the barber, the transfer was an assignment rather than a sublease, and the barber rather than the florist is in privity of estate for that period.

Answer to Question 133

(A) If Hank prevails, it will be because Bobby did not conform to the standard of care of a child of like age, education, intelligence, and experience. When the tortfeasor is a child, the standard of care generally imposed by the courts in negligence actions is that of a child of like age, education, intelligence, and experience. This permits a subjective evaluation of these factors. If Bobby failed to act according to the standard of care of a 12-year-old child who had flown model airplanes before, he has breached his duty to Hank, who was a foreseeable plaintiff because his car was parked nearby. This breach was the actual and proximate cause of damages to Hank's car, completing the prima facie case for negligence. (B) is incorrect because it applies the adult reasonable person standard; this standard has been applied to children only when they are engaged in activities that normally only adults engage in, such as driving an automobile or piloting an actual airplane. (C) is incorrect because the warning in the instruction manual may be a factor in establishing whether Bobby breached the standard of care applicable to him, but it is not determinative. Even if the instruction manual were silent about flying the airplane in the rain, Bobby may have been negligent by continuing to fly it when he had trouble controlling it. (D) is incorrect because trespass to chattels requires an intent to do the act that causes the damage to another's chattels. Bobby did not intend to fly the airplane at Hank's car; hence, he is liable only if he acted negligently.

Answer to Question 134

(A) Both Aaron and Sean are guilty of conspiracy. At common law, a conspiracy was an agreement between two or more persons to commit an unlawful act or to commit a lawful act in an unlawful manner. The elements are (i) an agreement between two or more persons, (ii) an intent to enter into an agreement, and (iii) an intent to achieve the objective of the agreement. When Aaron and Sean decided to kidnap Byrd, they were guilty of common law conspiracy. (While a majority of states now require an overt act in furtherance of the conspiracy, mere preparation, such as the surveillance here, will suffice.) (B) is wrong for two reasons. If a person withdraws from a conspiracy, he is no longer liable for future crimes committed in furtherance of the conspiracy, but he remains liable for the crime of conspiracy, which was complete at the time of the agreement. Second, to have a successful withdrawal, a person must communicate the withdrawal to his co-conspirators, which Sean did not do. Choice (C) is also wrong for two reasons. First, Sean is still liable for conspiracy. Second, even if his withdrawal relieved him from liability for subsequent offenses, Aaron could still be convicted of conspiracy. Answer (D) is wrong because, at common law, both parties must have the intent, at the time of the agreement, to commit the unlawful act. Since Ralph did not have the necessary intent, neither he nor Aaron can be convicted of conspiracy with respect to their conversations.

Answer to Question 135

(A) The most accurate statement is that Aaron will be found guilty of attempted kidnapping. Attempt requires a specific intent to commit the crime and an act beyond mere preparation in furtherance of the crime. The Model Penal Code and most state criminal codes require that the act or omission constitute a substantial step in a course of conduct planned to culminate in the commission of the crime. In addition, an act will not qualify as a substantial step unless it is strong corroboration of the actor's criminal purpose. Here, Aaron had the specific intent to commit a kidnapping, and took a substantial step toward committing the offense by paying Ralph to disable the security system, an act that strongly corroborates his intent. Hence, he can be found guilty of attempted kidnapping. (B) is incorrect because the conspiracy does not automatically result in attempt liability. For attempt, specific intent and a substantial step corroborative of intent must be established. Furthermore, under the modern (Model Penal Code) rules for attempt, Sean can raise withdrawal (renunciation) as a defense to attempt, because he voluntarily and completely abandoned his efforts to commit the crime (and took steps to prevent its commission) as a result of his "change of heart." (C) is incorrect because Ralph's response to Aaron is irrelevant for attempt. Because Aaron had the requisite intent and took a substantial step towards committing the offense by contacting Ralph, Aaron can be found guilty of attempted kidnapping. (D) is incorrect. Aaron and Sean did have the mental state necessary for attempt because they had the specific intent to kidnap Byrd.

Answer to Question 136

(B) The homeowner prevails because the painter gave no consideration for the purported modification of the contract. Terms of a contract may be modified by the parties to the contract. However, consideration generally is necessary to modify a contract (in other words, the modification must have a bargained-for exchange with some element of legal value to the parties). Where a modification would operate to the benefit of only one of the parties, it will be unenforceable unless some consideration is being given to the other party. Under the preexisting legal duty rule, the promise to perform or the performance of an existing legal duty will not be sufficient consideration. Here, the homeowner and the painter have attempted to modify their contract so that the homeowner will pay the extra $600. Because this modification would work to the painter's benefit only, it is unenforceable unless the painter has given some consideration to the homeowner for the modification. The painter was already under a binding contract to repaint the homeowner's house for $8,000. Thus, the painter's performance of a duty that he was already obligated to perform does not constitute sufficient consideration to support the modification. Consequently, the homeowner is obligated to pay only the originally agreed-upon $8,000. (A) is incorrect, because the homeowner's promise to pay the additional money need not be in writing to be enforceable. Under the Statute of Frauds, a writing signed by the party sought to be bound is required for: (i) a promise by an executor or administrator to pay the estate's debts out of her own funds; (ii) a promise to answer for the debt of another; (iii) a promise made in consideration of marriage; (iv) a promise creating an interest in land; (v) a promise that by its terms cannot be performed within one year; and (vi) a promise for the sale of goods of $500 or more. Because the homeowner's promise does not come within any of these categories, it need not be in writing. (C) is incorrect because, in repainting the homeowner's house, the painter was simply fulfilling his contractual obligation, rather than acting to his detriment in reliance on the homeowner's promise to pay the additional money. Even if unsupported by consideration, a promise is enforceable under the promissory estoppel doctrine to the extent necessary to prevent injustice if: (i) the promisor should reasonably expect to induce action or forbearance of a definite and substantial character; and (ii) such action or forbearance is in fact induced. The painter was legally bound to perform the work on the homeowner's house regardless of whether the homeowner agreed to pay the extra $600. Thus, it cannot be said that the painter incurred a detriment in reliance on the homeowner's promise. (D) is incorrect because there was no good faith dispute between the parties. An exception to the preexisting legal duty rule provides that, if the scope of the legal duty owed is the subject of honest dispute, a modifying agreement relating to it will be given effect. Here, the parties' legal duties were clearly specified: The painter was to repaint the homeowner's house, and the homeowner was to pay $8,000. There is no indication that the painter believed in good faith that he had legal grounds for avoiding the original contract because he could not otherwise make a profit. Therefore, the homeowner's promise to pay the extra money was not the settlement of a good faith dispute.

Answer to Question 137

(D) As an expert witness, the engineer may base her opinion on facts not in evidence that were supplied to her out of court, and that are of a type reasonably relied upon by experts in that particular field in forming opinions on the subject. In this case, expert testimony is admissible because its subject matter (*i.e.*, whether the closures caused the deflation panel to give way) is one where specialized knowledge will assist the trier of fact in determining a fact in issue. A structural engineer possesses the special knowledge and training sufficient to qualify her as an expert. An expert may base her opinion on facts not known personally but supplied to her outside the courtroom (*e.g.*, reports of technicians or consultants). Such facts need not be in evidence or even of a type admissible in evidence as long as they are of a kind reasonably relied upon by experts in the particular field. [Fed. R. Evid. 703] Consequently, if structural engineers reasonably rely on laboratory reports such as those at issue here, the engineer's testimony based on these reports should be admitted. (A) is incorrect because, as noted above, the engineer may base her opinion on facts not known personally to her. Thus, the admissibility of the engineer's testimony does not require that she have personally performed the tests on which the lab reports are based. (B) is incorrect because the facts upon which the engineer bases her opinion need not be of a type admissible in evidence. Thus, although the lab reports might be inadmissible hearsay, the engineer may base her testimony on them. (C) is incorrect because the engineer may base her opinion on facts that are not in evidence. Furthermore, while the engineer may be required to disclose the underlying facts on cross-examination, they may not be disclosed to the jury on the balloonist's direct examination unless the court determines that their probative value in assisting the jury evaluate the expert's opinion substantially outweighs their prejudicial effect.

Answer to Question 138

(B) Testimony as to the date of purchase of the panels should not be admitted because its minimal relevance is substantially outweighed by considerations of waste of time and confusion of the issues under Rule 403. Whether the balloonist actually purchased the deflation panels one week sooner than the date testified to by him has no bearing on the cause of the balloon's rapid descent, which is the issue in controversy. The only relevance of the clerk's testimony is to cast doubt on the balloonist's credibility, but it is not admissible for impeachment purposes either. When a witness makes a statement not directly relevant to the issues in the case, the rule against impeachment on a collateral matter bars his opponent from proving the statement untrue either by extrinsic evidence or by a prior inconsistent statement. As noted previously, the balloonist's statement as to the date on which he purchased the panels is not directly relevant to any other issue in the case. Thus, the manufacturer is not permitted to prove the statement untrue by means of the clerk's testimony that the balloonist made the purchase on a different day. (D) is incorrect even though it is true that the clerk's testimony tends to prove that the balloonist purchased the panels on a date other than that to which he testified. As detailed above, the limited relevance of the date for impeachment purposes is outweighed by considerations of waste of time and confusion of issues. (A) is incorrect because the clerk is not testifying to the content of the purchase order. Rather, she is simply testifying to the date of purchase from her own memory. Thus, the hearsay nature of the contents of the purchase order is not at issue. (C) is incorrect. Under the past recollection recorded exception to the hearsay rule, where a witness states that she has insufficient recollection of an event to enable her to testify fully and accurately, even after she has consulted a writing given to her on the stand, the writing itself may be introduced into evidence if: (i) the witness at one time had personal knowledge of the facts recited in the writing; (ii) the writing was timely made when the matter was fresh in the witness's mind; (iii) the writing was made by the witness or under her direction or adopted by her; and (iv) the witness is presently unable to remember the facts. Here, the clerk has not stated that she has insufficient recollection of the events to which she is testifying, and the manufacturer is not even attempting to introduce the purchase order into evidence. She is fully able to testify as to the date on which the balloonist purchased the panels, and is simply referring to the purchase order because of having seen the balloonist's unusual signature on it. Thus, the purchase order does not constitute a past recollection recorded.

Answer to Question 139

(B) Verdi has ownership of Lawnacre because he has exercised his power to terminate Tract's fee simple subject to condition subsequent in Lawnacre. A fee simple subject to a condition subsequent is created when the grantor retains the power to terminate the estate of the grantee on the happening of a specified event. On the happening of that event, the estate of the grantee continues until the grantor exercises her power of termination (right of entry) by bringing suit or making reentry. Here, Overhill conveyed a fee simple subject to a restriction against constructing multi-family dwellings, retaining a right of entry. She devised this interest to Verdi in her will, as the statute permitted, and Verdi exercised this right by bringing an ejectment action against Tract after the condition was violated. Hence, Verdi will have ownership of Lawnacre. (A) is not as good a choice as (B) because Tract's interest in Lawnacre was not automatically terminated once he violated the condition; it continued until Verdi took action to terminate it. Absent Verdi bringing an ejectment action, Tract would have superior rights in Lawnacre. (C) is incorrect because the Rule Against Perpetuities does not apply to a right of entry. A right of entry is a reversionary interest of the transferor, which is not subject to the Rule Against Perpetuities because it is vested. It retains its status as a reversionary interest even when it is transferred to a third party. Thus, Verdi had the power to exercise the right of entry. (D) is incorrect because the transaction was a valid conveyance of a defeasible fee simple. Restraints on alienation refer to restrictions in transferring property to others. There was nothing in the conveyance preventing Tract from transferring his interest to a third party. The restriction on the use of the property was a valid condition subsequent.

Answer to Question 140

(C) The testimony of the witness is inadmissible because it does not tend to prove or disprove any trait of the defendant's that is involved in the case. To be admissible, evidence must be relevant, *i.e.,* it must have some tendency to make the existence of any fact that is of consequence to the determination of an action more probable than it would be without the evidence. In a criminal case, the prosecution cannot initiate evidence of the bad character of the defendant merely to show that he is more likely to have committed the crime of which he is accused. However, the defendant may introduce evidence of his good character to show his innocence of the alleged crime. [Fed. R. Evid. 404(a)(1)] This is done by calling a qualified witness to testify to the defendant's good reputation for ***the trait involved in the case,*** or to give his personal opinion concerning that trait. [Fed. R. Evid. 405] The defendant is charged with assault with a deadly weapon. There is no indication that the defendant's honesty is at issue; rather, any traits of violence are at issue and are pertinent to the crime of which the defendant is accused. Because the testimony of the witness relates to the defendant's honesty, which is of no consequence to the determination of this criminal proceeding, such testimony is inadmissible as being irrelevant. (A) is incorrect because reputation evidence is not always admissible to establish a character trait. The trait sought to be established must be pertinent to the crime that is charged. (B) is incorrect because only the criminal defendant can put his character in issue. The prosecution cannot initiate evidence of the defendant's character, and the mere filing of criminal charges against a person does not put that person's character in issue. (D) is incorrect because reputation of a person's character in the community is an exception to the hearsay rule. [Fed. R. Evid. 803(21)] Thus, the evidence offered here would not be excluded on the ground that it is inadmissible hearsay.

Answer to Question 141

(B) The court will allow the historian to testify as to the identity of the voice simply because he is familiar with the uncle's voice. Where the identity of a speaker is important, the oral statements require authentication as to the identity of the speaker. A voice, whether heard firsthand or through tape recording, may be identified by the opinion of anyone who has heard the voice at any time. As long as such a foundation is laid to show familiarity with the voice, a lay opinion as to the identity of the speaker is permissible. Thus, because the historian became familiar with the uncle's voice when he made the tape recording, he will be permitted to testify that the voice on the tape was the uncle's. (A) is incorrect because, even assuming that the uncle is a party opponent, the historian is only testifying as to the identity of the speaker rather than any admissions that the uncle may have made. (C) is incorrect because, in contrast to the rule for handwriting verification, a person can become familiar with a voice after litigation has begun and for the sole purpose of testifying. Hence, the fact that the historian became familiar with the uncle's voice before the dispute arose is not critical to admissibility of his testimony. (D) is wrong because expert testimony is not required for identifying a voice on a tape recording. Because the historian's testimony is based on his previous familiarity with the uncle's voice and is needed to authenticate the tape recording, it will be admissible as opinion testimony under Federal Rule 701.

Answer to Question 142

(C) No contract was created because Multistate effectively revoked its offer. Under the U.C.C., an offer by a merchant to buy or sell goods in a signed writing that, by its terms, gives assurances that it will be held open is not revocable for lack of consideration during the time stated (not to exceed three months). If the term assuring that the offer will be held open is on a form supplied by the offeree, it must be separately signed by the offeror. Here, the school district supplied the form stating that the offer must be held open for four months. Smith's verbal assent to that requirement was not sufficient to qualify as a firm offer under the U.C.C. Thus, Smith was free to revoke his offer. (A) is wrong because the fact that a writing would not be required under the Statute of Frauds if a contract had been formed between the parties is irrelevant. A writing is required for a firm offer under the U.C.C. regardless of the value of the goods offered. (B) is incorrect because the school district lost its power of acceptance when Smith revoked the Multistate offer, regardless of the fact that three months had not passed. As discussed above, Multistate's offer did not constitute a firm offer under the U.C.C. (D) is incorrect because the fact that the term of the firm offer was more than three months does not invalidate it. If the stated period extends beyond three months, the firm offer will stand, but it will only last for the three-month maximum.

Answer to Question 143

(A) Dawson's motion should be denied as to the cocaine. As a general matter, to conduct a constitutionally valid search, the police must have a search warrant based on probable cause unless the case falls under one of the exceptions to the warrant requirement. One well-established exception to the warrant requirement is the automobile exception. If the police have probable cause to believe that an automobile contains contraband or evidence of a crime, they may search whatever area of the car that may contain the object of their search without having to get a warrant. Probable cause to search is defined as reasonable grounds for believing that a particular item of seizure is located at a particular place. From the facts given, the police clearly had reasonable grounds to believe that cocaine was in the trunk of the car. (B) is wrong. If the police make a valid arrest of the driver of the car, they can search the area within the immediate control of the driver as a search incident to an arrest. The area within the control of the driver would include the entire passenger area of the car, but not the trunk. The trunk cannot be searched as a search incident to an arrest. (C) is no longer the law. At one time, the officers were required to secure the closed container and then obtain a warrant. Under present law, the police can open the package if they have probable cause. (D) is wrong. Actual knowledge that it is the same package is not required. Probable cause—reasonable grounds to believe—is the criteria.

Answer to Question 144

(B) Dawson's motion should be denied as to the marijuana. A well-recognized exception to the general requirement of a search warrant is a search incident to a lawful arrest. If the police make a valid arrest of the driver of the car, they can conduct a warrantless search of the entire passenger compartment of the car as a search incident to the arrest. A valid arrest requires probable cause to arrest—reasonable grounds to believe that the person being arrested has committed a crime—but does not require an arrest warrant. From the facts given, the police had plenty of probable cause to arrest Dawson. Therefore, the search of the back seat where the marijuana was found was valid. (A) is too broad a statement. When the police stopped the car, they had probable cause to search the trunk and could search the trunk under the automobile exception without a warrant. They did not have probable cause to search the back seat. (C) is wrong. Even though the police did not have probable cause to search the back seat, it could be searched as a search incident to an arrest. (D) is wrong. Even after the driver has been arrested, the search incident to an arrest can take place.

Answer to Question 145

(D) Donna is not entitled to specific performance because she is unable to furnish Ed with such title to Whiteacre as to eliminate a reasonable probability that Ed will be subjected to a lawsuit.

Absent a provision to the contrary, a contract for the sale of land contains an implied promise by the seller that she will deliver to the buyer a marketable title at the time of closing. This promise imposes on the seller an obligation to deliver a title that is free from reasonable doubt; *i.e.,* free from questions that might present an unreasonable risk of litigation. Title is marketable if a reasonably prudent buyer would accept it in the exercise of ordinary prudence. An inability to establish a record chain of title will generally render the title unmarketable. If the buyer determines, prior to closing, that the seller's title is unmarketable, he must notify the seller and allow a reasonable time to cure the defect. If the seller is unable to acquire title before closing, so that title remains unmarketable, the buyer can rescind, sue for damages caused by breach, or obtain specific performance with an abatement of the purchase price. Here, the title search report fails to indicate how title to Whiteacre left Belle and was conveyed to Cornelius. This in turn indicates that some records are missing from the report. The fact that records are missing would create in a reasonably prudent buyer a doubt as to the probability of being subjected to a lawsuit by, *e.g.,* Belle or someone else who might claim rightful title to Whiteacre on the basis of Cornelius's conveyance to Donna being fraudulent or otherwise invalid. Consequently, Donna's title to Whiteacre was unmarketable. It is Donna's inability to make good her title by the closing date that permits Ed to rescind the contract and prevents Donna from being able to specifically enforce the contract. It is true that, as (C) states, there is a gap in the title. However, this gap does not by itself render title unmarketable. Rather, it is Donna's inability to establish a record chain of title or otherwise satisfactorily explain the gap by the closing date, after being notified of it, that renders title unmarketable. Therefore, (C) is not as good an answer as (D). It is also true that, as (A) states, the uniqueness of land makes it a proper subject for specific performance. However, as explained above, Donna's breach of her promise to deliver marketable title prevents her from specifically enforcing the contract, and permits Ed to rescind it. Thus, (A) is incorrect. (B) is also incorrect. Because Donna took title from Cornelius by warranty deed, she has received some assurance either that Cornelius had the authority to make the conveyance or that he will defend on her behalf against any lawful claims of title by a third party. However, even if such protections were extended to Ed (as Donna's transferee), title would still be unmarketable. Ed is not required to "buy a lawsuit," even if his ultimate success on the merits of such a suit seems likely.

Answer to Question 146

(A) The court will likely find the legislation to be a constitutional regulation of obscenity. Obscenity, which is not protected speech under the First Amendment, is defined by the Supreme Court as a description or depiction of sexual conduct that, taken as a whole, by the average person, applying contemporary community standards, appeals to the prurient interest in sex, portrays sex in a patently offensive way, and—using a national reasonable person standard—does not have serious literary, artistic, political, or scientific value. Thus, the legislation here is constitutional because it uses a reasonable person standard, rather than a community standard, for determining the value of the work. (B) is incorrect because while a statewide standard for determining whether the material is patently offensive is permissible, it is not mandatory. A state may use a "community standard" for making this determination. (C) is incorrect because, again, a statewide standard for determining whether the material is patently offensive is permissible. Only the "social value" element of the obscenity test requires a national standard. (D) is incorrect because the legislation is valid regardless of whether it is necessary to achieve the state's compelling interest in reducing violent crime. Speech that falls within the definition of obscenity is unprotected speech; the government does not need a specific compelling interest to ban it.

Answer to Question 147

(B) Because time was of the essence in the contract, the builder's tardiness in delivering the deed and certificate of completion was a material breach, thus excusing the buyer from her duty of performance. When a promisor is under an absolute duty to perform, and this duty has not been discharged, the failure to perform in accordance with the contract will constitute a breach of the contract. A minor breach (where the obligee gains the substantial benefit of her bargain despite the breach) affords a remedy to the aggrieved party but does not relieve her of her duty of performance under the contract. If the breach is material, the nonbreaching party may treat the contract as at an end (*i.e.,* any duty of counterperformance owed by her is discharged) and will have an immediate right to all remedies for breach of the entire contract. Generally, failure of a promisor to render timely performance, although a breach, will not be material. However, where the contract by its terms provides that time is of the essence, failure of timely performance will be a material breach. The contract between the buyer and the builder contained a clause stating that time was of the essence. Thus, when the builder failed to deliver the deed and certificate on time, as per his contractual duties, this failure constituted a material breach. Because the breach is material, the buyer may treat the contract as at an end, and the duty owed by her to pay the agreed-upon purchase price is discharged. Therefore, the builder will recover nothing. (C) is incorrect because, where time is of the essence, the shortness of the delay in performing will not render the breach minor. (D) is incorrect because, as explained above, the material breach by the builder discharges the buyer's duty of counterperformance. Therefore, even if the buyer suffered no damages as a result of the delay, she may treat the contract as ended, and the builder can recover nothing from her. (A) is incorrect because there is no indication that preparing a certificate of completion requires that degree of personal judgment and skill as to make the duty nondelegable, nor is there any indication that the buyer even contracted for a specific architect to prepare the certificate.

Answer to Question 148

(C) Under Article 2 of the U.C.C., an offer to buy goods for current or prompt shipment is construed as inviting acceptance either by a promise to ship or by current or prompt shipment of conforming or nonconforming goods. While shipment of nonconforming goods ordinarily is an acceptance creating a bilateral contract as well as a breach of that contract, the result is different if the seller seasonably notifies the buyer that a shipment of nonconforming goods is offered only as an accommodation to the buyer. In that case, the shipment is a counteroffer rather than an acceptance, and the buyer is free to accept or reject it, as stated by choice (C). Choices (A) and (B) are wrong because Bylon does not have any damage claim against Seltex, because its shipment of the gloves was a counteroffer rather than an acceptance and breach, and Bylon has the option to accept the offer on its terms or reject it, in which case no contract would be formed. (D) is incorrect because, as discussed above, the shipment of the gloves did not constitute an attempted acceptance and performance of Bylon's offer but rather a counteroffer by Seltex. Bylon did not have the power to accept only part of the goods.

Answer to Question 149

(C) The document at issue here expressed clearly Marty's agreement to grant to Howard the right of first refusal, exercisable within 45 days of any proposed transfer of ownership, which would include a transfer by will at his death. This agreement was supported by valuable consideration. Thus, the document creates in Howard a valid and enforceable interest. The only real question as to the validity of the document is whether it creates an unreasonable restraint on alienation. Generally, restrictions on the transferability of a legal interest in property are void. However, courts tend to uphold reasonable restrictions on transferability that arise in commercial transactions, because such restrictions appear in an agreement entered into by the parties, they are products of the parties' bargaining, and they serve a useful purpose in facilitating the parties' objectives. Marty's promise to grant Howard a right of first refusal may be considered a promissory restraint, in that any attempted transfer to anyone in derogation of Howard's right of first refusal breaches a promise, giving Howard a right of action against Marty or his estate. However, the restriction arose out of the brothers' commercial transactions with each other. These restrictions appear in agreements freely entered into by Howard and Marty, are products of their bargaining, and serve the useful purpose of facilitating the brothers' objective of seeing that their successful farming business would not be broken up by the death of either of them. In addition, the restrictions appear to contemplate that the party exercising the right must pay the price offered by a third party—here, the proposed contract price. Thus, a court would probably uphold the validity of the document. (A) is incorrect even though courts treat a right of first refusal as a contingent future interest that is subject to the Rule Against Perpetuities. Here, the interest of Howard and his heirs and assigns must be exercised, if at all, within 45 days after Marty (a life in being at the creation of the interest) has proposed a transfer of the property. This follows from the fact that the agreement refers to a sale or transfer "by me" (the party granting the right). Hence, the right would not exist if a transfer were proposed by the heirs or successors of the grantor, and is inherently limited in duration to 45 days after the grantor's death. (B) is incorrect because, as discussed above, a right of first refusal in a bargained-for agreement at a fair price is viewed as a reasonable restraint by the courts. (D) is incorrect because recordation of the document has no bearing on its validity as to Marty's children. Recording statutes protect only subsequent bona fide purchasers. Donees, heirs, and devisees are not protected because they do not give value for their interests.

Answer to Question 150

(B) Harry will have a fee simple determinable and Remus will have a possibility of reverter on Oscar's death. A fee simple determinable is an estate that automatically terminates on the happening of a stated event and goes back to the grantor. The interest that is left in a grantor who conveys a fee simple determinable is a possibility of reverter, which arises automatically in the grantor and can be devised by will in almost all jurisdictions. Here, Harry has a fee simple that is subject to automatic termination if dogs are no longer kept on the property. As discussed below, the ASPCA's interest is stricken because it violates the Rule Against Perpetuities. This leaves a possibility of reverter in Remus as Oscar's residuary devisee. (A) is incorrect because Harry's interest is a fee simple determinable (because it has "so long as" as part of the conveyance) that terminates automatically when the event occurs. In contrast, a fee simple subject to a condition subsequent is created when the grantor retains the power to terminate the estate (the right of entry) on the happening of a stated event, but the estate continues until the grantor exercises the power. (C) is wrong because the ASPCA's interest, if it were valid, would be an executory interest rather than a remainder. A remainder is a future interest that is capable of taking possession on the natural termination of the preceding estates created in the same disposition. Under modern law, this means that a remainder must always follow a life estate. If the present interest is a defeasible fee that has potentially infinite duration but can be cut short by the happening of a stated event, as in this question, the future interest created in a third party must be an executory interest. (D) is incorrect because the ASPCA's interest is void under the Rule Against Perpetuities and is stricken; the charity-to-charity exception to the Rule does not apply. The Rule Against Perpetuities provides that no interest in property is valid unless it must vest, if at all, not later than 21 years after one or more lives in being at the creation of the interest. It applies to executory interests created in third persons but not to reversionary interests of the grantor. Like any other gift, a gift for charitable purposes is void for remoteness if it is contingent on the happening of an event that may not occur within the perpetuity period. The only exception is when there is a gift to one charity followed by a gift over to another charity upon a possibly remote event (the charity-to-charity exception). Here, the first gift is to an individual and the gift over (a shifting executory interest) is to a charity; because the triggering event that will transfer the property (no dogs kept on the property) ***may*** occur more than 21 years after lives in being at the creation of the interest, the interest is stricken under the Rule Against Perpetuities.

Answer to Question 151

(C) The most likely basis for finding the waiting provision unconstitutional is that it improperly discriminates against Partridge's exercise of her fundamental right of interstate travel. An individual has a fundamental right to travel from state to state, and a state law that is designed to deter persons from moving into the state is likely to violate the Equal Protection Clause. When a state uses a durational residency requirement (a waiting period) for dispensing benefits, that requirement normally should be subject to the strict scrutiny test and will be found not to have satisfied that test. One such requirement that has been invalidated on this basis is a one-year waiting period for state-subsidized medical care. [Memorial Hospital v. Maricopa County (1974)] Thus, the most likely basis for Partridge to prevail is stated in choice (C). Choice (A) is not correct because the validity of state residency requirements will not depend on whether they have some theoretical rational relationship to an arguably legitimate end of government. Because a fundamental right is burdened, a higher standard of review is employed. (B) is wrong because the privileges and immunities protection of Article IV prohibits discrimination by a state against nonresidents when fundamental national rights are involved. Here, Partridge is a resident of the state whose legislation she is challenging; hence, the Equal Protection Clause will be the basis of her challenge. (D) is incorrect because a property interest entitled to protection under the Due Process Clause requires more than an abstract need or desire for the benefit. Here, the state is not attempting to take away from Partridge, without due process of law, a right for which she has already qualified; it is simply providing that the group to which she belongs (recent residents) is not entitled to certain benefits that are granted to other residents.

Answer to Question 152

(B) To recover in an action for indemnity, the owner must show that the manufacturer breached a duty that caused the injuries to the motorist and the other driver. Indemnity involves shifting the entire loss between tortfeasors. One of the circumstances in which indemnity is available occurs where one joint tortfeasor recovers against a co-joint tortfeasor due to a considerable difference in degree of fault. Where the tortfeasor is a retailer or user of a product who negligently failed to discover or guard against a product's defect, he can receive indemnification from the manufacturer who was liable for the defect on either a negligence or a strict liability theory. Here, if the claims of the motorist and the other driver against the owner are valid, then the owner must have been negligent in allowing the mower to reach the street. However, if the mower clutch engaged due to some defect in manufacture, then the manufacturer would be a joint tortfeasor. In such an instance, the manufacturer's conduct, either in negligently manufacturing the mower or in placing into commerce a mower that was so defective as to be unreasonably dangerous, actually and proximately caused the injuries suffered by the motorist and the other driver. Such wrongful conduct on the part of the manufacturer is considerably more culpable than that of the owner, who apparently was merely careless in losing control of the mower. Consequently, under these circumstances, the owner is entitled to indemnity from the manufacturer, which is the "more wrongful" tortfeasor. (A) is incorrect, because the age of the mower is not controlling. If it is shown that the clutch engaged because of some wrongful conduct by the manufacturer (such as a defect in manufacturing or design), the manufacturer will be considered a joint tortfeasor with the owner, despite the fact that it may have taken 15 years for the defect to show up. (C) is incorrect because, as explained above, the owner is entitled to indemnity if his negligence is appreciably less than any wrongful conduct by the manufacturer. Thus, the owner's recovery of indemnity is not dependent on a finding that he was not negligent. (D) is an incorrect statement of the law. A manufacturer is not strictly liable for all damages caused by its product. It must have breached its strict duty by producing a product that is so defective as to be unreasonably dangerous. (D) omits the requirement of a defect.

Answer to Question 153

(D) If a reasonable person under the circumstances would have restrained the mower before it entered the street, then the owner's failure to do so constitutes a breach of his duty of care, and this breach of duty caused the motorist's injuries and property damage. A prima facie case for negligence consists of: (i) a duty on the part of the defendant to conform to a specific standard of conduct for the protection of the plaintiff against an unreasonable risk of injury; (ii) breach of that duty by the defendant; (iii) such breach was the actual and proximate cause of the plaintiff's injury; and (iv) damage to the plaintiff's person or property. If a defendant's conduct creates a foreseeable risk of injury to persons in the position of the plaintiff, then the defendant's general duty of care is owed to the plaintiff. By failing to restrain the mower before it entered the street, the owner created a risk of injury to persons such as the motorist who might happen to be driving by at the time. If a reasonable person under the circumstances would have restrained the mower before it entered the street, then the owner breached his duty to the motorist (a foreseeable plaintiff) by allowing the mower to reach the street. This breach actually and proximately caused the motorist's personal injuries and property damage, because the sudden presence of the owner and the mower in the street caused the motorist to swerve violently and to strike another car. Thus, under the assumption stated in choice (D), the motorist will recover from the owner for her injuries and property damage. (A) is incorrect because, if a reasonable person would have restrained the mower despite being startled by the circumstances, the fact that the owner was startled by the mower's sudden movement will not preclude his being held liable. (B) is incorrect because the owner may be found liable for negligence in failing to restrain the mower, even if he was not negligent in maintaining the mower. (C) is incorrect for two reasons, regardless of what theory of liability the motorist is using against the owner: If she is using a strict liability theory against the owner, he will not be liable because strict liability requires that a defendant be a commercial supplier of the product in question. The owner is not a commercial supplier of the mower, but is merely someone who purchased it. The owner cannot be held strictly liable for damages caused by a defective product where he was not involved in the manufacture or commercial distribution of that product. If the motorist is alleging instead that the owner is liable on a negligence theory, she must prove that the owner knew or should have known of the defect and was therefore negligent in operating the mower while it was in such a defective condition. Merely showing the defective condition of the mower, without more, will not suffice to impose liability on the owner.

Answer to Question 154

(B) The President is empowered by the Constitution to grant reprieves and pardons for offenses against the United States, except in cases of impeachment. Here, the President seeks to pardon a person who has been convicted of a violent crime in a state. Thus, the President's pardon power does not extend to this prisoner, and the state will not be compelled to release him. (A) is incorrect because, pursuant to the Supremacy Clause of the Constitution, the Constitution, laws, and treaties of the United States take precedence over state laws. Any state law that is inconsistent with federal law will be superseded by the federal law. Although a state official may be acting pursuant to his state's constitution, that constitution may be in conflict with the United States Constitution or with other federal law. In such an instance, the state official will be required to abide by proper directives of a federal official issued in furtherance of the enforcement and execution of federal law. (C) is incorrect. As noted above, the President does have the power to pardon those convicted of federal offenses. Thus, an attempted pardon of a federal offender does not violate the President's sworn duty to see that the laws of the United States are faithfully executed; *i.e.,* the President is not "subverting" the law by issuing a pardon. It is in issuing a pardon for a crime that falls outside the scope of his pardon power that the President runs afoul of the Constitution. (D) is incorrect because the President's treaty power does not authorize his actions here. Although the Constitution gives the President the power to make treaties, he is not given the authority to use unconstitutional means to facilitate the making of a treaty. The President is acting here with the goal of advancing negotiations on a critical treaty. However, in doing so, the President may not disregard the Constitution by issuing a pardon that is outside the limits of his constitutionally derived pardon power.

Answer to Question 155

(B) The state has the burden of proving that the program is substantially related to an important government interest. When analyzing government action based on gender, the courts will apply an intermediate standard of review and strike the legislation unless it is substantially related to an important government interest. In these cases, the government bears the burden of proving this substantial relationship. Here, because the formula used to calculate termination of pension benefits depended on whether the surviving spouse was male or female, the legislation discriminates on the basis of gender. Thus, an intermediate scrutiny standard will be applied. (A) is wrong because the court will not apply the strict scrutiny standard in this case. A suspect class is not involved, and the program does not improperly burden a fundamental right. While marriage is a fundamental right, strict scrutiny applies only to legislation that directly and substantially interferes with the right to marry. Laws terminating certain benefits upon marriage do not directly and significantly interfere with that right, and thus are not subject to strict scrutiny. (C) is incorrect because the government, rather than the challenger, bears the burden of proof in gender discrimination cases. (D) is wrong for the same reason and also because it applies the incorrect standard; an intermediate scrutiny standard is applied rather than the minimal scrutiny of the rational basis test.

Answer to Question 156

(D) If, upon inspection, the machinery company failed to discover a defect that was discoverable in the exercise of reasonable care, then it breached its duty of reasonable care owed to the technician and would be liable in negligence. A prima facie case for negligence consists of: (i) a duty on the part of the defendant to conform to a specific standard of conduct for the protection of the plaintiff against an unreasonable risk of injury; (ii) breach of that duty by the defendant; (iii) the breach was the actual and proximate cause of the plaintiff's injury; and (iv) damage to the plaintiff's person or property. If the machinery company inspected the tunnel, it was under a duty to use the same care in such inspection as would an ordinary, prudent, reasonable person. This duty was owed to foreseeable plaintiffs, such as the technician, who might be working inside the tunnel. If the control system of the tunnel was defective, and the defect should have been discovered during an inspection in the exercise of reasonable care, the failure of the machinery company to discover the defect during the inspection would have created an unreasonable risk of injury to the technician and a breach of the duty it owed him. This breach actually and proximately caused the technician's death when the control system malfunctioned. Thus, under the circumstances in (D), the machinery company would be liable for negligently causing the technician's death. (A) is incorrect because liability ***in negligence*** will not lie merely because the wind tunnel was defective. There must be a showing of fault on the part of the machinery company with respect to the defect; *e.g.,* that the defect should have been discovered in the exercise of reasonable care. (A) would be correct if the technician's survivors were suing the machinery company on a strict products liability theory, but the call of the question indicates that the theory is negligence. (Always look carefully at the call of the question in Torts questions for the theory of liability that the plaintiffs are using.) (B) is incorrect even though the machinery company may have had a duty to inspect the control system before selling the tunnel to the lab. A retailer or other commercial supplier who labels a product as the retailer's own or who assembles component parts manufactured by others is subject to the same liability as the actual manufacturer of the defective component. This contrasts with the liability of an ordinary dealer, who has no duty under a negligence theory to inspect or test goods manufactured by another if there is no reason to anticipate that the product is dangerous. Because the machinery company assembled the wind tunnel from component parts manufactured by others and sold it to the lab as a completed unit, it will be liable not only for its own negligence but also for any negligence on the part of the manufacturers of the component parts. However, nothing in choice (B) indicates that either a component manufacturer or the machinery company was negligent. The existence of a defect does not by itself establish negligence, and the machinery company's failure to inspect the tunnel is not actionable negligence if the defect would not have been discovered even with a reasonably careful inspection. Hence, (D), which supplies the negligence element, is a better choice than (B). (C) is incorrect for the same reason: It omits the requirement that an individual conducting an inspection with reasonable care must have been able to discover the defect. It is possible that the defect was so well hidden that a reasonably careful inspection would not have revealed it. Thus, the failure of the machinery company to discover the defect upon inspection will not suffice by itself to create liability for negligence.

Answer to Question 157

(D) While the facts do not indicate that a reasonable inspection by the machinery company would have disclosed any defects, even if an inspection would have disclosed the defect, the machinery company's failure to do so would have no legal effect on the electronics company's liability. Regardless of whether the technician's survivors are using a negligence theory or a strict liability theory (you have to consider both because the call of the question does not supply the theory of liability), an intermediary's negligent failure to discover a defect is ***not*** a superseding cause, and the defendant who supplied the defective product will be held liable along with the intermediary. Thus, even if the machinery company's failure to inspect was negligent, it would not relieve the electronics company of liability. (A) is incorrect because it is a reversal of one of the situations in which indemnity is available. Where strict liability rules apply, each supplier of a defective product is liable to an injured person, but each supplier has a right of indemnification against all ***previous*** suppliers of the defective product in the distribution chain. Here, both the machinery company and the electronics company would be liable in a strict liability action as suppliers if they supplied a defective product. However, the electronics company, as the previous supplier in the chain, would be liable to the machinery company for indemnity, rather than the machinery company being liable to the electronics company for indemnity, as (A) states. (B) is incorrect because the failure of the machinery company to inspect is, at most, ordinary negligence. A superseding force is one that breaks the causal connection between the initial wrongful act and the ultimate injury. To be superseding, an intervening force must have been unforeseeable. Any ordinary negligence on the part of the machinery company was foreseeable and would not relieve the electronics company of liability for the consequences of supplying a defective product. (C) is incorrect because the machinery company and the electronics company do not have the type of relationship to which respondeat superior is applicable. Under the doctrine of respondeat superior, an employer is vicariously liable for tortious acts committed by his employee if such acts occur within the scope of the employment relationship. No facts suggest that the machinery company is an employee of the electronics company. The companies appear to be independent of each other; their only relationship is a contractual one. Therefore, any wrongful conduct committed by the machinery company will not result in the imposition of vicarious liability against the electronics company under respondeat superior.

Answer to Question 158

(B) The court will probably rule in favor of the government on the merits. Programs of aid to religiously affiliated grade schools and high schools are subject to the same three-part test as are other laws under the Establishment Clause: The program must (i) have a secular purpose, (ii) have a primary effect that neither advances nor inhibits religion, and (iii) not produce excessive government entanglement with religion. With respect to the first prong of the test, all government programs examined by the Supreme Court that provide aid for religiously affiliated grade schools or high schools have been found to have a secular purpose. With respect to the second prong, the program may be deemed to have a primary effect that advances religion if it results in governmental indoctrination of religion or defines its recipients by reference to religion. Here, the statute establishes a religiously neutral program that funds a supplemental service for the schools, and offers the instruction to all disadvantaged students regardless of whether they choose to attend public or private schools. [*See* Agostini v. Felton (1997)—government program providing remedial education services to all disadvantaged children at their schools, including children at parochial schools, held not to violate the Establishment Clause] Thus, (C) is incorrect. (D) is incorrect because the courts will not presume that the instruction provided by this program will be influenced by religion. Furthermore, with respect to the "excessive entanglement" prong of the test, there is no indication that the program requires detailed monitoring of the government employees to prevent them from incorporating religion in their instruction—the content and programs that they use in the private schools are the same as they use in the public schools. (A) is incorrect because the citizens' group has standing to challenge the expenditure on behalf of its members, who have a right to sue based on their status as federal taxpayers. The one recognized exception to the rule that people do not have standing as taxpayers to challenge the way tax dollars are spent by the federal government is if the expenditure was enacted under Congress's taxing and spending power and allegedly exceeds the specific limitation on that power found in the Establishment Clause. That exception applies here because the citizens' group is alleging that the federal appropriation is an unconstitutional attempt to provide government funds to religiously affiliated schools.

Answer to Question 159

(C) Purch has title to Blackacre because Merch's fee simple determinable automatically terminated when he sold tobacco on Blackacre. A fee simple determinable is created by the use of durational language such as "while" or "so long as" and is subject to automatic termination on the happening of the stated event. The corresponding future interest in the grantor, called a possibility of reverter, does not have to be expressly retained; it arises automatically when the determinable fee is created. In the majority of jurisdictions, a possibility of reverter can be transferred inter vivos or devised by will. Here, Ogden retained a possibility of reverter when he made the conveyance to Merch, and it was transferred to Devlin when Ogden devised all of his real property interests to Devlin. Devlin transferred the future interest to Purch by quitclaim deed, and it became a possessory present interest when Merch's fee simple determinable automatically ended. (A) is incorrect because the Rule Against Perpetuities does not apply to a possibility of reverter created in the grantor, regardless of whether the grantor later transfers or devises it to a third party. (B) is incorrect because, as discussed above, in most states the possibility of reverter is freely transferable inter vivos. (D) is incorrect because Merch's interest was a fee simple determinable rather than a fee simple subject to a condition subsequent. In the latter interest, the grantor retains the power to terminate the estate upon the happening of a specified event, but the estate will continue until the grantor exercises his power of termination (right of entry). In contrast, the fee simple determinable ends automatically when the event occurs.

Answer to Question 160

(A) Wanda can testify about the drug sale, but Dan can keep her from testifying about the 1997 statements. The federal courts recognize two separate and distinct spousal privileges. First, in a criminal case, a spouse can testify if she wants to testify, but the spouse cannot be compelled to testify. The privilege applies to all information that the spouse has gained before or during the marriage. This privilege ends when the marriage ends. Second, in any type of case, a spouse can refuse to disclose, or prevent a spouse from disclosing, confidential communications made between the spouses during the marriage. I. is false. Wanda can testify to Dan's 1996 statements if she desires, because they were not communications made during the marriage. She cannot testify to Dan's 1997 statements that were made during the marriage unless Dan does not object. II. is false. Wanda cannot be compelled to testify against Dan even with respect to information received before they were married. III. is true. Dan can object to Wanda's testimony concerning confidential communications during the marriage. IV. is true. While Dan can object to Wanda's testimony concerning confidential communications during the marriage, he has no privilege to object to other testimony by Wanda. It is clear that the 1997 drug transaction was not a confidential communication to Wanda, since Dan was not aware of Wanda's presence.

Answer to Question 161

(D) Because the burning in (D) was accidental, Leon did not have the intent required for arson. At common law, arson consisted of the malicious burning of the dwelling of another. The malice requirement does not imply ill will or any particular motive, nor is specific intent required. All that malice requires is that the defendant have acted with the intent or knowledge that the structure would burn, or with reckless disregard of an obvious risk that the structure would burn. On the other hand, it is not sufficient that the burning was accidental, even if the defendant was negligent. In (D), Leon's carelessness in setting the gasoline can next to the barbecue resulted in the burning of his neighbor's house. However negligent Leon may have been, he did not act with the malice required for arson. Thus, (D) is correct. (C) presents a close question, because Nancy apparently intended only to frighten the sorority members by the explosion of the firecrackers in the fireplace, rather than to cause a fire. However, Nancy's intentional placing of powerful firecrackers in a fireplace, knowing that they would be exposed to fire, might suffice to establish a reckless disregard of an obvious risk that the fire would escape from the fireplace and burn the structure. Thus, it is more likely that Nancy will be found to have acted with malice than that Leon will be found to have done so. In both (A) and (B), the defendants clearly acted with intent or knowledge that the structure would burn. Under common law, neither (A) nor (B) would constitute arson because the burnings were not of a dwelling. However, most statutes broaden the property that may be the subject of arson, and arson questions on the MBE will often assume without saying that the jurisdiction's arson law applies to other structures. Thus, (D) is a better answer than either (A) or (B), because in (D), the absence of malice means that the defendant could not be found guilty of arson under any circumstances, while a conviction would be obtained in (A) or (B) in most jurisdictions.

Answer to Question 162

(A) The court should admit the coat based on Victoria's testimony. Federal Rule of Evidence 402 provides that all relevant evidence is admissible unless a specific rule keeps the evidence out or limits its admissibility. In the case of real evidence, the object at issue is presented for inspection by the trier of fact. Such evidence can be presented to any of the senses of the jury from which the jury can obtain relevant information. Clearly the odor of the coat is a central issue in the case and the jury would obtain relevant evidence on that issue by smelling the coat. Admitting the coat for the stated purpose would violate no other rules of evidence. Choice (B) is wrong because Victoria's testimony is sufficient authentication. Federal Rule 901 does require, as a prerequisite to the admission of real proof, evidence sufficient to support a finding that the item is what the proponent claims. However, real evidence is commonly authenticated by recognition testimony, such as in the case here. Thus, Rule 901 has been satisfied by Victoria's testimony, and additional evidence would not be required. (C) is incorrect because the fact that Victoria had not been impeached would not matter. The coat is being offered for the purpose of having the jury smell it, because that is direct evidence of her claim; it is not being offered as evidence to bolster credibility. Answer (D) is not as good a choice as (A). While it is true that, under Federal Rule of Evidence 403, the coat could be rejected if the judge determined that its probative value was substantially outweighed by unfair prejudice, it is difficult to see any substantial prejudice that would result from smelling the coat.

Answer to Question 163

(B) Wanda's strongest argument, although by no means guaranteed of success, is that the height restriction is a gender-based classification that is not substantially related to important governmental interests. The Due Process Clause of the Fifth Amendment protects against action by the federal government. Although not expressly stated, this clause also provides an equal protection guarantee against federal action that generally applies to the same extent that the Fourteenth Amendment Equal Protection Clause applies to the states. If Wanda can show that the Park Service restriction actually establishes classifications of eligibility for the new position based on gender, then the restriction will be found to violate the Fifth Amendment Due Process Clause unless the government has an exceedingly persuasive justification that the restriction is substantially related to important governmental interests. However, if Wanda is only able to show that the restriction has a discriminatory impact without being able to prove discriminatory intent, the court will not treat it as a gender-based classification and Wanda will not be successful. Despite the difficulty of success, however, (B) is the correct answer because it provides the best possibility of a winning argument for Wanda. Remember that "best of the lot" questions are sometimes "best of a bad lot." You might need to work through all of the alternatives and arrive at the best answer by process of elimination. (A) is the most clearly incorrect, because it relies on the Equal Rights Amendment ("ERA"). The ERA was not ratified by the requisite number of states; thus, it has not become part of the Constitution and would provide no basis for arguing against the validity of the restriction at issue. (C) is incorrect because the Fourteenth Amendment is applicable only to states and not to the federal government. Because an agency of the federal government is being sued, Wanda must rely on the Fifth Amendment. (D) is incorrect because there is no evidence that Wanda has a property right in the newly created position in the Park Service. The Due Process Clause of the Fifth Amendment provides procedural safeguards against arbitrary deprivation by the government of a person's life, liberty, or property. One might have a property right in continued public employment if a statute creates a public employment contract. Here, Wanda is not being threatened with loss of the federal employment she currently holds, nor is there any statute or agreement from which she can derive an interest in or legitimate claim to the newly created position. Because Wanda does not have a property right in the position of Senior Ranger III, she cannot rely on her procedural due process rights. This leaves (B) as the only possible correct answer.

Answer to Question 164

(B) It would be least helpful to Dennis's defense if kidnapping were a general intent crime in the jurisdiction. While courts have not always clearly defined "general intent," the mental state required for the material elements of the offense are analogous to "recklessness" under the Model Penal Code: conscious disregard of a substantial or unjustifiable risk that the material element exists or will result from his conduct. Thus, the defendant need not be certain that his conduct will cause the result or that the attendant circumstances required by the crime exist; it is enough if he is aware of a high likelihood of that result or circumstance. In contrast, a specific intent crime requires the doing of an act with a conscious intent or objective. Most importantly for Dennis's purposes, defenses such as voluntary intoxication and unreasonable mistake of fact are not recognized as defenses to general intent crimes but are for specific intent crimes. If the jurisdiction treats kidnapping as a specific intent crime, Dennis's intoxication could be used to show that he was incapable of forming the requisite intent or that he mistakenly believed that Vinnie had consented to being left on the island. For specific intent crimes, any mistake of fact, even if unreasonable, is a defense. In contrast, voluntary intoxication is not a defense to a general intent crime, and any mistake of fact offered to negate a general intent must be reasonable to be valid. Hence, it would be helpful to Dennis's defense if the jurisdiction treated the offense as a specific intent crime, but not if it were treated as a general intent crime. Thus, (B) is correct because it is not helpful, and (C) is incorrect because it is helpful. (D) is incorrect because that fact may be helpful to Dennis's defense. If he believed that Vinnie wanted to be left on the island, he may not have had the intent required for the offense. (A) is incorrect because it is helpful to Dennis's defense. The offense is defined as the unlawful movement or concealment of a person without his consent. If Vinnie was not legally intoxicated, his consent would be a valid defense; if he was legally intoxicated, it could be argued that he was incapable of consenting, thus negating Dennis's defense.

Answer to Question 165

(B) Peter will prevail regardless of whether Darwin was exercising due care because Darwin intentionally entered onto Peter's property and had only a qualified privilege to do so. The elements of trespass to land are (i) an act of physical invasion of plaintiff's real property by defendant, (ii) intent on defendant's part to bring about the physical invasion of plaintiff's property, and (iii) causation. Here, although Darwin did not intend to harm Peter's land, he intended to enter upon it, and thus would have committed a trespass absent the privilege of necessity. A person may interfere with the real or personal property of another when the interference is reasonably and apparently necessary to avoid threatened injury from a natural or other force, as long as the threatened injury is substantially more serious than the invasion that is undertaken to avert it. However, when the act is solely to benefit any person or to protect any property from destruction or serious injury, this is considered private necessity and the defense is qualified; *i.e.*, the actor must pay for any injury that he causes. Hence, even though Darwin had a privilege to enter onto Peter's property (that superseded Peter's privilege of defense of property), he remains liable for any damages he caused on the land. (A) is wrong because Peter's damage action is based on Darwin's intentional entry onto Peter's land; therefore, he does not need to establish lack of due care to recover. (C) is incorrect because, as discussed above, Darwin's defense of necessity is not an absolute defense and he must pay for the damages caused by his entry on Peter's land. (D) is wrong because it is not relevant as a defense to Darwin's trespass to land. Darwin is not being sued for his negligence in driving too fast (and even if he were, it is doubtful that the tree in the road would be so unforeseeable as to qualify as a superseding force to cut off his liability); he is being sued for intentionally driving onto Peter's property to avoid hitting the tree. Thus, while the existence of the tree in the road may help establish the qualified defense of necessity, it does not cut off Darwin's liability for the damage to Peter's property.

Answer to Question 166

(B) The court should not grant the directed verdict because the jury could find that it was foreseeable that the son might cause damage to cars in the parking lot if he was left unattended. The common law rule is that a parent is not vicariously liable for the tortious conduct of her child. However, the parent may be held liable for her own negligence in allowing the child to do something that injures another's person or property. Under ordinary negligence principles, the mother owed a duty to the owners of other cars in the parking lot if it was foreseeable that her son might cause damage to them if left unattended. It is a question of fact for the jury whether she breached her duty to the other car owners by leaving her son unattended, and whether her conduct was an actual and proximate cause of the damage to the shopper's car. (A) is incorrect because it is doubtful whether the mother's violation of the statute is applicable here. The precise standard of care in a common law negligence case may be established by proving the applicability to that case of a statute providing for a criminal penalty. If that is done, the statute's more specific duty will replace the more general common law duty of care. Violation of the statute establishes negligence per se—a conclusive presumption of duty and breach of duty; plaintiff must then establish causation and damages to complete the prima facie case of negligence. In proving the availability of the statutory standard, plaintiff must show that (i) she is in the class intended to be protected by the statute, and (ii) the statute was designed to prevent the type of harm that she suffered. Here, it is more likely that the statute was designed to protect small children from harm if left unattended in a car, as choice (C) states, and the shopper would not be in the class intended to be protected by the statute. (C) is incorrect because it is not necessary for the statute to apply to find negligence on the part of the mother. As choice (B) states, the jury could find that the mother should have known that her son might cause damage to cars if left unattended, making her liable under ordinary negligence principles without resort to the statute. (D) is incorrect even though it is a true statement at common law. The shopper is not relying on vicarious liability to hold the mother liable but rather on the mother's own negligence in leaving her four-year-old son unattended.

Answer to Question 167

(C) Devlo can recover $50,000, which is the amount above the contract price that it will cost to get the building completed. In construction contracts, the standard measure of damages when the builder breaches depends on when the breach occurred. If the builder breaches after partially performing, the owner is entitled to the cost of completion plus reasonable compensation for any delay in performance (unless completion would involve undue economic waste). Most courts will allow the builder to offset or recover for work performed to date if necessary to avoid the unjust enrichment of the owner. Here, the cost of completion (the amount above the contract price that it will cost to get the building completed) is $50,000, which was a reasonable price considering the deadline. Hence, that is what Devlo can recover. (A) and (B) are incorrect because Devlo is not being unjustly enriched by the additional amount that Structo expended in performance over the progress payments that it received. Devlo still had to pay $50,000 more than the contract amount for completion of the warehouse because of Structo's breach; thus, that is Devlo's recovery. (On the other hand, if the cost of completing the building to specifications were only $150,000 after Structo's breach, Structo could recover $50,000 from Devlo on quasi-contract grounds because Devlo would have been unjustly enriched from Structo's breach.) (D) is incorrect because the cost of completion is determined from the perspective of the owner, *i.e.*, how much additional the owner has to pay to have the building completed. Devlo would be unjustly enriched if it could recover $50,000 more than the damages it suffered.

Answer to Question 168

(D) Applianceco will win because it has a valid security interest in the oven, and no other party has a superior interest. In a fixture case involving divided ownership, the majority rule is that, absent an agreement to the contrary, a tenant may remove a chattel that he has attached to the demised premises as long as the removal does not cause substantial damage to the demised premises or the virtual destruction of the chattel. Furthermore, if the landowner mortgages his land to a mortgagee and then leases it to a tenant who annexes a chattel to the premises, the mortgagee has no greater rights in the chattel than the mortgagor, provided that the original sufficiency of the security is not impaired (*e.g.*, removal would not cause substantial damage to the premises). Finally, as between the tenant-purchaser of the chattel and the holder of a properly created security interest, the holder of the security interest can reclaim possession of the chattel upon the purchaser's default according to the terms of the security agreement. Therefore, Applianceco has a claim to the oven that is superior to the other listed parties. (A) is wrong because it states the rule applicable to common ownership cases, *i.e.*, cases in which the person who brings the chattel on the land owns both the chattel and the real estate. To the extent that the owner of the real estate mortgages the realty, the mortgage attaches to all fixtures on the real estate in the absence of an agreement to the contrary. In that case, Applianceco's failure to make a fixture filing for its purchase money security interest would have caused it to lose priority. However, as discussed above, this rule does not apply in divided ownership cases where the tenant brings the chattel onto the premises. (B) is wrong because Terrance's rights are superior to those of Lester and Multistate, but not Applianceco. Absent the security agreement with Applianceco, Terrance would have been free to remove the oven that he purchased and retain possession of it because its removal would not substantially damage the leased premises. (C) is wrong because, as discussed above, the landlord would not prevail against a tenant who brought the chattel onto the leased premises, as long as the chattel can be removed without substantial damage to the premises.

Answer to Question 169

(A) The wife's conveyance of her interest in the property to the purchaser severed the joint tenancy between the wife and the husband, leaving the purchaser and the husband holding the entire parcel as tenants in common. A joint tenancy is a type of concurrent ownership of a parcel of land that is distinguished primarily by the right of survivorship; *i.e.,* when one joint tenant dies, the property is freed of his concurrent interest and the survivor retains an undivided right in the property that is no longer subject to the interest of the deceased co-tenant. To create a joint tenancy, a grantor must explicitly indicate in the conveyance that the parties are to hold as joint tenants. If one joint tenant conveys her interest, the joint tenancy is severed. The new tenant holds as a tenant in common with the remaining joint tenant, so that there is no longer a right of survivorship. Here, the mother, grantor of the property, expressly indicated in her will that the wife and the husband were to take the parcel of property as joint tenants with right of survivorship. When the wife quitclaimed her interest in the property to the purchaser, the joint tenancy between the wife and the husband was severed (despite the fact that the husband did not know of the conveyance to the purchaser). This left the purchaser and the husband holding the land as tenants in common, with no right of survivorship. The purchaser and the husband each own an undivided one-half interest in the property, and the purchaser will succeed in his suit to partition the property to reflect the respective interests of the co-tenants. (D) is incorrect because the husband no longer had a right of survivorship after the joint tenancy with the wife was severed. Thus, the wife's death is irrelevant to the current ownership interests in the property. (B) is incorrect because it suggests that the purchaser cannot prevail if the husband and the wife took as joint tenants (on the basis that the husband would take the entire property by right of survivorship upon the death of the wife). In fact, the husband and the wife did take as joint tenants, but the wife's conveyance of her interest to the purchaser severed the joint tenancy, thus eliminating the right of survivorship. Thus, the basic premise of (B)—that the purchaser can only prevail if the husband and the wife took as tenants in common—is incorrect. (C) is a trap for the unwary, because it implies that the marital status of the husband and the wife is relevant to the ownership of this property. Under the common law, a grant to husband and wife resulted in the creation of a tenancy by the entirety, which carried with it a right of survivorship that would not be eliminated by a conveyance to an outsider by one spouse alone. Divorce can terminate a tenancy by the entirety (leaving the parties as tenants in common with no right of survivorship), but separation does not terminate the estate. Hence, if this were a tenancy by the entirety, the husband would prevail rather than the purchaser. However, most states do not recognize a tenancy by the entirety. As noted above, the husband and the wife took the property as joint tenants. The husband and the wife did not receive this status by virtue of the fact that they were married, nor is their continuation in such status dependent on their remaining married. The wife's conveyance of her interest to the purchaser severed her joint tenancy with the husband and eliminated the right of survivorship, regardless of whether she and her husband were legally separated at the time.

Answer to Question 170

(C) The Commerce Clause provides the strongest support for Rudy's position, because the Eastern Seaboard legislation discriminates against out-of-state goods. A state may regulate local aspects of interstate commerce if such regulation is not in conflict with federal regulations and if: (i) the subject matter of the regulation does not require nationally uniform regulation; (ii) the regulation does not discriminate against out-of-state competition to benefit local economic interests; and (iii) any incidental burden on interstate commerce of the nondiscriminatory regulation does not outweigh the legitimate local benefits produced by the regulation. Laws that are designed to protect local businesses against interstate competition generally will be invalidated. Here, the Eastern Seaboard legislation discriminates against out-of-state manufacturers to protect local businesses by limiting the amount of units that can be sold by retailers of electronic products containing microprocessors manufactured out of state. There is no such limit on units that can be sold that utilize locally manufactured microprocessors. This law was enacted to encourage the development of local manufacturing operations. Because this law is designed to protect local businesses against interstate competition, it should fail a challenge under the Commerce Clause. (D) is incorrect because the Privileges and Immunities Clause of Article IV, which prohibits discrimination by a state in favor of its own citizens, applies only when citizens of other states are denied, without substantial justification, basic rights or the pursuit of essential activities. Although the Eastern Seaboard legislation does discriminate in favor of that state's manufacturers (and commercial activities are protected by the clause), Rudy is probably a resident of that state. Any burden that the legislation places on him is not based on his citizenship status but on the location of the supplier of his products. Hence, the Article IV Privileges and Immunities Clause does not provide the strongest support for his position. (A) is incorrect because, under the Fourteenth Amendment Equal Protection Clause, the validity of a classification that relates only to matters of economics or social welfare is determined by the rational basis test. Under this test, Rudy would have the burden of proving that the classification differentiating between resident and out-of-state manufacturers does not have a rational relationship to a legitimate governmental interest. Because this is a difficult burden to meet, the equal protection argument is not Rudy's strongest. (B) is incorrect because economic legislation such as this, which does not limit a fundamental right, will be sustained against a due process challenge as long as it is rationally related to a legitimate end of government. As with the Equal Protection Clause, relying on the Due Process Clause would impose on Rudy a heavy burden of proving the invalidity of the legislation.

Answer to Question 171

(B) The court should permit Petchow to introduce evidence of trade usage to support its definition of "cornmeal." Under the U.C.C., which governs contracts for the sale of goods, the parol evidence rule does not bar the introduction of evidence based on course of dealing, usage of trade, or course of performance to explain or supplement a contractual term. Here, Petchow is claiming that the parties understood the term "cornmeal" to have a narrower definition than the ordinary meaning of the term. Evidence that the term was used in the trade as Petchow used it is admissible to support Petchow's claim. [U.C.C. §2-202] (A) is incorrect because a latent ambiguity occurs where the expression of the parties' agreement appears perfectly clear at the time the contract is formed, but because of subsequently revealed facts, it may be reasonably interpreted in either of two ways. However, rather than using an objective test, the courts look to the subjective intention of the parties in determining whether an ambiguity existed. Here, Petchow is claiming that both parties subjectively understood the meaning of the term "cornmeal" in the context of the contract and that both parties intended the term to mean what Petchow is claiming; hence, Petchow's argument is that, as between the parties, there was no ambiguity as to the term. (C) is wrong because the U.C.C. does not require that an ambiguity be found in the writing before allowing an explanation by course of dealing, usage of trade, or course of performance. (D) is also incorrect. The general rule is that a writing that is a complete integration of the parties' agreement cannot be contradicted or supplemented by additional terms. However, the U.C.C. permits extrinsic evidence that explains or supplements a term through course of dealing, usage in the trade, or course of performance to date, even if the writing is otherwise a complete integration.

Answer to Question 172

(D) Petchow must allow Grainco until November 15 to ship cornmeal that conforms to the contract because that is the original date when performance was due. Under the U.C.C., if a buyer has rejected goods because of defects, the seller may within the time originally provided for performance "cure" the defective tender by giving reasonable notice of its intention to do so and making new tender of conforming goods, which the buyer must then accept. [U.C.C. §2-508] Here, Grainco promised to deliver cornmeal that conforms to the contract by the original date of performance. Thus, Petchow cannot declare the contract to be in breach and must accept Grainco's delivery of conforming goods if it occurs by November 15. (A) is incorrect not only because Grainco has the right to cure until November 15, but also because for contracts authorizing deliveries in separate installments, the buyer may declare a total breach only if the defects are such as to substantially impair the value of the entire contract. Hence, even if there were a specified time for the first shipment of cornmeal and it had expired, Petchow would not be entitled to declare a total breach of contract. (B) is incorrect because, as discussed above, Grainco has the right to cure the defective tender of the 50 tons by November 15, the date when performance is due under the contract. (C) is incorrect because it does not state the correct standard for determining when the defective tender can be cured in this case. Ordinarily, the seller has no right to cure beyond the original contract time. However, when the buyer rejects a tender that the seller reasonably believed would be acceptable, the seller, upon reasonable notification to the buyer, has a further reasonable time beyond the original contract time within which to make a conforming tender. This situation is not applicable here, however. In this case, the time for performance under the original contract has not expired and Grainco has promised to perform within that time.

Furthermore, there is nothing in the facts to suggest that Grainco believed its original shipment was reasonable; Grainco acknowledged that the shipment did not conform to the contract and there was no indication that Petchow had previously accepted nonconforming goods.

Answer to Question 173

(A) Brett will not prevail in his double jeopardy challenge. The Fifth Amendment provides that one may not be twice put in jeopardy for the same offense. Under the *Blockburger* test, two crimes do not constitute the same offense if each crime requires proof of an additional element that the other crime does not require, even though some of the same facts may be necessary to prove both crimes. Under *Blockburger*, reckless homicide and driving while intoxicated are separate offenses because the first requires proof that someone died, while the second requires proof that the defendant was intoxicated (and recklessness for the homicide offense can be shown by evidence other than intoxication). Thus, prosecution for the reckless homicide charge did not violate double jeopardy. (B) is incorrect. While imposition of cumulative punishments may be permissible even if two crimes constitute the same offense under *Blockburger* as long as this result was intended by the legislature, this situation applies only when the punishments are imposed at a single trial. Conversely, because the two charges are separate offenses, they could be tried together and cumulative punishments imposed without violating double jeopardy. (C) is incorrect because the fact that the two charges require proof of the same conduct is no longer relevant for purposes of double jeopardy. The *Blockburger* test governs regardless of whether the punishments are imposed at a single trial or multiple trials. [United States v. Dixon (1993)] (D) is wrong because it is irrelevant that the sentences were of different lengths and not concurrent. If the two charges had constituted the same offense, imposition of multiple punishments would be prohibited even if the two sentences had run concurrently. [Rutledge v. United States (1996)]

Answer to Question 174

(D) The transaction described in (D) does not present the problem of potentially unconstitutional state regulation of interstate commerce, state regulation of foreign commerce, or state regulation of federal government activities, as do (A), (B), and (C), respectively. (A) involves a sale to a manufacturer whose plant is located out of state. Because this law requires the out-of-state manufacturer to pay the government-set price for cheese even if the overall market price for cheese is lower, the law burdens interstate commerce even though it is nondiscriminatory. If this burden on interstate commerce outweighs the promotion of legitimate, nondiscriminatory local interests, the state law will violate the Commerce Clause. (B) involves a restriction on the price of cheese that was made in a foreign country and is being sold by a citizen of that country. This is a regulation of foreign commerce. The power to regulate foreign commerce lies exclusively with Congress. Thus, (B) presents a situation in which the statute would not be constitutionally applied. In (C), a sale is being made to an agency of the federal government. Application of the state statute to such a sale would result in state regulation of the federal government. The federal government and its agencies and instrumentalities are immune from state regulation that interferes with federal activities, functions, and programs. Thus, it would be impermissible for the state to attempt to compel the Air Force to comply with a state statute setting a minimum price for cheese. The transaction in (D) involves no contact with foreign commerce or with the federal government. In addition, the transaction is entirely intrastate and does not appear to involve an undue burden on interstate commerce. Therefore, (D) is most likely to be constitutionally applied.

Answer to Question 175

(B) Anne and Beth have a life estate because of the rule of convenience, and Tess's heirs have a reversion because of the Rule Against Perpetuities. When a gift is made to a group of persons generically described as a class, such as to someone's "nieces," the rule of convenience provides that the class closes when some member of the class can call for a distribution of her share of the class gift. Persons born after that date are excluded from the class. Here, the class of Tess's nieces entitled to the life estate closed when they became entitled to take, which was at the termination of the preceding estate (Harold's life estate). Since Caryn was not yet born at the time the class closed, she is not entitled to a share of the life estate. Thus, (C) and (D) are wrong. Tess's heirs have a reversion because the remainder to the children of the nieces violates the Rule Against Perpetuities. Viewed at the time the perpetuities period begins to run, which is Tess's death, the niece alive at that time, Anne, as well as her son Edward, could die and another niece not yet born could hold the life estate for more than 21 years after the death of Harold (the only other life in being at the time of Tess's death). Hence, the surviving children of the nieces would not take within the perpetuities period. Because their interest is void, Tess's heirs have a reversion, making (A) and (C) wrong.

Answer to Question 176

(C) Alphonse's mortgage remains on the property and Charter's mortgage is extinguished, and Patterson is personally liable to Charter for the deficiency. As a general rule, the priority of a mortgage is determined by the time it was placed on the property. When a mortgage is foreclosed, the buyer at the sale will take title as it existed when the mortgage was placed on the property. Thus, foreclosure will terminate interests junior to the mortgage being foreclosed but will not affect senior interests. The proceeds of the foreclosure sale are used first (after expenses and fees) to pay the principal and accrued interest on the loan that was foreclosed, and then to pay off any junior interests in the order of priority. Where the proceeds of the sale are insufficient to satisfy a mortgage debt, the mortgagee can bring a personal action against the mortgagor/debtor for the deficiency. Here, foreclosure by Bradford leaves Alphonse's senior mortgage interest intact on the property; the buyer at the foreclosure sale takes the property subject to that mortgage. On the other hand, Charter's mortgage interest, because it was junior to Bradford's interest, was extinguished by Bradford's foreclosure action. After Bradford's loan is paid off, the $20,000 that remains is used to reduce the amount of the debt owed to Charter. Charter can recover the balance against Patterson personally in a deficiency action. (A) is wrong because Alphonse's mortgage and Charter's mortgage are treated differently because of their priority in relation to Bradford's mortgage. (B) states the opposite of the actual result—Alphonse's mortgage (the senior interest) remains on Sandacre and Charter's mortgage (the junior interest) is extinguished. (D) is incorrect because, as discussed above, Alphonse's mortgage remains on the land; thus, all of the remaining proceeds from the foreclosure sale after Bradford's mortgage debt is satisfied go towards reducing the debt owed to Charter.

Answer to Question 177

(A) The child will prevail because he suffered physical injury as a result of the chemical company's engaging in an activity that involves a substantial risk of serious harm no matter how much care is exercised. A prima facie case for strict liability consists of: (i) an absolute duty on the part of the defendant to make safe; (ii) breach of that duty; (iii) such breach actually and proximately caused plaintiff's injury; and (iv) damage to the plaintiff's person or property. An activity is ultrahazardous or abnormally dangerous if it: (i) involves a risk of serious harm to persons or property; (ii) cannot be performed without risk of serious harm no matter how much care is taken; and (iii) is not a commonly engaged-in activity by persons in the community. In such cases, the duty owed is an absolute duty to make safe the ultrahazardous activity or condition, and liability is imposed for injuries to persons or property resulting from the danger. The duty is owed to persons to whom a reasonable person would have foreseen a risk of harm under the circumstances. The harm must result from the kind of danger to be anticipated from such ultrahazardous activity. The chemical company's maintenance of a deadly nerve gas system involves a risk of serious harm to persons and property through the release of harmful gas and heat energy, and cannot be undertaken without risk of serious harm no matter how much care is taken by the chemical company. Also, it is not common to maintain such a system in an urban area. Thus, this is an ultrahazardous or abnormally dangerous activity, imposing on the chemical company an absolute duty to make it safe. When the chemicals leaked, creating dangerous amounts of heat energy, the duty was breached. This breach actually and proximately caused the child's broken arm, which occurred as he was fleeing from the danger created by the heat. Harm to a person fleeing from the danger created by the activity is one of the kinds of danger to be anticipated from the activity. Thus, the chemical company is liable to the child for his injuries. (B) is incorrect because there is no indication that the chemical company was negligent with regard to the leakage of the chemicals. Apparently, the chemical company took all reasonable precautions under the circumstances. Thus, liability will be predicated on strict liability rather than on negligence. (C) is incorrect because, as explained above, injury to a person that is caused while fleeing from the immediate vicinity of a chemical leak is a kind of danger to be anticipated from maintaining a nerve gas system in an urban area. Thus, the harm incurred by the child flows from the normally dangerous propensity of the activity engaged in by the chemical company. In addition, even though the chemical company may not have known that children played in the chamber, a risk of harm is foreseeable to anyone (such as a city employee) who might enter the chamber. Hence, the child was within the "zone of danger" from the chemical company's activity. (D) is incorrect because the fact that the child was injured on property owned by the city is irrelevant to the chemical company's strict liability. The danger created by the chemical company's breach extended to the adjoining property, so the chemical company will be liable for injuries occurring there that were caused by the danger.

Answer to Question 178

(A) The ordnance company caused the accident by supplying a defective product; it will be liable under a strict products liability theory. To establish a prima facie case in products liability based on strict liability in tort, the plaintiff must establish (i) a strict duty owed by a commercial supplier, (ii) breach of that duty, (iii) actual and proximate cause, and (iv) damages. The ordnance company is a commercial supplier of the delivery systems because it contracted with the chemical company to design and manufacture them. The ordnance company breached its duty as a commercial supplier because it supplied a product that was so defective as to be unreasonably dangerous. Because of what the delivery systems were designed to contain, any kind of defect would probably make the systems unreasonably dangerous. And because the potential danger was lethal nerve gas, the zone of danger was broad; anyone who might be in range of the gas when it became toxic would be a foreseeable plaintiff. The facts indicate that the systems were either defectively designed or defectively manufactured, because they were intended to hold the chemical agents separate for at least 15 years and began leaking after three weeks. This defect was the actual and proximate cause of the child's injuries because he fell while trying to escape the danger. Even if the chemical company were negligent in storing the nerve gas, the ordnance company would not be relieved of liability. An intermediary's ordinary negligence, such as the failure to guard against a defect, would be foreseeable and therefore not a superseding cause. Thus, the child can recover damages against the ordnance company. (B) is not as good a choice as (A). Res ipsa loquitur may be used to establish breach of duty in a negligence action where no direct evidence exists of the defendant's negligence. The plaintiff must show that (i) the accident causing his injury is the type that would not normally occur unless someone was negligent, (ii) the negligence is attributable to defendant, and (iii) the plaintiff was not negligent in causing the injury. Attributing the negligence to the defendant means establishing that this type of accident ordinarily happens because of the negligence of someone in the defendant's position. Although it is not essential that the defendant have exclusive control of the instrumentality causing the injury, the plaintiff will have a harder time showing that the negligence is attributable to the defendant in the absence of exclusive control. Because the chemical company was in exclusive control of the delivery systems at the time of the injury, the child may have difficulty in proving that the negligence was attributable to the ordnance company. More importantly, a negligence action against the ordnance company for producing the defective delivery systems requires the child to show all of the elements of a strict products liability action as well as negligent conduct. Where the call of the question in a products liability action on the MBE does not indicate the theory of liability used by the plaintiff, your analysis should always begin with a strict liability theory. Because it relieves the plaintiff from proving negligence, strict liability is always the preferred theory if it is available. (C) is incorrect because, as indicated above, establishing that the instrumentality causing the injury was in the exclusive control of the defendant is just a common method of showing that the negligence causing the injury is attributable to the defendant. The fact that the canisters were in the control of the chemical company makes it more difficult for the child to attribute the negligence to the ordnance company, but he is not precluded from doing so. (D) is incorrect because the fact that the ordnance company was unaware that children were playing in the underground chamber does not make the child an unforeseeable plaintiff to whom the ordnance company would not owe a duty. The scope of the ordnance company's duty is defined by the risk of injury created by the ordnance company's negligence. Nerve gas escaping from the delivery systems created a broad zone of potential danger that would encompass not just employees of the chemical company but also any residents of the city who lived in the vicinity of the underground vaults, as well as anyone who happened to be in the adjacent storage chamber at the time.

Answer to Question 179

(C) The court should rule that Warden's testimony is admissible as circumstantial evidence that Denny was a member of a rival gang. Circumstantial evidence is evidence of a subsidiary or collateral fact from which, alone or in conjunction with a cluster of other facts, the existence of a material issue can be inferred. Under the Federal Rules, circumstantial evidence in the form of opinion testimony by a lay witness is admissible when (i) it is rationally based on the perception of the witness, (ii) it is helpful to a clear understanding of his testimony or to the determination of a fact in issue, and (iii) it is not based on scientific, technical, or other specialized knowledge. Here, Warden's testimony is based on his observation of the tattoo and his recognition, based on his experience, that it is worn by members of a gang that was a rival of the victim's gang. It is helpful to the determination of a fact in issue because it is circumstantial evidence contradicting Denny's claim that he was not a member of the rival gang and tending to support the prosecution's theory of first degree murder. It is not based on scientific, technical, or similar specialized knowledge. Hence, (A) is incorrect because Warden does not need to know that Denny is a member of the gang to testify that, based on his observation and experience, Denny's tattoo was the gang's symbol. (B) is incorrect because Warden does not need to be qualified as an expert to testify as he proposes. His personal observation of tattoos on gang members makes his testimony, even if considered an opinion, sufficiently helpful to the trier of fact to make it admissible without him having to qualify as an expert on gangs. (D) is incorrect because the availability of the tattoo for display does not affect whether Warden's testimony is admissible. The only context in which a preference is expressed for the "original" piece of evidence is the best evidence or original document rule, which applies when the terms of a writing are sought to be proved. Here, even assuming that the tattoo would constitute a writing under the broad definition in the Federal

Rules, the witness is not attempting to prove any terms or content of the "writing" that could be gleaned from the writing itself; thus, the rule does not apply.

Answer to Question 180

(D) Because the security chief's actions were merely part of a mock robbery, and the security chief had every reason to believe that the teller was aware of this, the security chief lacked the intent necessary to commit any of the crimes listed. Robbery is a taking of personal property of another from the other's person or presence by force or intimidation, with the intent to permanently deprive him of it. In taking from the teller the money, wallet, and wristwatch, the security chief simply intended to simulate the conditions of a bank robbery in as realistic a fashion as possible. The security chief did not intend to permanently (or even for any appreciable length of time) deprive the teller of any of his property. Because the intent required for robbery is missing, (A) is incorrect. Larceny is the taking and carrying away of tangible personal property of another by trespass with intent to permanently (or for an unreasonable time) deprive the person of his interest in the property. As explained above, the security chief lacked the intent to permanently deprive the teller of the property that was taken. In addition, the taking was not trespassory, because the security chief justifiably believed that the teller knew what was actually happening and that the taking was therefore consented to by the teller. Because of the absence of these elements of larceny, (B) is incorrect. An assault is either: (i) an attempt to commit a battery (*i.e.,* to unlawfully apply force to the person of another resulting in bodily injury or an offensive touching); or (ii) the intentional creation, other than by mere words, of a reasonable apprehension in the mind of the victim of imminent bodily harm. The security chief was not attempting to commit a battery, because at no time did he intend to apply force to the teller or otherwise cause the teller any injury. Although the teller may have had a reasonable apprehension of being shot, the security chief did not intend to create such an apprehension. The security chief was entitled to assume that the teller knew that this was merely a staged robbery, and that therefore there was no danger to the teller. Thus, under either definition of assault, the security chief is not guilty of this crime.

Answer to Question 181

(B) Clyde's testimony is admissible as evidence of habit. Habit describes one's regular response to a specific set of circumstances. Evidence of the habit of a person is relevant to prove that the conduct of the person on a particular occasion was in conformity with the habit. [Fed. R. Evid. 406] Testimony that, every morning for the past seven years, Bonnie has turned off the electric blanket immediately upon awakening describes Bonnie's regular response to a repeated specific situation. Thus, Clyde's testimony is evidence of habit. Such evidence is relevant to show that, on the day of the fire, Bonnie's conduct was in conformity with this habit (*i.e.,* that Bonnie turned off the blanket before leaving for work). Therefore, Clyde's testimony should be admitted. (A) misstates the rule as to admissibility of habit evidence. Evidence of habit is used to show that particular conduct conformed with such habit. However, evidence of prior conduct is not used to show conformity with habit. The testimony of Clyde is admissible because it is evidence of what Bonnie probably did the morning of the fire, not because it is evidence of what Bonnie did on prior occasions. (C) is incorrect because habit, as a regular response to specific circumstances, is in fact proved by evidence of specific conduct rather than by opinion or reputation evidence. (D) is incorrect because there is no requirement under the Federal Rules that habit evidence be corroborated to be admissible.

Answer to Question 182

(D) Lester, as the holder of a vested remainder, could ordinarily prevent the life tenant (Karen) from mining the property. However, the open mines doctrine permits Karen to continue to operate the mine because it was in operation at the time of the conveyance. Lester's future interest is a remainder, because it is capable of becoming a present interest upon the natural termination of Karen's preceding life estate. More particularly, Lester has a ***vested*** remainder, because his remainder is certain to become a present interest on termination of Karen's estate, it is not subject to being defeated, and it is not subject to being diminished in size. According to the general rule, Karen (as the life tenant) would not be permitted to mine the property absent an express conferral of such a right by Sutter, the grantor. This would allow Lester, the remainderman, to successfully maintain an action enjoining Karen from operating the mine. However, the open mines doctrine allows the life tenant to continue to operate a mine that was open at the time of conveyance. Golden Acres was conveyed to Karen upon Sutter's death, at which time the mine was already in operation. Therefore, under the open mines doctrine, Karen will be permitted to continue to operate the mine and the injunction will be denied. (B) is incorrect because, although Lester's status as the holder of a vested remainder would ordinarily provide the basis for a successful action seeking to enjoin Karen's operation of the mine, (B) fails to take into account the open mines doctrine, pursuant to which Lester's action will be defeated. (C) is incorrect because whether Karen's estate is a freehold estate is irrelevant to this analysis. (A) incorrectly characterizes Lester's vested remainder as subject to partial divestment. Such a remainder (also called a vested remainder subject to open) is a vested remainder created in a class of persons (*e.g.,* "children," "brothers and sisters") that is certain to take on the termination of the preceding estates, but is subject to diminution by reason of other persons becoming entitled to share in the remainder. The remainder here was created in Lester, not in a class of persons, so that Lester's remainder cannot be diminished as a result of other persons becoming entitled to share in the remainder. Therefore, Lester does not have a vested remainder subject to partial divestment; he has an indefeasibly vested remainder that is certain to become possessory in him (or his heirs) when Karen dies.

Answer to Question 183

(C) Ida owns a fee simple, albeit subject to a divesting condition subsequent (her dying without having had children). Thus, Ida is entitled to operate the Silver Creek mine, and the Society cannot prevent her from doing so. A defeasible fee is a fee simple estate that is of potentially infinite duration, but which may terminate on the happening of a specified event. One such estate is a fee simple subject to an executory interest. This estate is subject to a divesting condition subsequent that, if the condition occurs, will vest title in a third person rather than in the grantor. Here, according to the language of Sutter's will, Ida has a fee simple in Silver Creek. However, this fee simple is subject to a divesting condition subsequent, in that title will vest in the American Cancer Society if Ida dies without having produced issue. The Society is a transferee whose future interest is not capable of taking on the natural termination of a preceding life estate; *i.e.,* it divests the interest of another. Thus, the interest of the Society is classified as an executory interest, meaning that Ida has a fee simple subject to an executory interest. Although title will vest in the Society if Ida dies without having produced children, this may never happen. Thus, Ida's estate is of potentially infinite duration. As a result, the Society (in whom title may never vest) cannot prevent Ida from mining the property. (B) is incorrect because, although the Society has an executory interest, this does not confer on it the right to prevent the holder of the fee simple from mining the property. While a remainderman may assert certain rights against a life tenant, the holder of an executory interest cannot assert these rights against the holder of a fee simple. (A) incorrectly classifies the Society's interest. A remainder is a future interest created in a transferee that is capable of becoming a present interest upon the natural termination of the preceding estates created in the same disposition. Remainders follow life estates. Here, Ida has a fee simple, rather than a life estate. Thus, the Society's future interest will not take on the natural termination of the preceding estate, but will divest the interest of Ida (if Ida dies without having produced issue). Consequently, the Society's interest is an executory interest rather than a remainder. (D) is incorrect because the open mines doctrine is applicable to life estates. Generally, a life tenant may not consume or exploit natural resources on the land (*e.g.,* minerals) unless the grantor expressly confers such right on the life tenant. However, pursuant to the open mines doctrine, if the land was used in exploitation of natural resources (*e.g.,* a mine) prior to the grant, the life tenant can continue to operate the mines. It is assumed that, in granting the life estate, the grantor most likely intended the life tenant to have the right to continue to exploit. Here, Ida is not a life tenant. Thus, the open mines doctrine is inapplicable. As the holder of a fee, Ida could have mined the property even if no mine were already open when she took her interest.

Answer to Question 184

(D) Krell is not likely to prevail because the statute does not constitute a total taking of Krell's property and greatly promotes public welfare. If a government regulation denies a landowner all economic use of his land, the regulation may constitute a "taking" requiring the payment of "just compensation" under the Fifth Amendment. However, regulations that merely decrease the value of property do not necessarily result in a taking as long as there remains an economically viable use for the property. The court will balance the social goals intended by the legislation against the diminution in value of the property and the owner's reasonable expectations regarding use of the property. Here, the statute promotes the important public purpose of trying to reduce mudslides and flooding, and does not totally ban Krell from using his land for the harvesting of wortplants. Thus, the regulation does not constitute a "taking" of private property in violation of the Fifth Amendment. (A) is incorrect because even a substantial impairment of economic value does not necessarily constitute a taking. As long as there is some economically viable use for the property, the court will use a balancing test. (B) is incorrect because, as discussed above, the statute does not result in a taking of private property. (C) is incorrect because it does not accurately state the test used by the Supreme Court for determining whether a regulation constitutes a "taking," but instead states the test for determining whether a particular use is a "public use" for purposes of applying the "Taking" Clause.

Answer to Question 185

(D) Direction IV needs to be corrected in its course but not its distance. In land contracts and deeds, property may be described in various ways as long as the description is unambiguous. From a designated starting point that can be identified by reference to a government survey or a natural or artificial monument, the boundaries of the property can be described by successive calls of courses (*e.g.*, angles) and distances until returning to the starting point. A course is a statement of direction generally stated as some number of degrees east or west of due north or south. In each call a distance must be stated together with the course. Thus, the boundary in direction IV runs at an angle 45 degrees east of due south (*i.e.*, southeast) for a distance of 100 feet. However, since direction I went southeast, direction II went southwest, and direction III went northwest, the fourth direction has to be northeast for a distance of 100 feet to bring the final boundary back to the starting point. (In this type of question, diagram the boundaries as shown below to help you visualize the property.) Therefore, the correction in choice (D) is correct. (A), (B), and (C) are incorrect because none of those proposed changes in distance or direction would be sufficient to bring the final call back to the starting point.

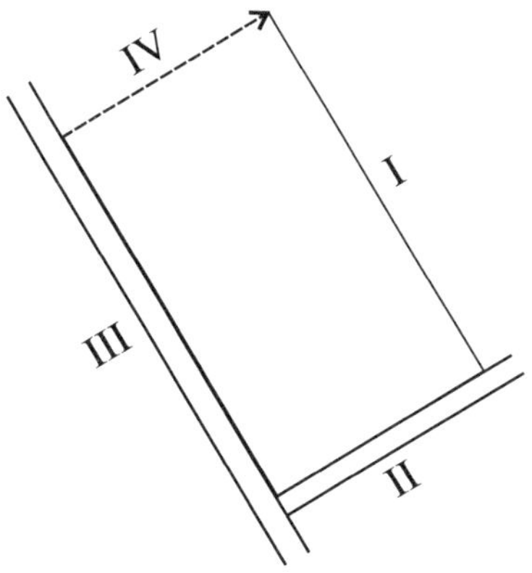

Answer to Question 186

(D) The reasonableness of the collector's belief that the length of his rifle did not violate the statute provides no defense to the crime charged. Unless the collector can establish a valid defense, he will be liable for violating the statute because he possessed a rifle less than 24 inches long. It is not a defense to a crime that the defendant was unaware that his acts were prohibited by the criminal law or that he mistakenly believed that his acts were not prohibited, even if such ignorance or mistake was reasonable. Here, the collector knew that the rifle he was purchasing was 22 inches long, but he was unaware that the statute prohibited possession of a rifle whose length was less than 24 inches. Such ignorance of the prohibition of the statute will not constitute a defense to the charge of possession of a sawed-off rifle, even if such ignorance remained after a reasonable investigation by the collector. (A) is incorrect because it would allow ignorance of the law to constitute a defense to a crime; *i.e.,* the collector would be acquitted because he did not know that the statute prohibited the possession of a rifle that is less than 24 inches in length. Where a statute specifically requires knowledge of some other aspect of law, ignorance of that aspect of law might negate a mens rea element of the offense, but here, even if the statutory language prohibited only a "knowing" possession of the weapon, it would not require knowledge of the statute. (B) is incorrect because the collector's ignorance of the law will not be deemed a valid defense merely because he conducted a reasonable investigation to ensure compliance with the statute. The statute is clear in its terms, and was reasonably available for the collector's perusal. The fact that he personally measured the rifle to confirm that its barrel was at least 16 inches long, so as to assure conformity with the part of the statute of which he was aware, does not excuse his failure to be aware of the rest of the statute. (C) incorrectly states that ignorance of the law is a defense if such ignorance is reasonable. As noted above, the reasonableness of the mistake or ignorance does not render it a valid defense.

Answer to Question 187

(A) The court will admit rehabilitation testimony of the witness's good reputation for truthfulness if her credibility was attacked by conviction of a felony. Under Federal Rule of Evidence 608, when the witness's general character for truth and veracity has been attacked, the party for whom the impeached witness has testified may call other witnesses to testify to the good reputation for truth of the impeached witness or to give their opinion as to the truthfulness of the impeached witness. The attack on the witness's veracity may have been not only by reputation or opinion evidence, but also by conviction of a crime under Rule 609. Here, the plaintiff's witness was impeached by conviction of a recent felony. (Because it is a felony, the crime does not have to involve dishonesty or a false statement.) This constitutes an attack on her general character for truth and veracity, allowing the plaintiff to present reputation or opinion evidence as to her truthfulness. (B) and (D) are both incorrect because impeachment by showing bias can be rebutted, but generally not by testimony as to the witness's overall good reputation for truthfulness (because showing bias usually is deemed not to be a broad attack on the witness's overall character for veracity). [*See* comments to Fed. R. Evid. 608] (C) is similarly not as good a choice as (A) because impeachment by showing a witness's sensory deficiencies usually does not constitute a general attack on the witness's character for truthfulness but rather is offered to show that the witness was mistaken as to her perception; hence, testimony as to the witness's good reputation for truthfulness probably would not be allowed under the circumstances here.

Answer to Question 188

(B) Pam is likely to prevail if Dottie acted in reckless disregard of a high probability that emotional distress would result. To establish a prima facie case for intentional infliction of emotional distress, plaintiff must show (i) an act by defendant amounting to extreme and outrageous conduct, (ii) intent on the part of defendant to cause plaintiff to suffer severe emotional distress, or recklessness as to the effect of defendant's conduct, (iii) causation, and (iv) damages—severe emotional distress. Here, Dottie's conduct was extreme and outrageous, and she caused Pam to suffer severe emotional distress. If, as choice (B) states, Dottie knew that it was very likely that Pam would suffer severe distress, she has acted with the mental state of recklessness, and Pam can establish the prima facie case for this tort. (A) is wrong because it is not necessary to show physical injury to recover for intentional infliction of emotional distress—severe emotional distress is sufficient. Physical injury is an element of negligent infliction of emotional distress, but that tort only arises when defendant negligently creates a foreseeable risk of physical injury to plaintiff, typically through threat of physical impact; it is not applicable to these facts. (C) is incorrect because it is too narrow. It is not essential for Pam to prevail that Dottie have had a purpose of causing Pam severe emotional distress; recklessness as to the effect of her conduct will also suffice to establish the prima facie case. (D) is incorrect because that factor would only be relevant if Pam were trying to recover for her emotional distress caused by physical harm inflicted on her boyfriend. Here, Dottie's conduct was directed at Pam rather than her boyfriend and is actionable if Dottie knew that it was very likely that Pam would suffer severe emotional distress.

Answer to Question 189

(D) The statement is inadmissible because it is hearsay not within any exception. It is an out-of-court statement being offered for the truth of the matter asserted, *i.e.,* that Debbie committed the crime. As will be explained below, the statement does not qualify for exception either as a dying declaration or as a declaration of Vanessa's state of mind. In addition, the statement does not constitute an excited utterance. Despite the fact that the declaration was made while Vanessa was still under the stress of a startling event, the statement does not qualify under the exception because it does not concern the immediate facts of the startling occurrence. The fact that Vanessa believes that Debbie would kill for her job does not concern what is happening to Vanessa at that moment except to give Vanessa's opinion of who did the deed. (A) is wrong for the same reason. The statement does not appear to concern the ***facts*** of the cause or circumstances of what she believed to be her impending death. A declaration of mere opinion that is not based on firsthand knowledge is inadmissible. While an argument could be made either way on this issue, a more certain reason why the statement is inadmissible as a dying declaration is that Debbie is being tried for ***attempted*** murder. Use of dying declarations ***in criminal prosecutions*** is limited to homicide cases. (B) is wrong because the state of mind exception covers statements of the declarant's then-existing state of mind, emotion, sensation, or physical condition, and is applicable only to show the declarant's state of mind when it is directly in issue or to show subsequent acts of the declarant. Neither of these situations is present here. Thus, this exception is inapplicable. (C) is wrong because it is too broad. While the declarant must be dead in a criminal prosecution because the use of dying declarations is limited to homicide cases, a dying declaration is admissible in a civil action even though the declarant did not die.

Answer to Question 190

(C) The manufacturer's best defense is that Doug's riding on a ledge at the bottom of the sleigh constituted a misuse of the sleigh that was not reasonably foreseeable, thus relieving the manufacturer of any potential strict liability. A prima facie case in products liability based on strict liability in tort consists of: (i) a strict duty owed by a commercial supplier; (ii) breach of that duty; (iii) actual and proximate cause; and (iv) damages. Breach of duty is established by showing that the defendant sold or produced a product in a defective condition unreasonably dangerous to users. Some products are safe if used as intended, but may pose serious dangers if used in other ways. Thus, suppliers must anticipate reasonably foreseeable uses (even if they are misuses) of the product. Here, the sleigh was designed to seat four children. If so used, there is no indication that the sleigh was unsafe. Doug's injury resulted from his losing his grip on the edge of the sleigh. Because the operator of the ride would be monitoring it to ensure that only children who had paid admission would ride, the manufacturer has a strong argument that it was not reasonably foreseeable that a child would ride the sleigh by holding onto an outer edge and riding on the outside. Thus, the manufacturer was not required to anticipate and guard against such a misuse of the sleigh. Consequently, the sleigh was not so defective as to be unreasonably dangerous. (A) is incorrect because privity is not required to apply the protection of strict liability. The strict duty is owed not only to buyers but also to family, guests, friends, and employees of the buyer, as well as foreseeable bystanders. Thus, the manufacturer will be unable to avail itself of the lack of contractual privity between itself and Doug. (B) is incorrect because ordinary contributory negligence is not a defense to a strict products liability action in contributory negligence jurisdictions. Only voluntarily and unreasonably encountering a known risk or misusing the product in an unforeseeable manner (as (C) states) would serve as a defense. (D) is incorrect because, even if Dick were negligent in his supervision of Doug, such ordinary negligence will not be deemed to be a superseding intervening force that breaks the causal connection between any initial wrongful conduct by the manufacturer and the ultimate injury. Thus, any negligence on the part of Dick will not relieve the manufacturer of liability for any consequences of its supplying a defective product.

Answer to Question 191

(C) If Dick is found to have been contributorily negligent, the shopping mall will have a complete defense in a jurisdiction that follows traditional contributory negligence rules. Dick is an invitee of the shopping mall because he entered for a purpose connected with the business. As such, the mall owed him a duty to make reasonable inspections to discover dangerous conditions and, thereafter, make them safe. The mall breached this duty by failing either to discover the pile of construction materials or to remove the pile, because it created an unreasonable risk of injury to shoppers, whose attention to where they are walking may be diverted by the store displays. [*See* Restatement (Second) of Torts §343A illus. 2] This breach actually and proximately caused Dick to fall, breaking his collarbone. Thus, Dick would prevail unless his attempt to hurdle the pile constitutes contributory negligence. Under traditional contributory negligence rules, a finding of contributory negligence would completely bar Dick's right to recover. (A) is incorrect because the fact that the mall's employees were unaware of the pile of materials may itself have constituted a breach of a duty owed to Dick. As noted above, the mall was under a duty to make reasonable inspections to discover dangerous conditions. If a reasonable inspection by its employees would have led to the discovery of the pile, the mall would be liable for any injuries to invitees resulting from such failure to discover. (B) is incorrect because the facts do not clearly indicate that Dick, knowing of the risk posed by the pile, ***voluntarily*** assumed such a risk by attempting to hurdle the pile. Dick could argue that the shopping mall, by negligently creating the danger to Doug, left Dick with no available alternative to proceeding in the face of the risk. Hence, it is not possible on these facts to arrive at the conclusion that Dick assumed the risk of injury. (D) is incorrect for the following reasons: Res ipsa loquitur is a doctrine of circumstantial evidence that permits the trier of fact to infer a defendant's liability. Here, it is not necessary to resort to a circumstantial evidence doctrine to establish negligence on the part of the mall. Direct evidence of the presence of the pile of construction materials probably demonstrates a failure of the mall to discover and make safe a dangerous condition that was discoverable in the exercise of reasonable care. (D) is also incorrect because it does not address the critical issue in the question. Res ipsa loquitur requires the plaintiff to establish that (i) the accident causing his injury is the type that would not normally occur unless someone was negligent, (ii) the negligence was attributable to the defendant, and (iii) the plaintiff was free from fault in causing the injury. The third element does not require plaintiff to be entirely free from contributory negligence; as long as the plaintiff's contributory negligence does not lessen the likelihood of negligence attributable to the defendant, plaintiff can still establish res ipsa loquitur. However, any type of contributory negligence will bar Dick's recovery here, even if he can establish the elements of res ipsa loquitur, because the jurisdiction follows traditional contributory negligence rules. Thus, (C) is a better choice because it addresses the critical issue of whether Dick was contributorily negligent.

Answer to Question 192

(B) Doug can recover all of his damages except the 10% for which he was at fault, but the shopping mall may obtain contribution from Dick for his share of the damages. Where two or more tortious acts combine to proximately cause an indivisible injury to plaintiff, each tortfeasor will be jointly and severally liable for that injury. Under joint and several liability, plaintiff may recover the entire judgment amount from any defendant. Under the rule of contribution, any defendant required to pay more than his share of damages has a claim against the other jointly liable parties for the excess. In jurisdictions that have adopted a comparative contribution system, nonpaying tortfeasors are required to contribute only in proportion to their relative fault. Here, the shopping mall and Dick are jointly and severally liable for Doug's injuries; hence, Doug can recover all of his damages from the shopping mall, reduced by 10% for the amount that he was at fault. Because Dick was 30% at fault, the shopping mall has a contribution action for $30,000 against him under the jurisdiction's comparative contribution rules. (A) is incorrect. Because the jurisdiction has retained joint and several liability, the shopping mall can be required to pay all of Doug's damages except the 10% for which he was responsible. (C) is wrong because it misstates a rule for partial comparative negligence involving multiple defendants. Comparative contribution rules do not have a threshold requirement; the shopping mall can recover from another jointly liable party regardless of its percentage of fault. (D) is incorrect because Doug cannot recover for the $10,000 in damages that the trier of fact determined was attributable to his negligence.

Answer to Question 193

(C) The situation in choice (C) is the only one in which Debbie intended to permanently deprive another of her interest in property. Debbie's mistake in thinking that such conduct is not proscribed by the criminal law will not afford her a defense. Larceny is the taking and carrying away of tangible personal property of another by trespass with intent to permanently (or for an unreasonable time) deprive that person of her interest in the property. In (C), Debbie ate the meal knowing of her inability to pay the bill. Thus, in eating the meal without intending to pay for it,

Debbie had the intent to permanently deprive Kim of her interest in the food, which Debbie clearly knew belonged to Kim unless and until Debbie paid for it. Although Debbie mistakenly believed that her conduct was not prohibited under criminal law, such a mistake of law is not a defense to a crime, even if the mistake was reasonable. Therefore, Debbie would be guilty of larceny under the circumstances in (C). (A) is incorrect because Debbie's intoxication prevented her from formulating the specific intent to permanently deprive Susan of her interest in the car. Because she was drunk, Debbie mistakenly thought that she was driving her own car. Consequently, Debbie did not intend to deprive another person of her interest in the car. (B) is incorrect because Debbie's mistake of law has prevented her from having the necessary intent to deprive the new homeowner of his interest in the porch swing. Although, as noted above, mistake of law is generally no defense, such a mistake may negate the state of mind required for a crime where it results in a mistake as to an element of the crime. In (B), Debbie mistakenly believes that the new homeowner has no legally cognizable interest in the porch swing. Because of this belief, Debbie does not have the intent to deprive the homeowner of his possessory interest in the swing, a necessary element of the crime of larceny. This is in contrast with (C), where Debbie's mistake of law did not prevent her from forming the requisite intent to deprive another person of her possessory interest in property. (D) is incorrect because Debbie's intent to borrow Jim's bicycle will not constitute the intent to permanently deprive. If a defendant intends to return the property within a reasonable time and at the time of the taking has a substantial ability to do so, the unauthorized borrowing does not constitute larceny. In (D), Debbie intended to return Jim's bicycle the next day, and apparently had the ability to do so at the time of the taking. Thus, her unauthorized borrowing will not constitute larceny.

Answer to Question 194

(B) Of all the alternatives, statement (B) most accurately reflects the balance between the scope of First Amendment protection for the dissemination of truthful commercial speech and the state's ability to enact narrowly drawn regulations to advance substantial governmental interests. Although commercial speech is protected by the First Amendment, it is subject to significant regulation. A state may outlaw commercial speech that proposes an unlawful transaction or that is misleading or fraudulent. If commercial speech concerns a lawful activity and is not misleading or fraudulent, the government regulation, to be valid, must directly advance a substantial governmental interest and must be no more extensive than necessary to serve that interest. The regulation must be narrowly drawn and there must be a reasonable fit between the legislation's end and the means chosen. If, as (B) states, the legislation here at issue does not prohibit the dissemination of truthful information about prices and product availability, and is otherwise narrowly tailored to serve a substantial state interest, the legislation probably will constitute a valid regulation of commercial speech. (A) is incorrect because it would overly limit the ability of the state to reasonably regulate commercial speech. This legislation does not necessarily violate auto dealers' rights of free speech. If it does not prohibit the dissemination of truthful information and is otherwise reasonable, the legislation is sufficiently narrow to pass constitutional muster. (C) incorrectly implies that the state's police power is broader than it actually is. This legislation does in fact potentially infringe the federal constitutional right of free speech (which extends to commercial speech). If the legislation does not satisfy the test for reasonable regulations of commercial speech, the police power of the state would not save it from being found invalid. (D) is a misstatement of the law. The Constitution prohibits any state from passing any law impairing the obligation of contract. This Contract Clause prevents state destruction of all rights or all enforcement of existing contracts. (D) refers to infringement of the right to enter into a contract rather than impairment of a currently existing contract. This is outside the purview of the Contract Clause.

Answer to Question 195

(A) The contractual term as to Bill's beginning construction on April 15 is a condition rather than a promise, and failure of occurrence of a condition is not a breach of contract. This two-part question is a good example of how the MBE will test your ability to distinguish between a promise and a condition. A promise is a commitment to do or refrain from doing something. A condition is an event, other than the passage of time, the occurrence or nonoccurrence of which will create, limit, or extinguish the absolute duty to perform in the other contracting party. There is no breach of contract until the promisor is under an absolute duty to perform. Failure of a condition is not a breach of contract, but it discharges the liability of a party whose obligations on the conditional promise never mature. Here, the term regarding the beginning of construction of the restaurant on April 15 merely fixes a tentative time of the start of performance, and does not involve an absolute promise by Bill to commence performance on April 15. This term is a condition, because its occurrence will create in Laura and Emily the absolute duty to make the initial $20,000 payment. Because Bill was under no absolute duty to commence construction on April 15, his failure to do so does not constitute a breach of the contract. However, this failure does mean that the condition that governs whether Laura and Emily have an absolute duty to pay has not yet occurred. Consequently, Laura and Emily need not make the initial payment. (B) is incorrect because, with the failure to satisfy the condition, Laura and Emily are not yet contractually obligated to make the initial payment. (C) and (D) are incorrect because Bill's failure to commence construction on April 15 is not a breach. As explained above, there can be no breach until there is an absolute duty to perform, and Bill had not absolutely promised to commence construction on April 15. An additional note: (C) states that, if Bill has breached the contract in a nonmaterial manner, then Laura and Emily need not make the initial payment. Actually, the usual effect of a minor breach would be simply to provide a remedy to the aggrieved party; the aggrieved party would not be relieved of her duty of performance under the contract. Only if the promise that is breached is also a condition for the aggrieved party's performance would the breach relieve the party's duty to perform. Hence, even if Bill's failure to begin on time were a minor breach, that fact alone would not have allowed Laura and Emily to suspend their performance.

Answer to Question 196

(C) Bill will recover the balance owing on the contract because he did not intend to assume the risk of the restaurant not making a profit. Once again, distinguishing between a promise and a condition is critical. If the provision regarding payment once the restaurant became profitable is a condition, its failure to occur will extinguish Laura and Emily's duty to pay Bill what they promised under the contract. The basic test of whether a contractual provision is a promise or a condition is the intent of the parties. Courts will examine the words of the agreement, prior practices of the parties, custom, and whether fulfillment of the provision is to be rendered by the promisee (in which case it is more likely to be a condition) or by the promisor. Under a provision that a duty is to be performed "once" an event occurs, if the event is not within the control of the promisee, it is less likely that he will have assumed the risk of its nonoccurrence and therefore less likely to be a condition of the promisor's duty to perform. In doubtful situations, courts will more likely hold that the provision is a promise rather than a condition because it supports the contract and preserves the reasonable expectations of the parties. Here, there is no evidence that Bill was agreeing to a joint venture with Laura and Emily whereby he would not get paid if they did not do well but would not receive any extra if they were very successful. Whether the restaurant made a profit was more within the control of Laura and Emily than of Bill; he was assuming nothing more than a risk of delay in receiving payment to allow Laura and Emily a chance to begin making a profit. His reasonable expectation was that ultimately he would be paid the balance owing on the contract, and the sale of the restaurant by Laura and Emily gives them the ability to pay him. (A) is incorrect because the provision governing payment is not a condition excusing the absolute duty of Laura and Emily to perform under the contract. The court will imply a promise to pay the balance after a reasonable time if the timing provision in the contract is not triggered. (B) incorrectly suggests that the contractual duty of Laura and Emily was discharged by frustration of the contract's purpose. Frustration exists if (i) some supervening act or event occurs that was not reasonably foreseeable at the time of entering into the contract; (ii) the act or event has completely or almost completely destroyed the purpose of the contract; and (iii) both parties realized the purpose of the contract at the time of making it. Here, the failure to earn a profit from a new restaurant was certainly not unforeseeable; in fact, the timing provision indicates that the parties realized at least some uncertainty as to the restaurant's profitability. (D) is not as good a choice as (C) even though it may be a true statement. While Bill's completion of the restaurant is not only a promise by him but also a condition precedent to Laura and Emily's duty to pay (and this condition has occurred), the issue in this question is whether the payment provision is a condition or merely a promise as to the timing of the monthly payments, and choice (C) specifically addresses that issue.

Answer to Question 197

(C) The fare increase probably will be upheld because the action undertaken by the city council will not require strict scrutiny. The Equal Protection Clause of the Fourteenth Amendment prohibits states from denying persons equal protection of the laws. Whenever a law treats certain classes of people differently from others, a potential equal protection issue is raised. If the governmental action classifies persons based on a suspect classification (such as race), a strict scrutiny standard will be applied and the action will be struck down unless the government proves that it is necessary to achieve a compelling interest. On the other hand, most classifications, including those based on income level, are reviewed under the rational basis standard and will be upheld unless they bear no rational relationship to any conceivable legitimate government interest. Here, the fare increase could be challenged on the ground that a suspect classification (race) is involved. However, the mere fact that a governmental action has a discriminatory effect is not sufficient to trigger strict scrutiny. There must be ***intent*** to discriminate on the part of the government. When the law does not discriminate on its face and is not applied in a discriminatory manner, a suspect classification will be found only if the lawmaking body enacted or maintained the law for a discriminatory purpose. While statistical evidence is admissible that the law has a disproportionate impact on one class of persons, such evidence will almost never be sufficient by itself to prove that the government had a discriminatory purpose in passing a law. In this case, the fare increase does not discriminate on its face and is not applied just to some classes of bus riders and not others. While the fare increase has a disproportionate impact on members of a minority group because they rely more heavily on the bus lines, there is no evidence that the increase was motivated by any other purpose than eliminating the operating deficit of the bus lines. Hence, the fare increase will be held not to involve a suspect classification based on race. The other group for which the fare increase creates a disproportionate impact is the poor. However, the Court has never held that wealth alone is a suspect classification. Unless a governmentally required fee deprives a person of a fundamental constitutional right, it will be judged under the rational basis standard (*i.e.,* it will be upheld if it is rationally related to a legitimate government interest). Here, the fare increase does not deprive poor persons of any fundamental right and it is rationally related to the legitimate purpose of reducing the operating deficit of the bus system. Therefore, the fare increase will be held constitutional. (A) is incorrect because there is no evidence that the voting system established for the election of city council members violates the Equal Protection Clause, which prohibits state dilution of the right to vote. In the absence of such evidence, the action of the city council cannot be challenged on the basis of inadequate representation. (B) is wrong because, as discussed above, the existence of a disparate impact on a suspect class is not sufficient by itself to trigger strict scrutiny; thus, the city will ***not*** need to show that the fare increase is necessary for a compelling state interest. (D) is incorrect because political questions are limited to those issues committed by the Constitution to another branch of government and those issues inherently incapable of resolution and enforcement by the judicial process. The fare increase is not a political question and will be subject to review by the courts, even though only the rational basis standard will be applied.

Answer to Question 198

(A) The court is likely to rule that the library board's meeting room policy is valid because it is reasonably related to a legitimate government interest. The library board, as a government body, may reasonably regulate speech-related conduct in public forums and designated public forums through reasonable time, place, and manner regulations. Some public property, such as streets, sidewalks, and parks, is so historically associated with the exercise of First Amendment rights that it is categorized as a traditional public forum. Other public property may become a designated public forum when the government, by policy or practice, opens it for expressive activity. However, most locations other than streets, sidewalks, and parks are not public forums and may be reserved by the government for their intended activity. When a nonpublic forum is involved, government regulations designed to reserve the forum for its intended use will be upheld if they are (i) viewpoint neutral, and (ii) reasonably related to the intended purpose of the nonpublic forum (which must be a legitimate government purpose). Here, a library meeting room is not a traditional public forum, and the library board has not designated it as a public forum because its use is limited to library groups for library purposes. Thus, the court would likely characterize it as a nonpublic forum. The restriction is viewpoint neutral (*i.e.*, it is not an attempt to limit the presentation of issues to only one viewpoint), and it is rationally related to the legitimate objective of alleviating the staff's scheduling burden. Hence, the library's policy would probably be upheld by the court. (B) is incorrect because it states part of the standard for restricting speech in public forums. Speech in public forums may be regulated by reasonable time, place, and manner regulations if the regulation (i) is content neutral (*i.e.*, subject matter neutral and viewpoint neutral), (ii) is narrowly tailored to serve a significant government interest, and (iii) leaves open alternative channels of communication. Here, as discussed above, the library meeting room probably would not be characterized as a public forum. (C) is incorrect because the library, as a nonpublic forum, is permitted to restrict speech based on content (*i.e.*, subject matter) as long as the restriction is not based on the viewpoint of the speech. (D) is wrong because the requirement of alternative channels of communication is a component of the public forum standard. Here, because the library meeting room is not a public forum, the policy is valid regardless of the availability of alternative meeting facilities.

Answer to Question 199

(B) Debby can be convicted of burglary and robbery. At common law, the elements of burglary are (i) a breaking (ii) and entry (iii) of the dwelling (iv) of another (v) at nighttime, (vi) with the intent to commit a felony therein. Here, Debby has committed a constructive breaking because she gained entry by means of a fraud. The hotel room constitutes a dwelling for purposes of burglary, and Debby apparently had the intent to commit larceny when she entered the room. Debby has also committed robbery, which is defined as (i) a taking (ii) of personal property of another (iii) from the other's person or presence (iv) by force or intimidation, (v) with the intent to permanently deprive the other of the property. Debby used the threat of force against Vernon to obtain the property, and obtained it while in Vernon's presence. Thus, she can be convicted of both burglary and robbery, making (C) and (D) incorrect. (A) and (C) are incorrect because the elements of larceny are contained within the more serious offense of robbery, which is basically an aggravated form of larceny.

Answer to Question 200

(C) A record of an arrest, even for a crime such as embezzlement, cannot be used to impeach the credibility of a witness. Since there was no criminal conviction, this would be classified as evidence of a prior bad act that demonstrates dishonesty. Federal Rule of Evidence 608 would allow an inquiry into such a prior bad act during cross-examination of the witness being impeached, but extrinsic evidence of such acts is not allowed under Rule 608, even if the witness denies the act on cross-examination. (A) might be admissible to impeach. Under Federal Rule 609, a prior felony conviction for crimes that do not involve dishonesty can be used to impeach if the trial judge determines that the probative value of the evidence is not substantially outweighed by prejudice or other Rule 403 considerations. (B) represents an acceptable method of impeachment. Prior inconsistent statements can be introduced to show that the witness is not always truthful. (D) is an acceptable impeachment method. Under Rule 608, a witness may be interrogated on cross-examination with respect to any act of misconduct that is probative of truthfulness (*i.e.*, demonstrates dishonesty). Lying on an expense report would be such an act.

barbri

BAR REVIEW

Multistate Exam Workshop

Lecture Handout

CONSTITUTIONAL LAW

Question 2

One of the provisions of federal anti-smoking legislation imposes restrictions on federal economic development grants, which were awarded to states to promote and assist small businesses in urban areas. The legislation mandates that grants will be reduced by 10% for any state that fails to require businesses engaged in the sale of cigarettes to take steps to avoid sales to minors, including checking drivers' licenses or photo ID cards. A tobacco-growing state that receives several million dollars under the federal grant program challenged the constitutionality of the provision in federal district court.

Should the court uphold the federal provision?

(A) No, if the federal provision affects state regulation of businesses that do not operate in interstate commerce.

(B) No, because state distribution of economic development funds is an integral government function.

(C) Yes, because Congress may condition grants of money under its spending power.

(D) Yes, because the provision is substantially related to the important government interest of restricting minors' access to cigarettes.

Question 85

If Congress enacted a statute that provided for direct money grants to the various states to be distributed by them to police agencies within their jurisdictions for the purpose of purchasing gas-efficient patrol vehicles, to help reduce the dependency of the United States on imported oil, which of the following would provide the best constitutional justification for the statute?

(A) The Commerce Clause.

(B) The power to tax and spend for the general welfare.

(C) The Necessary and Proper Clause.

(D) The power to conduct the foreign relations of the United States.

Question 74

In connection with its agricultural products price support program, the United States Department of Agriculture regularly sent marketing and price information via telephone and teletype to its numerous field offices in various states. Recently, problems arose because sophisticated criminals were using electronic devices to intercept the transmitted information, which they then used to gain an unfair advantage over other traders in the nation's commodities markets. To alleviate this situation, Congress enacted legislation making it a criminally punishable offense to "intercept marketing and/or price information in any fashion or to transmit such intercepted information to any other person in any fashion."

Delbert, who opposed the federal agricultural price support program, learned the identity of the individuals who are intercepting the Department of Agriculture transmissions, and, in exchange for not revealing their identities, obtained copies of every transmission they intercepted. He published these in his weekly newsletter, the "Market Ripoff Report."

If Delbert is prosecuted for violation of the federal statute prohibiting transmission of intercepted marketing or price information, what is Delbert's strongest argument that the statute is unconstitutional as applied to him?

(A) The statute denies him the equal protection of the law as guaranteed by the Fourteenth Amendment.

(B) The statute violates his right not to be deprived of liberty without due process of law.

(C) The statute violates his First Amendment right to free speech.

(D) The statute is an undue burden upon interstate commerce.

Question 94

One provision of the federal Return to Decency Act, recently passed by Congress and in effect for all relevant purposes of this question, provided that state governments may enact legislation regulating any form of pinball machine or video game, including location and hours of operation. Shortly thereafter, Arizona enacted legislation providing, among other things, that no establishment could operate more than five video games at a single location, that no location where any video games were operated could be within 1,000 yards of any other location operating video games, and that no video game could be operated in any location during the hours when any school with grades kindergarten through twelve was in session. The Arizona statute also mandated that any video game sold or operated within the state use a particular LCD screen designed to minimize eyestrain.

Funtime, Inc. is a California corporation that designs and manufactures video games for sale throughout the United States and in Europe. Approximately 10% of their gross sales arises from sales of their machines in Arizona. Funtime machines are not manufactured using the special eye-protecting LCD screens; to install such screens in all machines manufactured would cause the price of the machines to increase by 20%, and to use the screens in machines sold only in Arizona would increase the cost of the Arizona machines by 50%. Funtime files suit in federal district court in Arizona seeking to enjoin enforcement of the Arizona video game statute.

How should the court rule?

(A) For the state, because the challenged legislation is within the powers specifically reserved to the states by the Tenth Amendment.

(B) For the state, because Congress has acted within its power to authorize video game regulation by the states.

(C) For Funtime, because the challenged statute violates the Commerce Clause.

(D) For Funtime, because the challenged statute is overbroad and exceeds the permissible bounds of regulation as authorized by Congress.

Question 170

To encourage the development of local integrated circuit manufacturing operations, the state of Eastern Seaboard enacted legislation requiring that at least 50% of the units sold by retailers of electronic products within the state utilize locally manufactured microprocessors. Rudy, who owned several personal and business computer stores in Eastern Seaboard, sells electronic devices manufactured entirely in other states, primarily personal computers that he purchases from a manufacturer in the state of Oro.

If Rudy attacks the Eastern Seaboard legislation as being unconstitutional, which of the following would provide the strongest support for his position?

(A) The Equal Protection Clause of the Fourteenth Amendment.

(B) The Due Process Clause of the Fourteenth Amendment.

(C) The Commerce Clause.

(D) The Privileges and Immunities Clause of Article IV.

Question 174

The state of North Central's Commercial Code provides, in part, that "the minimum price of cheese sold in this state shall be $2.50 per pound."

As to which of the following persons would the North Central statute be most likely constitutionally applied?

(A) A resident of North Central selling cheese in that state to a manufacturer of snack foods whose plant is located in the neighboring state of South Central.

(B) A resident of Canada selling cheese made in Canada to the citizens of North Central.

(C) A resident of North Central selling cheese to the Commissary at the United States Air Force base in Capitol City, North Central.

(D) A resident of North Central selling cheese to the North Central State Department of Education for its use in its school lunch program.

Question 89

The state of Northern enacted a gross receipts tax on all businesses operating in that state. The tax was a proportional tax based on revenue derived by businesses in the state. Westco, which had its corporate headquarters and most of its manufacturing plants in Northern, was the leading manufacturer in the United States of widget assembly devices, known as widgebots, which are purchased by widget users across the country.

If Westco challenges the constitutionality of Northern's assessment of the tax against Westco, what is its strongest argument?

(A) Eighty percent of Westco's revenue is derived from widgebot purchases by the federal government.

(B) The tax applies to revenue derived from all of Westco's manufacturing plants, including those not located in Northern.

(C) The state of Northern also imposes a use tax on component parts purchased outside of the state by Westco to make its widgebots that is equivalent to Northern's sales tax for similar purchases within the state.

(D) Sales taxes are imposed by other states on Westco's widgebots sold in those states.

Question 36

A state statute prohibited the sale or possession of any food product containing more than one part per billion of a dangerous pesticide. An out-of-state driver taking her recreational vehicle through a corner of the state was stopped at a state inspection station. When the state trooper learned that the pantry of her RV was stocked with food, he asked to test a few samples of her baked goods. The samples contained about 600 parts per billion of the prohibited pesticide, and all of the other baked goods in her possession were tested and found to have the same level of pesticide. All of her baked goods, worth about $150, were confiscated and destroyed.

The state in which the driver lived has no laws governing the pesticide level of baked goods. A federal law designed to protect agricultural workers requires that any food product containing more than 500 parts per billion of the toxic pesticide must be labeled as such and be in special containers. The driver brings an action in federal court asserting that the state statute is invalid because it is preempted by the federal law.

How should the court rule as to this claim?

(A) For the state, because the purposes of the federal law are different from those of the challenged statute.

(B) For the state, because regulation of food quality is a power reserved to the states by the Tenth Amendment.

(C) For the driver, because the federal law does not expressly permit states to enact more stringent pesticide level controls.

(D) For the driver, because the federal law and the state statute regulate the same subject matter.

Questions 116-117 are based on the following fact situation:

NatureFoods, Inc. owned a number of natural food stores in the state of Vegas, and had contracted with landowners and construction firms in the neighboring state of Oro in preparation for the opening of several NatureFoods outlets in that state.

NatureFoods products are stored and sold in bulk, the consumers removing and packaging the amount of food they desire from large bins, and then presenting their assembled purchases at a checkout counter. Oro statutes prohibited the sale of food in bulk due to the health hazards associated with bulk storage and contamination from consumer access to food sold from bins. Oro has prosecuted other grocers' violations of the statute in the past.

116. NatureFoods, Inc. seeks an injunction in state court in Oro prohibiting that state from enforcing its statute barring bulk sale of foodstuffs on the ground that it is an unreasonable interference with interstate commerce. If the state court rules that the relevant statute is valid and denies injunctive relief, which of the following is the proper next step for the corporation to take to obtain review of the state court decision?

(A) Appeal to the state appellate courts.

(B) Petition for removal to the federal district court with jurisdiction in the state of Oro.

(C) Appeal to the federal circuit court of appeals with jurisdiction in the state of Oro.

(D) Petition for certiorari to the Supreme Court of the United States.

117. If NatureFoods had sought an injunction against state officials in the United States District Court with jurisdiction in the state of Oro, and the state officials had sought dismissal on the ground that the corporation lacked standing to sue, what would be the probable outcome?

(A) The suit would be dismissed, because NatureFoods has suffered no injury in the state of Oro.

(B) The suit would be dismissed, because the challenged state legislation had no effect on civil liberties.

(C) The federal court would hear the suit, because a federal question—interstate commerce—is involved.

(D) The federal court would hear the suit, because NatureFoods has undertaken substantial steps to open outlets in the state of Oro.

Question 110

Recently enacted legislation required farmers in certain counties of a western state to use drip irrigation systems instead of traditional methods in order to conserve water for agricultural and other uses. A farmer who refused to use the drip system was charged pursuant to the enforcement provisions of the legislation. A state court enjoined him from using other irrigation methods and fined him.

The farmer appealed to the state supreme court, renewing his trial court claims that the irrigation legislation violated a state constitutional provision prohibiting certain governmental intrusions into private commercial activities and that it was preempted by federal water management statutes. The state supreme court held that the state constitution prohibited the challenged legislation, and construed the relevant statutes as being within the parameters of the federal statutes, and thus preempted.

If the state petitions for certiorari to the United States Supreme Court, how should the Court rule on the petition?

(A) Grant the petition, if it appears that the state court's interpretation of the scope of the federal statutes was incorrect.

(B) Grant the petition, because, under principles of federalism, a state court cannot be the final arbiter of the validity of its own legislation when it is alleged to be in conflict with federal law.

(C) Deny the petition, because there is no substantial federal question that is dispositive of the case.

(D) Deny the petition, because a state government may not seek review of decisions of its own courts in the United States Supreme Court.

Question 130

Walter owned a large citrus farm in southern California. The marketing and sale of oranges was subject to the control of a local marketing authority created pursuant to federal legislation. The marketing authority determined what quantity of oranges could be sold by each grower, the price, and the location of sale. These decisions were made by a council of local growers whose members were selected by the federal Department of Agriculture.

The applicable federal legislation provided, in part, that when any grower subject to a marketing order challenged the propriety of that order, the council of the marketing authority must submit the controversy to the United States District Court with geographical jurisdiction for a recommendation as to whether the order should be confirmed, modified, or rescinded. After the hearing in district court, the council must revote on the challenged marketing order.

Walter brings suit in United States District Court, seeking to enjoin enforcement of the federal legislation providing for the marketing order that the council issued with regard to his orange crop. He asserts that the federal legislation is unconstitutional.

As to the constitutionality of the challenged legislation, Walter will probably:

(A) Lose, because the federal government may properly regulate items in interstate commerce.

(B) Lose, because the marketing order system is a necessary and proper means of effectuating the commerce power.

(C) Win, because the federal legislation permits the federal district court to give an advisory opinion.

(D) Win, because the federal legislation deprives him of his property without due process of law.

Question 131

Richard owned a skate rental business that he operated out of a specially equipped van. He would drive to various parks and public beaches in the southern California area and rent roller skates, related safety equipment and lightweight stereo/earphone sets to passersby on an hourly basis. He also sold skates and skating equipment.

About 50% of Richard's time is spent in the city of Beachfront, and he earns about 70% of his gross rental and sale income at its beach areas. After receiving numerous complaints from beachgoers about the sidewalks congested with roller skaters, the city council of Beachfront passed an ordinance prohibiting roller skating on public property between the hours of 7 a.m. and 9 p.m.

If Richard seeks to enjoin enforcement of the ordinance in federal district court on the basis that it is unconstitutional, that court will probably:

(A) Reach the merits of Richard's challenge to the ordinance, because it interferes with his right to free association.

(B) Reach the merits of the challenge, because enforcement of the ordinance will harm Richard's business and the rights of the public are linked to Richard's rights.

(C) Decline to hear the case, because the ordinance does not prohibit the rental of skating equipment.

(D) Decline to hear the case, because skating is not prohibited on private property, nor on public property from 9 p.m. to 7 a.m.

Question 59

Concerned about the number of households headed by single teenage mothers and the deleterious effects of overpopulation, the state of Northwest enacted legislation requiring that any person under the age of 25 must obtain a certificate of responsibility before having children. Any fetus whose parents do not both have a certificate of responsibility must be aborted under the terms of the statutes, and any child born into the same circumstances will be placed up for adoption. Parents who violate the statute are subject to fine, imprisonment, or both.

If Ben, a 22-year-old resident of Northwest, brings an action in federal court seeking to enjoin enforcement of the legislation on the grounds that it violates his constitutional rights, alleging that he plans to marry and father children before he is 25, which of the following provides the strongest justification for dismissing the action?

(A) It involves a nonjusticiable political question.

(B) It is not ripe for adjudication.

(C) There is no substantial federal question involved.

(D) Ben has no standing to sue.

Question 90

During a nationwide trucker's strike, striking drivers committed repeated acts of violence against independent truckers and railroad shipments that had replaced truck transportation. This prompted Congress to enact an emergency measure directing the President to dispatch United States Army troops to specified cities and rail and highway locations to preserve order and ensure the continued flow of commerce.

This enactment is probably:

(A) Unconstitutional, because it infringes on the President's authority to faithfully execute the laws of the United States.

(B) Unconstitutional, because it infringes on the President's authority as Commander in Chief of the armed forces.

(C) Constitutional, under Congress's power to regulate commerce.

(D) Constitutional, under Congress's power to raise and support the armed forces.

Question 154

To gain progress on critical treaty negotiations with another country, the President issued an official pardon to the leader of a radical group who was in a state prison after being convicted of a violent crime in the state. The President directed the governor of the state to free the leader but the governor refused. The Justice Department brought an action in federal district court seeking an order compelling his release.

The federal court most likely will rule:

(A) For the state, since a state official acting pursuant to his state's constitution need not obey inconsistent orders from a federal official.

(B) For the state, because the President's constitutional power to pardon prisoners extends only to those convicted of federal offenses.

(C) For the state, because the President's order and the pardon given the convicted leader violate his duty to see that the laws of the United States are faithfully executed.

(D) For the federal government, since the President's actions are authorized by his power to enter into treaties with other nations.

Question 184

The state of Idarodo was the sole habitat of the leafy wortplant, a large, fast-growing bush with a massive root system that grew naturally only on steep hillsides exposed to the sun. The roots of the wortplant were highly prized by chefs, who used them in numerous local recipes. The roots were also used for a very popular herbal remedy in the region. Krell owned several large tracts of hilly land in Idarodo that were covered with wortplants, and he regularly harvested a substantial quantity of the roots and sold them to local wholesalers.

After the most recent rainy season, a number of the communities in the lower-lying areas of Idarodo suffered flooding and mudslides that caused extensive property damage to public and private property. A study commissioned by the state legislature determined that the extensive removal of wortplants from the hillsides was a significant factor contributing to the floods and mudslides. The legislature passed a statute requiring, among other measures, that property owners leave intact at least 50% of the wortplants growing on any hillside.

Krell challenged the state statute on federal constitutional grounds, alleging that he had regularly harvested substantially more than 50% of the wortplants from his property and needed to do the same this year to meet the demand for the root.

Is he likely to prevail in his challenge?

(A) Yes, because the statute substantially impairs the economic value of Krell's land.

(B) Yes, because the statute effects a taking of private property for public use without just compensation.

(C) No, because the statute is rationally related to the legitimate government interest of preventing flooding damage to property.

(D) No, because the statute promotes an important public purpose and permits the continued use of Krell's property.

Question 10

The state of Palomar's legislature enacted a law that stated in relevant part, "No person who is not a citizen of the United States may be hired for Category C public employment positions by the state of Palomar or by any county, municipality, or other governmental unit within the boundaries of the state." One of the positions specified as Category C was civil engineer. At the time the statute was signed into law, Lourdes Delgado, a citizen of the Philippines, had been legally residing in Palomar for five years. She had been trained as an engineer in the Philippines and had been a public works engineer for 10 years in the Philippines before moving to Palomar. For the last three years, Lourdes has been taking additional classes at Palomar State University to stay abreast of the latest techniques and developments in her field. Lourdes read that the Palomar Department of Transportation needed a new drafting engineer. She applied for the position and had the required qualifications. However, Nekro, the assistant director of the Department, turned down her application, telling Lourdes, "I'd really like to hire you but I can't." The sole reason Nekro gave was the recently enacted statute. Lourdes really wanted the job and filed suit in federal court, claiming that the statute violates her right to equal protection under the Fourteenth Amendment.

If Lourdes prevails, it will most likely be because:

(A) Lourdes has proved that the statutory provision is not necessary to achieve a compelling government interest.

(B) Lourdes has proved that the statutory provision is not rationally related to a legitimate government interest.

(C) The state has failed to prove that the law is necessary to achieve a compelling government interest.

(D) The state has failed to prove that the law is substantially related to an important government interest.

Question 31

A state enacted health care legislation to provide comprehensive insurance coverage on prescription drugs for all of its citizens. The legislation provided state reimbursement for the cost of all prescription drugs with one exception. Specifically excluded from the benefit plan was a drug commonly known as the "abortion pill," which was prescribed to induce early term abortions without surgery. All other prescription drugs for pregnant women were covered. A pregnant woman who had received a prescription for the drug and was subsequently denied reimbursement filed suit in federal district court challenging the constitutionality of the state's prescription drug benefit plan.

Which of the following best describes the appropriate standard by which the court should review the constitutionality of the state legislation?

(A) Because the state legislation does not improperly discriminate against a suspect class or burden a fundamental right, the woman will have to show that the legislation is not rationally related to any legitimate state interest.

(B) Because the state legislation discriminates against women by not providing coverage for all of their prescription medications as it does for men, the state will have to demonstrate that the legislation is substantially related to an important government interest.

(C) Because the state legislation impinges on a woman's constitutional right to choose whether to terminate her pregnancy, the state will have to show that the legislation does not constitute an undue burden on that right.

(D) Because the state legislation discriminates against women seeking to exercise their fundamental right to terminate their pregnancy in favor of women incurring the regular expenses of pregnancy, the state will have to demonstrate that the legislation is necessary to vindicate a compelling state interest.

Question 155

The state of Sequoia's pension program provided supplemental state pension benefits to surviving spouses and children of state employees. The program provided that when the spouse remarried, that spouse's benefits would be gradually terminated based on a statutory formula. Because of statistics showing past disparities between the household income levels of male surviving spouses and female surviving spouses, different formulas were used for the termination schedule depending on whether the surviving spouse was male or female.

Paul, the widower of a state employee, was informed after he remarried that his pension benefits would be terminated in 90 days according to the applicable formula. Upon learning that a similarly situated widow would have continued to receive benefits for six months after remarrying, he decided to file suit in federal court, alleging that the state program is unconstitutional because it is discriminatory and it unfairly burdens his right to marry.

Which of the following best states the burden of persuasion in this case?

(A) The state must demonstrate that the program is narrowly tailored to achieve a compelling government interest.

(B) The state must demonstrate that the program is substantially related to an important government interest.

(C) Paul must demonstrate that the program is not substantially related to an important government interest.

(D) Paul must demonstrate that the program is not rationally related to a legitimate government interest.

Question 73

Concerned about the rising death toll on the state's highways, the legislature of the state of Red enacted a statute providing for a summary one-year suspension of the driver's license of any person convicted of three speeding violations within a 12-month period. The statute provided that an administrative hearing is immediately available upon request. However, that hearing is limited to a determination of whether the licensee is the same person who was convicted of the speeding violations.

Donna received three speeding citations in a three-week period and was convicted of all three charges. Her license was promptly suspended under the authority of the state statute. Without first seeking an administrative hearing, Donna files a suit in federal district court challenging the constitutionality of the statute.

The court should rule that the state law is:

(A) Constitutional, because driving an automobile on the state's highways is a privilege and not a right.

(B) Constitutional, because the state's interest in promptly removing unsafe drivers from its roads outweighs Donna's right to a prior hearing under these circumstances.

(C) Unconstitutional, because the law creates an irrebuttable presumption that all drivers falling within the ambit of the statute are unsafe.

(D) Unconstitutional, as a denial of due process without a prior hearing.

Question 20

The town of Lilyville was the county seat and had a population of about 250,000. The city council of Lilyville consisted of 20 members, each of whom was elected at large. Although at one time Lilyville had had individual member districts, the city charter was revised in 1954 to provide for at-large election of all council members. The political life of the town had been dominated by members of the Good Ole Boys Club, and its full slate of candidates almost always won election. Among the population of Lilyville are now 60,000 blacks, 20,000 Hispanics, 3,000 Asians, and 2,000 Native Americans. During the long period that Lilyville had used the at-large election system, only one black person had ever served on the city council. Fifteen years ago, the Good Ole Boys Club had decided to slate Bill Johnson, who had been an outstanding scholar and athlete at the state university. Johnson, although black, was duly elected to the council with the Good Ole Boys' support. However, Johnson, during the course of his term, asked embarrassing questions about the housing conditions in predominantly black areas of the city, and otherwise agitated for meaningful change. Although Johnson ran for reelection, he did not receive the Good Ole Boys' support and was soundly defeated, even though he received 95% of the black vote. Since then, no member of a minority group has served on the city council, nor has a member of a minority group been slated as a candidate by the Good Ole Boys Club.

If a minority coalition association brings suit to compel Lilyville to provide for single member districts, it would be most likely to win its case with arguments based upon which of the following provisions of the United States Constitution?

(A) Equal Protection Clause.

(B) Due Process Clause.

(C) The Fourteenth Amendment clause protecting the privileges and immunities of national citizenship.

(D) Article I, Section 2, Clause 4.

Question 151

Under recently passed health care legislation in the state of Lincoln, generous state-subsidized health benefits were provided to all residents who did not have an employer-funded program that met specified minimum requirements. To alleviate the burden on the state's budget, the legislation provided that a person must have resided in the state for at least one year to be entitled to any health benefits provided by the state. Partridge moved to the state of Lincoln last month to take a consulting job with a computer firm. The position does not provide health benefits, so she sought coverage through the state program and was denied. She then filed suit in federal district court, challenging the denial of the state benefits to her.

If the court finds in favor of Partridge, it will most likely be because:

(A) The restriction does not have a rational relationship to a legitimate state interest as required by the Equal Protection Clause of the Fourteenth Amendment.

(B) The restriction deprives Partridge of certain privileges and immunities in violation of the Interstate Privileges and Immunities Clause of Article IV, Section 2.

(C) The restriction improperly burdens the fundamental right of interstate travel in violation of the Equal Protection Clause of the Fourteenth Amendment.

(D) The restriction deprives Partridge of a property interest without due process of law in violation of the Due Process Clause of the Fourteenth Amendment.

Question 21

Andy Carnopolous was well-known as a philanthropist. To ensure that his name would be long remembered, he planned to build the crown jewel of museums. He mentioned his plans to Mike, his longtime friend and governor of Massamont, an eastern state. Mike decided that the museum would bolster the economy and stature of wherever it was located and told Andy that if Andy put the museum in Massamont, he would arrange for the state to purchase the land and grant it to the museum. Andy agreed and the museum was built.

Andy appointed Adolph, an amateur painter, to be curator of Carnopolous Hall. Adolph was of German descent and was ashamed of Germany's actions during World War II. To assuage his own conscience, Adolph refused to hire anyone whom he believed to be of German descent. Henry applied for a job at the museum, but Adolph refused to hire him because of his German background. Henry discovered Adolph's rationale, and he brings suit against the museum.

The court will most likely find that Adolph's hiring policy is:

(A) Constitutional, because the museum is a private entity and so may constitutionally hire and fire as it desires.

(B) Constitutional, to the extent necessary to remedy past discrimination.

(C) Unconstitutional under the Equal Protection Clause, because the grant of the land is sufficient state involvement to render the museum's actions state action.

(D) Unconstitutional under the Equal Protection Clause, because the state will benefit from the museum and this creates a sufficient nexus to find state action.

Question 163

Wanda is an employee of the National Park Service. The Park Service recently created a new personnel level for field employees—Senior Ranger III, which is the highest salaried position available to Park Service field employees. The position is restricted to employees over six feet in height. Wanda seeks your advice as to whether she can challenge the validity of the height restriction in federal court.

If you decide to file suit on her behalf (she is five foot three inches tall), which of the following would be your strongest argument against the validity of the restriction?

(A) Since most women are less than six feet tall, the restriction is unconstitutional as a violation of the Equal Rights Amendment.

(B) Since most women are less than six feet tall, the restriction is an invalid discrimination on the basis of gender in violation of the Due Process Clause of the Fifth Amendment.

(C) Since most women are less than six feet tall, the restriction is an invalid gender-based discrimination in violation of the Equal Protection Clause of the Fourteenth Amendment.

(D) The restriction denies Wanda a property right without an opportunity for a hearing before a neutral decisionmaker, in violation of the Due Process Clause of the Fifth Amendment.

Question 197

Belching Rapids was an industrial city in the Midwest with approximately 300,000 inhabitants. Of these, approximately 150,000 were members of a recognized racial minority, and the latest Census figures indicated that 33,501 minority residents of Belching Rapids could be classified as "poor" under federal poverty guidelines. Of the approximately 150,000 nonminority residents of Belching Rapids, only 7,328 could be classified as "poor." The 10-member city council of Belching Rapids, containing no minority members and no poor members, decided that it was time to deal with the large operating deficit incurred by the city-owned transit system. The council decided to raise bus fares during rush hour periods from 80¢ to $1. Because poor people and members of minority groups placed greater reliance on the city's bus lines than did the bulk of the nonpoor and nonminority population (many of whom drove to work), the effect of the transit-fare increase was hardest on the poor and minority communities. Several activist groups representing the poor, various minority organizations, and some community action coalitions vowed to fight the fare increase in federal court.

Which of the following statements most accurately describes the constitutional status of the fare increase?

(A) The fare increase is unconstitutional because the Belching Rapids city council is composed solely of nonpoor and nonminority members who cannot adequately represent the interests of poor persons, who need low bus fares to survive.

(B) The fare increase is unconstitutional, because the city cannot show that the resulting disparate impact of the fare increase is necessary for a compelling state interest.

(C) The fare increase is constitutional, because there is no evidence that the Belching Rapids city council acted irrationally or was motivated by an intent to discriminate on the basis of race.

(D) The fare increase is constitutional, because a political question is involved and fares and fees may be increased if the city council deems such increases appropriate to cure deficits.

Question 8

To encourage minority business and foster pride in minority heritage, a state adopted legislation exempting magazines and other periodicals from the state's receipts tax if 20% of the magazine is devoted to articles concerning minorities (a commission was set up to sample magazines to determine on a yearly basis whether they should be exempt).

A publisher produced a sports magazine in the state that occasionally contained articles about minority athletes, but the commission determined that the publisher's magazine was not eligible for the receipts tax exemption. After paying the tax assessed on her magazine, the publisher sued for a refund.

The court will most likely find:

(A) Against the publisher, because taxpayers do not have standing to challenge tax exemptions.

(B) Against the publisher, because the state has a compelling interest in encouraging minority business.

(C) In favor of the publisher, because the tax violates the Equal Protection Clause.

(D) In favor of the publisher, because the tax violates the First Amendment freedoms of speech and press.

Question 146

Based on recommendations of a state commission studying the effect of pornographic films on violent criminal activity, the state of Pilgrim adopted legislation banning films intended for commercial distribution that appealed as a whole to the prurient interest in sex of the average person in the community, portrayed sex in a patently offensive way to citizens of the state, and which a reasonable person in the United States would find had no serious literary, artistic, political, or scientific value.

In ruling on a constitutional challenge to the legislation from a film distributor in Pilgrim who was convicted of distributing films in violation of the legislation, the federal court will likely find the legislation:

(A) Constitutional, because it uses a national reasonable person standard for determining the social value of the work.

(B) Constitutional, because it uses a statewide standard rather than a community standard for determining whether the material is patently offensive.

(C) Unconstitutional, because it uses a statewide standard rather than a national standard for determining whether the material is patently offensive.

(D) Unconstitutional, unless the court finds that the legislation is necessary to advance the state's compelling interest in reducing violent criminal activity.

Question 194

The legislature of State, concerned that the numerous and strident television, radio, and newspaper advertisements by auto dealerships annoy and mislead the public, enacted comprehensive legislation regulating the timing and content of such ads, limiting their duration, frequency, and the types of claims and information made and given.

Which of the following statements is most accurate as to the constitutionality of the advertisement regulation of State?

(A) It is unconstitutional, because it infringes upon the First and Fourteenth Amendment rights of auto dealers to free speech.

(B) It is constitutional if it does not prohibit the dissemination of truthful information about price and the availability of products, and is narrowly tailored to serve a substantial government interest.

(C) It is constitutional, because it is within the police power of the state and no federal constitutional rights are infringed.

(D) It is unconstitutional, because it infringes upon the rights of the auto dealers to enter into contracts for advertising.

Question 198

On completion of a major expansion project, the Smallville Public Library Board adopted a usage policy for the new meeting room that was added to the facility. To alleviate the scheduling burden on the staff if the meeting room were open to all groups, the policy provided that the meeting room was to be used only for "library purposes" by the library staff, the library board, or groups affiliated with the library, such as the library's teen advisory group or volunteer "Friends of the Library" group. Dialog, a local organization that promoted the political interests of an ethnic minority in the Smallville area, requested use of the meeting room for an informational meeting that would be open to the public. Although no other event was scheduled for the meeting room at the time requested, the library director declined Dialog's request, citing the meeting room policy adopted by the library board.

Dialog filed suit in federal district court, challenging the library's policy and seeking access to the meeting room. How is the court likely to rule?

(A) The library's policy is valid, because limiting the meeting room's use to library purposes is reasonably related to a legitimate government purpose.

(B) The library's policy is valid, because limiting the meeting room's use to library purposes is narrowly tailored to serve a significant government interest.

(C) The library's policy is not valid, because limiting the meeting room's use to library purposes is restricting speech based on its content.

(D) The library's policy is not valid unless there are alternative facilities in the area available for groups to hold meetings.

Question 77

To combat fraud and misuse of driver's licenses, the state of Elbonia's Department of Motor Vehicles enacted new regulations for the issuance of driver's licenses. One of the regulations, which were authorized by state law, required for the first time that driver's licenses display a photograph of the person whose name is on the license. The regulations did not provide for any exemptions from this requirement. Living entirely within Elbonia was the Flemarite sect, which devoutly believed that allowing oneself to be photographed was sinful. However, because much of Elbonia was rural and sparsely populated, the Flemarites needed to travel by automobile to obtain necessary services and to gather for worship. A Flemarite who was refused a driver's license because he would not allow himself to be photographed challenged the state regulation in federal court.

Is the court likely to uphold the application of the regulation to the religious group?

(A) Yes, because exempting the church's members from the regulation would not have a secular purpose and would constitute improper state advancement of, and entanglement with, religion.

(B) Yes, because enactment of the regulation was not motivated by a desire to interfere with religion.

(C) No, unless the state shows that the regulation is necessary to promote a compelling governmental interest.

(D) No, because the opposition to the regulation arises from a sincerely held religious belief.

Question 158

As part of legislation enacted for the stated purpose of improving computer literacy of schoolchildren, Congress appropriated funds to permit public school teachers who had been certified by state school districts as remedial computer instructors to provide supplemental computer instruction to any students in either public or private schools who did not have access to computer resources. To help insure content neutrality, the statute required the instructors coming to the private schools to use the laptop computers supplied by the public school districts, which contained the programs that the instructors used for the same purpose in the public schools.

A citizens' group filed suit in federal district court to challenge the constitutionality of funding the computer teachers for private schools, alleging that most of the private schools covered by the statute were religiously affiliated schools. No members of the group have any children in either public schools or private schools affected by the statute.

How is the court likely to rule?

(A) Dismiss the case on the pleadings, because the citizens' group does not have a sufficient stake in the controversy to have standing to challenge Congress's expenditure, which was authorized under its power to spend for the general welfare.

(B) Decide the case on the merits in favor of the government, because the legislation defines the context in which instruction can be provided in private schools so as to avoid excessive government entanglement with religion.

(C) Decide the case on the merits in favor of the citizens' group, because the appropriation's primary effect advances religion in violation of the Establishment Clause of the First Amendment.

(D) Decide the case on the merits in favor of the citizens' group, because the court will presume that any instruction provided on the premises of a religiously affiliated school will be influenced by religion.

Question 70

The legislature of the state of New Shire enacted a program by which students in the public schools could request instruction as to specific religions and religious beliefs, and thus participate in public school programs in which leaders of the religions involved gave religious instruction and performed religious practices on school grounds. The program provided instruction on any religion requested by a student.

Which of the following, if true, would be relevant in assessing the constitutionality of the state religious instruction program?

I. The substantial effect of the legislation is to promote the religions studied.

II. The primary purpose of the statute is to foster belief in the religions studied.

III. The state does not have a compelling interest in instructing public school students about specific religions.

IV. The legislation requires that religious leaders and school officials interact constantly and frequently.

(A) I., II., and III.

(B) I., III., and IV.

(C) II., III., and IV.

(D) I., II., and IV.

CONTRACTS

Question 14

On one of her daily constitutionals through the local park, Nicelady came across a stray dog. Because she was a dog lover, she coaxed the dog home with her and placed an ad in the paper, under "Lost and Found," to try to find the dog's owner. Soon thereafter, Dawglost, the owner of the dog, contacted Nicelady and arranged to come see the dog to see if it was in fact his precious stud poodle, Rambo.

The next day, Dawglost came to Nicelady's and saw that the dog was his Rambo. He was so overwhelmed with joy at finding his dog that he offered Nicelady a $200 reward, although he told Nicelady that he would not be able to pay her the reward until February 14, when he would receive the down payment on Rambo's stud fee. Nicelady thanked Dawglost but told him that she was happy that he and Rambo were reunited, and she did not want any money from him.

By February 14, however, Nicelady had a change of heart. She decided that she could use the extra money, and so she called Dawglost and said that she would like the reward after all. Dawglost refused to pay.

If Nicelady sues Dawglost for breach of contract, what will she recover?

(A) No compensation, because she rejected Dawglost's offer.

(B) No compensation, because there was no consideration to support a contract.

(C) $200, because the technical defense of the Statute of Frauds will be overcome by Dawglost's moral obligation to pay.

(D) $200, because Dawglost could not have revoked his offer until February 14, and he failed to do so before Nicelady accepted.

Questions 15-17 are based on the following fact situation:

The food and beverage manager of an exclusive country club received a letter in the mail dated January 3 and signed by the sales director of a distiller. The letter offered to meet the club's requirements for vodka in the current year, stating: "Beginning January 15, we will supply your requirements on the 15th of each month at $120 per case throughout the calendar year." The manager promptly wrote back, "Regarding your letter of January 3, we agree to have you meet our requirements for vodka at the club during the coming year, on the terms stated." The manager placed a modest order for the distiller's vodka, which was duly delivered at the stated price on January 15. The vodka proved exceedingly popular with the club members and the manager placed increased orders for February 15 and March 15, which were duly delivered at the stated price.

However, on March 17, the manager received a letter from the sales director, stating in relevant part, "Due to extraordinary conditions of social upheaval in the distiller's country of origin and concomitant increased production and import costs, it will be necessary for us to increase the price of our vodka to you to $200 per case." The manager telephoned the sales director and told him, "Our members aren't going to be happy if we change brands. We have a contract." The sales director replied, "No we don't, and in any case there's no way we can supply our product to you now at $120 per case." The manager ordered vodka from one of the distiller's competitors. The best price the manager could get for that vodka was $135 per case. The competitor's vodka proved to be far less popular than the distiller's vodka (which was the leading brand of imported vodka) and vodka consumption at the club declined, as did profits from the sale of vodka drinks. The club sued the distiller for damages.

15. The original agreement between the distiller and the club can be best described as:

    (A) A single bilateral contract.

    (B) A series of unilateral contracts.

    (C) A series of option contracts.

    (D) Not an enforceable contract.

16. Assume for purposes of this question only that the court decides that a single bilateral contract existed between the distiller and the club. The court considers the following damages to which the club might be entitled:

    I. Nominal damages.

    II. $15 times the number of cases of the competitor's vodka purchased from April through December.

    III. The decline in profits that was caused by reduced sales of vodka drinks.

    The court should award:

    (A) I. only.

    (B) II. only.

    (C) III. only.

    (D) II. and III.

17. The distiller's best defense against the club's suit is:

    (A) The original promise by the club was illusory, because no maximum or minimum quantities were stated.

    (B) The agreement between the distiller and the club was a series of monthly unilateral contracts, cancelable at will.

    (C) Commercial impracticability.

    (D) The distiller never made a valid offer to the club.

Question 142

On March 1, School District 726 faxed a "quotation request form" to various suppliers of school furniture requesting offers for the sale of 20 student chairs. The form was on school district letterhead and signed by Paul Boone, the district's purchasing director. It specified that the offer must be held open for four months and that the price term must be no higher than $30 per chair. Joe Smith, the president of Multistate Institutional Furniture, telephoned the next week and told Boone that Multistate will sell the school district 20 chairs at $20 per chair, and agreed to hold the offer open for four months. Boone thanked Smith for the offer and indicated that he would get back to him within that time period. On May 1, before the school district had responded to Multistate's offer or taken any action in reliance on it, Smith faxed a letter to Boone stating that demand for student chairs had been higher than expected and that the offer was terminated. On May 2, Boone called Smith and told him that the school district was treating Multistate's offer as still being open and was accepting it on its terms.

Did Boone's call on May 2 create a legally enforceable contract with Multistate?

(A) Yes, because the contract is for the sale of goods valued at less than $500.

(B) Yes, because the school district accepted the offer within three months.

(C) No, because Multistate did not sign the form specifying the length of time that the offer would be held open.

(D) No, because a firm offer under the Uniform Commercial Code is not effective if its term is more than three months.

Questions 28-29 are based on the following fact situation:

Ken had a 1957 Chevrolet that he had restored using only original General Motors parts. He told his friend George that he was interested in selling it, but didn't know what price to ask. George said that he would pay $12,000 for the car, but would have to borrow the money and didn't know if he could get the financing. Ken said that he was going to put a classified ad in the auto section of the newspaper and really did not want to commit himself if George did not have the money. George then suggested that Ken postpone placing the ad in the newspaper and give him 10 days to obtain financing to buy the car. Ken agreed and wrote the following on a piece of paper and gave it to George: "I will sell my 1957 Chevrolet to George if he comes up with $12,000 within 10 days."

Later that day, Ken met an old college buddy, Lester, whom he had not seen in several years. Lester was in the business of selling customized cars, and when he learned of Ken's Chevrolet, said, "For 10% of the gross I could find you a buyer at no less than $15,000." Ken said nothing in reply.

The next morning, Lester telephoned Ken and told him that Mr. Jones was willing to pay $16,000 for the Chevrolet, sight unseen. Ken asked for Jones's phone number, which Lester gave, and then called Jones and arranged a sale. He then phoned George and said that he was revoking his offer.

28. Which of the following best describes the agreement between Ken and George?

    (A) A promissory estoppel situation.

    (B) A quasi-contract.

    (C) An offer for a unilateral contract.

    (D) An option contract.

29. If Lester is not paid by Ken and brings an action against Ken for breach of contract, seeking damages of $1,600, what will be the probable outcome?

    (A) Ken will win, because 10% is unconscionably large as a finder's fee in such a transaction.

    (B) Ken will win, because there was no consideration for any promise to pay that might have been implied from his conduct.

    (C) Lester will win, because he obtained a buyer for Ken's Chevrolet and a purchase price over $15,000 was paid.

    (D) Lester will win, unless Ken can show that he could have found another buyer who would pay at least $16,000 for the car.

Question 41

A homeowner offered a roofer $500 to replace the bad shingles on his roof if the roofer could finish the job by October 1. The roofer told the homeowner he would get back to him after he had checked out prices at a local builder's supply store. The next day, the roofer phoned the homeowner, who was not at home, and left a message on his answering machine that he could not do the roof for less than $650. The roofer did not hear from the homeowner for several days; since October 1 was still two weeks away, the roofer phoned the homeowner again and left another message on his answering machine stating that "$500 is O.K. for the roofing job. I'll do it this weekend unless that would be inconvenient." The homeowner replayed the second message just as he was leaving town on a business trip and did not contact the roofer. That weekend, unknown to the homeowner, the roofer took his tools and materials to the homeowner's house and repaired the roof. When the homeowner returned from his trip several days later, the roofer presented him with a handwritten invoice for $500.

If the homeowner refuses to pay the roofer, and the latter brings an action solely for breach of contract to recover the $500 contract amount, who will likely prevail?

(A) The roofer, because he accepted the homeowner's offer before the latter materially changed his position in reliance upon the first telephone message.

(B) The roofer, assuming that the work he did was actually worth $500.

(C) The homeowner, because he was unaware that the roofer was doing the roof repair while he was out of town.

(D) The homeowner, because he did not accept the roofer's offer to do the roof repair for $500.

Question 102

On July 26, a manufacturer of computer accessories received a purchase-order form from a retailer of computer and office equipment, in which the latter ordered 2,000 ergonomic mouse pads for delivery no later than September 1 for a total price of $10,000, as quoted in the manufacturer's current catalog. Two days later, the manufacturer faxed its own purchase-order acceptance form to the retailer, which had not previously done business with the manufacturer. The purchase-order acceptance form stated that it was an acceptance of the specified order, was signed by the manufacturer's shipping manager, and contained all of the terms of the retailer's form, but it also contained an additional printed clause stating that all disagreements under this sale are subject to arbitration by the American Arbitration Association.

Assuming that there was no further communication between the parties, which of the following is an accurate statement of the legal relationship between the manufacturer and the retailer?

(A) There is an enforceable contract between the parties whose terms do not include the arbitration clause in the manufacturer's form.

(B) There is an enforceable contract between the parties whose terms include the arbitration clause in the manufacturer's form.

(C) There is no enforceable contract between the parties because the manufacturer's form constituted a rejection of the retailer's offer and a counteroffer by the manufacturer.

(D) There is no enforceable contract between the parties because the manufacturer's form added an additional term that materially altered the terms of the retailer's offer.

Question 148

Bylon, the owner of an apparel store, faxed an order to Seltex, one of her regular suppliers, for 100 pairs of xylon gloves at $10 a pair, Seltex's list price, delivery within five days. Seltex checked its inventory and discovered that it only had 90 pairs of xylon gloves. It shipped to Bylon the 90 pairs of xylon gloves as well as 10 pairs of zeelon gloves, which also had a list price of $10 a pair. Seltex also faxed to Bylon the following message: "Did not have enough stock of xylon gloves to fill your order. In the hope that you will be able to use them, we are sending zeelon gloves at the same list price to make up the balance of the shipment."

Upon receipt of the shipment and the fax, what are Bylon's options?

(A) Bylon may accept the shipment, in which case she must pay Seltex $1,000 less any damages sustained because of the nonconforming shipment, or she may reject the shipment, in which case she has no further remedy against Seltex.

(B) Bylon may accept the shipment, in which case she must pay Seltex $1,000, or she may reject the shipment, in which case she may recover against Seltex for breach of contract.

(C) Bylon may accept the shipment, in which case she must pay Seltex $1,000, or she may reject the shipment, in which case she has no further remedy against Seltex.

(D) Bylon may accept the conforming part of the shipment and reject the nonconforming part, in which case she must pay Seltex $900 less any damages sustained because of the nonconforming part of the shipment, or she may reject the entire shipment, in which case she may recover against Seltex for breach of contract.

Questions 47-48 are based on the following fact situation:

Gordon's adult daughter Sheila smoked two packs of cigarettes a day, and he had often tried to persuade her to stop, to no avail. Gordon then learned that Sheila and her husband had decided to try to have a baby, and when he thereafter saw Sheila at a party, he told her, "If you will give up smoking for the next 11 months, at the end of that time I will give you $10,000." Sheila agreed to stop smoking that very day. After leaving the party, Sheila had second thoughts. She remembered that her father had once promised her that if she would refrain from wearing makeup until she was 16, he would buy her a car, and had never done so. Sheila called her mother, and asked her if she thought Gordon was serious. Nancy, her mother, said, "Go ahead and quit, honey—if your father won't pay, I'll see that you get the money he promised you from my own accounts."

Sheila quit smoking that day and never smoked again. Ten months after Gordon's conversation with Sheila, Gordon and Nancy were killed in an auto accident.

47. Assume for the purposes of this question only that, one month later, Sheila sought payment of the $10,000 only from her father's estate. Will Sheila prevail as to this claim?

    (A) No, because she will be unable to prove the terms of the oral contract between her and her father, because he is dead.

    (B) No, because her father's offer to pay was terminated upon his death.

    (C) Yes, because she has performed under a valid contract, and thus her father's estate must now perform.

    (D) Yes, because she changed her position for the worse in reliance on her father's promise, and thus his executor is estopped from denying that the contract existed.

48. Assume for the purposes of this question only that Sheila files a claim against her mother's estate for $10,000 on the promise her mother made to pay that amount if her father refuses to pay. She proves that she has submitted a claim for $10,000 to the executor of her father's estate and has been refused payment. What is the best argument for the probate court's rejecting this claim against Nancy's estate?

    (A) The contract between Nancy and Sheila was illusory.

    (B) Sheila has not been damaged by any breach because the only effect—that she quit smoking—was salutary.

    (C) The contract between Nancy and Sheila was oral.

    (D) No consideration flowed to Nancy under the contract.

Question 24

The nephew of a financially successful farmer inherited a nearby farm with a tractor that was badly out of date. Because the local bank refused to extend credit solely to the nephew to buy a new tractor, the nephew asked his uncle to guarantee the loan. The uncle told him, "I'll guarantee that loan if you'll let me use the new tractor for 10 days without having to pay you rent." The nephew readily agreed to the uncle's proposal, so the uncle went to the local bank, where he kept his accounts, and told his loan officer, "I'm willing to guarantee that tractor loan for my nephew." This prompted the loan officer to agree to extend the requested credit to the nephew. Although the loan officer did not make the uncle sign any papers, he considered the uncle's word to be his bond and issued the nephew a loan commitment statement. That very evening the uncle learned that his nephew had a reputation for financial irresponsibility among his former classmates at the state agricultural college. The next day, the uncle telephoned the loan officer, telling him, "You can forget about me guaranteeing any loan to my nephew." Despite the uncle's phone call, the loan officer did not stop the check from being issued, and the nephew received the money to purchase the tractor. The nephew drove the tractor over to the uncle's farm and told him, "Here, you can have it for 10 days, just like I promised." The uncle replied, "I don't want to use your tractor and I'm not guaranteeing your loan."

Six months later, the nephew defaulted on the loan. Because of gross misuse, the new tractor was in terrible condition and its value would not cover anywhere near the amount of the loan. The nephew has departed for parts unknown.

If the bank sues the uncle for the unpaid portion of the loan:

(A) The bank will win, if the suretyship agreement was supported by consideration between the bank and the uncle.

(B) The bank will win, if the uncle's main purpose in making the agreement with the bank was to benefit himself rather than his nephew.

(C) The uncle will win, because the suretyship agreement was not in writing.

(D) The uncle will win, because he withdrew his promise before the nephew received the money or the tractor.

Question 125

Alan wanted to have his driveway resurfaced. He called a number of commercial establishments which do such work and received bids ranging from $4,200 to $5,000. Bert submitted a bid to do the work for $4,000, and Alan entered into a contract with him to have the driveway resurfaced.

Shortly before Bert was scheduled to begin work, he called Alan and said, "I just found out my secretary made a mistake in adding figures. I know we signed a contract, but I couldn't possibly do the work for less than $4,400 or it would not be worth it."

Can Alan enforce the contract for $4,000?

(A) No, if Alan had reason to know that $4,000 was too low a bid.

(B) No, because there was no mutual assent.

(C) Yes, because a $400 change in price has a material effect on the agreement.

(D) Yes, because Bert assumed the risk of bid computation errors.

Question 136

A homeowner wanted to have his house repainted. He called a number of businesses which do such work and received bids ranging from $8,500 to $9,000. A local painter submitted a bid to do the work for $8,000, and the homeowner entered into a contract with him to have the house repainted. Shortly before the painter was scheduled to begin work he discovered that he could not make a profit unless the homeowner agreed to pay him $8,600. He called the homeowner with that information. The homeowner responded, "O.K., I'll pay you the extra $600, but I think you're being unfair." After the painter finished the painting he asked the homeowner for his money. The homeowner handed the painter $8,000 in cash and said, "This is all I'm going to pay you because you had no right to up the price on me."

If the painter sues the homeowner for the additional $600, who will prevail?

(A) The homeowner, because the promise to pay the additional money was not in writing.

(B) The homeowner, because the painter was already under a preexisting duty to paint the house for $8,000.

(C) The painter, because he relied to his detriment on the homeowner's promise to pay the additional money.

(D) The painter, because the promise to pay the additional money was the settlement of a good faith dispute.

Questions 171-172 are based on the following fact situation:

Grainco, a large grain dealer in the Midwest, contracted with Petchow, Inc., a pet food manufacturer, to supply "100 tons of cornmeal" to Petchow after Grainco had processed the grain from the fall corn harvest, but in any case no later than November 15. The purchase price and delivery terms were specified in the contract, which permitted partial shipments. On November 1, Grainco delivered 50 tons of cornmeal to Petchow with the notification that the balance would be shipped by November 15. Petchow rejected the shipment because the written documentation accompanying the shipment did not establish that the cornmeal came from corn that was not genetically modified, and therefore Petchow could not use it.

171. Assume for purposes of this question only that Grainco seeks an injunction to force Petchow to accept the shipment. Petchow claims that both parties to the contract understood that the term "cornmeal" meant only cornmeal documented to be from corn that was not genetically modified. If Petchow seeks to introduce evidence of trade usage supporting that understanding of the term, should the court permit it?

    (A) Yes, because there was a latent ambiguity in the expression of the parties' agreement.

    (B) Yes, because trade usage is admissible to explain or supplement the terms of a contract.

    (C) No, because the term "cornmeal" in the contract is not ambiguous.

    (D) No, if the court finds that the writing is a complete integration.

172. Assume for purposes of this question only that Grainco responded to Petchow's rejection by conceding that the shipment did not conform to the contract and promising Petchow that it would deliver all 100 tons of cornmeal by November 15 with proper documentation showing that it was not

from genetically modified corn. Which of the following best expresses Petchow's options?

(A) Petchow may notify Grainco that the entire contract is terminated and that Petchow is going to obtain the 100 tons of cornmeal from another source.

(B) Petchow may notify Grainco that the contract is terminated as to the 50 tons of cornmeal that was shipped and did not conform to the contract, but must accept the additional 50 tons when it is shipped if it conforms to the contract.

(C) Petchow must allow Grainco a commercially reasonable time to ship cornmeal that conforms to the contract before it can terminate the contract.

(D) Petchow must allow Grainco until November 15 to ship cornmeal that conforms to the contract before it can terminate the contract.

Questions 87-88 are based on the following fact situation:

On August 5, Walter and Yogi entered into a written agreement that specified, among other things, that "if the Seals win the pennant, Walter will deliver to Yogi's concession stand at Seals Stadium 500 hot dogs on each of the following days: September 5, 7, and 9. Price to be 25¢ per hot dog. Payment to be made by Yogi to Casey, a creditor of Walter, on September 10."

87. On August 15, Walter wants to avoid his obligation to deliver the hot dogs to Yogi. Casey has not become aware of any agreement between Walter and Yogi. Which of the following is the most accurate statement?

(A) Walter can rescind if Yogi and Casey give their permission.

(B) Walter can rescind if Yogi gives permission.

(C) Walter can repudiate the agreement because Yogi's promise to perform is illusory.

(D) Walter can revoke the offer to sell hot dogs if the Seals have not won the pennant.

88. Assume for the purposes of this question only that Casey first learned of the agreement between Walter and Yogi on September 5. On September 10, after Yogi refused to pay any money to Casey, the latter filed suit against Yogi for $375. Which of the following would provide a partial defense for Yogi in the litigation?

I. Walter and Yogi agreed on September 1 that the contract price for the hot dogs would be 20¢ instead of 25¢.

II. Walter and Yogi had originally agreed that the contract price for the hot dogs would be 15¢, but Walter had inadvertently written 25¢ in the contract, and neither Walter nor Yogi noticed before signing.

(A) I. only.

(B) II. only.

(C) I. and II.

(D) Neither I. nor II.

Question 3

A large insurance company with many employees instituted a supplemental employee benefit plan. The plan provided that any employee who had worked for the company for at least 25 years would be permitted to designate a charity to receive, upon the employee's retirement, a donation in the employee's name of six months' worth of the employee's salary. The plan gave participating employees an unqualified right to change the beneficiary at any time before payment was made. A veteran employee had worked at the company for 26 years when the program was instituted and was planning to retire in 10 months. He enrolled in the program and named his favorite church as the beneficiary of the donation. The church, which was undergoing a highly publicized restoration of its historic chapel, received a letter from the company informing it that the employee had named it beneficiary of his plan and indicating the approximate amount that it would receive upon the employee's retirement in 10 months. The letter did not inform the church of the employee's right to change beneficiaries before that time. Church elders, anticipating the gift, hired a European artisan to restore the stained glass windows in the chapel. They planned to put up a plaque in the employee's honor and pay for the work with the funds from the employee's benefit program.

Six months later, the employee converted to a different religion and changed the beneficiary of his plan to his new church. When the employee retired, the company paid the benefit to his new church. His old church, which had paid for the stained glass restoration work upon its completion, demanded payment of the benefit from the company.

If the employee's old church sues the company for payment of the benefit, the court should rule in favor of:

(A) The church, because the church took steps to restore the windows in reliance on payment of the benefit.

(B) The church, because the employee did not have the power to change the beneficiary of his plan after the church's rights as third-party beneficiary had vested.

(C) The company, because the agreement between the employee and the company allowed the employee to change the beneficiary of the benefit plan.

(D) The company, because it had a duty to pay the employee's new church as the named beneficiary of his plan.

Questions 34-35 are based on the following fact situation:

Agrigiant, Inc., a large midwestern farming corporation, and the Western Baking Company ("WBC"), a large food-selling corporation located on the Pacific coast, entered into a contract calling for Agrigiant to sell and WBC to buy 10,000 bushels of winter wheat for $5 per bushel. The contract stated that Agrigiant would deliver the wheat "F.O.B. St. Louis Railroad depot." Before the date on which performance was due, Agrigiant assigned all its rights under the contract to Pucker Farms, another large wheat producer. Pucker hired Acme Freight Lines to truck 10,000 bushels of winter wheat from the Pucker silos to a grain elevator in St. Louis, from which the wheat would be loaded onto Santa Fe Railroad hopper cars bound west. En route to St. Louis, the Acme trucks carrying the Pucker wheat were stopped by mobs of citizens maddened by the revelations that they and their children had been poisoned for years by the grain industry's practice of using highly toxic pesticides to fumigate grain and grain processing equipment. Although Pucker wheat was not fumigated with the pesticide, the mobs seized and burned the Acme trucks to protest the callousness and greed of the grain plutocrats and their government allies.

34. Pucker brings suit against WBC, which refused to pay the contract price for the wheat. What will be the probable outcome of this litigation?

    (A) Pucker will lose.

    (B) Pucker will recover the amount necessary to replace the destroyed wheat.

    (C) Pucker will recover the full contract price.

    (D) Pucker will recover the profits it would have realized under the contract.

35. WBC brings its own action against Agrigiant for breach of contract. What will be the probable outcome of this litigation?

    (A) WBC will lose.

    (B) WBC will recover the amount necessary to replace the destroyed wheat, over the contract price.

    (C) WBC will recover the full contract price.

    (D) WBC will be able to compel specific performance of the contract.

Question 124

Debbie owed Cyndy $1,250. Cyndy's best friend, Francis, had recently lost his job and was facing a number of serious financial problems. He told Cyndy that he might have to file for bankruptcy unless he could deal with some pressing overdue credit card bills. Cyndy wanted to help Francis, but most of her money was tied up in certificates of deposit, none of which came due in less than six months. Cyndy therefore told Debbie to pay the $1,250 to Francis when the debt became due in three days. Immediately after directing Debbie to pay Francis, Cyndy called Francis and told him he should expect to get $1,250 from Debbie in three days. Debbie did not know Francis and was doubtful of the wisdom of paying someone she did not know. When her debt became due, Debbie tendered $1,250 to Cyndy, and Cyndy accepted the money.

If Francis sues Debbie for $1,250, which of the following is the most likely result?

(A) Francis will recover, because Cyndy effectively assigned her right to collect the $1,250 to Francis.

(B) Francis will not recover, because Cyndy's acceptance of $1,250 from Debbie revoked Cyndy's gift to Francis.

(C) Francis will not recover, because Debbie was never indebted to Francis and cannot be forced to pay him.

(D) Francis will not recover, because Debbie's tender of $1,250 to Cyndy and Cyndy's acceptance thereof constituted a novation.

Question 108

A debtor owed a creditor $5,000, but the debt was barred by the applicable statute of limitations. During a conversation between the debtor and the creditor, the debtor agreed to assign to the creditor a debt of $4,000 that was owed to the debtor by a third party and was coming due in a week, and called the third party to inform him of the assignment. When the debt became due, the third party refused to pay the creditor.

If the creditor brings an action to collect the debt against the third party, will he likely prevail?

(A) Yes, because the creditor's agreement to accept a lesser amount than the original debt constituted consideration for the assignment.

(B) Yes, because an assignment need not be in writing to be enforceable.

(C) No, because the third party may raise the debtor's statute of limitations defense on the original debt.

(D) No, because a new promise to pay a legal obligation barred by law must be in writing.

Questions 61-62 are based on the following fact situation:

Decker owed Crieder $1,000 on a promissory note that was due on August 1. After Decker told Crieder that he might not be able to pay the note on its due date, Crieder agreed to extinguish the debt if Decker, who was the manager of a discount electronics store, purchased a new entertainment system that Crieder's girlfriend wanted and had it delivered to her home and set up by August 15. Since Decker would have to pay only $600 for the system because of his manager's discount, he agreed and the parties signed a writing to that effect on July 26.

61. Is the new agreement between Crieder and Decker legally enforceable?

(A) No, because Decker incurred no additional detriment that would serve as consideration for the new agreement.

(B) No, unless it would have cost Crieder $1,000 to purchase the entertainment system himself.

(C) Yes, because Decker incurred a different obligation than he originally had.

(D) Yes, because the new agreement between Decker and Crieder is enforceable with or without consideration as long as it was made in good faith.

62. Assume for purposes of this question only that Crieder filed suit against Decker on August 2 for failure to pay the $1,000 promissory note. May Decker have this action enjoined by introducing evidence of the July 26 agreement?

(A) Yes, because the July 26 agreement between Decker and Crieder suspended Decker's obligation on the promissory note.

(B) Yes, because the July 26 agreement between Decker and Crieder discharged Decker's obligation on the promissory note.

(C) No, unless Decker has already initiated the purchase of the entertainment system in reliance on Crieder's promise to extinguish the debt.

(D) No, because Decker's only remedy is to sue for damages for breach of the July 26 agreement.

Questions 105-107 are based on the following fact situation:

On January 1, Farnsworth entered into a written contract with Jones by which Farnsworth was to sing nightly at Jones's nightclub for a period of two years at $54,000 per year, commencing February 1.

105. Assume that on January 25 Farnsworth phoned Jones and told him, "I still haven't finished moving all my belongings into my new apartment. It's going to take me awhile to get settled and I might not be ready to start singing until February 10."

Can Jones bring an immediate suit against Farnsworth?

(A) Yes, because Farnsworth's telephone call was a repudiation.

(B) Yes, if Jones changes his position in reliance on Farnsworth's telephone call.

(C) No, because Farnsworth's telephone call did not constitute a repudiation.

(D) No, because a repudiation must be in writing to be given effect.

106. Assume that Jones had no communication with Farnsworth between January 1 and February 1. On February 1, Jones received a telegram from Farnsworth stating:

> Due to circumstances beyond my control, I will not be able to start my singing engagement at your club until February 10. I'm sorry for any inconvenience this causes you.

On February 10 Farnsworth appeared at Jones's nightclub, ready to sing.

May Jones cancel the contract?

(A) Yes, because Farnsworth failed to start singing when he contracted to do so.

(B) Yes, because Farnsworth's actions constitute a material breach.

(C) No, unless Jones was materially prejudiced by Farnsworth's failure to start singing on February 1.

(D) No, because Farnsworth notified Jones of his delay in performance in a timely fashion.

107. Assume that after Farnsworth failed to appear at Jones's nightclub on February 1, Jones read in the newspaper that Farnsworth had been in a traffic accident and was expected to be in the hospital for two months. Jones hired Young to sing in his nightclub for two months at a salary of $5,000 per month. Can Jones recover from Farnsworth the additional $500 per month salary he must pay Young?

(A) Yes, because Farnsworth failed to give Jones timely notice of his hospitalization.

(B) Yes, because Farnsworth knew that Jones had spent a considerable amount of money advertising live entertainment at his nightclub commencing February 1.

(C) No, because Farnsworth was not at fault for the delay since he did not cause the accident.

(D) No, because in a personal services contract, performance is excused by illness of the party performing the personal service.

Questions 195-196 are based on the following fact situation:

Laura and Emily wanted to open a restaurant, but were only able to raise $40,000 of the $160,000 needed for its construction. Bill, a contractor who had suffered greatly in the decline in residential construction, learned of Laura and Emily's problem and suggested that they enter into the following agreement: Laura and Emily would pay Bill $20,000 in cash on commencement of construction, scheduled for April 15 after the spring thaw. On completion of the restaurant on September 30, Bill would be paid an additional $20,000 in cash. He would agree to take the remaining $120,000 of the cost of building the restaurant in monthly payments of $1,000 principal plus 12% annual interest on the outstanding balance, once the restaurant started earning a profit. Laura and Emily were delighted, and a written contract setting forth those plus other terms was executed on March 30.

195. Assume for the purposes of this question only that the region had a late spring and that on April 30 Bill had not yet commenced construction of the restaurant. He has:

(A) Not breached the contract, but Laura and Emily need not make the initial $20,000 payment.

(B) Not breached the contract, and Laura and Emily must make the initial $20,000 payment.

(C) Breached the contract in a nonmaterial particular; thus, Laura and Emily need not make the initial $20,000 payment.

(D) Breached the contract in a material particular; thus, Laura and Emily may treat the contract as at an end and sue for damages.

196. Assume for the purposes of this question only that despite several months' effort, Laura and Emily are unable to attract enough customers to earn any profit from the operation of the restaurant. They are able to find a buyer who pays them $170,000 for the facilities. Bill brings an action against Laura and Emily for the remaining $120,000 owing on the contract. Will he recover?

(A) No, because Laura and Emily never earned a profit from their operation of the restaurant.

(B) No, because the failure to earn profits from the operation of the restaurant was an unforeseeable intervening event.

(C) Yes, because the provision governing payment of the outstanding balance of the construction cost merely established the time frame in which payment was to be made.

(D) Yes, because all of the conditions precedent to Laura and Emily's duty to pay had occurred.

Question 22

A retailer of personal watercraft and speedboats agreed to sell to a buyer a personal watercraft for $10,000. The written contract specified delivery within 30 days and a down payment of $2,000, but did not contain a liquidated damages clause. Two weeks after making the down payment, the buyer told the retailer that he lost his job and could not afford to go through with the purchase, and asked for his down payment back. The retailer, which could get as many of that model of watercraft as it required from the manufacturer for a wholesale price of $7,000, put the watercraft that it was going to deliver to the buyer back in its inventory. The retailer then sold it to someone else for $9,500.

The buyer sues the retailer to get back his deposit, and the retailer counterclaims for damages. Excluding incidental costs, which of the following amounts represents the most likely recovery?

(A) The buyer will recover $2,000.

(B) The buyer will recover $1,500.

(C) The retailer will recover $3,000.

(D) The retailer will recover $1,000.

Question 147

On March 1, a builder entered into a contract with a buyer to build a home on a specified lot and sell the lot and house to the buyer for $350,000. The buyer had the following language added to the contract: "Because my current lease will expire on September 1, time is of the essence on this contract." The builder and the buyer agreed that construction would be completed on August 1, and that escrow would close on the transaction on August 15.

State law required that a home builder have an architect's certificate of completion before any residence could be conveyed to a purchaser. The builder employed his own architect to design and oversee construction of his custom homes. Due to a materials shortage resulting from a dockworker's strike in early summer, construction of the buyer's house was not completed until August 5. On August 8, the builder discovered that his architect had left for a long-planned overseas trip without preparing the certificate of completion for the home. The builder was not able to obtain a certificate until August 20 from a local architect, who had to study the plans and make inspections that had already been completed by the builder's architect. When the builder attempted to place the deed and certificate of completion into escrow, he learned that the buyer had canceled escrow on August 16 and that she refused to proceed with the purchase.

The builder sold the home nine months later for its then reasonable market value of $330,000. He brings an action for damages against the buyer, seeking $20,000, the difference between the contract price and the amount he ultimately received for sale of the house.

Will the builder recover?

(A) No, because the duty to certify completion of the home cannot be delegated to an architect unfamiliar with the construction.

(B) No, because he was late in delivering the deed and certificate of completion into escrow.

(C) Yes, because the short time the builder was late in delivering the deed was not a material breach of the contract.

(D) Yes, unless the buyer can prove that she suffered damages as a result of the delay.

Question 167

Structo entered into a contract with Devlo to build a warehouse for $500,000 by August 1. The agreement provided for five progress payments of $100,000 each at various stages of completion. On June 20, after Structo had spent $350,000 on performance and received $300,000 in progress payments, Structo notified Devlo that it was not going to continue with the project because its crews were needed to start some other building projects. Devlo hired Buildco, another contractor, to complete the warehouse by August 1 for $250,000, which was a reasonable price given the short deadline.

Which of the following statements regarding the parties' remedies is correct?

(A) Structo can recover $50,000, the difference between the amount Structo expended on performance and the amount it was paid, to prevent Devlo's unjust enrichment.

(B) Neither party can recover anything, because the $50,000 extra that Devlo had to pay to complete the building is offset by the $50,000 difference between Structo's expenditures and the payments Devlo made to Structo.

(C) Devlo can recover $50,000, the difference between the contract price and the total amount it paid for completing the building.

(D) Devlo can recover $100,000, the difference between the contract price and the total amount expended in construction of the building.

CRIMINAL LAW

Question 54

Under which of the following circumstances would the named defendant be most likely to be convicted of common law murder?

(A) Huey, stopped by police for a traffic violation, gets into a fight with one of the officers and wrestles his gun away from him. The other officer fires his weapon, hitting Huey in the stomach. Rendered unconscious, Huey nevertheless fires the gun he took from the officer and hits the firing officer, killing him.

(B) Plagued by an infestation of rats in his house, Louie takes a flashlight and a pistol to the basement where the rats are worst, and begins picking off those that he can see. When one of the rats runs under a pile of gunny sacks, Louie aims at the movement he thinks is the rat burrowing to safety and shoots it. Unknown to Louie, the movement was a homeless person who had broken into Louie's home and crawled under the sacks for warmth, and who had been awakened by the previous shots. The person is killed by the pistol bullet.

(C) Despite the fact that he has had nine drunk driving arrests within the last year, and is on probation from his last drunk driving conviction, in which he pleaded guilty after smashing up another driver's car, Dewey drives to his favorite bar, gets extremely intoxicated, and then attempts to drive home. On his way, his car collides with another, killing the two occupants.

(D) While target shooting at some discarded soft drink cans on his ranch, Mickey takes aim at one of the cans and fires his rifle. The bullet passes through the can, hits a rock, ricochets to a nearby tree, ricochets off the tree, and strikes Mickey's companion, who is standing next to Mickey, and kills him.

Question 23

A fleeing bank robber ran into a school and took the principal hostage at gunpoint. The police, who had received a detailed description of the clothing the robber was wearing, surrounded the school and demanded that the robber come out with his hands up. When it began to get dark, the robber ordered the principal to undress, and the robber switched clothing with the principal. He tied the principal's hands to his side and pushed the principal out the door first. Seeing that the first person out of the door did not emerge with hands up and that the person was wearing clothing the robber was described as wearing, a police sharpshooter shot and killed the principal. The robber was captured and put on trial for the murder of the principal.

The jury should find the robber:

(A) Guilty, because the police were justified in using deadly force under the circumstances.

(B) Guilty, because changing clothes with the principal was an act taken with extreme indifference to an unjustifiably high risk to human life.

(C) Not guilty, because it was not foreseeable under the circumstances that the police would use deadly force.

(D) Not guilty, because the robber was not responsible for the police shooting the principal.

Question 118

In which of the following situations would the defendant be most likely convicted of manslaughter instead of murder (ignoring the felony murder doctrine)?

(A) Defendant, angry at his girlfriend for going out with another man, sets fire to the house he thinks is hers, but in fact the house set afire is the neighbor's very similar residence. The neighbor and his wife are killed in the blaze.

(B) Defendant, as part of a fraternity initiation ritual, throws a burning mattress onto the front porch of a sorority house late at night, intending to douse the mattress with a garden hose after the women inside the house have run outside in their nightclothes. He discovers that the hose has been disconnected and the sorority house burns down, killing several of the residents.

(C) Defendant, in order to punish his neighbor for filing a complaint with the city government about his (defendant's) pet hogs, ignites the utility shed a few feet from his neighbor's home. The blazing shed causes the house to catch fire, killing the neighbor.

(D) Defendant, seeking to gain a competitive advantage over a business rival, sets fire to the rival's warehouse in the deserted commercial district, not knowing that his rival decided to sleep in the warehouse that night to guard his inventory. The warehouse burns to the ground, killing the rival.

Question 126

Darryl and Ernie were 17-year-old seniors at Millard Fillmore High School. Ernie's father was a petroleum engineer whose work took him all over the world. He frequently brought back presents for his family from the exotic lands he visited. His last trip involved a mineral exploration project in Australia and he brought Ernie a boomerang, a heavy curved piece of dense wood used for the hunting of small game by traditional Australian Aborigines. The boomerang had beautiful hand carvings and felt good in Ernie's hand. He wanted to try the boomerang out, so Ernie telephoned his friend Darryl and asked Darryl to join him in Recreation Park where they could practice throwing the boomerang. Ernie threw the boomerang a couple of times and explained to Darryl that the knack to throwing it was all in the snap of the wrist.

Just as Darryl made his first throw, George, a Park District gardener, came riding into view on a large lawn mower. The boomerang missed George by about three feet and came sailing back to where Ernie and Darryl were standing. George began yelling curses at Darryl. Thus, Darryl decided to repeat his actions and so he hurled the boomerang in George's direction. It again passed over George's head by about three feet. However, when it sailed back in the direction from which it was originally thrown, it struck George on the head. The blow from the boomerang caused George to suffer a fatal cerebral hemorrhage.

Darryl was charged with homicide for George's death. At trial, the jury was given instructions on common law murder and manslaughter.

If the jury believes Darryl's testimony that he did not intend to hit George with the boomerang, the most serious crime for which the jury could find him guilty is:

(A) Murder.

(B) Voluntary manslaughter.

(C) Involuntary manslaughter based on criminal negligence.

(D) No homicide crime.

Question 49

Max was driving his beat-up old car along a narrow coast road overlooking the coastal bluffs when he was passed by Marcia in her new Mercedes. Marcia's daughter, Stephanie, was lying down in the back seat of the Mercedes and could not be seen. Max sped up, drew even with the Mercedes, and repeatedly rammed his car into the side of the newer car. After several collisions, the Mercedes was forced off the road, sliding down the cliff for several yards and being kept from falling the several hundred feet onto the rocks and surf below by a large tree growing out from the bluff.

Marcia and Stephanie were rescued and Max was charged with attempted murder of both of them. At his trial, he testifies that he was angry because of the cavalier way Marcia passed him in her new car, and that his only intent in smashing into her car was to scratch and dent it so that she would not be so haughty in the future.

Assuming that the trier of fact believes this testimony, Max may be convicted as to:

(A) Marcia.

(B) Stephanie.

(C) Both Marcia and Stephanie.

(D) Neither Marcia nor Stephanie.

Question 38

Howard became very intoxicated one Saturday night, which was his custom, and as he was staggering homeward, he came upon a construction site where several large pieces of earthmoving equipment were parked. Having had heavy equipment training in the Army, Howard decided it would be fun to rearrange all the machines so that the operators would be very surprised when they returned to work on Monday. He started up a huge Caterpillar and drove it toward the edge of the site, but because he was so intoxicated, he lost control of it, and it rumbled out into the street, weaved along for about a quarter mile, and then crashed into Webster's house, demolishing the living room and kitchen.

In this jurisdiction, it is a misdemeanor to tamper with heavy equipment on a construction site. Howard is prosecuted on the tampering charge as well as for reckless damage of Webster's property.

Should he be convicted of the reckless damage charge?

(A) Yes, because he was tampering with heavy equipment on a construction site, in violation of law, when he damaged Webster's house.

(B) Yes, because he was intoxicated while driving a huge piece of earthmoving equipment.

(C) No, because at most he could be found guilty of criminal negligence.

(D) No, because he must have been aware that his conduct would cause damage to Webster's property in order to be found guilty of reckless damage.

Question 39

Dudley sent a computer virus to Harry attached to an e-mail. Dudley believed that the virus would just disable Harry's e-mail program for a short period of time without causing any additional damage. However, because of a hidden bug in Harry's e-mail program, the virus infected the hard drive of Harry's computer, eventually rendering it unusable. Harry not only lost important data, he had to replace the computer's hard drive at a cost of over $200.

The jurisdiction in which this occurred has a modern criminal code patterned after the Model Penal Code. One of its statutes makes it a criminal offense to "knowingly cause over $200 in damage to another's property."

Can Dudley be found guilty of violating the statute?

(A) No, because Dudley did not know that the virus would cause damage to the computer's hard drive.

(B) No, because Dudley did not intend to cause the damage to the computer's hard drive.

(C) Yes, because Dudley knew that he was sending a virus to Harry's computer.

(D) Yes, if Dudley was aware that in a very small percentage of cases the virus could cause damage to a computer's hard drive.

Question 186

A gun collector ordered a rifle from a gun catalog. The rifle had a barrel 16 inches long and a pistol-type grip instead of the more usual rifle stock, so that the entire weapon was only 22 inches long. The collector was aware of a state penal statute that prohibited the possession of "any sawed-off shotgun or rifle." He was also aware that another statute defined sawed-off shotgun or rifle so as to include any such weapon whose barrel was less than 16 inches in length. He was unaware that the same statute also included in its definition of the prohibited weapons any shotgun or rifle whose overall length was less than 24 inches. When the rifle he had ordered arrived in the mail, he carefully measured it to confirm that its barrel was exactly 16 inches in length.

While driving to the target range one day, the collector was stopped for having a defective taillight, and the traffic officer saw the rifle he had ordered lying on the back seat of his car in plain view. The collector was arrested and subsequently prosecuted for possession of a sawed-off rifle.

What will be the probable outcome of the trial?

(A) He will be acquitted, because he honestly did not know that a weapon with an overall length of less than 24 inches was in violation of the statute.

(B) He will be acquitted, because he conducted a reasonable investigation to ensure that he was in compliance with the statute.

(C) He will be convicted, unless the trier of fact determines that his failure to realize that the overall length of the weapon was in violation of the statute was reasonable.

(D) He will be convicted, because his reasonable investigation does not vitiate violation of the statute arising from a mistake of law.

Question 67

A state statute prohibited, under criminal penalties, the sale or furnishing of any alcoholic beverage to a minor. A 16-year-old minor went to his neighborhood liquor store and asked a patron who was about to enter if the latter would purchase some beer for him. The patron agreed, took the minor's money, and returned with a six-pack of beer. At the moment that the beer changed hands, an official of the State Bureau of Alcohol Control leapt from behind a nearby car and announced that both the patron and the minor were under arrest. The patron ran to his car and escaped. The minor is now being prosecuted under the statute as having aided and abetted the patron in its violation.

Which of the following is his best argument in defense?

(A) He cannot be convicted as an aider and abettor unless the principal is first convicted.

(B) He cannot be convicted as an aider and abettor of violating a statute designed to protect the class of which he is a member—minors.

(C) He cannot be convicted of aiding and abetting any crime because he is a minor.

(D) He cannot be convicted alone of committing a crime that requires at least two parties to commit a violation.

Question 53

After a long period of marital problems, a wife told her husband that she was going to file for a divorce. Because the wife had recently inherited a large sum of money, the husband was determined not to let her go through with the divorce. He contacted an ex-convict and offered him $10,000 if he would kill his wife. The ex-convict agreed and they picked a time when the wife would be in the house by herself. When the ex-convict broke into the house, however, the wife called the police and fled out the back door. The ex-convict shot and wounded the wife as she was running away, but he was apprehended by the police before he could do any further harm.

After the ex-convict implicated the husband, both were charged with attempted murder and conspiracy to commit murder, and the husband was also charged with solicitation of murder. As part of a plea bargain, the ex-convict agreed to testify against the husband and plead guilty to aggravated battery in exchange for the attempted murder and conspiracy to commit murder charges being dropped.

Which of the following best states the crimes for which the husband can be convicted?

(A) Solicitation, attempted murder, and conspiracy to commit murder.

(B) Attempted murder and conspiracy to commit murder.

(C) Solicitation and attempted murder.

(D) Attempted murder only.

Question 63

Ron, Mike, and Dick decided that they could make some easy money by going to a shopping center that catered to wealthy people, finding elderly women who were wearing a lot of expensive jewelry and furs, then following the women home and robbing them before they could get into their houses. The three agreed to meet at the shopping center the next evening. At the appointed time, each arrived, armed either with a gun or knife, and the three began checking out the shoppers looking for a likely victim.

Ron began to have second thoughts when he considered that Mike had already done time for armed robbery and several assaults with deadly weapons, and that Mike had vowed that he would never "do time" again because "somebody finked to the cops." As Dick pointed out a frail-looking woman wearing what appeared to be a diamond necklace and a mink coat, Ron told Mike and Dick that he had changed his mind and wanted no part of the action. As the other two went off following the selected victim, Ron returned to his car and drove home.

The next day, Ron learned from the television news that an elderly woman had been robbed and brutally beaten as she got out of her car in her driveway after returning from a shopping trip the previous evening. Because of her ill health and age, the woman had died as a result of the beating.

The police later arrested Mike and Dick and obtained a full confession from Dick detailing the agreement and actions of all three, including the fact that Mike had beaten the woman to death after he and Dick had robbed her.

Ron is guilty of:

(A) No crime.

(B) Conspiracy.

(C) Murder.

(D) Murder and conspiracy.

Question 199

While checking her mail at the front desk of the hotel at which she was staying, Debby observed that Vicky, who had been wearing very expensive jewelry when she and her husband had checked in earlier in the evening, was no longer wearing any jewelry. After finding out Vicky's room number, Debby broke into a supply room and put on a bellhop's uniform. She then grabbed some flowers from a vase in the hall and knocked on the door to Vicky's room, announcing the delivery of a bouquet of flowers. After Vicky's husband, Vernon, let her in, Debby scanned the room for the jewelry while putting the flowers in a vase. When she did not see the jewelry, she pulled out a knife and forced Vernon to reveal the whereabouts of the jewelry. Since Vicky had stored the jewels in the hotel safe, Debby made Vernon call the front desk and ask that someone bring them up to the room. Debby then locked Vernon in the bathroom, changed out of the bellhop's uniform, and accepted the jewelry when it was brought to the room. She was apprehended a few days later trying to sell the jewelry.

Under these facts, what are the most serious crimes Debby can be convicted of?

(A) Burglary and larceny.

(B) Burglary and robbery.

(C) Larceny only.

(D) Robbery only.

Question 193

In which of the following situations is Debbie most likely to be guilty of larceny?

(A) Coming out of a bar quite drunk, Debbie mistakes Susan's car for her own and drives off.

(B) Mistakenly believing that a porch swing attached to the house that she had just sold was not a "fixture" that became part of the realty, Debbie goes onto the property while the new owner is away and removes the swing.

(C) Mistakenly believing that it is not a crime to accept services without paying for them, Debbie eats a meal at Kim's restaurant and cannot pay the bill.

(D) Debbie borrows Jim's bicycle without his permission, intending to return it the next day, but it is stolen from her before she can do so.

Question 19

Donald was a defenseman for a professional ice hockey team in Detroit. Donald had a reputation for being a dirty, vicious player. During a game with New York, Victor, a New York player, skated towards Donald at a high rate of speed; his hockey stick was raised in a threatening manner. Victor did not intend to actually harm Donald, but wanted to show him how it felt to be threatened by a large man traveling at a high rate of speed with a hockey stick. As Victor approached Donald, Donald smashed his stick into Victor's face, causing permanent eye damage.

If Donald is charged with the crime of battery and found not guilty, it will be because:

(A) He did not intend to injure Victor.

(B) Professional hockey players consent to being hit by hockey sticks during a game.

(C) He reasonably believed that he was under attack and his actions were reasonable.

(D) Victor was the original aggressor.

Question 180

The manager of a bank branch announced to bank employees at a meeting that the corporate security staff would be staging a mock bank robbery that evening just at closing time, so that the employees could learn the proper responses to such a stressful situation and view bank security measures. At closing time that evening, the main bank's security chief, dressed in grubby clothes, entered the bank with an assistant and pointed his empty handgun at a bank teller, shouting, "Put all your money in this bag now! Get moving or I'll blow your head off!" The teller, who had been too busy with a crossword puzzle to listen to the manager's announcement at the meeting, thought that a real robbery was in progress. He nervously attempted to stuff the contents of his cash drawer into the bag while the security chief was threatening him and waving the gun at him. Believing that the teller was playing along, the security chief then demanded the teller's wallet and wristwatch, threatening to shoot the watch off if he did not hurry up. After giving the security chief what he wanted and watching him exit, the teller collapsed into a chair and suffered a mild heart attack before the security chief could return with his "loot" to discuss the exercise with the bank employees.

Which of the following crimes has the security chief committed with regard to the teller?

(A) Robbery.

(B) Larceny.

(C) Assault.

(D) No crime.

Question 164

After drinking heavily at his bachelor party at a beachside resort, Vinnie was helped into a speedboat by a few of his friends and transported to a small island off the coast. They left him on the island, which had a small shelter but no communication facilities, without telling anyone else. As a result, Vinnie missed his wedding the next day.

One of the participants, Dennis, was charged with kidnapping, which is defined in the jurisdiction as the unlawful movement or concealment of a person without his consent. In his defense, Dennis claims that he was so intoxicated that he did not realize what he was doing, and that Vinnie had consented to his being left on the island.

Which of the following would be ***least helpful*** to his defense?

(A) Vinnie was not legally intoxicated that evening.

(B) Kidnapping is a general intent crime in the jurisdiction.

(C) Kidnapping is a specific intent crime in the jurisdiction.

(D) Dennis had overheard Vinnie say that he was not sure about going through with the wedding.

Question 161

Under which of the following circumstances would the named defendant ***least*** likely be found guilty of arson?

(A) Walter hires a "torch"—a professional firestarter—who burns down the restaurant of a competitor.

(B) Rico, angry because he has been ejected from a dance party at a private club, prepares a "Molotov cocktail" and throws it at the entryway of the club, causing a fire that destroys the building.

(C) Nancy, as a sorority initiation prank, puts several powerful firecrackers in the fireplace of another sorority, and when the members light their evening fire, the firecrackers explode, sending flaming debris into the room, which results in a fire that severely damages the sorority house.

(D) Leon, preparing to barbecue steaks in his backyard, douses the charcoal liberally with gasoline. When he throws a lighted match onto the charcoal, the gasoline explodes, igniting the can of gasoline that Leon had set down next to the barbecue. The resultant explosion sets both Leon's and his neighbor's houses afire, destroying both.

Question 109

A homeowner decided to destroy his home by fire in order to collect the insurance. A neighbor's house was located a short distance from the homeowner's home. The homeowner knew that there was a strong wind blowing towards the neighbor's home; while he did not want to burn the neighbor's home, he nevertheless set fire to his own home. The fire department was unable to save the homeowner's house. They did manage to put out the fire moments before it spread to the neighbor's home, which suffered damage from smoke and soot. The jurisdiction's arson statute covers burning one's own dwelling as well as the dwelling of another, but is otherwise unchanged from the common law.

If the homeowner is charged with attempted arson of the neighbor's home, he will most likely be found:

(A) Not guilty, because he did not intend to burn the neighbor's house.

(B) Not guilty, because the fire was put out before any part of the neighbor's home was burned.

(C) Guilty, because he intended to burn his own home and took a substantial step toward burning the neighbor's house.

(D) Guilty, because he acted with malice and took a substantial step toward burning the neighbor's house.

Questions 134-135 are based on the following fact situation:

Aaron and Sean hatched a scheme to kidnap an Australian film star, Russell Byrd, and hold him for ransom. After conducting a surveillance of Byrd's home, they decided that they would have to have inside help to disable the security system at the home. They agreed that Aaron would contact Byrd's gardener, Ralph, who they learned was heavily in debt and frequented a local racetrack during his time off. Ralph would be offered $10,000 to disconnect the security system on the night of the planned kidnapping. Shortly before Aaron was to go to the track to make contact with Ralph, Sean had a change of heart about the scheme and contacted Ralph. He warned Ralph not to have anything to do with Aaron. Ralph met with Aaron anyway and pretended to go along with his proposal, accepting the down payment that Aaron offered. After meeting with him, Ralph contacted the authorities.

134. Aaron and Sean are charged with conspiracy in a jurisdiction that follows the common law rule for conspiracy. The most likely result will be:

(A) Both Aaron and Sean are guilty of conspiracy because Sean agreed with Aaron to commit the offense.

(B) Sean is not guilty of conspiracy because he withdrew from the conspiracy by contacting Ralph.

(C) Sean is not guilty of conspiracy because he withdrew from the conspiracy by contacting Ralph, and Aaron is not guilty of conspiracy with Sean because one cannot be a conspirator by oneself.

(D) Aaron is guilty of conspiracy with Ralph.

135. Aaron and Sean are also charged with attempted kidnapping in a jurisdiction following the modern rules for attempt. Which of the following statements is most accurate?

(A) Aaron can be found guilty, because he paid Ralph to disable the security system.

(B) Aaron and Sean can be found guilty, because they conspired to kidnap Byrd.

(C) Aaron cannot be found guilty, because Ralph only pretended to agree to the proposal.

(D) Neither Aaron nor Sean can be found guilty, because they did not form the mental state necessary for attempt.

Question 93

Beavis and Butthead, both 15 years old, attended Southside High School, located in Arkla. They were best friends. For over a year, Butthead had been dating Ashley, but they broke up when Ashley declared that Butthead was "smothering her" and that she needed "more space." Both Beavis and Butthead knew that the real reason for the breakup was that Ashley had developed a crush on Tony, a new kid in school. Beavis appeared more upset over the breakup than Butthead. He continually urged Butthead to do something to embarrass Ashley and to get back at her. One day Butthead brought his pet snake, a small boa constrictor, to school to show to his science class. Beavis encouraged Butthead to put the snake in Ashley's desk, so that when she opened it up, she would scream, jump, and make a fool of herself. Butthead agreed and placed the snake in Ashley's desk. When she opened the desk, she screamed, jumped, and fell backwards, injuring her hip in the fall.

A statute in Arkla provides that "anyone who recklessly causes bodily injury to the person of another is guilty of battery in the third degree." In all other criminal matters, Arkla follows the common law.

If Beavis is charged with battery in the third degree under the theory of accomplice liability, he will most likely be found:

(A) Not guilty, because he did not engage in the act prohibited by the statute.

(B) Not guilty, if he did not intend to cause Ashley bodily injury and was not reckless with respect to her bodily injury.

(C) Guilty, because he intended to encourage Butthead, and Butthead recklessly caused bodily injury to Ashley.

(D) Guilty, because he encouraged Butthead to commit the crime.

Question 119

Oscar and Henry were suspected of having murdered, for pay, the rival of a local union leader. Both were under constant surveillance. One evening, the police arrested Henry at his home. After he was taken to the police station, the officers who remained at Henry's house asked Henry's housekeeper if she knew where any firearms could be found in Henry's home. She went into the bedroom and returned with a pistol. Ballistics experts established that the pistol had been used to murder the victim, and Oscar's fingerprints were all over the pistol. At subsequent grand jury proceedings, the district attorney introduces the pistol and the related ballistics and fingerprint evidence, and the grand jury indicts Oscar.

If Oscar seeks to quash the indictment, he will:

(A) Not prevail, because the evidence was offered before a grand jury, not a court.

(B) Not prevail, because the pistol was obtained by a private citizen, not the police.

(C) Prevail, unless the police had probable cause to seize the pistol.

(D) Prevail, because Henry's housekeeper was acting as an agent of the police when she obtained the pistol.

Question 1

In which of the following fact situations does the defendant have the best argument that he was the victim of an illegal search or seizure?

(A) The police notice that the defendant's car is weaving erratically on the highway. The officers pull the defendant over. The defendant emerges from the car and appears incoherent and disoriented. The defendant is arrested and charged with driving under the influence of alcohol or drugs. The police search the defendant's glove compartment and find a plastic bag containing a large quantity of marijuana.

(B) Without a warrant, federal narcotics officers cross the defendant's fenced-in field and look through a window into the defendant's horse barn. The barn is located about 150 feet outside of the fence surrounding his house. The federal agents observe a large quantity of recently harvested marijuana within the barn. The agents then go to a magistrate, swear out a warrant, and arrest the defendant.

(C) Narcotics officers attached to the state police learn from an informant that the semi-opaque panes of glass on the defendant's greenhouse, adjacent to his house, are being replaced during the night with a newer type of glass that lets in more light without an increase in visibility. They fly over the defendant's greenhouse in a helicopter that night. One of the officers focuses on the greenhouse with a pair of infrared "night-vision" binoculars supplied by the Department of Defense and not available to the general public. He determines that marijuana is being grown. The officers then go to a magistrate, swear out a warrant, and arrest the defendant.

(D) Using a small plane of the type used for crop-dusting, county sheriff's officers take aerial photographs of the fields surrounding the defendant's farm. The pictures are later developed and show that there is marijuana growing in the defendant's fields. The sheriff's officers go to a magistrate, swear out a warrant, and arrest the defendant.

Questions 143-144 are based on the following fact situation:

Rafael Guzman was an undercover agent for the United States Drug Enforcement Agency ("DEA"). He had infiltrated an international drug cartel in Juarez, Mexico. Through his position in the cartel, Rafael sometimes learned the details surrounding a shipment of illegal drugs to the United States. When that occurred, Rafael would notify the appropriate DEA agents in the United States. In August 1999, Guzman informed the DEA that a large amount of cocaine was being mailed from Mexico City to Ms. Mary Ash in Topeka, Kansas. The cocaine would be mailed in a large box, wrapped in bright-colored, festive paper with "Happy Birthday, Mary" printed in large letters on the package. Guzman further informed the DEA that Mary was not the purchaser of the cocaine, but was only acting as an intermediary. The cocaine would be picked up within a few days by the buyer, a businessman from Des Moines, Iowa.

The DEA immediately placed Mary's house under surveillance. In a few days, a large box wrapped in bright-colored paper was delivered by the post office. The DEA did not make an arrest, but kept the house under surveillance. Two days later, a well-dressed man driving a car with Iowa plates arrived at Mary's home. He entered the house and, within an hour, he came out carrying what appeared to be the same box. The suspect placed the box in the trunk of his car and drove off. Two blocks later, acting without a warrant, the car was stopped, the suspect arrested, and the DEA agents searched the entire vehicle. The box in the trunk was opened and cocaine was found.

In addition, the DEA agents found two pounds of marijuana in the back seat of the car.

The suspect, identified as Donald Dawson of Des Moines, Iowa, was charged with possession of cocaine and marijuana. At a preliminary hearing, Dawson moved to suppress evidence of both the cocaine and the marijuana.

143. As to the cocaine, the motion should be:

(A) Denied, because the DEA agents had probable cause to search the trunk.

(B) Denied, because the search was incident to a valid arrest.

(C) Granted, because the DEA agents should have obtained a warrant before opening the package.

(D) Granted, because the DEA agents had no way of knowing that it was the same package that was delivered to Mary Ash.

144. As to the marijuana, the motion should be:

(A) Denied, because when the police stopped the car, they had probable cause to search the car.

(B) Denied, because the search was incident to a lawful arrest.

(C) Granted, because the DEA did not have probable cause to search the back seat.

(D) Granted, because, after arresting the driver, the car should have been impounded and a warrant obtained before the search.

Questions 127-128 are based on the following fact situation:

Based on a tip from a reliable informant that an attorney was illegally selling automatic weapons and ammunition from his storefront office, the police obtained a warrant to search for weapons at the office. When they arrived at the building, they saw a client exiting the attorney's office and placing what appeared to be a weapon inside his jacket. The police stopped the client on the street and an officer patted down his outer clothing but found no weapon. However, the officer felt a bag with several small tube-shaped objects in it, and she immediately placed him under arrest. The contents of the bag were later determined to be marijuana cigarettes.

Meanwhile, other officers had entered the attorney's office and seized a quantity of weapons, records, and cash, and placed the attorney under arrest. The weapons seized from the attorney's office were determined to have been stolen. The records seized from the office indicated that the client had purchased a weapon, and the client's fingerprints were found on some of the cash that was seized. After further searching, the police found a gun in a trash bin near where the client was stopped that was the same type that he was recorded as having purchased. The client was charged with possession of illegal narcotics and purchase of an unlicensed and stolen weapon.

127. At a preliminary hearing on the narcotics charge, the client sought to suppress introduction of the marijuana as evidence. The arresting officer testified at the suppression hearing that, based on her long experience as a narcotics officer, she concluded immediately that the bag contained marijuana cigarettes when she first touched it. If the officer's testimony is believed, the motion to suppress the marijuana evidence should be:

(A) Denied, because the search was incident to a lawful arrest.

(B) Denied, because the police had a reasonable suspicion that the client might be armed and dangerous.

(C) Granted, because the scope of an officer's patdown during an investigatory detention is limited to a search for weapons.

(D) Granted, because the search warrant did not authorize the police to search the client despite the fact that he was just present at the place to be searched.

128. At a preliminary hearing on the weapons charge, the client established that, at the attorney's preliminary hearing, the court held that the search warrant for the attorney's office was not supported by probable cause and suppressed introduction of the evidence seized. The client moved to suppress introduction of the records and the cash on the same basis. If the court agrees that the search warrant of the attorney's office was not supported by probable cause, the client's motion should be:

(A) Granted, unless the police acted reasonably in relying on the issuance of the warrant.

(B) Granted, because the evidence is the fruit of an unlawful search.

(C) Denied, because the client's legitimate expectation of privacy was not constitutionally violated.

(D) Denied, because discovery of the gun would have led the police to the records and cash under the inevitable discovery exception to the exclusionary rule.

Question 6

A police officer went to the defendant's house and placed him under arrest for operating an auto theft ring. As the defendant was being arrested, he told his wife, "You had better call our lawyer; I don't want to sign anything unless she's with me." The defendant was given *Miranda* warnings on the way to the police station. Meanwhile, the defendant's lawyer called the station and told the desk sergeant that she was on her way and to have the defendant call her as soon as he arrived. The sergeant assured her that the defendant would be held without questioning for several hours until the district attorney arrived. When the defendant arrived at the station, the arresting officer and another officer immediately put the defendant in an interrogation room and questioned him about a bank robbery that had taken place two days ago. They did not inform him of the call from his lawyer, but he agreed to talk as long as he did not have to put anything in writing or sign anything without her okay. He made incriminating statements about the robbery, and he was eventually indicted for that crime as well.

At a preliminary hearing on the robbery charge, the defendant's lawyer moved to suppress the arresting officer's testimony about the defendant's statements. The court should:

(A) Deny the motion, because the questioning was about a different crime from the one for which the defendant was in custody.

(B) Deny the motion, because the defendant's statements were made voluntarily after receiving *Miranda* warnings.

(C) Grant the motion, because the defendant was not informed that his lawyer was trying to see him, and his lawyer was misinformed that he would not be questioned right away.

(D) Grant the motion, because the defendant's refusal to write or sign anything indicates that he did not knowingly and intelligently waive his right to the assistance of counsel.

Questions 81-82 are based on the following fact situation:

Late one night in Valleytown, a young couple in a small foreign car were struck by a speeding Cadillac as the couple's car crossed an intersection with the light green in their favor. The impact sent the smaller car spinning into one of the street light poles near the intersection, and the larger car rolled over several times before coming to rest in a nearby field. Witnesses saw a male get out of the Cadillac and run away, but could not describe him sufficiently to permit the police to make an arrest. The Cadillac was not registered with the State Department of Motor Vehicles, and its last registered owner lived in another part of the state and could prove that he had sold it several years ago.

Several weeks later, Jorge, awaiting trial on burglary charges, called the officer who had arrested him to the jail cell where he (Jorge) was incarcerated and asked to speak to a Highway Patrol officer. When the Highway Patrol officer came to the cell, Jorge told him that he had been the driver of the Cadillac that had struck the small foreign car. Jorge said that he just wanted to get it off his chest, since the female passenger in the small car had been killed in the accident. Jorge told the Highway Patrol officer that he had been drinking heavily before driving the Cadillac that night.

81. Jorge is tried for second degree murder on the theory that his driving of the Cadillac at high speed while intoxicated showed a wanton disregard for human life sufficient to provide the malice necessary to constitute murder. The prosecution seeks to introduce the statements made by Jorge to the Highway Patrol officer regarding the events of the night of the accident. Jorge's attorney objects, seeking suppression of the statements. Which of the following is the strongest argument for permitting the statements into evidence?

(A) Jorge had not been charged in connection with the auto accident at the time the statements were made to the Highway Patrol officer.

(B) Jorge made the statements spontaneously, without inducement or interrogation by the police.

(C) The Highway Patrol officer had no connection with the burglary investigation for which Jorge had been incarcerated.

(D) Jorge's statements were not the product of coercion by the police officers.

82. During Jorge's murder trial, a critical issue is the amount of alcoholic beverages he had drunk before driving his Cadillac that evening. At the start of the second day of trial, a bailiff conducting Jorge from his holding cell to the courtroom persuades Jorge to admit that he had had at least half a fifth of vodka shortly before driving the Cadillac and hitting the small foreign car. When the trial resumes, Jorge testifies that he had nothing to drink that night. In rebuttal, the prosecution attempts to put the bailiff on the stand to testify as to Jorge's statements, but Jorge's attorney again objects. Which of the following is the strongest argument in favor of excluding the statements from evidence?

(A) The bailiff did not give Jorge *Miranda* warnings.

(B) The bailiff did not tell Jorge's attorney that he was going to question him.

(C) The statements were made in the absence of Jorge's counsel.

(D) The statements were made to a law enforcement officer and therefore were not voluntary.

Question 69

A criminal statute in the state of Leland adopted the common law definition of larceny. Another Leland statute provided as follows:

> It shall be an affirmative defense to a crime if the defendant establishes by clear and convincing evidence that, due to a mental disease or defect, he was unable to appreciate the criminality of his conduct or conform his conduct to the requirements of the law.

Victor Victim was leaving town for two weeks and he asked his cousin, Don, to stop by the house each day and water the plants. While at Victim's home, Don found the keys to Victim's new Corvette that was parked in the garage. Don took the car and drove it into town to show his friends. Don told all of his friends that he had purchased the Corvette. Victim returned home three days early, saw that the Corvette was missing, and called the police. Later that day, Don was arrested and charged with larceny.

At Don's trial, Don testified that he intended to return the car. In addition, two psychiatrists testified that, due to a mental defect, Don suffered from an extreme inferiority complex and delusions of grandeur. The doctors further testified that his mental condition caused him to take the car and to tell other people that he owned it. At the conclusion of the evidence, the court's instructions to the jury included the following:

I. If you find by a preponderance of the evidence that the defendant intended to return the car, you should find the defendant not guilty.

II. If you find by a preponderance of the evidence that, due to a mental disease or defect, the defendant was unable to appreciate the criminality of his conduct or conform his conduct to the requirements of the law, you should find the defendant not guilty.

Don was found guilty and he appealed, claiming that the jury instructions violated his constitutional rights. The appellate court should rule that:

(A) Both instructions were constitutional.

(B) Both instructions were unconstitutional.

(C) Instruction I was unconstitutional; Instruction II was constitutional.

(D) Instruction I was constitutional; Instruction II was unconstitutional.

Question 173

After winning a long and grueling civil trial, Brett and several other attorneys from a prestigious litigation firm went out to celebrate at a private club. After consuming numerous alcoholic beverages over a period of two hours, Brett attempted to drive home, ignoring the pleas of others in his group. Two blocks away, he allowed his car to cross over the center line because of his intoxicated condition and the car collided head-on with Terry's car, killing her instantly. The district attorney, who was an acquaintance of Brett's from law school, charged Brett with driving while intoxicated. After a bench trial, he was convicted and sentenced to two years of probation. The resulting public outcry and media attention cost the district attorney the next election. His successor immediately filed a charge of reckless homicide against Brett for causing Terry's death while driving drunk.

Brett was tried and convicted of the reckless homicide charge and sentenced to five years in prison. If Brett asserts on appeal that his trial and conviction on the reckless homicide charge violates the Fifth Amendment provision against double jeopardy, will he be likely to prevail?

(A) No, because the driving while intoxicated charge and the reckless homicide charge each require proof of an additional element that the other crime does not require.

(B) No, because the fact that the charges arose out of the same transaction does not prevent the imposition of separate punishments as long as they are imposed in separate trials.

(C) Yes, because the reckless homicide charge will require proof of the same conduct that constituted the driving while intoxicated charge.

(D) Yes, because the sentence for the reckless homicide conviction was greater than, and not concurrent with, the driving while intoxicated sentence.

Question 75

Cheryl had a bumper crop in her garden this year and decided to sell her surplus at a busy intersection near her home. She loaded her fruits and vegetables into her pickup truck and drove to the intersection, parking on the corner where there was a vacant lot, and put up a small sign advertising her products and prices. Business was fairly good, so she returned for the next four days. A statute provides that it is a misdemeanor, punishable by a fine of up to $500 and/or imprisonment in county jail for up to one year, to sell any product without a business license, except for informal sales held on the property of the seller no more often than once every three months.

At Cheryl's trial, she requested but was refused appointed counsel. Assuming that she would otherwise qualify as indigent, if she is convicted of violating the statute, what is the maximum penalty that may be imposed upon her?

(A) Imprisonment for six months.

(B) A $500 fine.

(C) Imprisonment for six months and a $500 fine.

(D) No penalty, because her conviction is void as having been obtained in violation of her right to counsel under the Sixth Amendment.

EVIDENCE

Question 40

In Robert's prosecution for robbery, the prosecutor asks the court to take judicial notice of the fact that at that latitude, the sun is still up at 5:30 p.m. on June 21. The court so finds.

The effect of the court's action is that:

(A) The burden of persuasion is now on the defendant to prove otherwise as to the fact judicially noticed.

(B) The fact judicially noticed is established beyond a reasonable doubt.

(C) The prosecutor's burden of producing evidence on the fact judicially noticed is satisfied.

(D) The fact judicially noticed is conclusively established.

Question 68

In a civil action tried to a jury, Defendant objected to the introduction by Plaintiff of certain evidence without the judge first making a preliminary ruling on the admissibility of the evidence.

For which evidence is Defendant's objection ***not*** appropriate?

(A) Opinion testimony regarding the structural integrity of a building by an engineer called by Plaintiff, without a preliminary determination by the judge that the engineer is an expert.

(B) Hospital records pertaining to Plaintiff offered by Plaintiff, without a preliminary determination by the judge that they were made as a regular activity of the hospital staff.

(C) Contract negotiations between Plaintiff and a third party, without a preliminary determination by the judge that the third party was Defendant's agent.

(D) A paramedic's testimony that Plaintiff's wife, before she died, said that Defendant's car went through a red light before hitting her, without a preliminary determination by the judge that she made the statement under a sense of impending death.

Question 50

At the trial of the plaintiff's breach of contract action against the defendant, the plaintiff called as a witness her accountant to testify about the difference in gross sales, gross income, and net profit caused by the defendant's failure to supply the promised quantity of ice cream to the plaintiff's boutique ice cream shop/bookstore. When the plaintiff's attorney asked the accountant to state the gross income figures for the year prior to formation of the contract between the plaintiff and the defendant, the accountant replied that he could not remember the exact amounts. The plaintiff's counsel then handed the accountant a copy of the federal tax return submitted by the plaintiff for that year, and asked him to read it. Counsel then asked, "Now that you have read the tax return, can you remember what the gross income of the plaintiff's ice cream shop was for the relevant period?" The defendant's counsel objects.

How should the court rule?

(A) Sustained; the plaintiff's counsel is seeking to elicit testimony based on inadmissible hearsay.

(B) Sustained; the accountant's testimony is not the best evidence.

(C) Overruled; the accountant's hearsay testimony is admissible as a past recollection recorded.

(D) Overruled; the accountant's testimony is admissible evidence relating to the plaintiff's damages.

Question 179

Denny is on trial for first degree murder for the shooting of a rival gang member. Denny's defense is that the gun accidentally discharged while he was cleaning it and that he is not in any gang. The prosecution seeks to offer the testimony of Warden, an experienced police officer in the gang crimes unit who interrogated Denny. Warden is prepared to testify that he saw a distinctive tattoo on Denny's leg and that he recognized the tattoo as one worn by members of a gang that was a rival of the victim's gang. Denny's attorney objects to this testimony.

How should the court rule?

(A) The testimony is inadmissible because Warden does not have personal knowledge that Denny is in the gang.

(B) The testimony is inadmissible unless Warden is qualified by the court as an expert on gangs.

(C) The testimony is admissible as circumstantial evidence that Denny was a member of the rival gang.

(D) The testimony is admissible only if the tattoo is either displayed in court or shown by the prosecution to be no longer available.

Question 187

In a civil lawsuit arising from a car accident, the plaintiff's witness testified that she observed the defendant drive through a red light before striking the plaintiff's car. The defendant then presented evidence impeaching the plaintiff's witness. The plaintiff now wishes to call someone else to testify as to his witness's good reputation for truthfulness.

The court is most likely to permit this testimony if the impeachment was by evidence that:

(A) The plaintiff's witness was convicted of the felony of aggravated battery five years ago.

(B) The plaintiff's witness had a previous dispute with the defendant.

(C) The plaintiff's witness was not wearing her prescription eyeglasses at the time of the accident.

(D) The plaintiff's witness was his mother.

Question 60

State A's defamation statutes require as a prerequisite for the filing of a libel suit against a public newspaper that the plaintiff demand in writing that the defendant retract the allegedly defamatory material. In Rupert's defamation suit against Cellulose Corporation, publisher of the *Metropolis Times,* a public newspaper, Rupert calls as a witness Wilma, a former employee of the *Times* who was the secretary to the editor during the period in which the events underlying Rupert's suit occurred. Wilma will testify that two days after the allegedly defamatory story was run in the *Times,* she remembers receiving a letter to the editor of the *Times* delivered by Rupert. Rupert has already testified that he wrote a letter to the editor demanding a retraction, and that the letter was delivered by him the same day that the defamatory story was published.

Should the court admit Wilma's testimony over Cellulose Corporation's objection?

(A) No, because Wilma is no longer employed by the *Times.*

(B) No, because the letter itself is the best evidence.

(C) Yes, because Wilma's testimony is evidence of a matter in issue.

(D) Yes, because Wilma's testimony is an admission by a party-opponent.

Question 43

Libby and her daughter Kimberly were driving home from an evening of Christmas shopping on December 21 when their car, which Libby was driving, was struck broadside by a car driven by Herman at an intersection controlled in all directions by stop signs. Libby and Kimberly were taken by ambulance to the hospital. In a personal injury action brought by Libby and Kimberly against Herman, pretrial discovery revealed that both cars were in perfect mechanical condition just before the accident, and Herman was on his way home from work at the time of the accident, but had stopped off at a bar before he reached the intersection at which he struck Libby's car.

At trial, Libby calls a co-worker of Herman, who testifies over objection that Herman has a reputation as a hard drinker who tolerates alcohol well but who always drinks a great deal at any one drinking occasion. Was it error for the trial court to admit his testimony?

(A) Yes, because in a civil matter, evidence of a party's character may not be introduced until he has put his character at issue.

(B) Yes, because Libby may not attempt to prove that Herman acted in a particular way on one occasion in conformity with his reputation as to that behavior.

(C) No, as long as the co-worker had personal knowledge of Herman's drinking habits from having observed him while drinking.

(D) No, unless an unbiased eyewitness exists who can testify as to how much Herman actually drank at the bar before he had the accident with Libby.

Question 100

After a routine background check of his references, John Jones was hired as a security guard at First Bank. Jones had been a security guard at another local bank, First Federal, but took the job at First Bank for a higher salary. The bank issued Jones a gun that he was allowed to take with him during his off-duty hours. However, First Bank policy required that all bullets be removed from the gun when the guard was off duty. Each security guard was required to sign a statement that he would abide by the unloaded gun policy.

One evening, John was driving home on the expressway. Another car, driven by Victor, cut sharply in front of John's car. John and Victor exchanged obscenities as their cars traveled at a high rate of speed on the expressway. On one occasion, John almost ran Victor off the road. Both vehicles took the same exit and when they pulled up next to each other at a stop light, the argument intensified. In a rage, John jumped out of his car, waving his gun. It was loaded and accidentally went off. Victor suffered a gunshot wound.

Victor brought an action against both First Bank and John Jones for his injuries. He alleged that First Bank was negligent in entrusting the weapon to John, and that John was negligent in his handling of the weapon. Victor offers the testimony of Warren, a security guard who worked with Jones for 10 years at First Federal. Warren is prepared to testify that, while an employee at First Federal, Jones had a reputation for being a hothead, keeping his weapon loaded during off-duty hours, and threatening people with his gun whenever he got into an argument.

Assuming proper objection, how should the court rule regarding the admissibility of Warren's testimony?

(A) Warren's testimony is character evidence, inadmissible in a civil case.

(B) Warren's testimony is character evidence admissible against First Bank if it can be established that First Bank knew of John's reputation.

(C) Warren's testimony is character evidence admissible against First Bank whether or not First Bank knew of John's reputation.

(D) Warren's testimony is admissible to help establish that John may have acted negligently at the time of the accident.

Question 181

Bonnie brought an action against a major national department store alleging that the electric blanket she bought from them overheated, causing a fire that destroyed her home and all that it contained. The defendant contends that its blanket could not have overheated unless it was left on after Bonnie left for work on the day of the fire. Bonnie offers in rebuttal the testimony of her husband, Clyde, who will state that he has been married to Bonnie for seven years, that he has slept in the same bed with her for most of that period, and that the first thing Bonnie does every morning upon awakening is to turn the control on the electric blanket to "off."

Should this testimony be admitted?

(A) Yes, because prior conduct may be used to show conformance with habit.

(B) Yes, because evidence of habit may be used to show that a person acted in conformance with the habit on a particular occasion.

(C) No, because habit may only be established by opinion or reputation evidence, not specific conduct.

(D) No, because there is no corroboration of Clyde's testimony by a nonparty witness.

Question 140

At a defendant's trial for assault with a deadly weapon, the defendant's counsel calls a witness to the stand and asks him, "What is the defendant's reputation for honesty and veracity in your community?" The prosecutor objects before the witness can answer.

Should the court admit the testimony?

(A) Yes, because reputation evidence is admissible under these circumstances to establish a character trait.

(B) Yes, because the prosecution put the defendant's character at issue when they filed charges against him.

(C) No, because the evidence offered is irrelevant to any material issue in the case.

(D) No, because the evidence offered is inadmissible hearsay.

Question 83

At Jason's trial for armed robbery, the prosecutor offers evidence tending to show that Jason committed two other armed robberies in the year preceding the present offense, and that Jason committed all three robberies to obtain money for his heroin habit.

Should the court admit this evidence over Jason's objection?

(A) No, unless Jason was convicted of the other robberies.

(B) No, if Jason has not testified at his trial.

(C) Yes, unless the court determines that the probative value of the evidence is substantially outweighed by its prejudicial effect.

(D) Yes, if the prosecution establishes by clear and convincing evidence that Jason committed the robberies.

Question 91

In which of the following cases would the offered evidence most likely be admissible?

(A) In a civil defamation action arising from media allegations that the school board president had embezzled funds, testimony from the director of a homeless shelter that the president volunteers her services at the shelter every weekend.

(B) In a criminal action for aggravated battery in which a witness for defendant has testified that defendant is a peaceful and law-abiding citizen, a certified copy of defendant's two-year-old felony conviction for armed robbery.

(C) In a civil fraud action for making false and misleading statements in a stock offering, evidence that defendant had made intentional misrepresentations on other stock offerings.

(D) In a criminal action for shoplifting, testimony by a restaurant cashier that defendant, a regular customer, had several times corrected an undercharge on her bill.

Question 44

Paul Port spent the evening drinking at O'Hara's Bar in West Philadelphia. At 1 a.m., Port left O'Hara's to drive home. While driving home, Port passed out at the wheel. His car went through a red light at an intersection and was struck by a car driven by Dan Dane. Port, under the influence of alcohol, staggered from his car. Dane, believing that Port had been injured in the accident, said "It's my fault. I was not paying attention. I'll take care of all your medical bills." Later that night, Port was treated for minor injuries at a nearby hospital.

Port sued Dane for damages, alleging that Dane was driving negligently at the time of the accident. Port offered the testimony of Wally Witness. Witness was prepared to testify that, after the accident, Dane stated in a clear, calm voice, "I was not paying attention. I'll take care of all your medical bills."

Assuming the proper objection, should Witness's testimony concerning Dane's statement be admitted?

(A) No, because Dane's statement is a settlement offer.

(B) Yes, as an admission by Dane.

(C) Dane's statement "I was not paying attention" should be admitted but the statement "I'll take care of all your medical bills" should not.

(D) No, if Port was negligent per se.

Question 123

While walking down a city street, Paul was seriously injured when a rotten limb fell off of a tree and hit him on the head. The tree was located on a vacant lot next to Don's house. The lot appeared to be a part of Don's property. Paul sued Don to recover damages for his injuries, alleging that Don was negligent with respect to the care of the tree. Don's defense was that he did not own the lot or the tree, and that both the lot and the tree were the property of the city. At trial, Paul calls Wally to testify that shortly after Paul was taken to the hospital, he observed Don cutting down the rotten limbs on a number of trees on the vacant lot.

Wally's testimony is most likely:

(A) Admissible, to help prove that Don was negligent in not removing the rotten limbs sooner.

(B) Admissible, to help prove that Don owned the lot.

(C) Inadmissible, because subsequent repairs are encouraged for reasons of public safety.

(D) Inadmissible, because the evidence does not prove that Don owned the lot.

Question 57

Parker is suing Driver for injuries Parker suffered when his car was struck by Driver's truck, allegedly because Driver had fallen asleep at the wheel after driving all night. At trial, Glenda, Driver's girlfriend, testified that she had been with Driver in the truck and had taken over the driving duties for several hours that night while Driver napped. Parker calls Walker, an acquaintance of Glenda, to testify that Glenda told him that she had been unable to get out of bed the weekend the accident occurred because of severe back pain.

Walker's testimony is:

(A) Admissible for impeachment purposes only.

(B) Admissible for impeachment purposes and as substantive evidence as a declaration of physical condition.

(C) Inadmissible, because this means of impeachment can be done only through cross-examination.

(D) Inadmissible, because Parker has not first given Glenda an opportunity to explain or deny the statement.

Question 200

As a result of an automobile accident at the intersection of First and Main, Paul sued Dennis, claiming that Dennis's car was traveling at a high rate of speed and went through a red light just before the crash. Walter, a witness for Paul, testified that he observed the accident and that Paul's car was traveling at a low speed with a green light at the time of the accident.

Which of the following is the court ***least*** likely to allow to impeach the credibility of Walter?

(A) A certified copy of a certificate of conviction for felony assault and battery seven years ago.

(B) The testimony of Daisy that, last month, while having a drink at a bar, Walter told her that Paul's light was red.

(C) A record of an arrest one week ago for embezzlement.

(D) On cross-examination of Walter, the question "Isn't it a fact that you lied to your employer last year concerning your meal expenses on a business trip to Chicago?"

Question 103

A defendant was charged with embezzling $1 million from his employer, a bank. The theory of the government's case was that $1 million of the bank's funds had been wired to a secret, off-shore account in the bank's name, and that only the defendant and a bank vice-president were authorized to draw funds from the account. The vice-president had been indicted with the defendant but had committed suicide on the day that the grand jury indictments came down.

At trial, the defendant testified that he had wired $1 million to the account but had done so at the direction of the vice-president, who had told him that the bank was acting as a secret agent for one of its largest depositors, which was attempting to acquire an off-shore property with a minimum of publicity. The defendant stated under oath that he had no intent to embezzle bank funds. The government's cross-examination of the defendant concentrated exclusively on his relationship and conversations with the vice-president.

The defense now seeks to call a second witness, who is prepared to testify that he had worked with the defendant for 10 years and that the defendant had a reputation in both the business and general communities as being a very honest person.

The witness's testimony is:

(A) Admissible, because a defendant has a constitutional right to call witnesses in his own behalf.

(B) Admissible to help show that the defendant did not embezzle funds.

(C) Inadmissible character evidence.

(D) Inadmissible, because you cannot bolster the credibility of your own witness unless the credibility of the witness has been attacked.

Question 32

Pam sued Good Eats Restaurant, claiming that she injured her teeth, gums, and mouth when she bit into a hamburger that contained a large jagged piece of glass. Walter, working as a waiter for Good Eats at the time of the alleged incident, testified for Pam. Walter testified that, when he heard Pam scream, he looked in her direction and saw her remove a piece of glass from her bleeding mouth. On cross-examination, the defense asked Walter, "Isn't it a fact that three months ago you were fired by Good Eats for serving drinks to your friends and not charging for them?" Walter responded, "Yes, but I wasn't trying to steal anything. I just forgot to charge them." The defense then asked, "Isn't it a fact that last month you threw a rock through the plate glass window at Good Eats?" Walter replied, "That's not true; I was there but I didn't throw the rock." The defense then offered the testimony of Margaret. Margaret was prepared to testify that she also was there when the window was broken and that she saw Walter throw the rock.

Assuming that there have been no criminal charges filed as a result of the broken window, Margaret's testimony is:

(A) Inadmissible, because specific acts of misconduct that did not result in a conviction cannot be used to impeach a witness, either on cross-examination or through extrinsic evidence.

(B) Inadmissible, because specific acts of misconduct that did not result in a conviction cannot be established through extrinsic evidence.

(C) Admissible as evidence of bias.

(D) Admissible to establish that Walter lied under oath.

Question 33

In a wrongful death action for the death of his wife in an automobile accident, the plaintiff, Poshard, alleged that the accident was caused by a mudflap assembly that fell off the truck of Dean, the defendant. Poshard wishes to introduce the testimony of Willis, another truck driver who was on the same highway at the time, who heard someone tell Dean over CB radio that he had noticed at the truck stop that Dean's mudflap assembly on his truck was loose. Willis does not know the identity of the person who gave the warning.

If Dean objects to admission of the testimony, the court should rule that it is:

(A) Admissible to prove that Dean was notified that the mudflap assembly was loose.

(B) Admissible both to prove that Dean was notified that the mudflap assembly was loose and as substantive evidence that it was loose.

(C) Inadmissible, because Willis cannot identify who made the statement.

(D) Inadmissible, because it is hearsay not within any recognized exception.

Question 5

A moving company specializing in local moves sent two employees on a typical job: a driver and a helper. The driver's responsibility was to drive the truck and load and unload the cargo. The helper's responsibility was to load and unload the cargo and generally assist the driver. While transporting furniture in a company truck, the driver failed to stop at a stop sign and collided with a car, causing the motorist to be seriously injured in the accident.

In a lawsuit brought by the motorist against the moving company on the theory of negligence by its employee, the motorist offered into evidence a written statement of the helper. The statement said that the driver was adjusting his portable radio and not observing the road when the accident occurred.

The helper's written statement is admissible if:

(A) The helper takes the witness stand and testifies that the driver was adjusting his radio and not observing the road.

(B) The helper is unavailable to testify.

(C) Evidence is introduced to establish that the helper is an employee of the moving company and his written statement is in the scope of his employment.

(D) The helper's statement was given under oath at a trial or other proceeding.

Questions 120-122 are based on the following fact situation:

Linda is charged with arson for hire in the burning down of an old office building, Watson Towers, in downtown River City.

120. The prosecution offers to introduce the testimony of Libby, an acquaintance of Linda, who will state that the day after the fire, she went to Linda's apartment. Linda had burnt a roast in her oven, and the apartment was full of smoke. Libby, coughing and choking, said, "What did you do, burn down Watson Towers again?" Linda made no reply. Should this evidence be admitted over Linda's objection?

    (A) No, it is hearsay not within an exception.

    (B) No, if the court determines that Linda would not reasonably deny such a statement under the circumstances.

    (C) Yes, it is an admission by silence.

    (D) Yes, it is a declaration against penal interest.

121. The prosecution offers to introduce the testimony of Officer Brown, who will testify that he showed a photographic lineup containing Linda's picture to a witness who saw the arsonist run from the Watson Towers, and the witness selected Linda's picture. The witness has moved out of state and cannot be persuaded or compelled to return to testify. Should this evidence be admitted over Linda's objection?

    (A) Yes, it is a past recollection recorded.

    (B) Yes, it is a prior identification.

    (C) No, it is hearsay not within an exception.

    (D) No, unless the picture of Linda is properly authenticated.

122. During the prosecution's case in chief, evidence was introduced establishing that a can of turpentine, a highly flammable liquid, was discovered in Linda's closet when she was arrested. On direct examination by her own attorney, Linda states that when she was arrested and the can of turpentine was found, she told the officers, "I use that to clean my paint brushes after art class." If the prosecution moves to strike this testimony, how should the court rule?

    (A) For Linda, since it is a prior consistent statement.

    (B) For Linda, since it tends to explain prosecution evidence.

    (C) For the prosecution, because it is hearsay not within an exception.

    (D) For the prosecution, because it is a self-serving statement.

Question 96

Norma was injured when the bus in which she was riding braked too abruptly and threw her into a support stanchion, breaking her hip. She has brought an action against the bus company for damages from personal injuries on theories of respondeat superior and negligent hiring.

During its case in chief, the bus company counsel calls Walden, personnel director for the company, as a witness and asks him if the driver of the bus had been required to provide proof that he had had no convictions for crimes relating to vehicle use before being hired. Walden answers, "It's been several years since he was hired, but my best recollection is that we did not ask for such proof." Counsel then prepares to question Walden about his statement, made at a deposition taken 18 months before trial, that he had personally requested and received a statement from the driver before he was hired that he (the driver) had no such convictions.

May counsel for the bus company pursue this matter in this fashion?

(A) Yes, if it is being done to refresh Walden's recollection.

(B) Yes, but the jury must be instructed that the evidence may only be considered for impeachment of Walden.

(C) Yes, the evidence may be admitted for both impeachment and substantive purposes.

(D) No, counsel may not impeach its own witness.

Question 113

At trial of Priscilla's personal injury action against Delbert, Bill, who was near the accident scene but did not see what happened, testifies that Oscar, a witness to the accident, shouted, "Good Lord! The green car just ran through a red light and hit the red car!" Previous evidence had established that Delbert drove a green car and Priscilla a red one. Delbert offers to call as a witness Arthur, who will testify that he spoke with Oscar the next day, and Oscar said that the light was green when the green car drove through the intersection. Oscar had moved to Sri Lanka prior to trial.

Should this evidence be admitted over Priscilla's objection?

(A) No, because Oscar is not available to explain or deny the contradiction.

(B) No, because it is hearsay not within any exception.

(C) Yes, for the purpose of impeachment and as substantive evidence.

(D) Yes, for the purpose of impeachment only.

Question 189

Vanessa collapsed at her desk while drinking her morning coffee. Her secretary, Will, came rushing to her aid. Gasping for breath, Vanessa said, "I don't think I have much time left. I want you to remember when they come looking for suspects that I believe Debbie would kill for my job." Vanessa soon lost consciousness. She regained consciousness briefly after arriving at the hospital, but the doctors would not allow her to speak to anyone, including the police. She again lapsed into a coma, and she remains in this vegetative state. It was determined that she was poisoned. Debbie is arrested and charged with attempted murder.

At Debbie's trial, the prosecution wishes to call Will to testify to Vanessa's statement to him at the office before the ambulance arrived.

The court should find the statement:

(A) Admissible, because it is a dying declaration.

(B) Admissible, because it is a declaration of Vanessa's state of mind.

(C) Inadmissible, because dying declarations are not admissible unless the declarant is dead.

(D) Inadmissible, because it is hearsay not within any exception.

Question 76

Porter sued Data Exchange, a computer dealer engaged in buying and selling used computers, alleging that he was not given credit for a CD-ROM drive that he had on the computer that he had sent back for resale. Warden, the bookkeeper, testified that it was company practice when a boxed computer was returned to have one clerk open the box and identify the type of computer and its components and have another clerk record the information in the inventory ledger. Data Exchange seeks to enter into evidence the original ledger entry, which Warden authenticated, showing that a CD-ROM drive was not checked off on the components list for Porter's computer. Porter objects to the admission of the ledger.

The ledger is:

(A) Admissible, because it is a record of a transaction for which Warden does not have any present recollection.

(B) Admissible, because it was regular company practice to record receipt of the components in the inventory ledger.

(C) Inadmissible as hearsay within hearsay, because even if a hearsay exception permits introducing the record itself rather than requiring testimony by the employee who made it, that employee was just recording hearsay because he had no personal knowledge of what he was recording.

(D) Inadmissible hearsay, because absence of the notation implies a statement that no CD-ROM return was received, and the evidence is being offered as proof of that assertion.

Question 162

Victoria sued Specialty Cleaners, claiming that Specialty had permanently ruined her $10,000 mink coat. The theory of her case was that Specialty had cleaned the mink coat with a solvent that left an extremely offensive odor that smelled like "skunk." Further attempts to have the odor removed by other cleaning services were unsuccessful. The odor was so bad that she could no longer wear the coat.

At the trial, Victoria testified to the above facts. She then identified a mink coat as her coat that the defendant had ruined. She testified that it still smelled the same as it did after Specialty had cleaned it. Victoria's counsel offered to introduce the coat for the purpose of having the jury smell it. Defense counsel objected.

How should the court rule?

(A) The coat is admissible based on Victoria's testimony.

(B) The coat is admissible, but only if Victoria presents extrinsic evidence sufficient to support a finding that the coat is the coat that she had cleaned at Specialty.

(C) The coat is not admissible because Victoria's testimony has not been impeached.

(D) The coat is not admissible because its limited probative value in resolving the case would be substantially outweighed by the prejudice that would result from the jury smelling the coat.

Question 141

In litigation over whether an uncle conveyed a parcel of land to his nephew, the nephew wishes to offer into evidence a tape recording of his uncle made by a well-known oral historian at the nearby state university. The voice on the tape is discussing various conveyances of the parcel of land and other property owned by the uncle. The nephew wishes to have the historian testify that the voice on the tape is the uncle's.

If the court allows the historian to testify, it will be because:

(A) The historian is testifying regarding an admission by a party-opponent.

(B) The historian has heard the uncle speak before.

(C) The historian became familiar with the uncle's voice before the dispute over the property arose.

(D) The historian's experience as an oral historian qualifies him as an expert in voice recognition.

Questions 137-138 are based on the following fact situation:

A balloonist sued the manufacturer of deflation panels for hot air balloons after one of the panels failed while his balloon was descending, causing the balloon to crash and the balloonist to suffer severe injuries.

137. At trial, the balloonist calls as a witness a structural engineer, who testifies that she read several reports done by an independent laboratory on the burst strength and material composition of the deflation panel closures. His attorney then asks the engineer whether, in her opinion, the closures caused the deflation panel to give way. The manufacturer objects. Should the court admit this testimony?

   (A) No, unless the balloonist establishes that the engineer performed the laboratory tests herself.

   (B) No, because the laboratory reports are hearsay not within an exception.

   (C) Yes, if the balloonist offers into evidence the reports to which the engineer referred, so that the manufacturer may cross-examine as to them.

   (D) Yes, if structural engineers reasonably rely on such reports in the course of their profession.

138. During his testimony, the balloonist stated that he purchased the deflation panels two days before installing them and taking the test flight. During its case in chief, the manufacturer presents the testimony of a clerk at the aviation supply store where the balloonist purchased the panels. The clerk testifies that she remembers the balloonist coming into the store and purchasing the panels a week before the date testified to by him, because he signed the purchase order with such an unusual signature. If the balloonist objects to this testimony, should the trial court admit it?

   (A) No, because the content of the purchase order is hearsay not within any exception.

   (B) No, because the date of purchase of the panels is a collateral matter.

   (C) Yes, because the purchase order is a past recollection recorded.

   (D) Yes, because the clerk's testimony is relevant evidence as to the date the panels were purchased.

Question 58

Robert is charged with having been one of two men who robbed the Roundup Bar and its patrons at gunpoint at 5:30 p.m. on December 16.

Robert calls Leon as a witness. Leon will testify that he was at Robert's house about 9:30 a.m. on December 16, and that as he was leaving, Robert said to him, "I'm going to my mother-in-law's house this afternoon for a birthday party."

Is Leon's testimony admissible?

(A) No, it is hearsay not within any exception.

(B) No, it is irrelevant.

(C) Yes, it is not being offered to prove the truth of the matter stated, so it is not hearsay.

(D) Yes, it is hearsay within an exception, and thus admissible.

Question 160

In January of 1996, Dan, a drug dealer in south Florida, became engaged to Wanda. During the engagement, Dan confided in Wanda about various drug deals in which he was participating. Wanda, hopelessly in love, swore to Dan that she would never reveal any of his confidences. On January 1, 1997, Dan and Wanda were married. Dan continued to share with Wanda information concerning his illegal drug activity. Wanda's only rule was that Dan could not participate in any illegal drug transactions in their home. On one occasion, Wanda came home unexpectedly and saw Dan completing a drug transaction in the living room. Dan was not aware that Wanda had observed the event. In 1998, Dan was charged with 57 counts of illegal drug sales that occurred between 1995 and 1998. The prosecutor wishes to call Dan's wife, Wanda, as a witness for the state.

Assuming that Dan's attorney makes appropriate objections, which of the following statements is correct regarding testimony by Wanda?

I. Wanda can testify about Dan's 1996 and 1997 statements if she desires.

II. Wanda must testify to the 1996 statements of Dan.

III. Dan can keep Wanda from testifying about his 1997 statements.

IV. Wanda can testify to the drug sale that she observed if she wants to.

(A) Only III. and IV. are correct.

(B) Only I. and IV. are correct.

(C) Only II. and III. are correct.

(D) None of the above.

REAL PROPERTY

Question 18

Among his properties, Tommy owned Greenacres, a 300-acre operating farm. The farm was profitable, but Tommy received income from many other sources as well. When Tommy died, one of the provisions in his will left Greenacres "to my wife, Wanda, for life, then to my three daughters, Debi, Doreen, and Donna, in fee simple absolute."

Wanda occupied the farmhouse on Greenacres and operated the farm herself, occasionally hiring additional hands for busy times, such as planting and harvesting. After expenses of operation, Wanda earned about $25,000 per year from Greenacres. Neither Debi, Doreen, nor Donna did anything to assist Wanda with farm chores or expenses. Wanda has consistently failed to pay the annual $2,000 county tax assessment and continues to refuse to pay it, despite threats from county tax collection authorities.

With the taxes three years in arrears, the tax authorities made good on their threats. Using proper procedures authorized by state law, the county has ordered a tax sale of Greenacres.

You are an attorney with offices located in the county seat. Donna consults you regarding her rights and obligations.

You should advise her that:

(A) Wanda, as life tenant, is personally liable for the taxes, but a tax sale will cut off the rights of the remaindermen.

(B) The remaindermen are personally liable for the taxes if the life tenant does not pay them.

(C) Donna will have to pay one-third of the taxes if Debi and Doreen pay two-thirds.

(D) Wanda, as life tenant, is personally liable for the taxes, and the tax sale will affect only the rights of the life tenant and not the rights of the remaindermen.

Question 159

Ogden owned Blackacre, a one-acre tract of land containing a gift shop and general store, that was located adjacent to a national park. Thirty years ago, he delivered a deed of Blackacre "to Merch for so long as tobacco is not sold on the premises, because careless smokers are the second leading cause of fires in the park." The deed was promptly and properly recorded. A few years later, Ogden died, leaving Harry as his only heir but devising "all of my interests in any real property" to Devlin by a duly probated will. The next year, Devlin conveyed "all of my interest in Blackacre" to Purch by means of a quitclaim deed supported by valid consideration. Purch promptly and properly recorded the deed. Two months ago, Merch began selling tobacco at the general store located on Blackacre.

In a jurisdiction in which the common law Rule Against Perpetuities is unmodified by statute, who currently has title to Blackacre?

(A) Harry, because Devlin received an executory interest that was void under the Rule Against Perpetuities.

(B) Devlin, because the interest he holds in Blackacre is not transferable inter vivos.

(C) Purch, because tobacco is being sold on Blackacre.

(D) Merch, because no party has taken action to terminate his interest in Blackacre.

Question 139

Overhill owned Lawnacre, a 20-acre tract of land in a formerly rural area that was rapidly becoming developed. She conveyed Lawnacre "to Tract and his heirs, provided that no multi-family dwellings may be built on the property for a period of 25 years. If such construction is undertaken, the grantor may terminate the conveyance and retake Lawnacre." Two years later Overhill died, leaving her nephew, Verdi, as the sole beneficiary under her will. Shortly thereafter Verdi discovered that Tract was constructing multi-family dwellings on Lawnacre. He promptly brought an ejectment action against Tract.

The jurisdiction in which Lawnacre is located has a statute providing that all future interests are freely devisable and alienable inter vivos. There are no other applicable statutes.

The court should rule that ownership of Lawnacre belongs to:

(A) Verdi, because Tract began constructing multi-family dwellings on Lawnacre.

(B) Verdi, because Tract began constructing multi-family dwellings on Lawnacre and Verdi brought an action for ejectment.

(C) Tract, because the Rule Against Perpetuities applies.

(D) Tract, because the restriction in the conveyance is an invalid restraint on alienation.

Questions 182-183 are based on the following fact situation:

Sutter owned a gold mine in California and a silver mine in Nevada. His will provided that the property on which the gold mine was located, Golden Acres, would go "to my wife Karen, for life, remainder to my nephew, Lester." The property on which the silver mine was located, Silver Creek, was devised "to my sister Ida, her heirs, and assigns; but if Ida should die without producing issue, then to the American Cancer Society."

When Sutter died, the gold mine was producing a net annual value of $100,000 in gold and had proven reserves valued at $2 million. The silver mine was producing a net annual value of $25,000 in silver and had proven reserves of $250,000.

182. Shortly after Sutter's death, Lester brings an action to enjoin Karen from operating the Golden Acres mine. What should be the outcome of this litigation?

(A) Issue the injunction, because Lester has a vested remainder subject to partial divestment.

(B) Issue the injunction, because Lester has a vested remainder.

(C) Deny the injunction, because Karen has a freehold estate.

(D) Deny the injunction, because of the open mines doctrine.

183. Shortly after Sutter's death, the American Cancer Society brings an action to enjoin Ida from operating the Silver Creek mine. What should be the outcome of this litigation?

(A) Issue the injunction, because the Society has a contingent remainder.

(B) Issue the injunction, because the Society has an executory interest.

(C) Deny the injunction, because Ida has a defeasible fee simple.

(D) Deny the injunction, because of the open mines doctrine.

Question 150

Oscar, the owner of Wolfacre, conveyed Wolfacre by will as follows: "To Harry Lupus, so long as one or more dogs are kept on the property; if dogs are no longer kept on the property, then to the American Society for the Prevention of Cruelty to Animals (ASPCA)." The will also provided that the residuary estate would go to Oscar's nephew, Remus.

In a jurisdiction that has not modified the common law Rule Against Perpetuities, what are the respective interests in Wolfacre on Oscar's death?

(A) Harry has a fee simple subject to a condition subsequent and Remus has a right of entry.

(B) Harry has a fee simple determinable and Remus has a possibility of reverter.

(C) Harry has a fee simple determinable and the ASPCA has a remainder.

(D) Harry has a fee simple determinable subject to an executory interest and the ASPCA has a shifting executory interest.

Question 175

Tess, the owner in fee simple of Farmacre, made the following provision in her will:

> I grant Farmacre to Harold, my husband, for life, then to my nieces for life, then to the children of my nieces in fee simple.

When Tess died, she had one niece, Anne, who had a son, Edward. While Harold was alive, another niece, Beth, was born. One year after Harold died, another niece, Caryn, was born. At the time Caryn was born, Anne, Anne's son Edward, and Beth were also alive. The jurisdiction's Rule Against Perpetuities is unmodified by statute.

What are the respective interests of the parties in Farmacre at this point in time?

(A) Anne and Beth have a life estate, and Edward has a remainder.

(B) Anne and Beth have a life estate, and Tess's heirs have a reversion.

(C) Anne, Beth, and Caryn have a life estate, and Edward has a remainder.

(D) Anne, Beth, and Caryn have a life estate, and Tess's heirs have a reversion.

Question 25

Hal and Wallene, a married couple, owned Blackacre in joint tenancy. They conveyed a 10% interest in Blackacre to their daughter, Donna. Six months later, they conveyed a 10% interest in Blackacre to Donna's husband, Dan.

If the jurisdiction within which Blackacre is located does not recognize tenancy by the entirety, which of the following best describes the ownership of Blackacre after the conveyances?

(A) Hal and Wallene have an 80% interest as joint tenants, Donna has a 10% interest as tenant in common, and Dan has a 10% interest as tenant in common.

(B) Hal and Wallene have an 80% interest as tenants in common, Donna has a 10% interest as tenant in common, and Dan has a 10% interest as tenant in common.

(C) Hal and Wallene have an 80% interest as tenants in common, and Donna and Dan have a 20% interest as joint tenants.

(D) Hal and Wallene have an 80% interest as joint tenants, and Donna and Dan have a 20% interest as joint tenants.

Question 169

A parcel of oceanfront property was devised to a husband and wife "as joint tenants with right of survivorship" through the will of the husband's mother. After title had passed to them, the husband and wife experienced marital difficulties. Unknown to the husband, the wife quitclaimed her interest in the oceanfront property to a bona fide purchaser for value. Shortly thereafter, the husband and the wife reconciled. The next month, the wife was killed in an auto accident.

The purchaser of the wife's interest filed a suit for partition of the property so that he could build a beach house on the portion of which he would become sole owner. The husband filed an appropriate counterclaim for quiet title, asserting that he was owner of the entire parcel by right of survivorship.

How should the court rule?

(A) For the purchaser, because he owns an undivided one-half interest in the property.

(B) For the purchaser, if the husband and the wife are found to have taken title from the mother as tenants in common.

(C) For the purchaser, if he can show that the husband and the wife were legally separated when he purchased his interest from the wife.

(D) For the husband, because he succeeded to the entire ownership when the wife died.

Question 114

A developer with a large plot of unimproved land divided it into 30 small plots and two much larger ones, intending to develop a "flea-market" or "swap meet" where nontraditional retailers could market their wares. He built covered stalls on the small plots and larger, permanent buildings on the two large plots. He leased the small plots and stalls to retailers for lease terms ranging from six months to two years. One of the larger plots and the building thereon were offered for lease to an auctioneer, who planned to use the building mainly for storage and as a "show area," while auctions would be conducted outside, from the raised porch at the front of the building. Because rain was frequent in the area, the auctioneer insisted that the developer construct a structure in front of the building that would keep rain off the heads of the auctioneer's prospective customers. The developer agreed to do so and the auctioneer signed a 10-year lease. The developer built a large wooden roof supported by wooden columns. A term in the auctioneer's lease stated, "Lessor agrees to maintain all structures on the property in good repair." The auctioneer's business was a success.

Four years after the auctioneer entered into the lease, the developer sold the property to a buyer. The buyer did not agree to perform any obligations under the lease. As instructed, the auctioneer began paying rent to the buyer. In the fifth year of the lease, the wooden roof began to leak. Citing the lease terms, the auctioneer asked the buyer to repair the roof. He continually refused to do so. The auctioneer finally repaired the roof herself at a cost of $2,000. The auctioneer then brought an appropriate lawsuit to recover the money.

Absent any other facts, the auctioneer is likely to recover:

(A) $2,000 from the developer only, because the sale of the property did not sever his obligation to the auctioneer.

(B) $2,000 from the buyer only, because a covenant to repair runs with the land.

(C) $1,200 from the buyer and $800 from the developer, because that represents their pro rata shares.

(D) $2,000 from either the buyer or the developer, because they are both in privity with the auctioneer.

Question 129

Turbo entered into a written five-year lease to rent an office from Blaze for $6,000 per year. The lease term was scheduled to begin on October 1, and the lease required that rent in the amount of $500 be paid on or before the first of each month. During Turbo's occupancy, he paid his rent promptly each month. Two months before the five-year term was up, Turbo received a letter from Blaze. It contained a new lease identical to the lease Turbo had already signed, except that the lease term began on the upcoming October 1 and the stated amount of rent per month was $600. The envelope also contained a note stating: "The rent goes up to $600 per month on October

1. If you want to renew, sign this and return it to me by September 15. Sorry about the rent increase. Taxes went up. —Blaze." Turbo returned the lease to Blaze unsigned, with a letter stating that he did not intend to renew the lease, and would be moving on September 30. Turbo did not move on September 30, and would not return Blaze's phone calls. On October 1, Blaze received a check for $500 from Turbo. The notation on the check indicated that it was for the October rent. Blaze deposited the check in her account. She then sent a letter to Turbo stating that he was $100 in arrears in his rent. Turbo did not move out of the office during October, and Blaze did nothing to remove him.

Most courts would hold that:

(A) Turbo has a month-to-month tenancy at a rent of $500.

(B) Turbo has a month-to-month tenancy at a rent of $600.

(C) Turbo has a year-to-year tenancy at $500 per month.

(D) Turbo has a year-to-year tenancy at $600 per month.

Question 132

A landowner owned a strip mall in a suburban commercial district. She leased one of the stores to a grocer for a term of five years at $10,000 per year, payable in monthly installments. The lease permitted assignments and subleases. After occupying the premises for two years and paying the rent, the grocer transferred the remaining three years of the term to a florist. The agreement between the parties did not have a specific provision regarding payment of rent, instead just referring to the original lease provisions. The florist occupied the premises for two years but paid rent only for the first year. With one year left on the original lease, the florist transferred her leasehold interest to a barber. The barber occupied the premises for one year but did not pay any rent.

The landowner brought an appropriate action against the grocer, the florist, and the barber to recover the rent. Against whom may the landowner recover?

(A) The grocer and the florist jointly and severally for $10,000, and the grocer individually for $10,000.

(B) The grocer and the florist jointly and severally for $10,000, and the grocer and the barber jointly and severally for $10,000.

(C) The grocer and the florist jointly and severally for $10,000, and the grocer, the florist, and the barber jointly and severally for $10,000.

(D) The grocer and the florist jointly and severally for $20,000.

Question 46

The owner of three acres of lakefront property subdivided it and sold two acres to a buyer, retaining the one acre actually fronting upon the lake. The deed for the two acres expressly included an easement over the westernmost 30 feet of the one-acre parcel retained by the owner; the easement was for access to the lake for recreational purposes. Shortly after the transaction was completed, the buyer recorded his deed in the county containing the land. The county maintained an alphabetical grantor-grantee index only.

Fifteen years later, the owner died, leaving the one acre of beachfront property to his wife. She sold it to a real estate developer that planned to build beachfront condominiums. A month later, the buyer died, and his two acres passed by testamentary gift to his nephew. Three weeks after taking title to the property, the nephew and his family drove to the property, intending to spend a weekend of waterskiing at the lake. When they arrived, they discovered that the developer had erected a chain link fence all along the boundary between the nephew's land and the acre of beachfront land.

The nephew brings an action to enjoin the developer from obstructing his easement across the acre of beachfront property. Which of the following best describes why the nephew should prevail in this litigation?

(A) Since the developer and the nephew can trace their predecessors in interest to a common grantor whose covenants run with the land, the developer is estopped from interfering with the nephew's use of the easement.

(B) The nephew's easement is a legal interest that the developer has record notice of, even though there is no tract index.

(C) Since there is no tract index, the developer was under an obligation to determine the riparian rights of any adjacent landowners before erecting the chain link fence.

(D) The nephew's easement is a legal interest that attaches not just to a legal estate but to the land itself, and, running with the land, it binds successive owners of the servient estate whether or not they have notice of it.

Question 51

Edward owns 15 acres of undeveloped property near the outskirts of Middleville. The land is mostly covered with grass and some old trees, and a small stream meanders through a portion of it. The parcel is adjacent to a small public park. Edward has been negotiating with the professional football league for assignment of an expansion franchise to Middleville, and believes that he has an excellent chance of being awarded a franchise two years from now. If so, he will build a stadium complex on the 15 acres to house the team. Until then, he would like to gain the goodwill of the city council and to get the citizenry in the habit of spending leisure time at or near his property. He wants to open the 15 acres to public use for picnicking and similar activities, and has asked you, his lawyer, for advice on the best manner of doing so while retaining the greatest freedom of action if the football franchise is awarded.

Which of the following would best suit Edward's needs?

(A) Dedicate the 15 acres for use as a public park.

(B) Lease the 15 acres to the city for two years.

(C) Grant the city an easement for public recreational uses for two years.

(D) Covenant that the city may use the 15 acres for recreation for two years.

Question 37

A developer owned several acres in an old, dilapidated area of downtown. He was delighted when the city council decided to try to revitalize the city center, restoring some of the hundred-year-old buildings and creating a mixed use development that combined a variety of boutique shops and restaurants with small townhouse developments. The developer prepared a subdivision of his various parcels, filed a subdivision map showing commercial lots, obtained all the necessary approvals, and began selling the lots to merchants and businesspersons eager to join in the new prosperity of the development. Each of the deeds conveying lots sold by the developer contained the following:

It is hereby covenanted by the seller that the property conveyed shall be used for commercial or residential purposes only, that no industrial, warehouse, or other manufacturing structures shall be erected or maintained thereon, and that this covenant shall bind the buyer, his heirs and assigns, and their successors.

Two years later, after all but two of the lots had been developed as small businesses, the developer was forced to raise funds immediately and sold his remaining two lots to a real estate speculation firm. The deed to the firm did not contain any language restricting the use of the property. The firm then sold the property to a giant supermarket chain, which intended to construct a warehouse and distribution center for its retail operations in the western states. The warehouse would involve the constant movement in and out of large trucks 24 hours per day, seven days a week.

A shopkeeper who had purchased a lot from the developer located next to the proposed warehouse operated a coffee shop specializing in local folk entertainment and poetry readings. She brings suit against the supermarket chain seeking to enjoin construction of the warehouse. Her attorney argues that the lots sold by the developer to the firm and then to the supermarket chain are bound by the same restrictions on use that are contained in the deed by which the shopkeeper took her property.

What is the likely outcome of this litigation?

(A) The shopkeeper will win unless the firm and the supermarket were not aware of the restrictions when they purchased the property.

(B) The shopkeeper will win if she can show that the developer established a common development scheme for his entire subdivision and that the subdivision appeared to conform to the scheme.

(C) The shopkeeper will lose because the restrictions in her deed binds only the purchaser of the land.

(D) The shopkeeper will lose because the deed by which the firm took the property from the developer did not contain any restrictions on use.

Question 168

Lester owned Forestacre, a parcel of land on which he built a single-family residence. To pay for the construction, he obtained financing from Multistate Mortgage Company in exchange for a mortgage on Forestacre. Multistate promptly and properly recorded its mortgage in the appropriate recording office. When the house was completed, Lester agreed to lease the house to Terrence for a three-year term. At the time Terrence moved in, the house was complete except for the absence of an oven in the kitchen, and there was no provision in the lease agreement regarding kitchen appliances. Terrence bought a state-of-the-art professional chef model oven from Applianceco and had it installed in the space provided around the built-in cabinets in the kitchen. To make the purchase, Terrence signed a security agreement with Applianceco granting it a security interest in the oven in exchange for financing. Applianceco did not file or record its security interest in the oven.

By the end of the lease term, Lester was in serious default on his mortgage payments to Multistate and Terrence was in serious default on his loan payments to Applianceco. In preparing foreclosure proceedings against Lester, Multistate learned that Terrence was planning to remove the oven and take it with him when he moved out within the next few weeks. Multistate filed an action against Terrence claiming ownership of the oven, and joined Lester and Applianceco as parties.

Which party has a superior claim to the oven?

(A) Multistate, because its mortgage interest attaches to all fixtures on the real estate and it has priority over Applianceco.

(B) Terrence, because removal of the oven will not cause substantial damage to the real estate.

(C) Lester, because the oven was annexed to the real estate after the mortgage was given.

(D) Applianceco, because it has a valid security interest in the oven even though it was not recorded.

Question 42

Ogden owned Pineacre, an unimproved parcel of wooded land, in fee simple. He orally agreed to sell Pineacre to Burton under an installment land contract whereby Burton agreed to pay $5,000 down and $100 a month for the next 10 years, and Ogden would retain the deed until Burton finished paying the installments. Because Ogden and Burton were friends, they saw no need for a written contract and shook hands on the deal. After making the down payment, Burton moved onto the property and began clearing some of the trees for a road and a cabin. Ten months later, Burton, who had regularly made the monthly payments, was killed when a tree he was cutting fell on him. His estate consisted of a small quantity of personal possessions, $200,000 in cash, and his interest in Pineacre. His properly executed will conveyed his real estate to Rhonda and the remainder of his estate to Patrick. During the next several months, Burton's estate failed to make payments on the installment contract. Ogden then notified the estate that he was rescinding the deal and asserting ownership of Pineacre, and offered to return the amount Burton had paid him, less expenses, as restitution.

Burton's estate initiated a quiet title action, naming Ogden, Rhonda, and Patrick as parties. Papers filed in court by the estate indicated that it was prepared to pay the accelerated full balance of the contract from the proceeds of the estate in order to complete the conveyance and take title to the land, which it was permitted to do by the state's equity of redemption statutes.

If the court determines that Rhonda will receive title to Pineacre in fee simple free of any obligation on the installment contract, which of the following doctrines will the court use to reach this determination?

I. Doctrine of equitable conversion.

II. Doctrine of part performance.

III. Equitable mortgage doctrine.

(A) I., II., and III.

(B) I. only.

(C) I. and II.

(D) II. and III.

Question 145

Donna and Ed entered into a written contract whereby Donna contracted to sell and Ed to purchase Whiteacre at a price of $200,000. The closing date was set at August 8. Before the closing date, Ed received the title search report. The records on Whiteacre in the County Recorder of Deeds office indicated that Alan conveyed Whiteacre to Belle by quitclaim deed in 1975 and that Cornelius conveyed Whiteacre to Donna by warranty deed in 1987. Ed notified Donna that the records did not indicate how Whiteacre was conveyed to Cornelius (Donna's immediate transferor), and that Ed was concerned about this. Donna replied that she had no knowledge of the matter, but that she would look into it. At the date and time appointed for closing, Donna informed Ed that she could not locate Cornelius, or obtain any information as to the conveyance of Whiteacre to him. Upon hearing this, Ed refused to tender the purchase money, and told Donna that he was rescinding the contract. Donna sued Ed for specific performance.

Which party is more likely to prevail?

(A) Donna, because land is unique and therefore a proper subject for a specific performance action.

(B) Donna, because she took title from Cornelius by warranty deed.

(C) Ed, because there is a gap in the title.

(D) Ed, because Donna cannot supply marketable title.

Question 13

A parcel of property was located in a state with a statutory adverse possession period of 15 years. The current owner purchased the property 25 years ago. It was a suburban property containing a single-family dwelling in which the owner lived. Immediately adjoining the property was a five-foot-wide strip, which was a private right-of-way. When the owner took possession of the property, she was not sure where the exact boundaries of her property were located. Therefore, when she planted a garden and enclosed it with a wire fence two weeks after taking up occupancy, the five-foot right-of-way strip was included within the bounds of the fence.

The owner maintained the fence and garden for 20 years, at which time she tired of gardening chores. When she gave up gardening, she also removed the fence and smoothed out the ground where the garden had been located.

Five years later, the owner entered into a written contract to sell the property to a buyer. The description in the contract included the five-foot strip. After research in the county recorder's office, the buyer discovered that the strip was a private right-of-way when the owner purchased the property. After properly notifying the owner of the problem prior to closing, the buyer refused to tender the purchase money to the owner when the closing day arrived. The owner sued the buyer for specific performance of the real estate sales contract.

Who will prevail?

(A) The buyer, because the owner failed to provide a marketable title.

(B) The buyer, because the owner surrendered her adverse possession rights when she removed the fence, because her possession was no longer open, notorious, and continuous.

(C) The buyer, because one may not adversely possess a right-of-way.

(D) The owner, because she held the right-of-way for a longer time than the minimum required by the state adverse possession statute.

Questions 97-98 are based on the following fact situation:

Proctor and Gamble owned large adjoining tracts of land. The boundary line between the two properties was never properly determined or clearly known.

In 1976, Proctor installed a gas-powered generator on land he thought he owned, but which was in fact owned by Gamble. The generator was housed in a small shed and surrounded by a fence. During the summer months, Proctor ran electrical wires from the generator to a guest house across land he knew belonged to Gamble. Gamble orally consented to the wiring's crossing his land.

In 1989, Gamble was found to be mentally incompetent. He died in 2000, and his executor filed suit to eject Proctor and quiet title. The statute of limitations in ejectment is 20 years.

97. With respect to the land on which the generator was installed:

(A) Proctor cannot claim title by adverse possession because the statute of limitations was tolled by Gamble's incompetency.

(B) Proctor cannot claim title by adverse possession because his occupation was not under claim of right.

(C) Proctor has acquired title by adverse possession.

(D) Proctor has acquired a prescriptive easement.

98. With respect to the land over which the electrical wires were laid:

(A) Proctor has acquired title by adverse possession.

(B) Proctor has acquired a prescriptive easement.

(C) Proctor cannot claim any right on title because his use of the land in question was not continuous.

(D) Proctor cannot claim any right on title because Gamble consented to his use of the land for the wires.

Question 111

Rupert's uncle decided, as a surprise birthday present, to give Rupert a beach house which Rupert had visited often and expressed his great admiration for. The uncle's attorney prepared and the uncle validly executed a deed conveying the property to Rupert, and the attorney then validly recorded the deed.

Unknown to the uncle, Rupert was experiencing severe financial difficulty and was contemplating filing for bankruptcy. When Rupert learned of the recordation of the deed at his birthday party, he immediately told his uncle that he did not want the beach house and could not accept such an expensive gift anyway.

Later, Rupert filed for bankruptcy and the trustee in bankruptcy asserted an ownership interest in the beach property on behalf of the debtor's estate. The bankruptcy court ruled that the property belonged to Rupert's uncle and not to Rupert, and thus was not part of the debtor's estate subject to distribution.

Which of the following is the strongest reason in support of the bankruptcy court's ruling?

(A) There was no presumption of delivery created by recordation of the deed because Rupert did not know of the recordation.

(B) Rupert's statements to his uncle at the birthday party were a constructive reconveyance of the property.

(C) There was never an effective acceptance of delivery of the deed by Rupert.

(D) The recordation of the deed was invalid because it was done without Rupert's permission.

Question 185

Venn entered into a written contract with Purch for the sale of Scrubacre, a large tract of land in a sparsely populated area of the state. The contract set forth an accurate metes and bounds description of the land based on a survey that Venn had undertaken before putting the property up for sale. At closing, Purch discovered that the deed was incorrectly transcribed and did not agree with the description of the land in the contract. Purch refused to proceed with the closing and brought an action to reform the deed to make it conform to the intention of the parties.

The deed described the property to be conveyed as follows:

I. From the southwest corner of Section 25 of Township 2 North, Range 6 West, Cimmaron Base and Meridian, proceed South 45 degrees East 200 feet to the Scrub Basin Irrigation Canal;

II. From that point, proceed South 45 degrees West 100 feet along the Scrub Basin Irrigation Canal to its intersection with State Highway 11;

III. From that point, proceed North 45 degrees West 200 feet along State Highway 11;

IV. From that point, proceed South 45 degrees East 100 feet to the starting point.

Which of the following corrections should be made for the deed to properly describe Scrubacre?

(A) Direction I. should be changed to "South 45 degrees East 100 feet."

(B) Direction III. should be changed to "North 45 degrees West 100 feet."

(C) Direction III. should be changed to "North 45 degrees East 200 feet."

(D) Direction IV. should be changed to "North 45 degrees East 100 feet."

Question 78

Billy entered into a contract with Sherm to purchase Sherm's farm, upon which the latter grew wheat and soybeans. The contract of sale referred to the farm by name and location, and recited that it contained 250 acres of prime farmland. The agreed-upon price was $1 million. Before the date upon which escrow was to close, Billy learned from a surveyor he had hired that the farm actually contained 248 acres. On the date the sale was to close, Billy instructed the escrow agent to release all but $8,000 of the purchase money. Sherm refused to proceed with the sale.

If Billy brings an action for specific performance and also seeks a reduction of the agreed-upon contract price, what will be the probable outcome of the litigation?

(A) Sherm will win, because Billy refused to tender the contract price when Sherm tendered substantially what the contract called for him to perform.

(B) Sherm will win, because both parties had seen the farm before the contract was formed.

(C) Billy will win, because he is not receiving what he bargained for under the contract.

(D) Billy will win, if the difference of two acres is found to be material and if the reduction in price is not an excessive variance from the parties' agreement.

Question 149

Howard and Marty were brothers who each owned 80-acre parcels of farmland adjacent to each other. They decided to combine their acreage in order to benefit from economies of scale, and operated the combined 160 acres as a single farm. After a few years, during which each got married and had children, they began to worry that the very successful farm would be broken up if either of them died, since at least half might be divided among the deceased brother's survivors. Consequently, they each executed identical documents providing: "I hereby grant to my brother and his heirs and assigns a right of first refusal as to my 80 acres, exercisable within 45 days of any proposed sale or transfer of ownership by me." Each brother gave the other valuable consideration for his respective agreement. Each brother promptly recorded his document in the county where the land was located.

Fifteen years later, Marty died, devising his interest in his 80 acres to his oldest child, Charlene. Two weeks later, Howard learned that Charlene had entered into a contingent contract with Boxhomes Developers for the sale of the 80 acres, the contract to take effect when the property was out of probate. Howard notified the executor of Marty's estate that he wished to purchase the 80 acres at the contract price, but on instructions from Charlene, the executor refused. The jurisdiction in which the land is located has a Rule Against Perpetuities unmodified by statute.

If Howard brings an action for specific performance of the agreement giving him a right of first refusal, how should the court rule?

(A) Against Howard, because the interest created by the document violates the Rule Against Perpetuities.

(B) Against Howard, because the document created an unreasonable restraint on alienation.

(C) For Howard, because the document granted him a valid and existing interest in Marty's property.

(D) For Howard, because the document was recorded prior to Marty's death.

Question 112

An elderly woman who lived alone in a large house invited her niece, a registered nurse, to live with her. The niece accepted and moved into the house. For the next several years, the niece took care of most of the housework and the shopping despite her busy schedule. The aunt decided that when she died she should reward the niece by giving her the home. The aunt had her attorney prepare a valid warranty deed conveying the property to the niece, then executed and delivered it to the niece. The niece did not record the conveyance.

Two years after the conveyance, the aunt was involved in an auto accident that left her bedridden. She had allowed her auto insurance to lapse and the other driver's insurance company obtained a judgment against her for $100,000, which it recorded. A statute in the jurisdiction provides: "Any judgment properly filed shall, for 10 years from filing, be a lien on the real property then owned or subsequently acquired by any person against whom the judgment is rendered."

When the aunt died five years later, her will left all of her property to the niece. The insurance company filed a claim in probate against the estate for $100,000. The niece, as executrix, seeks a determination from the probate court that the home is not part of the aunt's estate, having already been conveyed to the niece.

What should the court's ruling be?

(A) That the home is part of the estate and must be utilized to satisfy the $100,000 claim.

(B) That the home is part of the estate, but is not subject to the $100,000 claim.

(C) That the home is not part of the estate and thus is not subject to the claim.

(D) That the home is not part of the estate, but is nevertheless subject to a $100,000 lien in favor of the insurance company.

Question 26

When Blandings decided to invest in the futures market, he borrowed $50,000 from Ace Financial Corporation, secured by a mortgage on his home. Shortly thereafter, when the bottom dropped out of the pork belly futures market, Blandings needed some ready cash, so he agreed to sell his home to Grant for $70,000. With the deed conveying the property to Grant was a recital signed by both parties stating that title passed "subject to" the indebtedness of $50,000 in favor of Ace, "which obligation grantee expressly assumes." Grant then paid Blandings $20,000, took possession of the house, and began making monthly payments of principal and interest to Ace. A few years later, Giant & Insensitive, Inc., a chemical manufacturing firm, built a huge sulfur processing plant just down the road from the home, which caused the house to immediately decline in value to $35,000. Grant's career as a dramatic actor similarly went into decline, and he was unable to continue making the monthly payments to Ace. Ace exercised its contractual right of nonjudicial foreclosure, and sold the house at a public auction for $34,000. Ace then brought suit against Blandings and Grant for $14,000, the difference between the proceeds of the foreclosure sale and the $48,000 principal remaining due on the original loan to Blandings. The jurisdiction does not bar deficiency judgments.

Ace should be granted a judgment for $14,000 against:

(A) Both Blandings and Grant.

(B) Only Blandings.

(C) Only Grant.

(D) No one.

Question 4

A landowner sold a parcel of land to an investor for $100,000. The investor put the deed in her desk drawer without recording it and left for an extended sojourn in a foreign country. The landowner, aware of the investor's departure and seeing an opportunity to make a quick profit, partitioned the parcel of land and sold the front half to a friend in exchange for $50,000. The friend, who knew nothing about the investor's interest in the property, promptly recorded his interest. Two months later, the friend found a job in another city and sold the front parcel to a buyer in exchange for $55,000. The buyer was acquainted with the investor and was aware of her interest in the property but did not believe that she would return from her sojourn anytime soon. The buyer promptly recorded her deed to the front parcel. Meanwhile, the landowner executed a mortgage on the back half of the property to a bank in the amount of $40,000. The bank knew nothing of the landowner's transaction with the investor but neglected to record its mortgage interest. Six months later, the investor returned home and recorded her deed to the parcel of land.

The recording statute in the jurisdiction reads, in relevant part: "Any conveyance of an estate in land, other than a lease for less than one year, shall not be valid against any subsequent purchaser for value, without notice, unless the conveyance is recorded."

If the investor brings an action to quiet title in the parcel of land, which of the following statements is most accurate?

(A) The investor's claim to the parcel of land is superior to the landowner's rights in the back half and the buyer's rights in the front half, and not subject to the bank's mortgage on the back half.

(B) The investor's claim to the parcel of land is superior to the landowner's rights in the back half, inferior to the buyer's rights in the front half, and subject to the bank's mortgage on the back half.

(C) The investor's claim to the parcel of land is superior to the landowner's rights in the back half, inferior to the buyer's rights in the front half, and not subject to the bank's mortgage on the back half.

(D) The investor's claim to the parcel of land is superior to the landowner's rights in the back half and the buyer's rights in the front half, but subject to the bank's mortgage on the back half.

Question 30

The following provision is on the statute books of the state of Central:

> No conveyance or mortgage of real property shall be valid against a subsequent purchaser for value and without notice whose conveyance is first recorded in accordance with the laws of the state of Central.

The following events all took place within the state of Central:

In January, Smith, the owner of Midacre, a parcel located in Lake County, executed and delivered a mortgage on the property to Senior Bank to secure a $50,000 loan. Due to a clerical error, the appropriate filing papers languished in the desk drawer of a bank officer, and so the mortgage was not recorded at that time. On February 15, Smith entered into a contract to sell Midacre to Jones for $150,000. On February 16, Smith took out a $30,000 mortgage on Midacre with Junior Bank. Junior Bank promptly and properly recorded the mortgage. Knowing nothing about either of the mortgages, Jones closed on Midacre on April 1, tendering $150,000 to Smith. Smith gave Jones a warranty deed to Midacre.

On April 3, the officer at Senior Bank finally found the papers for the Midacre mortgage in his drawer and properly recorded the mortgage that same day. Jones recorded his deed to Midacre on April 6.

Senior Bank brought an appropriate action to determine the status of its mortgage on Midacre. The court should hold that:

(A) Jones holds Midacre subject to both mortgages, and the Senior Bank mortgage is subordinate to the Junior Bank mortgage.

(B) Jones holds Midacre subject to both mortgages, and the Senior Bank mortgage is superior to the Junior Bank mortgage.

(C) Jones holds Midacre subject only to the Junior Bank mortgage.

(D) Jones holds Midacre subject only to the Senior Bank mortgage.

Questions 55-56 are based on the following fact situation:

Barton entered into a contract with Currier to buy Texacre for $70,000. Although Barton was expecting to receive a large sum of money from an inheritance in a few weeks, he had very limited funds on hand and was able to obtain financing from Arco State Bank only in the amount of $40,000. He executed a promissory note in that amount secured by a mortgage on Texacre. To cover the remaining balance, Barton went to Currier and obtained a loan for $30,000, giving Currier a promissory note in that amount secured by a mortgage on Texacre and orally promising to pay Currier in full when he received his inheritance money. At the time the sale of Texacre was consummated, neither Currier nor Arco knew about the other's mortgage.

Currier learned from Barton a few days later that he would be receiving his inheritance sooner than he had thought. Currier promptly negotiated the mortgage note to Darwin for $25,000 without informing Barton. Darwin had no notice of Arco's interest in Texacre. The next day, Currier received a check from Barton in the amount of $30,000. A few days later, Currier left the country with the $95,000 he had made on the sale of Texacre. That same day, Arco properly recorded its mortgage on Texacre.

A statute in the jurisdiction provides:

> No conveyance of an interest in land, other than a lease for less than one year, shall be valid against any subsequent purchaser for value, without notice thereof, unless the conveyance is recorded.

The jurisdiction also permits a deficiency judgment against the mortgagor if the proceeds of a foreclosure sale are insufficient to satisfy the mortgage debt.

55. If a foreclosure action is instituted by Darwin, which of the following correctly states his rights against Barton?

   (A) Darwin has no enforceable interest in Texacre and no rights against Barton because Currier did not transfer the mortgage to him and Barton paid the mortgage amount in full.

   (B) Darwin has an enforceable interest in Texacre to the extent of $25,000, but cannot recover against Barton personally for any deficiency.

   (C) Darwin has an enforceable interest in Texacre to the extent of $25,000, and can recover against Barton personally for any deficiency.

   (D) Darwin has an enforceable interest in Texacre to the extent of $30,000, and can recover against Barton personally for any deficiency.

56. Assume for purposes of this question only that Darwin has an enforceable mortgage interest in Texacre. Which of the following correctly states Darwin's interest in relation to Arco's interest?

   (A) Arco's interest is superior to Darwin's interest because Arco has recorded its interest.

   (B) Arco's interest is superior to Darwin's interest because Arco provided a purchase money mortgage for Texacre.

   (C) Darwin's interest is superior to Arco's interest because neither Currier nor Darwin had notice of Arco's interest at the time of their transactions.

   (D) Darwin's interest and Arco's interest are equal in priority because they are both purchase money mortgages.

Question 176

Patterson purchased Sandacre from Alphonse for $100,000. She financed the purchase by obtaining a loan from Alphonse secured by a mortgage on Sandacre. Alphonse promptly and properly recorded his mortgage. Shortly thereafter, Patterson obtained a loan from Bradford Credit Union secured by a mortgage on Sandacre for remodeling. Bradford promptly and properly recorded the mortgage. One year later, Patterson obtained a home equity loan from Charter Bank secured by a mortgage on Sandacre. Charter promptly and properly recorded its mortgage. A few months later, Patterson stopped making payments on the debt owed to Bradford. With proper notice to all parties, Bradford brought an action to foreclose on its mortgage. At that time, Patterson owed $20,000 on the Alphonse mortgage, $25,000 on the Bradford mortgage, and $30,000 on the Charter mortgage. At the foreclosure sale, the property was sold for $45,000. The jurisdiction in which Sandacre is located permits deficiency judgments.

After the $25,000 debt owed to Bradford is satisfied from the proceeds, which of the following statements is most correct?

(A) Alphonse's mortgage and Charter's mortgage are both reduced by $10,000 and remain on Sandacre.

(B) Alphonse's mortgage is satisfied in full and extinguished, while Charter's mortgage remains on Sandacre.

(C) Alphonse's mortgage remains on Sandacre, while Charter's mortgage is reduced by $20,000 and extinguished, leaving Patterson personally liable to Charter for the deficiency of $10,000.

(D) Alphonse's mortgage is satisfied in full and extinguished, and Charter's mortgage is also extinguished, leaving Patterson personally liable to Charter for the deficiency of $30,000.

Question 66

Upacre and Downacre are located in the state of New Cossack, which has a statutory 10-year prescription and adverse possession period. New Cossack follows the riparian doctrine of reasonable use.

Uri owned Upacre, a 15-acre undeveloped parcel of land, through which Timur Creek ran. Timur Creek also ran through Downacre, a 35-acre parcel located downstream from Upacre. Downacre was owned by Dmitri, and Dmitri began using Downacre to grow cotton and for other agricultural purposes. Dmitri drew off water from Timur Creek to irrigate his land and to water livestock thereon. Dmitri's use of Downacre and Timur Creek water has been continuous and uninterrupted for 18 years. Two years ago, Uri constructed a residence on Upacre, and began to draw off the waters of Timur Creek for his domestic use. During the first summer that Uri occupied the Upacre residence, there was adequate water in Timur Creek for all of Uri's domestic purposes and for all of Dmitri's agricultural purposes. However, the flow of Timur Creek is irregular and the water level dropped dramatically this summer. The amount of water in Timur Creek is sufficient to meet either all of Dmitri's needs and none of Uri's or all of Uri's needs and one-half of Dmitri's. Both Uri and Dmitri claim they are entitled to sufficient water from Timur Creek to meet all their respective needs. Each files suit against the other to enforce his rights.

In the resulting trial of the case, who will prevail?

(A) Dmitri, because he has a prior reasonable use of the water.

(B) Dmitri, because he is entitled to the water by prescription.

(C) Uri, because his use of the water does not totally deprive Dmitri of water for his needs.

(D) Uri, because Dmitri's use of the water is not a natural use.

TORTS

Question 45

Chuck had obtained a permit from the national forest service to cut some firewood in the national forest, and had driven his pickup to the designated area and had begun to cut down a marked tree with his axe when Chloe, a member of the Save the Vegetation movement, approached him and began berating him for cutting the tree. Chuck told her that he had a permit to cut and to leave him alone. Chloe persisted, however, shouting that Chuck was "a moronic, murdering plantkiller." Intending to frighten Chloe away, Chuck said, "Get away or I'll start cutting on people!" and swung his axe as if to strike her. The manufacturer of the axe had neglected to insert a metal pin that secured the axe handle to the blade, and Chuck's previous chopping had so loosened the head that it flew off the handle and struck Chloe in the upper chest, crushing her clavicle.

If Chloe brings an action for battery against Chuck, will she recover?

(A) No, if a reasonable person would have been angered by Chloe's remarks.

(B) No, because the defective axe was the cause in fact of Chloe's injuries.

(C) Yes, because Chuck intended to frighten her.

(D) Yes, unless she intended to provoke Chuck.

Question 92

Abigail was scheduled to undergo surgery for removal of her appendix. Doctor Smith, her family doctor, was to perform the operation. The day of the surgery, Doctor Smith was called out of town because of a family illness. Even though there was no emergency, it was decided by the hospital to go ahead with the operation and substitute Doctor Michaels for Doctor Smith. Doctor Michaels is considered to be an expert in appendectomies. Abigail was not informed of the switch in doctors.

If Abigail sues Doctor Michaels on a battery theory, who will prevail?

(A) Abigail, only if the operation did not improve her physical well-being.

(B) Abigail, regardless of whether the operation improved her physical well-being.

(C) Doctor Michaels, because he was at least as qualified as Doctor Smith.

(D) Doctor Michaels, if Doctor Smith approved the substitution of doctors.

Questions 64-65 are based on the following fact situation:

An elderly grocery store customer was doing his weekly shopping at the supermarket, and had left his grocery list at home. Somewhat absentminded, he occasionally would reach into his coat pocket to take out the list, forgetting for the moment that it was not there. A clerk who saw the customer take his hand out of his pocket more than once alerted a security guard that the customer was shoplifting. After the customer had passed through the checkout counter, the security guard stepped in front of him and said, "Okay, Pops, what's in your pocket?" When the customer replied, "My car keys," the security guard said, "Let's go to the manager's office." The customer refused to move, demanding to know why he was being harassed. The security guard said, "Have it your way, then." Pulling a pair of handcuffs from his belt, he reached for the customer's arm. "I'll go," said the customer, and he went with the guard to the manager's office as some of his friends and neighbors looked on. The security guard told him to sit in a chair, left the office, and locked the door behind him from the outside with a key. An hour later, the manager, who had been supervising installation of a computer inventory system in another part of the store, returned with the security guard to his office, and told the employee who had originally alerted the security guard to identify the customer. After explaining what he had seen, including that he had never actually seen the customer put anything in his pocket, the employee left. When the customer explained the situation, the manager apologized profusely and escorted him out of the store.

64. If the customer brings an action against the supermarket for assault based on the security guard's attempt to handcuff him, will he likely recover?

(A) No, because he suffered no injury from the guard's actions.

(B) No, if the guard did not intend to injure the customer when he pulled out the handcuffs and reached for the customer's arm.

(C) Yes, if the security guard was unreasonable in suspecting that the customer was a shoplifter.

(D) Yes, because he was afraid that the guard was going to handcuff him.

65. If the customer brings a false imprisonment action against the supermarket, will he be able to recover for the humiliation that he felt on being seized and taken to the manager's office in front of his friends and neighbors?

(A) No, humiliation is not actionable.

(B) No, unless the security guard and employee were negligent in suspecting that he was a shoplifter.

(C) Yes, but only if the store's actions were extremely outrageous.

(D) Yes, because he was falsely imprisoned.

Question 9

A homeowner whose lawn mower broke down started borrowing his neighbor's mower once a week to mow his lawn. A running joke developed between the two men as to when the homeowner would break down and purchase a new mower. One fall day the homeowner decided to blow the leaves off his lawn before mowing. The homeowner went to the neighbor's house to borrow the neighbor's leaf blower, but the neighbor was not at home. His leaf blower, however, was in his unlocked garage with his other garden tools, and the homeowner took it. Unbeknownst to the homeowner, the neighbor had drained the oil from the leaf blower's motor. The homeowner ran the leaf blower for an hour; the motor was totally destroyed because it had no oil.

The value of the leaf blower at the time that the homeowner took it was $300. An identical, new leaf blower costs $500. The cost of repairing the motor is $150. A new motor will cost $250.

If the neighbor sues the homeowner on a theory of conversion and is successful, he is entitled to:

(A) $300, but the homeowner will keep the leaf blower.

(B) $500, but the homeowner will keep the leaf blower.

(C) $150.

(D) $250.

Question 79

Pinkerton owned Lowacre, a strawberry farm that he held open to the public for a fee. Pinkerton's business consisted primarily of families, who would often eat as many strawberries out in the field as they would bring home with them. Accordingly, Pinkerton advertised that no chemical pesticides or fertilizers were used on his strawberries, so that they could be eaten right off the plant. Adjacent to Lowacre was Highacre, owned by Dalton, on which a soap factory was located. Flakes of calcium silicate, a chemical byproduct of the process, would drift over onto Lowacre whenever the wind was blowing in that direction and settle onto the strawberry plants. The flakes caused no harm to the plants themselves, but detracted from the appearance of the strawberries as well as their taste if eaten right off the plant; consequently, Pinkerton's business sharply declined. On several occasions, Pinkerton complained to Dalton about the discharge, but Dalton did nothing, in part because a visit to the county recorder of deeds office had convinced him that he was the true owner of a large part of Lowacre. After a heavy discharge had ruined what should have been a peak weekend of berry picking, Pinkerton sued Dalton.

Can Pinkerton recover damages for the harm caused to his business?

(A) Yes, because the discharge from Dalton's factory entered Pinkerton's land.

(B) Yes, because Dalton intended to conduct the activities that caused the particles to fall on Pinkerton's land.

(C) No, because Dalton had no intent to cause harm to Pinkerton's property.

(D) No, if Dalton's belief that he owned the property, although erroneous, was reasonable.

Question 165

Darwin was driving his expensive sports car down the highway at 90 m.p.h. in a heavy rainstorm. Just after cresting a hill, Darwin observed a large tree that had been hit by lightning and was blocking the highway. To avoid hitting the tree, Darwin drove off the road and onto the property of Peter. In so doing, Darwin destroyed Peter's mailbox and flower bed.

If Peter sues Darwin for damages to his mailbox and flower bed, he will:

(A) Prevail, but only if he can establish that Darwin was not exercising due care.

(B) Prevail, regardless of whether Darwin was exercising due care.

(C) Not prevail, because Darwin was acting under necessity when he drove onto Peter's property.

(D) Not prevail, because even though Peter was exceeding the speed limit, the tree in the road was an act of God, and a superseding intervening cause.

Question 188

When Dottie learned that the boyfriend of her roommate, Pam, had a motorcycle, she advised Pam that they should both wear helmets when they were on it. Pam responded that they had no intention of wearing helmets because they were too restricting. Dottie, whose brother died in a motorcycle accident because he was not wearing a helmet, wanted to impress upon Pam how important helmets were. One day when Pam was at work, Dottie called her and left a message that her boyfriend was in a motorcycle accident and was in the hospital on life support. Pam was very upset when she got the message and left immediately for the hospital. When she found out later that the message was not true, she became even more upset.

If Pam brings an action against Dottie to recover for her emotional distress, is she likely to prevail?

(A) Yes, if Pam suffered physical injury from her distress.

(B) Yes, if Dottie knew that it was very likely that Pam would suffer severe emotional distress.

(C) No, unless Dottie's purpose was to cause Pam severe emotional distress.

(D) No, because Pam and her boyfriend were not related.

Questions 11-12 are based on the following fact situation:

Eddie suffered from a physical condition that caused him to periodically lapse into unconsciousness without symptoms that would indicate such a seizure was about to occur. Four years ago, Eddie visited Dr. Dock. At that time, Dock put Eddie on the medicine "Noseeze." Eddie was required to take six Noseeze pills daily. The medication successfully ended Eddie's lapses into unconsciousness. However, Noseeze caused some unpleasant side effects, such as periodic nausea. After one year on Noseeze, Dock cut Eddie's dosage in half, and one year later, Dock took Eddie off the medication altogether, although Eddie was required to visit Dock for a check-up every two months. In the two years since he was removed from the Noseeze medication, Eddie regularly appeared at his check-up appointments and told Dock that he had suffered no seizures while off the medication.

One day, Eddie was driving his automobile along a busy highway. Eddie suddenly suffered a seizure and lapsed into unconsciousness. While Eddie was passed out, his car crossed the center line, which divided his lane from traffic proceeding in the opposite direction. The center line was marked with a double yellow line, and by statute the jurisdiction declares that it is illegal for any person operating a motor vehicle on the highways of the state to cross a double yellow line. When Eddie's car passed into the lane containing oncoming traffic, his car collided with a vehicle driven by Pompeia. Pompeia's car was damaged and Pompeia suffered physical injuries that required hospitalization.

11. If Pompeia sues Dr. Dock for personal injuries and property damage arising from the accident, is she likely to recover?

    (A) Yes, if it was reasonably foreseeable that removing Eddie from medication could cause harm to third parties.

    (B) Yes, if but for the removal of Eddie from medication, the accident would not have occurred.

    (C) No, unless Dr. Dock failed to warn Eddie about driving without medication.

    (D) No, if it was reasonable as to Eddie's treatment to suspend the medication.

12. Is Eddie liable to Pompeia?

    (A) Yes, because the vehicle he was operating crossed a double yellow line in violation of statute.

    (B) Yes, if Eddie lapsed into unconsciousness on prior occasions.

    (C) No, because Eddie was unconscious.

    (D) No, unless Eddie had reason to believe that he might lapse into unconsciousness.

Question 7

A landowner who had owned and operated a small airport notified the electric company that he was discontinuing operations and that it should shut down the electrical current that had supplied his communications equipment, which was surrounded by a fence with signs warning of high voltage. Because the electric company maintained a transformer next to the landowner's communications equipment that contained many valuable and reusable parts, it decided to leave the power on to prevent theft until it could schedule removal of the transformer. Three days later, a trespasser who knew that the airport had closed went onto the property looking for something to steal. He could find nothing of value except the transformer. He noticed the signs warning of the high voltage but believed that the power had been turned off by now. He scaled the fence with the intent to dismantle the transformer. As soon as he touched the transformer, he was seriously injured by the electric current.

If the trespasser asserts a claim against the electric company to recover damages for his injuries, the trespasser will:

(A) Prevail, because the electric company was not the owner of the land on which the trespasser trespassed.

(B) Prevail, because the electric company used unreasonable force to protect its property.

(C) Not prevail, because the trespasser was a trespasser on the landowner's land.

(D) Not prevail, because the trespasser intended to steal the electric company's transformer.

Question 166

A state statute prohibits leaving a child under the age of five years unattended in an automobile. A mother parked her car at a supermarket parking lot. She left her four-year-old son in the car with his seatbelt fastened while she did her grocery shopping. While the mother was shopping, the son undid his seatbelt, left the car, and started riding on the grocery carts that customers had left in the parking lot. The son crashed one of the carts into another shopper's car, causing damage.

The shopper brought a negligence action against the mother to recover for the damage caused by the son. At trial, the shopper presented evidence of the statute and the facts stated above. At the conclusion of the shopper's case, the mother moved for a directed verdict in her favor.

Should the court grant the mother's motion?

(A) No, because the shopper has established negligence per se based on the mother's violation of the statute.

(B) No, because the jury could find that it was foreseeable that the son would cause damage to cars in the parking lot if the mother left him unattended.

(C) Yes, because the shopper has not presented evidence that the statute was designed to prevent children from causing damage to the cars of other customers.

(D) Yes, because a parent is not vicariously liable for the negligence of her child.

Question 84

Darrel was out backpacking with friends when he came upon another hiker, who had been bitten by a rattlesnake. Darrel and his companions carried the bitten hiker back to Darrel's four-wheel-drive vehicle, and Darrel drove him toward the nearest hospital. On the way there, while exceeding the posted speed limit, Darrel lost control of his vehicle and crashed into a tree by the side of the road. He was uninjured, but the snakebitten hiker's leg was broken. An ambulance soon arrived and took the hiker to the hospital. The emergency room physician committed malpractice that resulted in the loss of the hiker's leg. The hiker is now suing Darrel.

Which of the following is the most likely reason why Darrel will be held liable for the hiker's injuries?

(A) Having undertaken to rescue the hiker, Darrel is strictly liable for injuries resulting from the rescue.

(B) The emergency room physician's malpractice is a foreseeable intervening cause that does not relieve Darrel of liability.

(C) Darrel did not conduct himself as a reasonably prudent person in carrying out the rescue of the hiker.

(D) Darrel committed negligence per se when he exceeded the posted speed limit.

Question 95

Lamont applied for a job at the Jones Security Agency. He was required to fill out an application listing references and indicating whether he had any prior convictions of felonies or violent misdemeanors, which would disqualify him from a position as a security officer. Lamont listed as references some aunts and uncles who had not seen him in some time, and stated that he had no prior convictions. In fact, Lamont had several times been convicted of violent assaults using firearms as a juvenile, but the official records were sealed to the public when he attained age 21, several months before he applied for the job at Jones. Lamont was hired, given training in security procedures and firearm use, and placed on assignment at a shopping mall.

After he had been working for a month, Lamont was at a bar with his girlfriend when he got into an argument with another patron over whether the city's football team would make it to the Super Bowl. When the patron made a remark disparaging the abilities of a certain running back, Lamont drew the pistol he had been given at work, which he kept in his waistband, and shot the patron in the chest, killing him.

If the survivors of the dead patron bring an action against Jones Security Agency for wrongful death, who is likely to prevail?

(A) Jones, because Lamont's actions occurred while he was acting outside the scope of his employment.

(B) Jones, because it owed no duty to the patron which was violated.

(C) Plaintiffs, because Jones employed Lamont and gave him the pistol he used to kill the patron.

(D) Plaintiffs, if they can show that a reasonable employer would have discovered Lamont's prior convictions.

Question 104

Prex came to Doctor Dillamond, a dermatologist, for treatment of a skin condition on his face that had resisted standard treatment. Doctor Dillamond prescribed a new topical antibiotic cream that was recommended by an associate of hers. Doctor Dillamond gave Prex instructions on how and when to apply the cream but did not discuss potential side effects. Prex purchased the cream at his local pharmacy and applied it as instructed. Shortly thereafter his skin turned a vivid shade of green and he felt a strong burning sensation when he tried to wash it off. The color took almost a week to fade away, during which time he avoided going out in public and took time off from work.

The cream was packaged with a lengthy printed insert that listed a number of possible side effects of varying degrees of probability. A "green pallor" and "irritation" were listed as uncommon side effects.

If Prex sues Doctor Dillamond for prescribing the medicine, is he likely to prevail?

(A) No, if a reasonable person in Prex's position would have used the cream even when told of the potential side effects.

(B) No, because the printed insert that came with the cream listed possible side effects similar to the reaction Prex experienced.

(C) Yes, unless the severity of the reaction Prex experienced was unforeseeable.

(D) Yes, because Doctor Dillamond, as a specialist, owes a high duty of care and is liable even for slight negligence.

Question 133

Bobby, age 12, was dedicated to his hobby of flying radio-controlled model airplanes that he built himself. One Saturday, Bobby invited his friends to the park to watch him fly his plane. The weather that day was rainy, and the instruction manual for the plane warned against flying it in the rain, but Bobby did not want to miss this opportunity to impress his friends with the tricks it could do. He therefore forged ahead and was able to get the plane off of the ground, but he had trouble controlling it with the transmitter because of the rain. He tried to have the plane make a loop but it veered off course and crashed through the fabric roof of Hank's convertible, which was parked nearby on the street.

If Hank sues Bobby for damages to his car and prevails, it will be because:

(A) A child of Bobby's age, education, intelligence, and experience would not have flown the airplane that day.

(B) A reasonable person would not have flown the airplane that day.

(C) The airplane instruction manual warned against flying in the rain.

(D) Bobby committed a trespass to chattel with his airplane.

Question 115

On the way out of Dinah's Diner after enjoying a wonderful meal, Eaton made a detour into the kitchen to personally compliment the chef. However, before he could get the attention of the chef, he slipped on a puddle of grease that had congealed on the floor by the stove. He fell, hitting his head and sustaining a severe head injury.

If Eaton sues Dinah's for damages, is he likely to recover?

(A) Yes, because Dinah's Diner is a place of public accommodation and breached its duty of care owed to its patrons.

(B) Yes, because a Dinah's employee could have discovered the dangerous condition of the floor by making reasonable inspections.

(C) No, unless patrons were welcomed into the kitchen to compliment the chef.

(D) No, if the puddle of grease was visible on the floor.

Question 86

Peron was a passenger on a commuter train operated by Northeast Transit, Inc. During the commute, Peron left his seat to go to the lavatory at the front of the car. While he was in the aisle, the car moved across intersecting tracks, causing the car to rock. He stumbled and bumped his knee against the lavatory door, aggravating a preexisting circulation problem in his leg that had been controlled by medication. As a result, he had to have several surgeries to correct the circulation problem.

Peron brought suit against Northeast for his damages. At the jury trial, the following evidence was presented: Peron testified as to how he was injured and introduced evidence of his medical expenses. His physician testified that the bump aggravated the circulation problem. The engineer of the train testified that the train had not been exceeding the speed limit for that stretch of track, and Northeast introduced a report indicating that a subsequent inspection disclosed no problems with the track.

At the close of the evidence, Northeast moved for a directed verdict. The court should:

(A) Grant the motion, because there is no evidence that Northeast operated the train negligently.

(B) Grant the motion, if Northeast introduced uncontroverted evidence that a person in normal health would not have been injured by the bump.

(C) Deny the motion, because the jury could find that Northeast, as a common carrier, breached its high duty of care to Peron.

(D) Deny the motion, because the fact that the severity of Peron's injuries was not foreseeable does not cut off Northeast's liability.

Question 101

A petroleum company operated refineries in several states and was also engaged in the manufacture of a variety of petrochemical products. The company hired an industrial cleaning service to thoroughly clean one of its refineries. While one of the cleaning service's employees was engaged in routine cleaning activities at the refinery, one of the support legs on a crane suddenly gave way, causing part of the crane to fall onto a pipe carrying hot oil, cracking it open. The employee had his back to the pipe at the time and hot oil squirted over his back and legs, causing severe burns. The employee filed suit against the petroleum company for his injuries.

The parties stipulated for trial that the crane had been designed and constructed by a crane construction specialist and was serviced at regular intervals by a reputable crane maintenance company selected by the crane construction company. The employee testified at the trial that he was injured when the pipe cracked open and submitted his medical bills and other evidence of damages. The employee introduced no further evidence. At the conclusion of the employee's case, the petroleum company moved for a directed verdict in its favor.

Should the directed verdict be granted?

(A) Yes, because the employee has done nothing to connect the petroleum company to any negligent activity that might have caused the accident.

(B) Yes, because the petroleum company did not owe a duty to an employee of an independent contractor.

(C) No, because the petroleum company is strictly liable to the employee for his injuries.

(D) No, because based on the evidence presented by the employee, a jury could reasonably conclude that the petroleum company was negligent.

Questions 156-157 are based on the following fact situation:

A testing lab used a wind tunnel to test the aerodynamic characteristics of components of vehicles, boats, and planes. The wind tunnel was sold to the lab as a complete unit by a machinery company, which contracted with an electronics company for the design and installation of the electronic systems that regulated air speed and triggered the emergency shut-off devices.

A technician was installing a scale model of a prototype aircraft that was to be tested in the wind tunnel when the electronic control system of the tunnel malfunctioned and started the huge fans that created the air flow. The powerful air flow pinned the technician against the grating covering the intake ducts, asphyxiating him before he was discovered and the fans could be shut off.

156. If the technician's survivors bring an appropriate action against the machinery company for negligently causing the technician's death, they will recover if they prove that:

(A) The control system of the wind tunnel was defective.

(B) The control system of the wind tunnel was defective and the machinery company failed to inspect it before selling the tunnel to the lab.

(C) The control system of the wind tunnel was defective and the machinery company inspected it but failed to discover the defect.

(D) The control system of the wind tunnel was defective, the machinery company inspected the tunnel and failed to discover the defect, and the defect was such that it should have been discovered in the exercise of reasonable care.

157. The technician's survivors bring an appropriate action against the electronics company for damages. Proof by the plaintiffs that the machinery company failed to inspect the wind tunnel has which of the following legal effects?

(A) If the electronics company is held liable to the plaintiffs, it may bring an action for indemnity against the machinery company based upon the failure to inspect.

(B) The failure of the machinery company to inspect the tunnel is a superseding cause that relieves the electronics company of liability to the plaintiffs.

(C) The failure of the machinery company to inspect the tunnel is attributable to the electronics company under the doctrine of respondeat superior.

(D) The failure of the machinery company to inspect the tunnel has no legal effect on the electronics company's liability.

Question 71

A motorist purchased a new sport utility vehicle from his local dealer. Standard equipment on the vehicle included a set of top-of-the-line tires from a premium tire company. However, the motorist was able to save $400 on the purchase price by allowing the dealer to substitute a lower priced tire manufactured by a discount tire manufacturer. Unbeknownst to the motorist and the dealer, the tire manufacturer had negligently designed the tires, with the result that a tire would occasionally blow out when the car was traveling at a high rate of speed in hot weather. On July 4, the motorist was traveling 80 m.p.h. in a 55 m.p.h. zone. A tire exploded, resulting in damage to the vehicle and injury to the motorist.

If the motorist sues the dealer on a theory of strict liability, is he likely to prevail?

(A) Yes, because the tire was in a dangerously defective condition when the motorist purchased the car.

(B) Yes, because the dealer is responsible for the negligence of the tire manufacturer, because the dealer used its tires.

(C) No, because the motorist assumed the risk when he substituted the discount tires in exchange for $400.

(D) No, because the motorist was misusing the tire when he was traveling at 80 m.p.h.

Questions 190-192 are based on the following fact situation:

Dick took his six-year-old son Doug to the shopping mall to do some Christmas shopping. As Dick was looking at the mall directory in order to locate a store he was seeking, Doug walked over to a nearby "Santa's Reindeer Ride," a small electric trolley made to look like a sleigh being pulled by reindeer, which traveled over a small oval track in a winter holiday setting. The sleigh held four children, and as Doug watched, four youngsters whose parents had paid the 50¢ admission climbed into it for a ride. Doug climbed over the low fence surrounding the ride and ran to the rear of the sleigh, catching onto the upper edge and riding on a narrow ledge at the bottom. Dick, who looked up and saw Doug on the end of the sleigh, ran toward it, attempting to hurdle a small pile of construction materials that had been left by workers who set up the ride. Dick sprawled onto his face, breaking his collarbone. Doug, who turned to see what the commotion was about, lost his grip on the sleigh and fell backward onto the track, injuring his head.

190. Doug brings an action, through his guardian ad litem, against the manufacturer of the sleigh ride on a theory of strict liability. Assume that the jurisdiction follows traditional contributory negligence rules. Which of the following would provide the best defense for the manufacturer in this litigation?

(A) There is not privity of contract between Doug and the manufacturer.

(B) Doug was contributorily negligent in riding on the rear of the sleigh.

(C) The sleigh was not being used by Doug in a reasonably foreseeable manner.

(D) Dick was negligent in his supervision of Doug.

191. Dick brings an action in negligence against the shopping mall to recover for his injury. Assume that the jurisdiction follows traditional contributory negligence rules. Who will prevail?

(A) The mall, if its employees were unaware of the pile of construction materials left by the sleigh ride builders.

(B) The mall, because Dick assumed the risk of injury when he attempted to vault the pile of materials.

(C) Dick, unless he is found to have been contributorily negligent when he attempted to vault the pile of materials.

(D) Dick, on a theory of res ipsa loquitur.

192. Assume for purposes of this question only that the jurisdiction has adopted pure comparative negligence and has replaced its traditional contribution rules with a pure comparative contribution statute, but has retained joint and several liability. Assume further that parent-child immunity does not apply in this situation. Doug brought a negligence action, through his guardian ad litem, against the shopping mall. The trier of fact determined that Doug has suffered $100,000 in damages and that the shopping mall was 60% at fault, Doug was 10% at fault, and Dick was 30% at fault in failing to supervise Doug. How much can Doug recover from the shopping mall?

(A) $60,000, because the jurisdiction has adopted comparative contribution rules.

(B) $90,000, but the shopping mall can recover $30,000 from Dick.

(C) $90,000, and the shopping mall cannot recover from Dick because its fault was greater than the combined fault of Dick and Doug.

(D) $100,000, because the jurisdiction has retained joint and several liability.

Question 99

Douglas Corporation manufactured parachutes, which it sold exclusively to the United States Army. To meet the standards required by the Army, each parachute was subjected to a 15-point inspection by Douglas before it could be approved for sale. When a parachute did not pass inspection, it was stored in another section of the Douglas plant. At a later time, a further inspection of the defective parachute would be made to determine whether the defects could be corrected or whether the parachute should be destroyed.

One night, the Douglas plant was burglarized and a large number of parachutes, including the defective ones, were stolen. The defective parachutes eventually were sold on the black market to Paul, the president of High-Flying Sky Divers, a private group of parachute enthusiasts. Sky Divers members were delighted to get Douglas parachutes, as the parachutes were seldom available to nonmilitary people. One week later, Paul was killed when his Douglas parachute failed to open.

If Paul's estate brings a wrongful death action against Douglas on a theory of strict liability in a jurisdiction retaining traditional contributory negligence rules, Douglas's best defense would be that:

(A) Douglas acted reasonably in storing the defective parachutes.

(B) Douglas did not sell or place into the stream of commerce the defective parachute.

(C) Paul did not purchase the parachute from Douglas.

(D) Paul was negligent when he purchased the parachute on the black market.

Questions 152-153 are based on the following fact situation:

The owner of a self-propelled mower started the engine in preparation to mow when the clutch of the mower suddenly engaged, and it jerked forward rapidly. The owner was unable to grab the handle in time before the mower was out of reach and heading for the street. As he caught up with the mower and attempted to restrain it in the street, a motorist driving down the street swerved to avoid the mower and struck another car traveling in the opposite direction. Both the motorist and the other driver were injured and their cars damaged. The jurisdiction follows traditional contributory negligence rules. The owner purchased the mower 15 years ago.

152. The owner brings an action against the manufacturer of the mower for indemnity based on claims asserted against him by the motorist and the other driver. Assuming for the purpose of this question only that the latter claims are valid and that traditional indemnity rules are followed by the jurisdiction, what will be the probable outcome of this litigation?

(A) The owner will lose, because the mower was 15 years old.

(B) The owner will lose, unless he can show that the mower clutch engaged because of some defect in manufacture.

(C) The owner will win, if his conduct is found not to have been negligent.

(D) The owner will win, because the manufacturer is strictly liable for damages caused by its product.

153. In the motorist's action for personal injuries and property damage against the owner, will she prevail?

(A) No, because the owner was so startled by the mower's sudden movement that he was unable to react swiftly enough.

(B) No, unless the owner was negligent in his maintenance of the mower.

(C) Yes, because her damages resulted from the defective condition of the owner's mower.

(D) Yes, if a reasonable person under the circumstances would have restrained the mower before it entered the street.

Question 72

Jimmy McFinn, a resident of New Oregon, kept a pet bear, Horace, at his farm. Horace was very old in bear years. He had no teeth, no claws, and very little energy. The joke in the community was that Horace could not squeeze a lemon. Horace had not always been so tame. When Jimmy first obtained Horace, he had a large steel cage constructed to house the animal. The cage had an electronic lock that only opened with a security code. Even though Horace was currently harmless, he was always kept locked in the cage. One night during a severe storm while Jimmy was out of town, a bolt of lightning hit the cage and the door opened. Horace left the cage and wandered off. The next morning, 10-year-old Victoria was waiting on a rural road for her school bus. Horace emerged from a wooded area about 100 feet from where Victoria was standing and headed towards her. She screamed and turned to run, tripping on the road and breaking her arm when she fell.

If Victoria sues Jimmy on a theory of strict liability for her bodily harm, will she prevail?

(A) No, because Horace was in fact a nondangerous animal.

(B) No, because the damage she suffered was not the type of damage that a bear would normally cause.

(C) Yes, because Horace is a wild animal.

(D) Yes, but only if she can establish that pet bears were uncommon in the community.

Questions 177-178 are based on the following fact situation:

A chemical company located in a small city manufactured the components of a deadly nerve gas under government license. It contracted with an ordnance company to design and manufacture the delivery system, which would hold the chemical agents in chambers and then combine them effectively upon deployment. The chemical company's detailed specifications for creation of the delivery systems required that the chemical agents be held harmlessly in the separate chambers for at least 15 years without deterioration. After receiving the filled delivery systems from the ordnance company, the chemical company stored them in its underground vaults, which were adjacent to an old underground storage chamber of the city's cable car system. Unknown to the chemical company or the city, children living nearby had gotten access to the city's underground chamber and played in there from time to time.

About three weeks after the nerve gas weapons had been placed in their underground storage vaults, several of the canisters in the delivery systems began to leak, permitting mixture of the two harmless agents into the deadly nerve gas. The chemical reaction of the mixture released a great deal of heat energy, which eventually melted through the walls of the storage vault where it adjoined the city's underground storage chamber. The children playing in the chamber at the time were able to scramble out through a ventilation shaft, but one of the children fell and broke his arm while escaping. Fortunately, the intense heat of the chemical reaction rendered the nerve poison inert, and no one was harmed by its effects.

177. Through his parents, the injured child brings an action against the chemical company. Will he prevail?

(A) Yes, because the chemical company was engaged in an abnormally dangerous activity.

(B) Yes, because the chemical company was negligent.

(C) No, because his injuries were not foreseeable.

(D) No, because the underground chamber in which the child was injured was owned by the city, not by the chemical company.

178. Through his parents, the child brings an action against the ordnance company. Will he prevail?

(A) Yes, because the ordnance company caused the accident that resulted in his injuries.

(B) Yes, because the ordnance company will be found negligent pursuant to the doctrine of res ipsa loquitur.

(C) No, because the canisters that leaked were most recently in the custody and control of the chemical company before they caused the injuries to the child.

(D) No, because the ordnance company was unaware and could not have discovered that the children were playing in the underground chamber.

Question 52

After leaving ceremonies at which Judge Burger had been named distinguished jurist of the year, while both Judge Burger and Judge Douglas were being interviewed by the press on the courthouse steps, Judge Douglas stated to a reporter, "Burger is a senile imbecile who lets his clerks write all his opinions. He hasn't had a lucid thought since 1975. In addition, he has been on the payroll of the mob for a decade." Enraged, Judge Burger attempted to choke Judge Douglas into unconsciousness, and was only pried away by the intervention of several reporters. Burger subsequently brought an action for defamation against Douglas.

Which of the following, if established by Burger in his defamation action, would permit recovery against Douglas?

(A) Douglas negligently made the statements, which were false, and caused Burger actual injury.

(B) Douglas made the statements knowing they were false.

(C) Douglas made the statements because he hated Burger and wished to destroy his reputation in the legal community.

(D) Douglas made the statements in order to ensure that Burger's political career was nipped in the bud.

Question 27

A patient sought psychiatric treatment from a psychiatrist. During the treatment, which consisted of hour-long analysis sessions twice a week, the psychiatrist, unknown to the patient, videotaped her. No sound recording was made of the sessions, but the psychiatrist was conducting a study on "body language" and planned to use the videotapes in those experiments. The patient learned that the psychiatrist had been videotaping their analysis sessions and brought an action against him on a theory of invasion of privacy.

Which of the following arguments best supports the patient's claims in this action?

(A) The psychiatrist has placed the patient in a false light.

(B) The psychiatrist has publicly displayed private facts of the patient's life.

(C) The psychiatrist has misappropriated the patient's likeness.

(D) The psychiatrist has intruded upon the patient's physical seclusion.

Question 80

At Donald's BAR-B-QUE Restaurant, the barbecue was prepared in a large, outdoor pit in the back of the restaurant. Cooking meat outdoors in a commercial establishment violated a city health code regulation, designed to assure that the food was not exposed to flies and other insects. On windy days, smoke from the barbecue pit sometimes blew into Paul's backyard. Paul had extremely sensitive eyes. They watered and stung every time that he was exposed to any form of smoke. When the barbecue smoke drifted onto his property, Paul could not use his backyard.

If Paul sues Donald's on a theory of private nuisance, should Paul prevail?

(A) Yes, because Donald's action interfered with Paul's use and enjoyment of his yard.

(B) Yes, because Donald's was violating a health code regulation.

(C) No, if the smoke would not disturb a person of ordinary sensibilities in the community.

(D) No, because the health code regulation was not designed to protect against the type of harm suffered by Paul.